DATA DIVINATION:
BIG DATA STRATEGIES

PAM BAKER

Cengage Learning PTR

CENGAGE
Learning·

Professional • Technical • Reference

Australia • Brazil • Japan • Korea • Mexico • Singapore • Spain • United Kingdom • United States

CENGAGE Learning

Professional • Technical • Reference

Data Divination: Big Data Strategies
Pam Baker

Publisher and General Manager, Cengage Learning PTR: Stacy L. Hiquet

Associate Director of Marketing: Sarah Panella

Manager of Editorial Services: Heather Talbot

Product Manager: Heather Hurley

Project/Copy Editor: Kezia Endsley

Technical Editor: Rich Santalesa

Interior Layout: MPS Limited

Cover Designer: Luke Fletcher

Proofreader: Sam Garvey

Indexer: Larry Sweazy

For product information and technology assistance, contact us at **Cengage Learning Customer & Sales Support, 1-800-354-9706**.

For permission to use material from this text or product, submit all requests online at **cengage.com/permissions**.

Further permissions questions can be emailed to **permissionrequest@cengage.com**.

All trademarks are the property of their respective owners.

All images © Cengage Learning unless otherwise noted.

Library of Congress Control Number: 2014937092

ISBN-13: 978-1-305-11508-8

ISBN-10: 1-305-11508-2

Cengage Learning PTR

20 Channel Center Street

Boston, MA 02210

USA

Cengage Learning is a leading provider of customized learning solutions with office locations around the globe, including Singapore, the United Kingdom, Australia, Mexico, Brazil, and Japan. Locate your local office at: **international.cengage.com/region**.

Cengage Learning products are represented in Canada by Nelson Education, Ltd.

For your lifelong learning solutions, visit **cengageptr.com**.

Visit our corporate website at **cengage.com**.

Printed in the United States of America
1 2 3 4 5 6 7 16 15 14

To my daughter Stephanie and my son Ben; you are my inspiration each and every day and the joy of my life. To my mother Nana Duffey; my profound gratitude for teaching me critical thinking skills from a very early age and providing me with a strong, lifelong education and living example of exemplary ethics.

ACKNOWLEDGMENTS

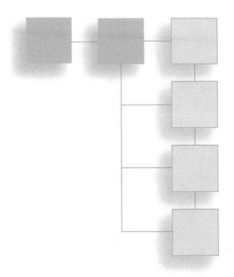

First and foremost, I would like to thank the publishing team at Cengage Learning PTR for their hard work and patience during this time. Specifically, thank you Stacy Hiquet for publishing our text. Thank you Heather Hurley for facilitating this book and being the marvelous person that you are. Your professionalism is second to none but your demeanor is an absolute joy. Thank you Kezia Endsley for your calm management of the editing and deliverables, despite the challenges I inadvertently presented to you. Your many talents, eternal patience, and wise guidance were invaluable to this effort. You are by far the best editor I have had the pleasure of working with and I sincerely hope to have the honor of working with you again one day. Thank you Richard Santalesa for your thorough tech review and insightful suggestions. You are and always will be the greatest legal resource and tech editor a writer can ever have, not to mention the truest of friends. Thank you to the entire team at Cengage.

Many thanks also to my family for their patience and support during this time. Spending long and seemingly unending hours finishing the book is not only hard on the authors, but our families as well. A special thanks to two of my brothers—Steven Duffey and John Duffey—for pitching in to create screenshots and such to exacting specs to help speed completion of the book on such a tight deadline.

ABOUT THE AUTHORS

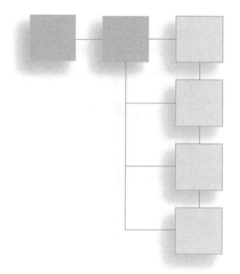

Pam Baker is a noted business analyst, tech freelance journalist and the editor of the online publication and e-newsletter, FierceBigData. Her work is seen in a wide variety of respected publications, including but not limited to *Institutional Investor* magazine, *ReadWriteWeb,* CIO (paper version), CIO.com, *Network World, Computerworld, IT World, LinuxWorld, iSixSigma,* and *TechNewsWorld.* Further she formerly served as a contracted analyst for London-based VisionGain Research and Evans Data Corp, headquartered in Santa Cruz, California. She has also served as a researcher, writer, and managing editor of *Wireless I.Q.* and *Telematics Journal* for ABI Research, headquartered in New York.

Interested readers can view a variety of published clips and read more about Pam Baker and her work on these websites: Mediabistro Freelance Marketplace at http://www.mediabistro.com/PamBaker and the Internet Press Guild at http://www.netpress.org/ipg-membership-directory/pambaker. There are also numerous professional references on her LinkedIn page at http://www.linkedin.com/in/pambaker/.

She has also authored numerous ebooks and several of the dead tree variety. Six of those books are listed on her Amazon Author Central page. Further, Baker co-authored two books on the biosciences for the Association of University Technology Managers (AUTM), a global nonprofit association of technology managers and business executives. Those two books were largely funded by the Bill and Melinda Gates Foundation.

Among other awards, Baker won international acclaim for her documentary on the paper-making industry and was awarded a Resolution from the City of Columbus, Georgia, for her news series on the city in *Georgia Trend Magazine*. The only other author to receive such recognition from the city was the legendary Carson McCullers. Baker is a member of the National Press Club (NPC) and the Internet Press Guild (IPG). You can follow or chat with her on Twitter where her handle is @bakercom1 or on Google + at google.com/+PamBaker. You can also reach her through the contact form at FierceBigData where she is the editor (see http://www.fiercebigdata.com/).

Bob Gourley is a contributing writer in *Data Divination*. He wrote a significant portion of the chapter on use cases in the Department of Defense and Intelligence Community given that is the area he focuses on in his work with big data. Gourley also wrote the chapter on Empowering the Workforce. He is the editor in chief of CTOvision.com and is the founder and Chief Technology Officer (CTO) of Crucial Point LLC, a technology research and advisory firm.

Bob was named one of the top 25 most influential CTOs in the globe by *InfoWorld*, and one of DC's "Tech Titans" by *Washingtonian*. Bob was named one of the "Top 25 Most Fascinating Communicators in Government IT" by the Gov2.0 community GovFresh. In 2012 Bob was noted as "Most Influential on Twitter for Big Data" by *Forbes*.

Bob holds three master's degrees including a master of science degree in scientific and technical intelligence from Naval Postgraduate School, a master of science degree in military science from USMC university, and a master of science degree in computer science from James Madison University. Bob has published over 40 articles on a wide range of topics and is a contributor to the January 2009 book titled *Threats in the Age of Obama*. His blog, CTOvision, is now ranked among the top federal technology blogs by *WashingtonTech*.

Bob is a founding member and member of the board of directors of the Cyber Conflict Studies Association, a non-profit group focused on enhancing the study of cyber conflict at leading academic institutions and furthering the ability of the nation to understand the complex dynamics of conflict in cyberspace. You can follow and chat with him on Twitter where his handle is @bobgourley. You can also find him on Twitter as @AnalystReport and @CTOvision and online at http://ctovision.com/pro.

CONTENTS

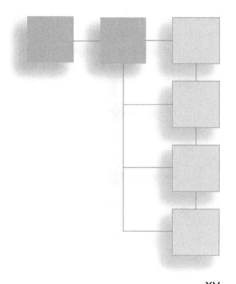

Introduction

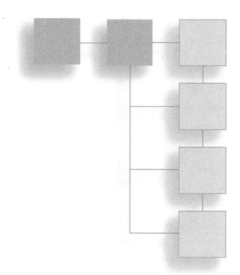

Amidst all the big data talk, articles, and conference speeches lies one consistently unanswered question: What can we actually do with big data? Sure, the answer is alluded to frequently but only in the vaguest and most general terms. Few spell out where to begin, let alone where to go with big data from there. Answers to related questions—from how to compute ROI for big data projects and monetize data to how to develop a winning strategy and ultimately how to wield analytics to transform entire organizations and industries—are even rarer. That's why *Data Divination* was written—to answer all of those most pressing questions and more from a high-level view.

This Book Is for You If

If you are interested in the business end of big data rather than the technical nuts and bolts, this book is for you. Whether your business is a one-man operation or a global empire, you'll find practical advice here on how and when to use big data to the greatest effect for your organization. It doesn't matter whether you are a data scientist, a department head, an attorney, a small business owner, a non-profit head, or a member of the C-Suite or company board, the information contained within these pages will enable you to apply big data techniques and decision-making to your tasks.

Further, many of the chapters are dedicated to use cases in specific industries to serve as practical guides to what is being and can be done in your sector and business. Ten industries are addressed in exquisite detail in their own chapters. There you'll find use cases, strategies, underlying factors, and emerging trends detailed for the governments, department of defense and intelligence community, security, healthcare, small businesses and farms, transportation, energy, retail, banking and insurance, and manufacturing sectors. However, it is a mistake to read only the chapter on your own industry, as changes wrought by big data in other industries will also affect you, if they haven't already.

If there is one thing that big data is shaping up to be, it is a catalyst of disruption across the board. Indeed, it is helping meld entire industries in arguably the biggest surge of cross-industry convergence ever seen. It therefore behooves you to note which industries are converging with yours and which of your customers are reducing or eliminating a need for your services entirely. It's highly likely that you'll find more than a few surprises here in that regard.

STRATEGY IS EVERYTHING

Data Divination is about how to develop a winning big data strategy and see it to fruition. You'll find chapters here dedicated to various topics aimed at that end. Included in these pages are the answers to how to calculate ROI; build a data team; devise data monetization; present a winning business proposition; formulate the right questions; derive actionable answers from analytics; predict the future for your business and industry; effectively deal with privacy issues; leverage visualizations for optimum data expressions; identify where, when, and how to innovate products and services; and how to transform your entire organization.

By the time you reach the end of this book, you should be able to readily identify what you need to do with big data, be that where to start or where to go next.

There are some references to tools here, but very few. Big data tools will age out over time, as all technologies do. However, your big data strategies will arch throughout time, morphing as needed, but holding true as the very foundation of your business. Strategy then is where you need to hold your focus and it is where you will find ours here.

From your strategy, you will know what tools to invest in and where and how you need to use them. But more than helping you pick the right tools and to increase your profits, your strategy will see you through sea changes that are approaching rapidly and cresting on the horizon now. The changes are many and they are unavoidable. Your only recourse is to prepare and to proactively select your path forward. We do our best to show you many of your options using big data in these pages to help you achieve all of that.

CHAPTER 1

WHAT IS BIG DATA, REALLY?

One would think that, given how the phrase "big data" is on the tip of nearly every tongue and top of mind for most, everyone knows what big data is. That's not quite the case. Although there is a technical definition of sorts, most people are unsure of where the defining line is in terms of big versus regular data sizes. This creates some difficulty in communicating and thinking about big data in general and big data project parameters in particular.

This chapter considers the different interpretations of the meaning of the term "big data."

TECHNICALLY SPEAKING

As discussed in more detail in the next chapter, big data does not mean more of the same data, simply boosting gigabytes to terabytes, although obviously it includes the expected growth of existing data sets. Rather, big data is a collection of data sets, some structured and some unstructured, some "onboarded" from physical sources to online sets, some transactional and some not, from a variety of sources, some in-house and some from third parties. Often it is stored in a variety of disparate and hard-to-reconcile forms. As a general rule, big data is clunky, messy, and hard, if not impossible, as well as significantly expensive, to shoe-horn into existing computing systems.

Furthermore, in the technical sense there is no widely accepted consensus as to the minimum size a data collective must measure to qualify as "big." Instead the technical world favors a definition more attuned to data characteristics and size relative to current computing capabilities.

You'll commonly hear big data defined as "containing volume, velocity, and variety" which is the three-legged definition coined by a 2001 Gartner (then Meta) report. These days, some people throw in a fourth "v,"—veracity—to cover data quality issues too.

But in essence big data is whatever size data set requires new tools in order to compute. Therefore, data considered big by today's standards will likely be considered small or average by future computing standards.

That is precisely why attaching the word "big" to data is unfortunate and not very useful. In the near future most industry experts expect the word big to be dropped entirely as it fails to accurately describe anything essential to the concept. For what makes "big data" truly valuable are the "big connections" it makes possible—between people, places, and things—that were previously impossible to glean in any coherent fashion.

Even so, there are those who try to affix a specific size to big data, generally in terms of terabytes. However this is not a static measurement. The measure generally refers to the amount of data flowing in or growing in the datacenter in a set timeframe, such as weekly. Conversely, since data is growing so quickly everywhere, at an estimated rate of 2,621,440 terabytes daily according to the Rackspace infographic in Figure 1.1, a static measurement for a "big data" set is frequently meaningless after a very short time. (This infographic can also be found online at http://www.rackspace.com/blog/exploring-the-universe-of-big-data-infographic/.)

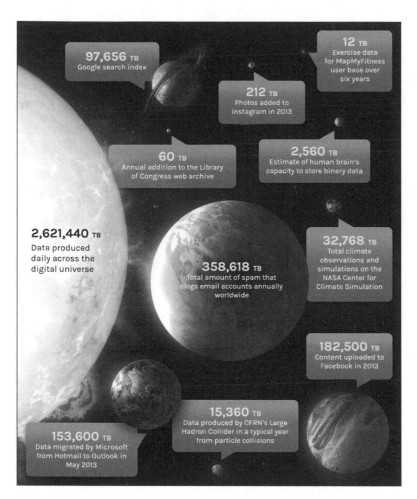

Figure 1.1
This interactive infographic has a counter at the top that shows how many terabytes of data were added to the digital universe since the user opened the infographic. The speed in which the counter counts gives you a good idea of just how fast data is growing overall. By rolling a mouse over the different planets, the user reveals the size of data in different categories relative to the size of all data generated (represented here as the sun) such as in email spam, in the Google search index, and in Facebook.

Source: Infographic courtesy of Rackspace. Concept and research by Dominic Smith; design and rendering by Legacy79.

Already we know that bigger data is coming. Data sets so big that we don't yet have a measuring term for it. But until then we'll use the measurements we do have: first up is zettabytes and then yottabytes. To give you an understanding of the magnitude of a yotta-byte, consider that it equals one quadrillion gigabytes or one septillion bytes—that is a 1 followed by 24 zeroes. Consider Figure 1.2 for other ways to visualize the size of a yottabyte.

What is a yottabyte?
1000 GB = 1 Terabyte (TB)
1000 TB = 1 Petabyte (PB)
1000 PB = 1 Exabyte (EB)
1000 EB = 1 Zettabyte (ZB)
1000 ZB = 1 Yottabyte (YB)
In other words, a Yottabyte = 1,000,000,000,000,000 GB.

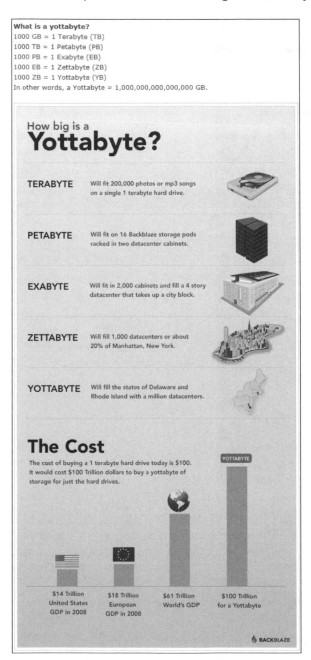

Figure 1.2
This graphic and accompanying text visualize the actual size of a yottabyte.
Source: Backblaze; see http://blog.backblaze.com/2009/11/12/nsa-might-want-some-backblaze-pods/.

As hard as that size is to imagine, think about what comes next. We have no word for the next size and therefore can barely comprehend what we can or should do with it all. It is, however, certain that extreme data will arrive soon.

WHY DATA SIZE DOESN'T MATTER

Therefore the focus today is primarily on how best to access and compute the data rather than how big it is. After all, the value is in the quality of the data analysis and not in its raw bulk.

Feel confused by all this? Rest assured, you are in good company. However, it is also a relief to learn that many new analytic tools can be used on data of nearly any size and on data collections of various levels of complexities and formats. That means data science teams can use big data tools to derive value from almost any data. That is good news indeed because the tools are both affordable and far more capable of fast (and valuable) analysis than their predecessors.

Your company will of course have to consider the size of its data sets in order to ultimately arrange and budget for storage, transfer, and other data management related realities. But as far as analytical results, data size doesn't much matter as long as you use a large enough data set to make the findings significant.

WHAT BIG DATA TYPICALLY MEANS TO EXECUTIVES

Executives, depending on their personal level of data literacy, tend to view big data as somewhat mysterious but useful to varying degrees. Two opposing perceptions anchor each endpoint of the executive viewpoint spectrum. One end point views big data as a reveal all and tell everything tool whereas the other end of the spectrum sees it is simply as a newfangled way to deliver analysis on more of the same data they are accustomed to seeing in the old familiar spreadsheet. Even when presented with visualizations, the second group tends to perceive it, at least initially, as another form of the spreadsheet.

There are lots of other executive perceptions between these two extremes, of course. But it is useful for your purposes here to consider the two extremes—omniscience and spreadsheet upgrade—in order to quickly assess the executive expectations. This will better prepare you to deliver data findings in the manner most palatable and useful to your individual executives.

The "Data Is Omnipotent" Group

For the first group, it may be necessary to explain that while big data can and does produce results heretofore not possible, it is not, nor will it ever be, omniscience as is often depicted in many movies. In other words, data, no matter how huge and comprehensive, will never be complete and rarely in proper context. Therefore, it cannot be omnipotent.

This group also tends to misunderstand the limitations of predictive analytics. These are good tools in predicting future behavior and events, but they are not magical crystal balls that reveal a certain future. Predictive analytics predict the future assuming that current conditions and trends continue on the same path. That means that if anything occurs to disrupt that path or significantly change its course, the previous analysis from predictive analytics no longer applies. This is an important distinction that must be made clear to executives and data enthusiasts. Not only so that they use the information correctly but they also understand that their role in strategizing is not diminished or replaced by analytics, but greatly aided by it.

Further, most big data science teams are still working on rather basic projects and experiments, learning as they go. Most are simply unable to deliver complex projects yet. If executives have overly high initial expectations, they may be disappointed in these early stages. Disappointment can lead to executive disengagement and that bodes ill for data science teams and business heads. This can actually lead to scrapping big data projects and efforts all together. Therefore, it's important to properly and realistically manage executive expectations from the outset.

On the upside, executives in this group may be more open to suggestions on new ways to use data and be quicker to offer guidance on what information they most need to see. Such enthusiastic involvement and buy-in from executives is incredibly helpful to the initiative.

The "Data Is Just Another Spreadsheet" Group

At the other extreme end of the spectrum, the second group is likely to be unimpressed with big data beyond a mere nod to the idea that more data is good. This group views big data as a technical activity rather than as an essential business function.

Members of this executive group are likely to be more receptive to traditional visualizations, at least initially. To be of most assistance to this group of executives, ask outright what information they wish they could know and why. Then, if they answer, you have a solid and welcomed way to demonstrate the value of the company's big data efforts by presenting exactly what was needed but heretofore missing.

If they can't or don't answer the question, work proactively to find ways to demonstrate the value of data analysis in ways that are meaningful to those executives.

Expect most executives to have little interest in how data is *cooked*—gathered, mixed, and analyzed. Typically they want to know its value over the traditional ways of doing things instead.

Whether executives belong to one of these two extreme groups or are somewhere in between, it is imperative to demonstrate the value of big data analysis as you would in any business case and/or present ongoing metrics as you would for any other technology.

However, your work with executives doesn't end there.

Big Data Positioned in Executive Speak

Although data visualizations have proven to be the fastest and most effective way to transfer data findings to the human brain, not everyone processes information in the same way. Common visualizations are the most readily understood by most people, but not always. Common visualizations include pie charts, bar graphs, line graphs, cumulative graphs, scatter plots, and other data representations used long before the advent of big data.

The most common of all is the traditional spreadsheet with little to no art elements. Figure 1.3 shows an example of a traditional spreadsheet.

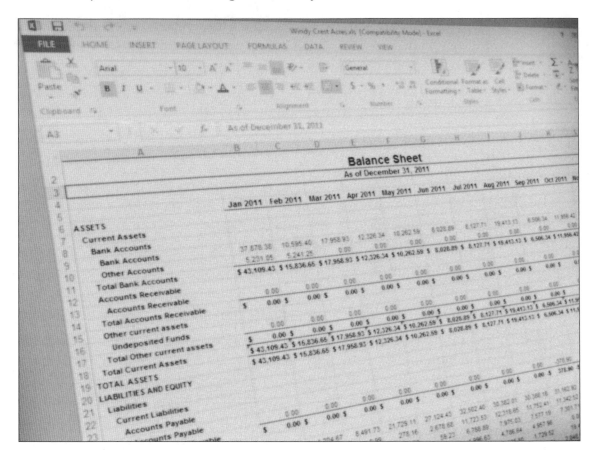

Figure 1.3
An example of a traditional spreadsheet with little to no art elements.
Source: Pam Baker.

Newer types of visualizations include interactive visualizations wherein more granular data is exposed as the user hovers a mouse or clicks on different areas in the visual; 3D visualizations that can be rotated on a computer screen for views from different angles and zoomed in to expose deeper information subsets; word clouds depicting the prominence of thoughts, ideas, or topics by word size; and other types of creative images.

Figure 1.4 is an example of an augmented reality image. Imagine using your phone, tablet, or wearable device and seeing your multi-dimensional data in an easy-to-understand form such as in this VisualCue tile. In this example, a waste management company is understanding the frequency, usage, and utility of their dump stations.

Figure 1.5 shows an example of a word cloud that quickly enables you to understand the prominence of ideas, thoughts, and occurrences as represented by word size. In this example, a word cloud was created on an iPad using the Infomous app to visualize news from several sites like FT, *Forbes, Fortune, The Economist,* The Street, and Yahoo! Finance. The size of the word denotes its degree of topic prominence in the news.

Figure 1.4

Augmented reality visualization. Imagine using your phone, tablet, or wearable device and seeing your multi-dimensional data in an easy to understand form such as in this VisualCue tile. In this example, a waste management company is understanding the frequency, usage, and utility of their dump stations.

Source: VisualCue™ Technologies LLC. Used with permission.

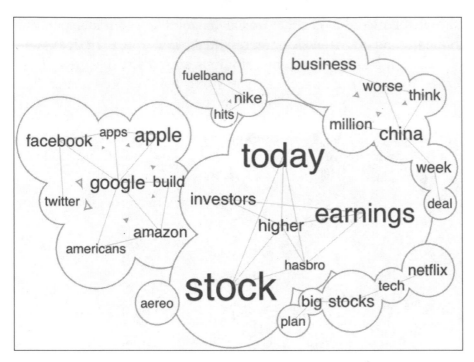

Figure 1.5
A word cloud created on an iPad using the Infomous app to visualize news from several financial sites. The size of the word denotes its degree of topic prominence in the news.
Source: Infomous, Inc. Used with permission.

Both traditional and new visualizations range from the overly simplistic to the mind-bogglingly complex, with most falling somewhere in the middle. The function of any visualization is to convey meaningful information quickly. The effectiveness of such is not measured by its aesthetic value but by how well and quickly the information is received by the viewer.

"The best approach is to build visualizations in the most digestible form, fitted to how that executive thinks," John Lucker, principal at Deloitte Consulting, said in a phone interview. "You will have to interact with executives, show them different visualizations, and see how they react in order to learn which forms work best for them. Be ready to fail often and learn fast, particularly with visualizations."

In short, one man's perfect visualization is often another's modern art nightmare scenario. Some executives will continue to prefer a spreadsheet format or the old familiar pie charts and bar graphs while others will prefer newer visualizations that not only convey the information easily but also enable the user to consider the same information from different viewpoints and to drill down for more granular information.

In any case, it is imperative to figure out how each executive best learns, values and absorbs information and then tailor the visualizations accordingly.

As a result, it is a common mistake to develop a "one set of visualizations fits all" to share with all executives. Given the inexpensive visualization tools available today and the ease in which they generate the same data results into a large variety of visualizations, there is simply no reason to standardize or bulk-produce visualizations.

Personalize visualizations instead. It's not much more work and the effect on improved communications with executives is invaluable.

"Whichever visualizations you decide to use, be consistent throughout your report," advises Lucker. "Consistency in forms makes it easier to understand and follow as the viewer doesn't have to stop and figure out each new visualization before they can grasp the information within. Frequently changing visualization forms in your report creates user exhaustion."

Figures 1.6 and 1.7 show more examples of new visualization types available today.

Figure 1.6 is in VisualCue's "tile" format, whereby you can understand numerous organizations at a glance, leveraging scorecard colors (red, yellow, and green) and intuitive pictures. In this case, you see one organization and the relevant financial market data. You make decisions with the full picture and then you can employ traditional views (graphs, charts, and so on) later once you know who or what you really want to study further.

Figure 1.7 is an example of how you can view your data on a map, but not just with one or two dimensions. Understand relationships as well as the overall picture of your organization. Such visualizations inspire you to ask questions you didn't even think to ask! In this example, a school franchise is understanding how their total operation is performing (main middle VisualCue tile) and then each corresponding student.

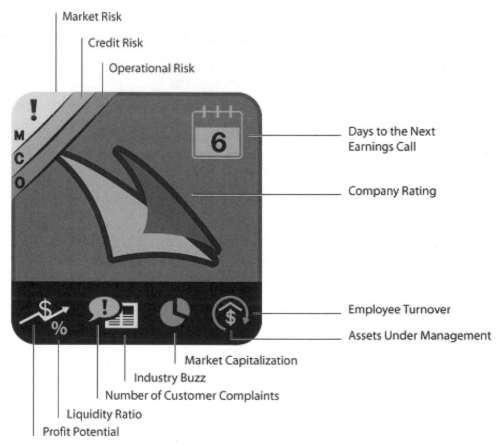

Figure 1.6

VisualCue's "tile" format, where you can understand numerous organizations at a glance leveraging scorecard colors (red, yellow, green) and intuitive pictures. In this case, you see one organization and the relevant financial market data.

Source: VisualCue™ Technologies LLC. Used with permission.

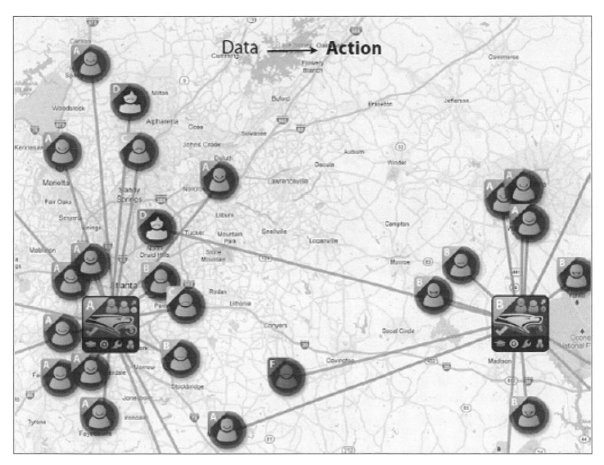

Figure 1.7
Another example of the wide range of new visualization types you can use to get people excited about your big data. In this example, a school franchise is understanding how their total operation is performing (main middle VisualCue tile) and then comparing each corresponding student.
Source: VisualCue™ Technologies LLC. Used with permission.

However, even traditional spreadsheets are becoming more powerful and versatile in providing data visualizations these days. Figure 1.8 shows a new way to use bar graphs in Microsoft Excel. There are several ways to use new data visualizations in Microsoft Excel now, particularly in the Enterprise version with Microsoft's Power BI for Office 365.

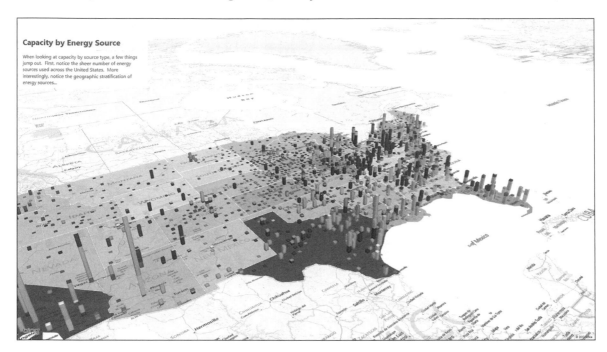

Figure 1.8
An image of a new way to use bar graphs in Microsoft Excel.
Source: Microsoft Inc.

Focus on delivering the findings and skip the explanations on how you got to them unless the executive expresses interest in such.

Summary

In this chapter you learned that the term "big data" is imperfect. There is no widely accepted consensus as to the minimum size a data collective must measure to qualify as "big." Instead, the technical world favors a definition more attuned to the data characteristics and size relative to current computing capabilities. Therefore the focus today is primarily on how best to access and compute the data rather than how big it is. After all, the value is in the quality of the data analysis and not in its raw bulk. However, it is certain that extreme data is a near-term inevitability.

Fortunately, many new analytic tools can be used on data of nearly any size and on data collections of various levels of complexities and formats. Data size doesn't much matter as long as you use a large enough data set to make the findings significant.

Executives, depending on their personal level of data literacy, tend to view big data as somewhat mysterious but useful to varying degrees. Two opposing perceptions anchor each endpoint of the executive viewpoint spectrum. One endpoint views big data as omnipotent, capable of solving any problem and accurately predicting the future, whereas the other end of the spectrum sees it simply as a spreadsheet upgrade. The latter group views big data as a technical activity rather than as an essential business function. There are lots of other executive perceptions between these two extremes, of course. But in any case, executive expectations must be managed if your big data projects are to succeed and continue.

Although data visualizations have proven to be the fastest and most effective way to transfer data findings to the human brain, not everyone processes information in the same way. It is imperative to figure out how each executive best learns, values, and absorbs information and then tailor the visualizations accordingly. Focus on delivering the findings and skip the explanations on how you got them unless the executive expresses interest in such.

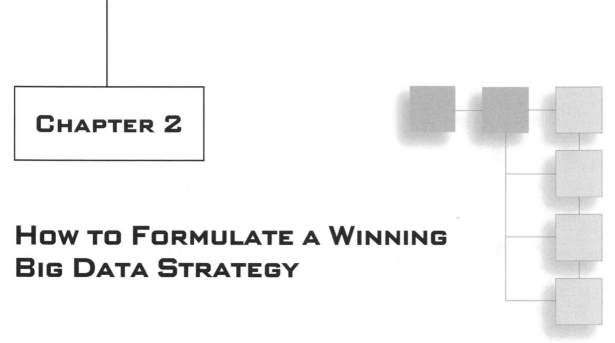

CHAPTER 2

HOW TO FORMULATE A WINNING BIG DATA STRATEGY

Strategy is everything. Without it, data, big or otherwise, is essentially useless. A bad strategy is worse than useless because it can be highly damaging to the organization. A bad strategy can divert resources, waste time, and demoralize employees. This would seem to be self-evident but in practice, strategy development is not quite so straightforward. There are numerous reasons why a strategy is MIA from the beginning, falls apart mid-project, or is destroyed in a head-on collision with another conflicting business strategy. Fortunately, there are ways to prevent these problems when designing strategies that keep your projects and your company on course.

However, it's important to understand the dynamics in play first so you know what needs to be addressed in the strategy, beyond a technical "To Do" list.

THE HEAD EATS THE TAIL

The question of what to do with data tends to turn back on itself. Typically IT waits for the CEO or other C-level executives and business heads to tell them what needs to be done while the CEO waits for his minions, in IT and other departments, to produce cunning information he can use to make or tweak his vision. Meanwhile department heads and their underlings find their reports delayed in various IT and system queues, or their selections limited to a narrow list of self-service reports, quietly and fervently wishing someone at the top would get a clue about what needs to be done at their level. In other words, everyone is waiting on everyone else to make the first move and all are frustrated.

The default is business gets done in the usual way, meaning everyone is dutifully trudging along doing the exact same things in the exact same ways. And that is why so much data sits fallow in data warehouses. No one is using it. No one is entirely sure what data is there. Few can imagine what to do with it beyond what is already being done at the moment.

The typical CEO continues to depend on data fed to the same fields he's accustomed to looking at on his trusty and familiar spreadsheet (see Figure 2.1). IT continues the daily struggle of trying to store and integrate data, learning and deploying new big data tools plus other technology and online initiatives, and managing a growing number of service and support tickets. Department heads consult the same reports they always have, often populated with too little data and which commonly arrive too long after the fact to accurately reflect current conditions. Staffers scratch their heads in confusion over the fruitlessness or inefficiency of the entire process.

It's not that anyone in this scenario is deliberately thinking that improving things is not their job; rather they are usually unsure what needs to change or how to go about making these changes. They are also not thinking about how these changes would affect others in the organization or the organization at large; rather they are focused on how their desired changes will affect their own domain within the business.

People are simply unaccustomed to thinking in terms of using big data to decide the way forward and to predict business impact. Some are even afraid of using big data, should it become a driver to such an extent that it results in a loss of power or worse, a loss of job security.

But for the most part, it simply hasn't occurred to many people that data analysis can address and even resolve most of their problems. That's why few think to turn to it first.

Those who do think data-driven decision making is a logical and worthy approach often do not have the authority, data literacy, or the resources, skills, and tools to put it fully in action. The end result is that almost no one knows what to do differently and therefore the status quo is maintained.

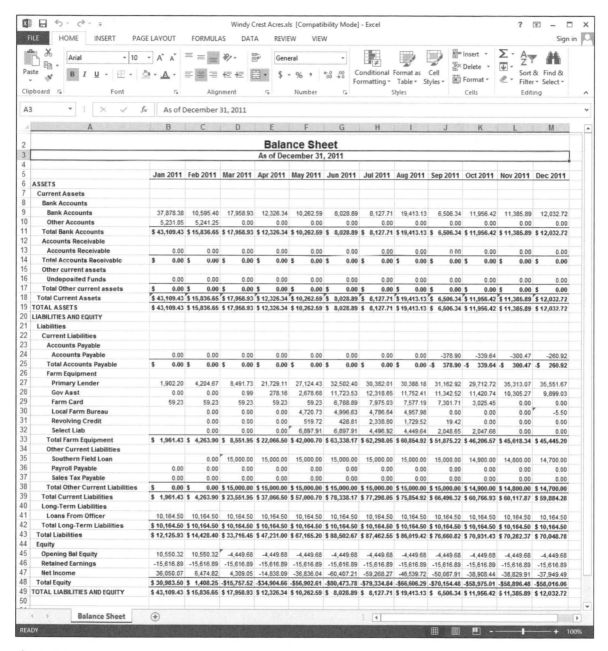

Figure 2.1

A common, traditional spreadsheet used by executives.

Source: Pam Baker.

In other words, the head eats the tail and everyone in the organization is trapped in this circular reasoning. But as you shall see in a moment, the way to end this circle is not with a linear strategy but with a non-linear one and yes, sometimes even with another circle, albeit one of a far different nature.

How to End the "Who's on First" Conundrum

That is not to say that using data is a foreign experience to everyone. Virtually all people already use data to some extent in their daily work. What is different now, however, is *not* that there is more data, that is, big data, but that there are more ways to use that data than most people are accustomed to.

Unfortunately, the difference gets muddied in conversations about big data, leading to muddied efforts as well.

Changing Perspectives of Big Data

When we focus on the word "big," our minds most often translate that to mean "more of the same." For example, a big person is just one person no matter how big or tall, and not a big collection of several different people. Big means more and not a diverse and growing collection of connections in the minds of most people. As a consequence, when most people hear the term "big data," they tend to think of more of the same data.

That mental translation of the term happens commonly in everyday conversations about big data. Perhaps you will hear someone say something like, "big data is so big we have trouble storing and retrieving it" or "big data is too big for normal computing methods." It's not that these statements are untrue, for they are indeed often correct. It is that the average human mind conjures the image of more of the same data clogging the system, and not diverse and disparate data sets tumbling in from every direction.

How humans professionally and personally relate to the word "data" also adds weighty perceptions to the mental baggage carried into big data conversations, bringing to mind the old fable of the Blind Men and The Elephant, where each man, based on their limited perception, concluded that an elephant was far different from what it actually is when all the parts are recognized and assembled properly. Big data allows us to see the elephant; not merely a trunk, leg, or tail in isolation.

In such conversations, each participant is automatically relating what they perceive to what they do. Their reference points are their job, their personal behavior, and their past experiences. These filter their interpretation and perception of how data can be used.

User Perception Versus the Data-Harvesting Reality

For example, a Facebook user will typically think in terms of what they personally post when they hear Facebook is gathering data on them. Most people have trouble immediately comprehending that Facebook can track far more than merely what they have posted. Is this ignorance of how data is collected? Yes, in many cases it is. But even when such ignorance is not present, the average person will immediately first think of what they shared or used intentionally on Facebook and not necessarily what they did on their computer overall while Facebook was accessed or their smartphone's Facebook app was running in the background. Why? Because their personal experience on Facebook is their reference point.

The reality of Facebook's work in data harvesting far exceeds that of simply recording and analyzing posts users put on their Facebook wall. Here is just one example of how Facebook gathers data on both non-users and users, tracking them across websites, none of which are Facebook owned, as reported in a November 16, 2011 article in *USA Today*:

> *Facebook officials are now acknowledging that the social media giant has been able to create a running log of the web pages that each of its 800 million or so members has visited during the previous 90 days. Facebook also keeps close track of where millions more non-members of the social network go on the Web, after they visit a Facebook web page for any reason.*
>
> *To do this, the company relies on tracking cookie technologies similar to the controversial systems used by Google, Adobe, Microsoft, Yahoo!, and others in the online advertising industry, says Arturo Bejar, Facebook's engineering director.*

Of course the information Facebook gathers from actual user activity on their website is staggering too. Bernard Marr explains some of it in his February 18, 2014 SmartDataCollective post this way:

> *We as the users of Facebook happily feed their big data beast. We send 10 billion Facebook messages per day, click the Like button 4.5 billion times and upload 350 million new pictures each and every day. Overall, there are 17 billion location-tagged posts and a staggering 250 billion photos on Facebook.*
>
> *All this information means, Facebook knows what we look like, who our friends are, what our views are on most things, when our birthday is, whether we are in a relationship or not, the location we are at, what we like and dislike, and much more. This is an awful lot of information (and power) in the hands of one commercial company.*

Facebook has also invested in image processing and "face recognition" capabilities that basically allow Facebook to track you, because it knows what you and your friends look like from the photos you have shared. It can now search the Internet and all other Facebook profiles to find pictures of you and your friends.

Face recognition allows Facebook to make "tag suggestions" for people on photos you have uploaded but it is mind boggling what else they could do with technology like that. Just imagine how Facebook could use computer algorithms to track your body shape. They could analyze your latest beach shots you have shared and compare them with older ones to detect that you have put on some weight. It could then sell this information to a slimming club in your area, which could place an ad on your Facebook page. Scary?

There is more: a recent study shows that it is possible to accurately predict a range of highly sensitive personal attributes simply by analyzing the "Likes" you have clicked on Facebook. The work conducted by researchers at Cambridge University and Microsoft Research shows how the patterns of Facebook "Likes" can very accurately predict your sexual orientation, satisfaction with life, intelligence, emotional stability, religion, alcohol use and drug use, relationship status, age, gender, race and political views among many others. Interestingly, those "revealing" likes can have little or nothing to do with the actual attributes they help to predict and often a single "Like" is enough to generate an accurate prediction."

The Reality of Facebook's Predictive Analytics

As if this data wasn't enough intimate information about users, Facebook also studies a user's posting patterns and moods to predict a future romantic relationship. I reported on this activity in a February 19, 2014 FierceBigData post:

"During the 100 days before the relationship starts, we observe a slow but steady increase in the number of timeline posts shared between the future couple," writes Facebook data scientist Carlos Diuk in his "The For-mation of Love" post. "When the relationship starts (day 0), posts begin to decrease. We observe a peak of 1.67 posts per day 12 days before the relationship begins, and a lowest point of 1.53 posts per day 85 days into the relationship. Presumably, couples decide to spend more time together, courtship is off and online interactions give way to more interactions in the physical world."

In other words, Facebook knows when you are about to become a couple, perhaps before you know, and certainly long before you announce your new couplehood on your own Facebook posts. Further, Facebook determines that the physical part of your relationship begins when your online activity decreases. Facebook tactfully calls this phase "courtship" in the posts but we all know that courtship actually occurred during the exchanges Facebook initially tracked to predict the coupling.

What is the business value in tracking the innocently love struck and the illicitly entangled? Possibly so flower retailers, chocolatiers, condom and lubricant retailers and essentially any company that can make a buck off of love can place well-timed ads.

Further, Facebook uses posting patterns and moods to detect a romantic breakup before it happens. In a February 15, 2014 post on Facebook titled "When Love Goes Awry," Adrien Friggeri, Facebook data scientist, said:

> To conclude this week of celebrating love and looking at how couples blossom on Facebook, we felt it was important not to forget that unfortunately sometimes relationships go south and people take different paths in life. In this context, we were interested in understanding the extent to which Facebook provides a platform for support from loved ones after a breakup.
>
> To that end, we studied a group of people who were on the receiving end of a separation, i.e. who had been in a relationship for at least four weeks with someone who then switched their relationship status to Single.
>
> For every person in this group, we tracked a combination of the number of messages they sent and received, the number of posts from others on their timeline and the number of comments from others on their own content, during a period starting a month before the separation to a month after.
>
> We observed a steady regime around the baseline before the day the relationship status changes, followed by a discontinuity on that day with a +225% increase of the average volume of interactions which then gradually stabilize over the course of a week to levels higher to those observed pre-breakup.

This means that Facebook now has the means to accurately predict romantic breakups, often long before the poor, dumped soul may suspect anything is wrong. Rest assured that Facebook is likely using similar analysis to predict other intimate details about its users beyond mere romantic relationships.

Facebook's Data Harvesting Goes Even Further

Facebook officials say they are even going further in data collection but they will do so in an increasingly secretive mode. On April 18, 2014, Dan Gillmor reported in his post in *The Guardian*:

> Facebook may be getting the message that people don't trust it, which shouldn't be surprising given the company's long record of bending its rules to give users less privacy. CEO Mark Zuckerberg told The New York Times' Farhad Manjoo that many upcoming products and services wouldn't even use the name Facebook, as the company pushes further and further into its users' lives. The report concluded:
>
> If the new plan succeeds, then, one day large swaths of Facebook may not look like Facebook—and may not even bear the name Facebook. It will be everywhere, but you may not know it.

If Facebook does indeed proceed down that route, users will be even less likely to be able to correctly identify what data the social media giant is collecting about them and how it is being used. Meanwhile Facebook's big data projects, whatever they may be, will become increasingly accurate, thus enabling the firm to substantially increase revenues and accelerate innovation.

Using Facebook to Open Minds on the Possibilities and Potential of Big Data

Because the average Facebook user has no direct knowledge or experience with Facebook's data collection activities and data usage practices, they often fail to see the harm such can cause. Instead, the average user tends to perceive Facebook's use of data as relatively harmless and little more than an annoyance. They mistakenly believe that as long as they don't post anything on their wall of a personal or detailed nature that no harm can come of it.

Facebook is not the only corporate giant engaging in wide scale data harvesting. These days almost all corporations do so to some degree. Some of these efforts are benign and others not so much. Worse still, none of us know how this data will be used in the future nor to whom it is being sold and for what purpose it is being bought.

While the average person is fully attuned to the potential danger in the government collecting large amounts of data on them, they are blinded to the dangers in the private sector doing so.

It is this limited perception based on personal experience alone that can cloud discussions of the potential in big data within an organization. While many business heads are personally using Facebook and other social media, they may not be aware of how Facebook uses their and other users' data and thus have difficulty imagining how their own organization could do so. Therefore, Facebook serves both as an excellent example of what is possible with big data from the business side, and as a warning of the dangers to privacy on the individual side. In any case, Facebook is an excellent case study to use in broadening the thinking of business leaders in your organization.

Professional Perceptions Versus Data Realities

The same holds true with perceptions stemming from professional reference points. For example, a marketing person will think in terms of customer and prospect data and metrics that they are somewhat familiar with or already use extensively. They will not necessarily extend the thought to what else they might learn from big data analysis, particularly when gleaned from sources they have never used or heard of. Marketers almost universally cheer the concept of gathering and using more data. Unfortunately many of them are unsure what to do with that data once it is gathered.

Further, professionals in all disciplines tend to think of data only as it pertains to their specific job or current tasks.

Members of the C-suite will typically act similarly. They tend to think in terms of the data they use now and rarely what other types of data and analysis they might use, at least not in any specific detail. Even CIOs, presumably skilled in taking the broader data picture, may think in terms of the specific data and related reports they regularly deliver to departments and to the CEO, and not necessarily about the data in storage that no one has accessed or requested in ages.

Because data analysis is performed piecemeal in this way, analysis becomes fragmented and siloed, even if the data itself isn't, and the organization overall typically fails to realize full benefit. It isn't that data democratization is a problem, for such is actually a strong advantage in nearly every case. The problem is that no one in the typical organization is asking the larger questions, those that exist outside their normal tasks, beyond their job scope or perhaps entirely outside of it. Innovation comes from looking at things differently rather than using new tools to perform the same tasks for the same reasons and in the same way. For innovation and extraordinary competitive advantage to be realized, this mold must be either augmented or broken.

From Perception to Cognitive Bias

Relying on your personal or professional reference point is a totally human thing to do. It is a useful way to organize your thoughts and actions most of the time. However, it is a clear example of "cognitive biases," a term which coincidentally grew out of studies examining humans' innate inability to correctly recognize and rationally factor decisions in situations involving huge numbers or statistical probabilities counter from commonly expected results. This leads to actions counter-productive to innovation in general and to data use in particular.

In other words, in order to consider information from a perspective not related to one's own cognitive biases or reference points, most people need to see a clear example or for someone to show them what can be done before they can begin to imagine what else can be done with data.

Finding the Big Data Diviners

This is why it's important for someone or some team to take the lead on exploring new data uses rather than merely hope such will spontaneously and organically appear within the organization. It is also important to understand these dynamics to better communicate the details and worthiness of big data projects and thereby increase executive buy-in, user adoption, overall collaboration, and widespread innovation.

Fortunately there are a few people in every organization who possess sufficient intellectual curiosity, analytical and critical thinking skills, and a fearlessness of change who can power true innovation via data use. The big surprise is that they are generally peppered throughout the organization and almost never conveniently grouped entirely in IT or as business analysts. Occasionally one of those people happens to hold a seat in the C-suite or at the boardroom table, but that is relatively rare given their great distance from the troops on the ground and the sanctum of the datacenter and data warehouse.

Characteristics of a Big Data Diviner

Remember your data diviners will be peppered throughout your organization and often where you least expect them to be. Look for these characteristics to help you find them:

- Insatiable curiosity. A tendency to explore information even when not directly required to do so.

- A love for knowledge. These individuals are constantly learning on their own and on the job. But they may not be enrolled in training classes or formalized education. Whether they are enrolled in a class or not, they are absorbing new information around them constantly and they do so naturally and eagerly.

- Easily make connections between seemingly disparate information. It has been said that the nature of genius is to "connect the dots" between sets of information. You're looking for this kind of genius. Like big data tools, data diviners naturally and easily see connections between information points that others either don't recognize at all or are far slower in recognizing.

- Intuitive intelligence. This relates to the ability to make connections between disparate information but goes beyond that to include the ability to put such newly "connected information" to work. In other words, they don't just see the connections and divine a new thought from them, but also can intuitively sense an appropriate action based on that information.

- Ease with change and new technologies. Because this group loves to learn, they're quick to accept change based on new information. In other words they are quick to discard old ideas in favor of new ones as information and logic dictates. They are also quick to adopt new technologies at work. They may not possess a technical understanding of it, and they may flounder in learning how to use it, but they're usually eager to take the new tech for a spin and see what it can do.

- Good critical thinking skills. They are highly logical in their approach to work and life. These people are natural thinkers and logical, effective planners.

- Easily understand patterns. Whether they purposefully do so or not, data diviners naturally see patterns everywhere: in how people act and think, the flow of work, the nature of office politics, the information in any chart they see, and pretty much in everything they observe.

- Science lovers. This group tends to be interested in science to some degree because of the logic and patterns they find there and because of their love for learning. They may not be in science professions, but they have an affinity for science all the same.

- Typically good at math. Typically this group has strong math skills, or least they have stronger math skills than the average person. But not always. Some may be truly awful at statistics and higher maths but possess such high pattern recognition and critical thinking skills that they can divine data easily with the help of software that does the math for them.

- Natural problem solvers. These are the "fixers" in your ranks. When data diviners see a problem they're usually the first to suggest a solution or even to just fix it outright.

- Easily bored with repetitive work. They may be doing repetitive work, after all jobs are still relatively hard to come by so they may have taken whatever job they could find, but they're not happy there. This group much prefers mental exercise to accompany their work.

- Purpose driven. This group is not at all interested in busy work. They want to know the purpose behind their work and they want to work purposely. It is this innate search for purpose that enables them to find faster and better ways to accomplish the same thing. They don't work harder; they work smarter.

- Values production over time clocking. These are clock haters. They don't want their work time tracked because they tend to find such activity annoying and useless. Instead they value actual production. In other words, it doesn't matter to this group if a task takes five minutes or five weeks, what matters is producing a worthy result. They want to be judged by results and not by how much time they took or didn't take in getting them. But don't worry, they tend to be hard workers who will stay at the task for whatever time is necessary to complete it. But if they accomplish it early, don't expect them to fill the rest of the time on the clock doing busy work. They'll want another challenging task to do. They are highly focused on efficient production and this is what makes them exceptionally good at innovating.

- Highly focused. This group is not easily distracted from a task. They tend to be highly focused and detailed in their work. While any human can make a mistake, this group makes far fewer than others, simply because they are so conscious of detail.

- Often teach peers. Because this group learns well and easily, they are the first among their peers to learn and master new things. Usually they are also quick to teach their peers or at least answer their questions. Usually a data diviner is the person others in their work group turn to for help in understanding a task or process.

These people, the data diviners, whomever they are and wherever they are, need to be identified and their skills put into play, not necessarily on the data science teams, although they are very helpful there too, but in any position where they can have a direct impact on how data is used in the organization. At the very least, they should be encouraged to share their thoughts and to show their peers the very real gains to be had in data analysis beyond the norm.

It's only when people with these tendencies are actively seeking new ways to use data that the company will see the full promise of big data come to fruition.

Until such people can be identified and their skills leveraged, the beginning big data play almost always rests on IT and/or the data science teams. Certainly the average team can work on the low-hanging fruit in data analysis if only by enhancing existing reports and processes. But for there to be any ground-breaking realizations of big data benefits and any truly imaginative innovations, those teams need members who are cross-disciplined and extremely knowledgeable of the business.

In other words, you need people on your data science teams who can bridge the gaps between disciplines and find the intersections. This is where creative thinking in terms of honing the company's competitive edge begins and thus where innovative ideas are found.

However, it is a mistake to limit your data efforts to only data science teams. Granted, they are the foundation on which the company can pivot to a better position but they are not, nor should they ever be, the company's only innovative engine. Start here but move quickly to recruit talented data diviners to the ongoing effort.

Start at a single point, such as with your data science team, but move quickly and steadily toward a large and fluid collaboration throughout the organization.

NEXT STEP: EMBRACING IGNORANCE

Understand that you and your team will always be saddled with a degree of ignorance. It is not possible to foresee everything or to know every question that needs to be asked. Learn to be comfortable with that ignorance and a near constant degree of uncertainty. After all, if you knew everything already, there would be no need to analyze the data in the first place.

Further, if you are aware of and acknowledge the ignorance, you can more easily identify what needs to be known. Use ignorance; consider it your friendly conspirator in big data explorations. It is when you are sure of the answer beforehand that you are more likely to fail because it then becomes more likely that you'll inadvertently introduce confirmation biases, manipulate the outcome, or overlook additional data.

Build your project strategy as tightly as you can in order to keep it on course but also allow some "ignorance flexibility" to enable the capture and leverage of knowledge heretofore unknown that you may find along the way.

Where to Start

You should develop an overall big data strategy as well as more pointed project-specific strategies. The overall data strategy should be focused on continuously discovering ways to improve the business through refinement, innovation, and solid returns, both in the short and long terms. Project-specific strategies should lead to a specific measurable and actionable end for that effort. This should be immediately followed with ideas about what can be done from there, which in turn should ultimately lead to satisfying the goals in the overall big data strategy and reshaping it as necessary too.

Figure 2.2 illustrates how big data projects form from your overall big data strategy, but each project also has its own strategy. As these projects come to fruition, your company grows and changes to become more competitive and profitable. When this happens, new ideas and needs form which then should return to shape, inform or instruct your overall big data strategy and to dictate new big data projects.

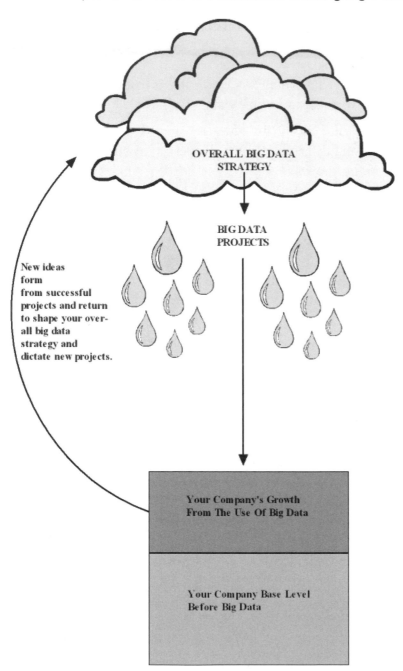

Figure 2.2
Big data projects form from your overall big data strategy, but each project also has its own strategy.

Source: Pam Baker. Illustration by John Duffey.

Begin at the End

The key to developing a winning big data strategy is to focus on actionable insights rather than on simply delivering information. This in not to say that knowledge isn't useful in its own right but merely an acknowledgment that even the best fishing expeditions are not satisfying unless you also bring home a basketful of fish at the end of the day. In other words, you must produce actionable insights for there to be measurable gain, that is, an appreciable return on investment (ROI). However, it is smart to also "fish" for new knowledge that may not result in an immediate payload, as that new knowledge will often point you to opportunities and avoidable pitfalls that you may not have otherwise discovered.

For projects designed to deliver actionable insights, you begin at the end by identifying what you need to know, and that which you can actually act upon, in order to solve a specific business problem or to reach a specific goal. From there you work backward to formulate the questions you need to ask of data in order to arrive at the needed insights.

If your defined goal is too broad, such as "increase sales," then you can't easily determine what information you'll need to look for within your data, nor will you be able to pinpoint a specific action to bring about the desired outcome. By contrast, if your defined goal is more specific, such as "to increase purchases of Product X by 10% in the 'best customers' group" then you will know what you need to look for inside your internal and externally imported data in order to develop a winning strategy.

For example, some of the things you would likely need to know in the "to increase purchases of Product X by 10% in your 'best customers' group" scenario are the following:

- A list of your top customers in general
- A list of your top customers who bought Product X in the past
- A list of your top customers who bought products similar to Product X in the past
- A list of top customers who have not purchased Product X but have bought similar or related products
- A determination of common characteristics and triggers among top buyers of product X and similar products that you can then use to identify other top customers in general who share the same characteristics and high response rate to the same triggers

- An understanding of how Product X compares with competing products on the market and with current trends overall; determine how that information affects "salability" of Product X

- An understanding of which price points moved Product X best in the past; which moved products similar to Product X best in the past

- Knowledge of which price points moved Product X well in the past and also delivered the best margin

- An understanding of which price points slowed Product X sales; find out whether those price points were the sole problem or whether there were other circumstances present that also affected Product X sales in the same time period

- A determination of what seasons, weather, and other external factors affected an uptick or downturn in Product X sales

- Insight into which sales people and stores are currently moving the most Product X and what they have in common (pricing, ad campaigns, in-store merchandising or window displays, weather conditions, sales contests, and so on)

- Metrics on what website positioning has moved the most Product X in the past

- Comparatives of all A/B and multivariate testing regarding or impacting Product X sales online

- A performance comparative of past ad and marketing campaigns aimed at moving Product X

- A study of loyalty programs that affected past sales of Product X and similar products to evaluate how well such worked in the past and to determine if a new loyalty tie-in is needed to move more of Product X now

- Analysis of what your competitors are doing to move Product X and similar products (pricing, ad/marketing campaigns, merchandising displays online and off, and so on)

Using analytics to explore new ideas and discover and address issues and opportunities is done much the same way. Start with a "what if" or "why is this so" or "could this be" question and work your way back to identify what questions you need to ask of data. Even if the answer is not actionable in some of these cases, the knowledge gleaned will likely be useful in other actionable situations.

Once you know what questions you need to answer, you can effectively mine data. When you find the answers to those and other related questions, you can combine them for a concise view that will then reveal an action. Evaluate the action in terms of logistics and cost as well as in terms of public relations, customer relations, and regulatory compliance. Take action accordingly.

When Action Turns into Inaction

Ideally your company will be willing, able, and prepared to take action as soon as you have the insights necessary to do so. Unfortunately this is sometimes not the case.

Industry analyst Joshua Greenbaum, who is also an IEEE Computer Society member and principal at Enterprise Applications Consulting, said in an interview following his presentation at the 2013 Rock Stars of Big Data event that the "number of companies that walk away from taking action after they have the insights from big data is unbelievable."

He cited as one example a manufacturer that used big data to discover counterfeiters who were stealing millions of dollars from the company by producing look-alike products complete in every detail, including packaging and the company logo. After the counterfeiters were busted via big data analysis, one would think the company would immediately act to protect future revenues. But that's not what happened, says Greenbaum. "They shrugged and walked away because they had no budget with which to act."

If you would like to hear Greenbaum's full presentation, you can find it on YouTube. The video is titled "Joshua Greenbaum: Imagineering Big Data—How to Bring Rock Star Analysis to Your Company." But rest assured that many industry observers have noted the all-too-common phenomenon of companies walking away from the answers found in data analysis.

This begs the question of why companies bother going to the expense and effort of analyzing big or small data if they have no plans to then act upon the findings? This is a frequent occurrence across industries. Why? Frequently, companies find they don't have the resources or the leadership commitment to follow through. Other times, says Greenbaum, "the company culture gets in the way."

In other words, if the analysis is counterintuitive to decision makers, if the action indicated is costly or threatens to disrupt other activities already budgeted and prioritized, and/or if the implementers perceive the action to be threatening to their job security or department, the recommended action is not taken and the big data project fails to produce a return on investment (ROI). This then, not surprisingly, tends to lead to a huge drop in morale among data science team members and users who were eagerly looking forward to having a solution.

Therefore it is prudent to consider at the beginning of strategy development both the availability of the means to take action on the results and the likelihood that action will be taken. There simply is no point in searching for a solution to a problem that the powers-that-be don't want solved or can't afford to act upon.

However, quite frequently you will not know in advance how the end results will be received or whether they will be acted on. Many big data efforts will thus be a bit of a gamble. To offset this risk, mix data projects so that you are running some you know will be seen to fruition with some you are unsure will ever see the light of day. In this way, you can steadily show a return on investment while also pushing forward into new territory.

Otherwise, consider big data analysis largely a "what if" game on a huge scale. However, time can be lost and efforts scattered if you simply begin by exploring all the "what ifs" you and your team can think up.

Identifying Targets and Aiming Your Sights

It is smarter to begin by looking at the reports and processes the company already uses.

In regard to reports, begin by noting the questions posed and the report requests made to IT and reporting systems. Also look at what reports are generated and what information they contain. Then ask the data science team to discern from this information what specific insights are being sought and why, and then figure out how those insights can be delivered more effectively and efficiently through big data analysis.

In regard to processes, follow a similar line of inquiry. Why does the process exist, that is, what ultimately is it designed to achieve? Look for inefficiencies in those processes that can be eliminated by a smarter use of data analytics. Sometimes you'll even discover that a process is no longer needed and should be replaced or eliminated outright.

This is where the "what if" game begins. This is where the team asks "what if we did it this way?" or "what other analysis can we add to help?" until an optimum answer is found. From there, mapping out a data project right down to the user interface and dashboard is relatively straightforward.

It's when you get past this low hanging fruit that the what-if game gets truly challenging. At that point you'll need creative, analytical thinkers who are unusually knowledgeable about the business and who are capable of intellectually exploring what lies beyond anything the company has ever analyzed or done before. The failure rate will increase at this stage since a good bit of this exercise is experimental or trial-and-error. Make sure your strategy accounts for this in terms of budget, ROI calculations, and the time and effort needed for multiple iterations.

Covering All the Bases

Beyond the previously mentioned considerations in strategy development, use this checklist to ensure your strategy is covering all the bases before you call it done:

- Is your strategy in line with the CEO's vision and the company's stated objectives? If not, are you confident you can sell your strategy to the C-suite? If not, your project is likely doomed to failure no matter how good your overall strategy is.

- Is your data project ethical? If you are unsure, check the ethics rules from reputable organizations and associations, including those in your specific industry or market. Some examples are the American Statistical Association (ASA); The National Science Foundation (NSF) supported Council for Big Data, Ethics, and Society; and the Data Science Association.

- What is the potential backlash from customers, society, or regulators? Make sure you understand those risks and ensure they are within an acceptable range before you finalize your strategy. And discuss your project in detail in advance with legal counsel. Otherwise, you will end up recommending or implementing actions that could prove costly to the company.

- Do you need data from third-party sources? If so, identify the sources in your strategy and make sure you know what costs and restraints exist before proceeding.

- Will the results move the company forward in some way? If not, label the project as experimental and feed it into the project stream in such a way that it neither slows the company's advance nor unduly reflects negatively in ROI calculations.

- What buy-ins do you need for this project to succeed? Solicit support from top management and users early and reinforce that support as often as needed going forward. Make part of your strategy a detailed plan to develop, nurture, and maintain all necessary buy-ins.

- Is your strategy free of human cognitive bias? In other words, is your team, or any member on it, seeking a specific outcome or approaching the project with an agenda other than finding an accurate answer to the question? If so, your strategy is compromised at the outset and the analysis will be highly questionable if not outright wrong.

■ Are your projects balanced between short-term, mid-term, and long-term returns? It's common for companies to focus on short-term ROI and thus ignore the long-term. Such tunnel vision is inadvisable as it can hurt the company over time. Make sure your overall strategy includes long-term projects and thinking too.

These guidelines will put you well on the way to devising a winning strategy.

How to Get Best Practices and Old Mindsets Out of Your Way

Because big data is relatively new, at least in terms of tools and the things those tools now make possible, everyone is busy trying to figure out how to best leverage and manage data. A goodly number of industry experts try to shed light by sharing use cases and what those success stories have in common. Inevitably, this list of commonalities becomes a set of oft-repeated "best practices."

While the concept of best practices works well in mature technologies and industries, it can actually be counter-productive in newer ones such as big data. Ironically in the case of big data that is because too little data is used to determine what practices are indeed the best. Most companies are experimenting today with big data and almost all of those are going for the simplest of projects in order to learn enough to take on more complex projects. Of those, many fail for a variety of reasons, some of which have nothing to do with their big data practices.

By all means note what successful companies are doing and how they are doing it, but remember always that the practices that will be successful for your company do not necessarily come canned and will always be measured in terms of business outcome. Take a hard look at what others are doing with big data and learn from it. Just don't blindly follow in those footsteps. Instead, apply what you learned only to the extent that it helps you arrive at your goals. That may mean skipping or adding steps or even leaving that path altogether.

Established mindsets, however, tend to be a heavily ingrained problem and one much harder to overcome than a lack of skills or project uncertainties. People—be they on your data science team, in the C-suite or end-users—are rarely inclined to leave their current brain rut or abandon lessons learned through previous experience. Some of those mindsets will need to change, however, if your company is to move to a data-driven model rather than a human intuitive model. Be prepared, for that task is not an easy one.

Addressing People's Fears of Big Data

Human stubbornness is, of course, part of the problem but so are negative personal experiences and perceptions. For example, in some companies the culture has been poisoned by punitive use of technology. In others, staffers perceive new technologies to be punitive even if they aren't. Whether purposefully punitive or not, employees may fear big data tools will be used to punish them or eliminate their jobs, particularly after witnessing or experiencing job losses through automation or outsourcing, time tracking tools applied to their work, and other technologies perceived to punish or replace workers.

When the personal experience or perception is one of punitive technology use, resistance to data-driven decision making is naturally high. Be aware of these mindset scenarios: stubbornness, intellectual and job pride, fear of job loss or punishment, fear of change, turf protection, budget protection, and fear of loss of control, among others. Build into your strategy the steps you need to take to acknowledge and then change negative or resistant mindsets from the outset.

Usually that begins by demonstrating early on how data analysis actually can make each person's job easier—particularly in decision making. Without making a big deal of it, stress that data-driven decisions also offer a degree of cover. When one makes a decision based on quantifiable data that can be clearly pointed to, win or lose, it is easier to justify.

Ending the Fear of the Unknown

Take for example, a national or district restaurant manager. It is his or her job to continuously increase sales for the company. The data he or she traditionally considers in this effort is generally dated and limited information. It is essentially a snapshot of occurrences in the past with little to no indication of context. Even if more current or real-time information is flowing in through various systems such is often incomplete, siloed rather than integrated, and also often out-of-context.

Yet it is all the information the national or district manager has to go on because he or she cannot physically be in all store locations all the time to personally observe each situation. Therefore the manager travels throughout the territory he is responsible for, and holds many meetings with managers beneath him in the hierarchy, trying to augment the data he has on hand.

Even so, he really has no idea what is happening in every store. In the end, he'll make an educated and possibly instinctive guess as to what actions should be taken to increase sales in each store and over the entire territory. That guess may or may not prove to be correct but he won't know which until much later.

By contrast, with big data the national or district manager will be able to see in near real-time or real-time, everything that is happening at each restaurant in the territory, including external factors such as weather, local events, and road construction that may be negatively or positively affecting sales for the duration.

But he can also see which servers are the best sellers and whether they are on duty, how food inventory is holding up to demand or wasting away for lack of it, which marketing campaigns are working where and which are not, and react to all of that and more in real-time to adjust each restaurant's performance immediately. Now he can do his job better and with less stress. It's less stress because now he can see what needs to be done rather than blindly guess at it. He can rapidly correct course as needed rather than suffer the consequences afterwards.

The national or district restaurant manager need not fear big data because big data cannot do his job for him; it cannot take action, only suggest it. But if he embraces big data, he can outperform on the job and thus actually protect his job because his performance remains high. Should something negative happen anyway, he can justify his actions based on the data analysis.

Tempering Assurances for Change Is About to Come

Explain to fearful workers that data analysis is not an automated process that replaces jobs but an enhancing element to help workers get the work done. Be careful with such claims because obviously if there is a department or group of people solely dedicated to producing the same reports month after month, big data tools could eliminate their jobs or necessitate transfers. For the most part, data analysis does not replace people; it enhances their performance. At least it isn't replacing people yet.

However, big data analysis will ultimately lead to job losses through a wide assortment of automations and process refinements stemming from the analysis. Further, there will be less and less human involvement in decision-making once all is said and done.

Andrew McAfee, principal research scientist at the Center for Digital Business in the MIT Sloan School of Management and author of *Enterprise 2.0*, succinctly made this point in his December 9, 2013 blog post in *Harvard Business Review*.

> *The practical conclusion is that we should turn many of our decisions, predictions, diagnoses, and judgments—both the trivial and the consequential—over to the algorithms. There's just no controversy any more about whether doing so will give us better results.*

When presented with this evidence, a contemporary expert's typical response is something like "I know how important data and analysis are. That's why I take them into account when I'm making my decisions." This sounds right, but it's actually just about 180 degrees wrong. Here again, the research is clear: When experts apply their judgment to the output of a data-driven algorithm or mathematical model (in other words, when they second-guess it), they generally do worse than the algorithm alone would. As sociologist Chris Snijders puts it, "What you usually see is [that] the judgment of the aided experts is somewhere in between the model and the unaided expert. So the experts get better if you give them the model. But still the model by itself performs better."

Things get a lot better when we flip this sequence around and have the expert provide input to the model, instead of vice versa. When experts' subjective opinions are quantified and added to an algorithm, its quality usually goes up. So pathologists' estimates of how advanced a cancer is could be included as an input to the image-analysis software, the forecasts of legal scholars about how the Supremes will vote on an upcoming case will improve the model's predictive ability, and so on. As Ian Ayres puts it in his great book Super-crunchers, "Instead of having the statistics as a servant to expert choice, the expert becomes a servant of the statistical machine."

Humans should take heart at that last bit of the quote as it is proving to be a smart move to incorporate expert opinions in algorithms at least for now.

The Feared Machine's Reign Is not Certain; Mankind Still Has a Role

However, there is solid reason to doubt that we'll soon see a day when machines will completely replace human reasoning and work. While well-designed algorithms perform nearly flawlessly, they are relatively rare today. One need only look at the ill-fitting ads regularly served by the likes of Facebook and Google, two of today's top algorithm builders, to see how far from hoped-for targets such algorithms can stray.

One can safely assume that algorithms will improve over time and machines will begin developing algorithms as often or more often as people do. But until machines come enabled with imagination and the ability to absorb and use context creatively, it is unlikely they will take over completely—at least not in a world dominated by humans.

However, it is a mistake not to acknowledge ongoing advancements in artificial intelligence (AI), much of which is big data driven. AI machines will indeed supplant most human workers one day but that day is not today.

Do not mislead people about the role of big data analysis in the workplace but do not feed fears of a data dominated world either because such fears may never be realized. And if they do come to be, it is likely they will materialize in a far less scary form. As McAfee pointed out in his post, adding human expert input to the algorithm dramatically improves the outcome. Human roles are more likely to adapt than to be eliminated in a data-driven world.

Reaching the Stubborn Few

As to reaching the more stubborn and negative people in the organization, that's a bit trickier to overcome. Identify them early if they are in key positions and dedicate part of your strategy to addressing this obstacle. The goal should be to find ways to convince them to positively view adoption of the results and to take action if they are in a position to do so. But in cases where individuals can't be educated or swayed, you'll need to find other ways around their resistance. The point is that the "human" factor, particularly in changing negative or resistant mindsets, must be a part of your overall strategy.

Eventually data-driven decision making will become as routine as email and negative mindsets will become less common. Until then, you must prepare to win hearts and minds or you may find your projects sabotaged from within.

ANSWER THE QUESTIONS NO ONE HAS ASKED

Other things to consider in your strategy development are the questions no one thought to ask. If you're waiting on other people in the organization to tell you what they need, you may be in for a long and fruitless wait. Generally speaking, people don't realize what is possible in the realm of data analysis and therefore don't know what to request.

And, if in response to the resulting sound of crickets, all you're doing with big data is rethinking and reworking existing processes and reports, you are missing the greater benefits to be had. It's perfectly fine to start out reworking existing projects, as they provide solid learning exercises and build on established results and parameters, not to mention they are the fastest route to solid ROI. However, you will need to move past those pretty quickly if your business is to have and retain a competitive edge.

One of the easiest ways to build in this forward movement is to add the "and then" questions to your "what if" questions in every project strategy.

For example, follow a big data analysis on financials by asking a question such as "what if finance could drill down to small data and drag selected data sets into a grouping in any way they want to create a new analysis on demand using just that data subset"? Certainly that would be a brilliant mix of standard reporting and self-serve analysis through the simplicity of visualization. Kudos should be given all around. But why stop there?

Keep Asking What Is Possible

Part of the strategy should be to follow that moment of clarity brought on by a "what if" question with another question: "and then what is possible?"

By creating a culture where data teams naturally follow a successful answer to the "what if" question with an "and then what is possible?" question, people will begin viewing each project not as an end in itself, but as a step along a continuum. It is easier to see next steps, particularly innovative steps, if you ask what you can do next once you are able to do "this."

Another way to find an answer to questions that no one has asked but clearly should is to combine results from earlier projects and wonder aloud what can be done from there. Some combinations will lead to a dead end. Others will lead to innovations either through their direct use or by sparking related Eureka moments. But this too is not an end unto itself; it is the beginning of yet another purpose-driven data exploration.

Look for End Goals

Yet another way is to observe how people work in specific jobs. What data do they use? How do they use it? What do they do with the results? Further, are those results shared with anyone else in any other job and, if so, why do they need it and what do they do with it? In other words, observation can enable you to detect, follow, and analyze the information trail within the business in order to see what knowledge is sought and why.

But most importantly, you should wonder about why any of the people involved in the business do any of the tasks they do. If you ask them, they'll probably just explain that the task is part of their job or that they do a specific task or set of tasks in order to arrive at point C, or D, or E. But that often is not the real, or at least not the entire answer to why they do what they do. Further, there may no longer be a need to arrive at point C, D, or E. In other words, that route may have worked in previous years but a new route to a different end may work better now.

For example, let's consider someone in the organization who is charged with managing fleet fuel costs. The manager may spend a goodly portion of their day gathering fuel costs from different fueling outlets, watching the energy market, and forecasting future fuel cost estimates. The data science team could improve that existing process by providing that manager with a stream of data from one or more reliable third parties, such as from the U.S. Energy Information Administration (EIA). In this way, the manager uses more of her day making management decisions rather than in gathering the information.

But improving efficiencies in that process may not be enough to positively deliver the end goal—which is to manage and ultimately decrease fuel costs. Big data analytics could reveal that changing the vehicles' routes to leverage lower prices available from other fueling stations not previously considered, or adding alternative fuels, will lower fleet fuel costs. Further the analytics may reveal that switching to self-driving vehicles will reduce overall operational costs and maintain even vehicle speeds (as opposed to a human driver who may change speeds unnecessarily, especially if tired) to further reduce fuel costs.

In the first scenario, the existing process is made more efficient but it remains essentially the same. In the second, the process is changed in order to better achieve a well-defined end goal—in this case managing and lowering fuel costs.

This is why digging to discover the actual reason behind actions and processes is imperative and why weighing the efficiency and usefulness of that reason and action is equally important.

Mull it over. Figure out what ultimately it is they are trying so hard to know and do. If you can discover the answer to that, you can form the question they don't know to ask, and then you can deliver an answer that is relevant to the work at hand.

CROSS-POLLINATE THE INTERPRETATIVE TEAM

As previously discussed, it is important for members of the data science team to be multi-disciplined. They need to understand the business and at least one discipline other than data science. The reason for this is clear. Tools are useful only in the hands of master craftsmen with a clearly-defined purpose. That "clearly-defined purpose" can only come from understanding what the business needs built, repaired, or adapted.

For example, a data science team member who is well-versed in financials and data tools will prove invaluable in providing financial data insights. This logic follows with other disciplines and other department projects. Is it too much to ask for a single member of the team to possess such a mix of skill sets? Not really, but they can be difficult (and expensive) to find.

Start by looking in your ranks for skilled IT professionals who have served time servicing a specific department. Those people should have a strong understanding of the business and how that department in particular works. They will have at least some data skills because that is a goodly part of what IT does—delivers data in a variety of reports.

However, they may not have all of the necessary big data skills and you may need to supplement the team with individuals who possess a working knowledge of advanced data science, data mining, data sourcing, and new big data tools. Or, you may elect to train these workers on using big data tools instead. In any case, it is typically easier and faster to train people how to use the tools than it is to train a skilled big data scientist on the nuances of your business as a whole and any given department or division in particular.

Keep in mind that not all big analysis, as Greenbaum calls it, requires the use of big data proper. It's not like data analysis is an entirely new, never-before-heard-of business tactic. It's only that the new tools are better, cheaper, and faster than the traditional ones. Therefore, you may be able to build a productive team from your existing IT ranks that can function just fine until you can train them further and/or find and hire supplemental talent specifically trained in big data.

Add Business Analysts and Key End Users to the Team

But that is only part of the solution. You'll also need multi-disciplined or cross-pollinated data and business analysts. It's one thing for data science teams to feed insights to a given department or a member of the C-suite. It's another thing entirely to interpret the results correctly and form appropriate action plans.

For this reason, part of the strategy must include building rapport and collaboration between business and data analysts, as well as other key end users, who are not already a part of the data science team. In this way, the entire organization becomes one giant big data engine where innovative ideas can flow in any direction. Big data use becomes ubiquitous and a renewable energy that forever powers the organization.

To that end, increasing data literacy throughout the company, or at the very least among key personnel, either through training existing employees or through acquiring new ones who already possess this skill, is imperative. That part of the company's overall big data strategy should be shared with human resources so they can begin to act on it now.

Add a Chief Data Officer to Gather and Manage the Data

Mario Faria, an affable and brilliant guy originally hailing from Brazil, bills himself as the world's very first chief data officer (CDO), and perhaps he is. He certainly holds that title at ServiceSource. He's also a big data advisor to the Bill & Melinda Gates Foundation. Whether or not he is the very first CDO, he is certainly a passionate supporter of the concept and the practice.

"A CDO does not own the data, he or she is the caretaker of the data and, importantly, an agent of change in helping to establish a data driven culture inside the organization," he said. "From here they are account-able for data strategy, bringing a data management view on how a company can make money using its data assets. The importance of this role is coming to light and will be a part of the discussions among C-level and the board of directors."

Indeed, it's a brilliant idea packing a ton of potential benefits and many companies are taking advantage of it now. In other words, the addition of a CDO to executive ranks is no longer an anomaly.

Mark Raskino, vice president and Gartner Fellow in the Executive Leadership and Innovation group of Gartner Research, reported in November 2013 that the number of chief data officers doubled over the number in 2012 to a total of 100 (see Figure 2.3). Interestingly over 25% of them were women, almost twice the number of female CIOs. The majority of CDOs (65%) were based in the United States, but they were also found in over a dozen countries.

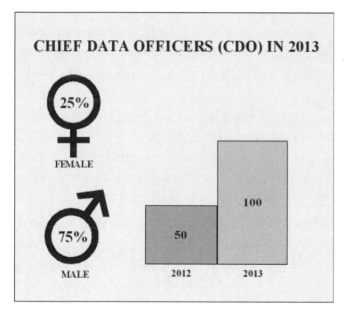

Figure 2.3
Depiction of Gartner Research findings on the growth of Chief Data Officers and gender breakdown in 2013.
Source: Gartner Research. Bar graph drawn by Pam Baker. Illustration by John Duffey.

Traditionally data has been kept and managed by IT as one of its many daily duties. But that was back in the day when data was only generated and used in-house and it rarely if ever took center stage in company affairs.

Today we are in a data economy and data-driven decision making is the goal at nearly every level of business. Data has officially come out of the warehouse closet and now sits center stage like a prima donna with all eyes upon it. In short, data is a major tangible asset now.

Critically, the data needed to complete the transition from information to knowledge is no longer housed entirely on-premises as it once was. It's not even always solely within the company's ownership or control. A good chunk of such data may typically be in the cloud or in the possession of other entities.

Someone needs to be in charge of managing this new asset across many fronts, not only in terms of housekeeping and cataloging, as was once the primary focus, but also in regard to actively developing and implementing strategies, standards, policies, and governance.

Make no mistake, a chief data officer is not simply a caretaker but also a strategic thinker, a champion of projects, and ideally a master of all things data related.

It makes sense to have a chief data officer or someone charged with CDO duties in place. There needs to be a point person ultimately responsible and accountable for the company's data currency in this new data economy. After all, none of us would treat any other form of valuable asset with any less diligence or without actively seeking to maximize its return, so why would we treat this new currency any differently?

However you choose to manage data, do not take the task lightly. Make sure someone in the organization stays on top if it constantly.

START SMALL AND BUILD UP AND OUT

While you should think big in developing your overall big data strategy, it is wise to begin implementation with small, well-defined projects. This enables the team to rapidly turn projects to meet ROI expectations and to learn as they go. The value of the on-the-job training cannot be overstated.

One of the many striking comments Foster Provost made at an October 2013 press luncheon at Strata/Hadoop World in NYC was that there is "no consensus on what data scientists should know." Provost is a professor of information systems and NEC faculty fellow at New York University's Stern School of Business as well as coauthor of the book *Data Science for Business*. He said he was often asked what skills companies should look for in data scientists but there's no firm answer to that question.

Hence the need for your data science teams to learn on the job. Yes, they need some hard and soft data science skills from the outset but don't expect those to be complete or adequately refined. At least not yet.

It will take time for universities and others to be able to accurately define needed skills for this group and to refine their teachings accordingly. It will also take considerable time for enough data scientists to gain the experience necessary to hit peak performance. Meanwhile, there's work to be done.

Make gaining experience part of your strategy. Start with small, purpose-driven projects that can double as training exercises and move to larger projects when the team is more experienced with the tools and the concepts.

PROTOTYPES AND ITERATIONS STRATEGIES

Because big data is relatively new and few end users understand it, it's important to present work in stages so they can focus on one element at a time. In this way, you will increase adoption and collaboration and you will find what changes need to be made early on.

Sapana Patel, senior director of BI and Software Development at Spirit Airlines, demonstrated how her company achieved this during her presentation at the 2013 Big Data Summit in Arizona. Patel explained that her team shared prototypes in stages so users could evaluate design and ease of use before they worried about the actual data. In this way the team could finalize the design of reports and dashboards before they plugged the data in. Such an approach saves time and effort, decreases complaints, and increases adoption. Once the final rollout happens, none of the end users were surprised by how it looked and worked or by the data it contained.

There should be few if any surprises in successive iterations either. Collaborate with users on the front-end, get feedback early, and roll out what was expected by all. Changes in each iteration should be handled the same way. Make these steps part of your project strategy so that they are never overlooked or bypassed.

A WORD ABOUT ADDING PREDICTIVE ANALYTICS TO YOUR DATA STRATEGY

Predictive analytics is something everyone talks about but few actually use. Everyone would like a crystal ball to peer into and see the future but most have their hands full dealing with the here and now. That's unfortunate because predictive analytics can be key to plotting the company's future and its just-in-time innovations.

It is imperative to include predictive analytics in your overall big data strategy. For some, it will be easiest to accomplish that by following projects based on real-time or traditional analysis with projects centered on predictive analytics addressing the same questions in a future timeframe. This tactic helps pace the addition of predictive analytics and focuses its use on known areas of need.

At some point in your overall big data strategy there should be definite plans to broaden the use of predictive analytics. As with other potential long journeys though, taking initial small steps is better than delaying starting. After all, there will never be a time when data science teams are not busy. Plan its use now or it will never happen.

DEMOCRATIZE DATA BUT EXPECT FEW TO USE IT (FOR NOW)

There is much talk in the industry about democratizing data and analytics so that anyone in the business can tap into them however and whenever they need to. In theory, under such a scheme everyone will use the data, at least everyone who is duly authorized will, and the company will move smoothly and rapidly forward as a result. In practice, it is highly unlikely that more than a few people will actually regularly use such data.

"People will buy analytics and workbenches and expect everyone to use them to write their own reports," explained John Lucker, principal at Deloitte Consulting. "But an audit of licenses in actual use typically reveals a fairly big ratio of unused licenses which is costly in itself but also means the company is not getting use out of the data."

At this moment in time, data literacy rates are incredibly low in the average organization. This is true even among the millennial generation who grew up in a highly technical world. This situation exists because people are more likely to be experienced in using technology, particularly consumer technology, than they are in understanding how it works. While the average person can readily use analytical results, they typically have no idea how those results came to be or what else they can be used for nor do they necessarily have the desire to find out.

For example, people are generally familiar with checking the analytical results provided by a service like Expedia and making a decision based on that information. This is a data-driven decision although they may not recognize it as such. However, they do not necessarily understand how Expedia or a related service works or what else they could do with the information. They generally accept the analytical results as accurate and use them for the intended purposes only. The same holds true with data and analytics that people use at work. The average person only uses them to perform a previously set task without considering what else the information could be used for or whether the information is even accurate.

If this is the case, why should any company democratize data? Simple. It is the quickest way to find and identify those employees who do have an affinity for data and analytical thinking. Those employees *will* use the data and often in very creative and unexpected ways. Make sure part of your overall strategy is to take note of who is using the data and how, and that it includes a plan to leverage this previously hidden talent pool.

Your Strategy Is a Living Document; Nourish It Accordingly

While no plan works if it isn't executed accordingly, rigidity in adhering to the plan can also be self defeating. Treat your overall big data and project strategies as living documents that will adapt and grow in response to changes, new discoveries, and, yes, additional data. This is not the same thing as scope or mission creep. You need to keep projects planned and focused but within parameters that allow flexibility so that you can leverage elements, processes, and new knowledge as you discover them.

Further, it is important to consciously plan to routinely revisit and rework your big data strategy on a regular basis. As time passes, new knowledge is discovered and skills improve. Make sure your strategy is refined regularly to reflect and leverage those advancements.

Summary

In this chapter you learned how confusion leads to inertia in using big data for decision-making throughout the organization and how to overcome that. You learned how to formulate both an overall big data strategy and successful project-specific strategies, as well as show to build more projects off of successfully completed ones. The reasons that strategies fail, ROI is not delivered, and actionable insights are not acted on, became clear and tactics to resolve or overcome these issues were revealed. The human factor, and all the issues contained within, was explained and tactics were explored to successfully address these too. Further, you learned several ways to build a successful team, including finding and recruiting "data diviners" scattered throughout your organization. In short, you now know how to strategize and drive big data efforts in your company.

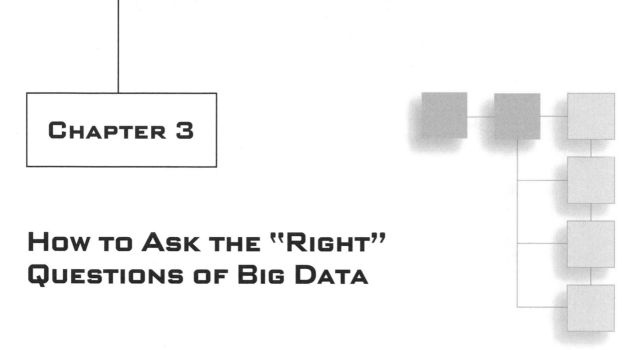

CHAPTER 3

HOW TO ASK THE "RIGHT" QUESTIONS OF BIG DATA

While data analysis has always been important to business decisions, traditionally it has been possible only as an after-the-fact process. For example, analysis of the effectiveness of a marketing campaign could be conducted only once a campaign ran its course. Financial analysis similarly was done at the end of a week, a quarter, or a year. In other words, no matter what was analyzed, the findings came too late to "feedback" into the process and change anything in the now. Instead they became "lessons learned" to be applied to the next marketing campaign, next quarter's financial planning, or the next endeavor. One of the most valuable features about today's analytical tools is the ability to see what is happening in real-time, or near real-time if you prefer, which means you can change course as needed to affect outcomes immediately.

Unfortunately, as in many aspects of work (and life), "data paralysis" can set in given there is so much data available. When this happens, instead of spurring companies to the next phase of data analysis, they can become confused over what data to use and what to measure. To change this dysfunctional dynamic, start by forming the questions the company most needs answers to, rather than forming them based on what data is currently or potentially available. Think in terms of what instant knowledge would make the biggest difference in moving the company or the department ahead immediately. At least for the moment, forget about the data and tools and focus only on what insights offer the most business value.

Eight Ways to Overcome Data Paralysis

Try these eight helpful ways to overcome data paralysis:

- **Base your questions on a current business objective; follow the money.** Think in terms of what instant knowledge would make the biggest difference in moving the company or the department ahead immediately. At least for the moment, forget about the data and tools and focus only on what insights offer the most business value.

- **Stop worrying about the size of your company data.** You can and should use data from multiple sources to get the best results. Fortunately, data is everywhere and a good bit of it is even free. This means that there is enough data available to you right now to use big data tools regardless of how much—or how little—data your company owns.

- **Race with the data analysts you already have.** Make no mistake, big data is changing everything in every industry and it waits for no one. In this race it's better to just get moving and go with the data analysts you have rather than wait until you can hire newly minted data scientists. Your own analysts know your business and are experienced in data analysis; all they need is some training on using the tools. A newly hired data scientist, on the other hand, may know how to use the tools but he or she will need months to learn your business.

- **Don't wait until you master big data; learn as you go.** Seriously, you do not have time to learn all there is to know about big data before you start using it. Start with small projects and learn as you go. Grow your own experts by doing one project after another and moving steadily ahead in project complexity.

- **Stop worrying about front-end cost; the real cost is in failing to use big data at all.** Storage is cheap and analytics are getting steadily cheaper. Besides, your business is already storing and using data now and odds are those costs are actually higher than the cost of new big data alternatives. Cost and ROI should not be your focus; gaining competitive advantages should be. What do you suppose the cost to your company will be if it suddenly finds it can no longer compete?

- **Stop worrying that employees outside of IT won't know how to use it.** Newsflash: People are already using big data every day by using apps like Expedia, Yelp, Kayak, Google Earth, and many others. These apps serve up the results of big data analytics on mobile and other devices and most people are comfortable with using them. So stop thinking big data analytics is a totally foreign concept. Most of your employees will adopt your company analytics with little fuss.

- **Start with evolution before you join the revolution.** Add more inputs to the algorithms you already use to get better outputs immediately. In other words, improve the data analysis your company is already doing—evolve those into something better and stronger before you join the big data revolution and start changing everything about your business.

- **Face the change.** Whether you or your company is comfortable with change, change is coming and much of it is big-data driven. You really only have two choices here—manage the change or get run over by it. Either way, you can't avoid change.

Remember always that this process is part scientific, part creative, and part sheer necessity because you need to develop every possible competitive advantage to stay profitable. Data analysis has never been, nor will it ever be, about simply parsing data and serving up whatever you find in the hopes that someone, somewhere in the organization might one day put that analysis to use.

All fundamentally useful data analysis must be purpose-driven. And that purpose is defined by the question(s) asked of the data. If you ensure the questions asked are highly relevant to the business at hand, then the answer(s) returned will be something you can take action on (or conversely, stop or forego an action if analysis indicates it's fruitless) in meaningful ways.

COLLABORATE ON THE QUESTIONS

While it is possible for IT staff to develop questions for further data analysis by reviewing existing reports for clues, such a tactic is merely a starting point. Generally, forming the right questions requires a collaborative effort between people in the data science team and those outside of IT. Sometimes the collaboration will be a true and equal partnership, other times it will be more one-sided with one party taking the lead or pushing the other. Regardless, for data analysis to be highly useful and truly actionable, the initial question formation cannot occur in isolation.

Unfortunately, many companies attempt exactly that. Typically this is due to a low data literacy rate, which results in the data literate second-guessing what the data illiterate need to know. Second-guessing is often unavoidable because many people do not understand or make the leap to what can be learned from data beyond how they use it now. They therefore cannot coherently express what else they need. However, a second-guessing-driven data analysis approach is limited at best and fundamentally flawed at worst.

The far better approach is to ask key individuals or department teams what specific information they need (or would like to have) to make their work more efficient or that they can see as impacting the company or the department's bottom line. Ask what information or measurements they currently seek and use—and why—in the course of their work. Then determine together what additional or improved information will correlate or expand the knowledge gained from their current use of data. The more focused people are in considering the issue, the better. By collaborating in this way, you can determine a useful direction and form more specific questions.

THE MAGIC 8 BALL EFFECT

Another accomplishment from collaborating on question formation is narrowing the initial scope from the general to the specific. Asking too general a question can lead to vague answers that can be tough to effectively act upon. Think of this as the "Magic 8 Ball effect." The familiar Magic 8 Ball toy gives quick general answers at the turn of the ball, and while the answers can be entertaining or interesting, they aren't really useful. The same type of effect can happen in big data analysis. However, general questions are useful for sparking more specific questions down the chain.

An example of a too general question is asking for the characteristics of the typical Facebook user. The result may be interesting (the Magic 8 Ball effect) but not particularly useful to your marketing campaign since it doesn't depict a real person. A narrower question would serve you better, such as which Facebook users liked XYZ with XYZ representing something that correlates with the product you are promoting in your marketing campaign or a buyer characteristic. The answer to that question will be useful to your marketing efforts. It will also lead to even narrower questions that will ultimately provide you with a list of qualified prospects you can then target in your campaign.

Note

A paper published in the journal Proceedings of the National Academy of Sciences (PNAS) by researchers at Cambridge's Psychometrics Centre, in collaboration with Microsoft Research Cambridge, revealed that few Facebook users click Likes that explicitly reveal intimate personal attributes, perhaps in an attempt to conceal such. Instead, researchers can best find this information by inferring from less obvious Likes. Surprisingly accurate conclusions can be drawn from seemingly innocuous liking behavior. For example, the study found correlations between likes for curly fries with high user IQs and likes for the That Spider is More Scared Than U post with non-smokers. Currently information on Facebook Likes is publicly available by default. The Cambridge researchers said that "observation of Likes alone is roughly as informative as using an individual's actual personality test score."

From the summary on that study published on the University of Cambridge website:

Researchers created statistical models able to predict personal details using Facebook Likes alone. Models proved 88% accurate for determining male sexuality, 95% accurate distinguishing African-American from Caucasian American and 85% accurate differentiating Republican from Democrat. Christians and Muslims were correctly classified in 82% of cases, and good prediction accuracy was achieved for relationship status and substance abuse—between 65 and 73%.

But few users clicked Likes explicitly revealing these attributes. For example, less that 5% of gay users clicked obvious Likes such as Gay Marriage. Accurate predictions relied on "inference"—aggregating huge amounts of less informative but more popular Likes such as music and TV shows to produce incisive personal profiles.

Even seemingly opaque personal details such as whether users' parents separated before the user reached the age of 21 were accurate to 60%, enough to make the information "worthwhile for advertisers," suggest the researchers.

Specific questions help guide the project from data selection to the metrics used. But sometimes even a specific question is the wrong thing to ask if it misses the intended mark. This is why collaboration on formation of questions is so important.

Further, collaborations will often reveal whether there is the will and the means to take action on the results. If action can't or won't be taken in some fashion, asking the questions may be a fruitless exercise.

Translating Human Questions to Software Math

Once you have set priorities on what answers and information you need from the data and have formed your questions accordingly, you'll need data scientists and engineers to translate the question into an algorithm. Popular languages for data analysis include R, Python, Julia, Java, Hadoop and Hive, Scala, Kafka, Storm, and MatLab.

It will be up to the data science team to determine the modeling, identify the needed data sources, and do the data mining. Further, the team will eliminate outliers that could taint or distort results and test relationships between metrics and subsets, among other technical duties. In the end, a stream of analysis or a combination of streams will result. From there, humans must interpret what these results mean to the organization and how to act upon them.

It is important to understand that data analysis will not pop out a detailed and convenient answer that says "do this" with a big arrow pointing the way. Instead it should quickly provide what you need to know in order to make a fact-based decision. Even stand-alone desktop data visualization and analysis tools—such as Tableau and MicroStrategy Analytics Desktop—deliver results in this way. This is primarily why this book is titled *Data Divination* and not *Automated Decision-Making*!

Checklist for Forming the "Right" Questions

The "right" questions to ask of the data is determined largely by the information you need in order to address a specific business problem or objective and by properly identifying the data set(s) containing that information. However, a few general guidelines can help refine the questions and improve the outcome.

- Is the question specific and measurable?
- Will the answer be actionable and do the will and means exist to take action?

- How quickly and how often do you need the information? Real-time? Near real-time? Weekly? Monthly?

- Does this information have a shelf life? For example, is your question tied to a specific marketing campaign or an ongoing need for marketing information? Crystallizing context before hand will help you refine the question.

- Will this information replace or enhance existing information in a meaningful way?

- Is this a quest for new information or a rehashing or validation of existing information? Are you trying to learn something new here or are you simply repeating old processes and old thinking? Certainly there is nothing wrong with validating existing information or plans, but the true value in big data analysis is in thinking creatively and reaching beyond traditional limitations.

If you get the questions right, the rest will logically follow. But be prepared, most questions lead to more questions. That is as it should be; how else can you discover what else there is to know?

Summary

In this chapter you learned about the importance of correctly and precisely forming questions for big data analysis. You learned that often the best questions to ask are not the obvious ones and that interdepartmental collaboration is invaluable to question formation. Further, you learned several ways to overcome data paralysis. You now even have a checklist you can use to make sure you are asking the right questions.

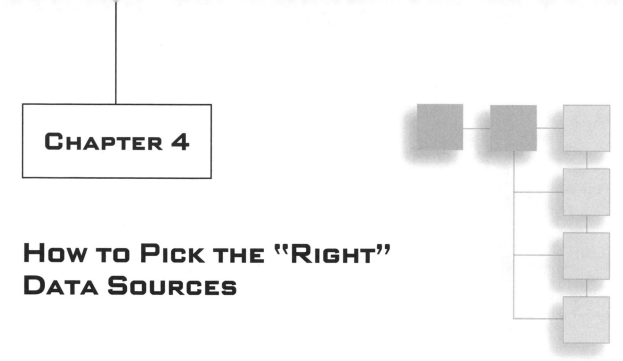

Chapter 4

How to Pick the "Right" Data Sources

In the minds of data scientists and IT pros who deal with the intricacies of analyzing and storing data, the source of any given data set is not nearly as important as its form. "We ignore the source and focus on working with data based on whether it is structured or unstructured," said Sunil Kakade, IT Director at Sears, in an interview for this book. And that is as it should be from a technical perspective, because unstructured data is raw and unorganized. Structured data is the opposite: it is highly organized and suited for automated analysis and database integration. Examples of unstructured data are social media posts, emails, the content of books, and a wide assortment of business and personal documents. Examples of structured data are machine data and customer transactional data. However, from a business perspective the source of one's data sets matters a great deal.

You Need More Data Sources (Variety), Not Just More Data (Volume)

Variety in data calls for more sources, but not necessarily a fire hose of data from those sources. The value is found in layering data from multiple sources, not in simply adding bulk to the final data count.

Indeed, this is a good time to review data volume, i.e. size, and its relative unimportance to most analytical projects. While it's true that too small a data set can lead to insignificant or misleading results, it's also important to understand that a bigger data set can do the same. Bigger is not necessarily better. However, if your company has amassed, or amasses over time, great volumes of data, there are tools and applications to handle that volume of data. You'll likely find a good bit of that data to be useful but some of it will merely be flotsam.

On occasion you'll find entire data sets, big and small, to be useless, irrelevant or without a clear use case. Sometimes companies lose sight of this and hoard all the data they can find in a vague hope that one day it will prove useful. Such a strategy, if one can call it that, often leads only to higher data storage and management costs, not to mention increasing potential legal and other liabilities in the event of a data breach resulting in loss of stored data.

The confusion over the volume of data that is needed for analysis stems in part from the unfortunate moniker we've saddled the tools and discussion with: "big data." While it is true that new data analysis tools were initially designed to manage and analyze large amounts of data, it turns out that these tools, such as real-time and predictive analytics, work extremely well on smaller (although still sizeable) data sets too. As previously discussed in Chapter 1, "What Is Big Data, Really?," there is no real consensus on what size a data set must reach to technically be classified as "big." Certainly the largest data collections easily qualify as such but once you slide down the size scale it's harder to find a definitive line. Further, data from outside sources can be layered with company owned data thus creating a larger size of data to be analyzed. Therefore, the size of the data you own doesn't dictate whether or not you can use big data tools. But that is not to say that big data tools should be used for every analysis nor that data of any given size can solve every business problem.

Finding key insights and solutions to problems that can be solved through data analysis depends significantly on the quality of the data used, in terms of its accuracy, authenticity, and the reliability of its source. We'll come back to this important point in a moment.

WHY YOUR OWN DATA ISN'T ENOUGH AND WILL NEVER BE ENOUGH, NO MATTER HOW LARGE IT GROWS

Certainly internal data stores are helpful in solving a number of business problems, particularly in improving internal processes. Because internal data is generated by ongoing business operations it contains some (but not all) answers pertinent to addressing existing problems and/or pointing to overlooked opportunities. For example, a quick look at how your company's logistics managers are currently tracking, calculating, and predicting fuel costs will point to ways that company owned data can be better used to achieve the same ends faster and more efficiently. In other words, big data tools allow fast and frequent analysis of data, which in turn illuminates process changes that are also faster and more efficient. You aren't reinventing the wheel here; you're just adding nitrogen filled rubber tires, puncture-proofing, run-flat capabilities, and fuel efficiency, as well as stronger rims.

This is precisely why most companies use big data first to improve existing operations. It is relatively easy to identify where problems or shortfalls exist in internal processes that can be solved by more data and better, faster analysis of it.

However, even efforts to improve internal processes are hobbled to some degree if you're limited to analysis of only internal data. Why? For one thing, it usually doesn't account for competitor actions or emerging disruptive forces unless, of course, you're gathering data on that as well and storing it internally.

By working in isolation and applying analysis only to internal data, you may find yourself improving processes and products that are on their way to becoming obsolete or unprofitable. Conversely, if you are collecting and storing data on outside forces—such as competitor actions and emerging industry disruptors—you may find yourself allocating too much money to data collection and storage.

DATA HOARDING VERSUS CATCH AND RELEASE

Your aim should be to avoid hoarding data from either external or internal sources. Purge outdated or irrelevant data as needed and do not collect data if there is no clear or present business use for it.

Storing data for eternity "just in case" there might be a use for it only impedes your work and drives up your costs and potential liabilities. Consider using a "catch and release" approach in some cases. In that approach you collect and store data, usually but not always from an outside source, for the purposes of a specific project but then dump it when you are done. You can always return to that third-party source for updated data should you need it later. Why then would you go to the expense and effort of storing it?

One-Dimensional Traps

Similar drawback scenarios exist in other departments. Take marketing, for example. If the only customer data being analyzed is transactional, then the picture of customers is one dimensional and incomplete. Why? For one thing it is exceedingly rare for a person to buy everything from one company. Therefore, you can't know a customer's complete buying profile just from analyzing their transactional history with your company.

It's not that you need to know *every* intimate detail about the customer, but rather you need to know enough to infer correctly what that customer's buying triggers actually are. If you know or can infer those triggers, you can induce more and larger purchases, and that is, after all, why you're using big data in marketing efforts, isn't it?

Using only your company transactional data, you can't be sure of the frequency of total product or product category buys let alone why they were purchased. Any given customer can buy the same product from numerous stores and in different brands and that activity will not show in your internal data, resulting in mistaken conclusions or missed opportunities.

THE MYSTERIOUS CASE OF THE DIAPER-BUYING DOG-OWNER

A perfect example is diapers. A customer may buy one brand from Walgreens when on sale but an entirely different brand from CVS a week later during another sale. Such behavior may be driven by temporary price discounts on the two brands, customer reward programs from either or both chains, or by sheer happenstance of proximity of either store when need for more diapers arises. It behooves the seller to know the motivation(s) behind the buy in order to leverage that buying trigger over and over again. However, there could be other or more motivations behind these purchasing decisions than those the seller initially suspects. Perhaps the buyer is a grandmother buying brands according to her grandchildren's parent's preferences on her way to their respective houses, hence the stops at different stores. Or maybe the buyer is using the diapers inconsistent with its expected use, perhaps for a new puppy to prevent accidents in the house. It is not uncommon for children's diapers or adult incontinence pads to cost less than puppy diapers sold in pet stores. To a price-conscious consumer, cutting a hole in a diaper meant for a human child to accommodate the puppy's tail or attaching a self-adhesive adult incontinence pad to the inside of a washable dog diaper may be a perfect and cheaper solution. Good luck in detecting that with pure transactional data run through your current algorithms.

Now, you may be wondering at this point what difference the buyer's motivation for buying the product makes as long as the product is sold. Knowing or being able to infer the precise buying trigger is essential to reducing waste in marketing, retaining the customer and selling more products.

In the case of the buyer who uses diapers for her dog, any marketing offers for baby related items will result in a no sale and are therefore a wasted effort. However, knowing or correctly inferring that the diaper-buyer is not a mother but a grandmother, makes it possible to send her offers on diapers *and* offers for other products appealing to her demographic.

THE VALUE IN UPSIZING TRANSACTIONAL DATA

Knowing or correctly inferring the customer's motivation for making a purchase is also key to upselling, moving the buyer to buy a more expensive product or one with a higher margin for your company, and cross-selling, moving the buyer to buy additional items in the same or a related product category.

Remember also that transactional data reveals past purchases and may or may not have any bearing on future purchases. If items were bought as one-time gifts or a favor for a neighbor, for example, those transactions muddy rather than clarify the customer's buying profile.

Further, when transactional data is taken out of context, it blinds you to other selling opportunities. Take for example, a customer who recently bought outside patio furniture from your store. If you are only using internal transactional data you might pitch that customer garden gnomes and outdoor lighting. By contrast, if you also used social media data and public data on home deeds, you might discover that this customer bought patio furniture to use by the pool at their newly purchased home. Now you are instantly able to pitch a vast array of home products instead of the few you otherwise would have offered and thus gain more sales from this one customer.

By relying only on internal data, at best you can gain but an inkling of what the customer does. You can't fully understand the customer's buying habits or motivations. Relying on your internal data alone further stymies understanding of actionable motivations and may undercut efforts to successfully move a potential customer to buy from your company.

THE LIMITS TO SOCIAL MEDIA ANALYSIS

Some companies try to resolve this problem by analyzing social media data as a stand-alone project. The thinking behind this is that social media can reveal customer sentiments about products, brands, and stores and their buying motivations. While social media analysis can provide many useful insights, these have largely proved unsatisfactory when used as sole source for analysis because the data is often incomplete and mostly reveals correlation rather than causation.

The resulting data problems are painfully evident. As any social media user can attest, ad algorithms often fall woefully short of the mark. Today, typically ads appear in social media for a product the user has already purchased, complained about in a post, or that is in no way relevant to the user. This is because social media analysis at present presents one-dimensional measurements of three-dimensional people.

Again, it is better to layer data from multiple sources to gain dimensions in your understanding of the customer than it is to try to use one source alone.

Further, attempts at predictive analytics where a user's future actions are gauged in the social media context tend to fail because:

- Social media users do not typically provide all and/or true aspects of their thoughts and feelings in social media posts, which muddies an accurate view of them.

- Analysis is based almost entirely on past online behavior, without the benefit of the emotion or causation behind such behavior. This limits your ability to predict the likelihood of their future buying behavior. As collective big data skills and tools improve, the goal is to eventually gain a better understanding of customers and prospects. But for now, adding social media to your internal data stores and analysis efforts is insufficient for the task. You have essentially two choices at this point:
  - Accept the shortcomings and go for the best results possible under the circumstances.
  - Improve the blend of data via layering to gain more accurate views of customers now and to create more accurate predictions of customers' behaviors in the future.

Either way, the data you have now, no matter how large, is not and will not ever be enough to complete the puzzle. Variety (well, the correct variety) in data trumps sheer volume. Every time.

THE MONETARY VALUE OF DATA BOUGHT AND SOLD

By now, most companies are at least peripherally aware of the vast expanse of "data brokers." While the definition of "data broker" varies, for the purposes here, it is a company that collects and then sells data about consumers or market segments. Most data brokers are hard at work peddling their wares and many of their buyers are equally hard at work learning how to sell the data they own too. To their dismay, many newcomers are finding that there is a glut of "raw" data.

"If you just sell your data, you are commoditizing it and the price you can get for it will steadily decline," said Mario Faria, chief data officer at ServiceSource and a Big Data Advisor for the Bill and Melinda Gates Foundation, during a panel discussion on monetizing data at the 2013 Big Data Summit in Arizona.

And that's pretty much what has happened in the larger data market. So many companies rushed to sell their data that it indeed became a commodity. There's too much data for sale these days, and vast amounts of it are duplications of the same information. You didn't really think data brokers were going to sell any proprietary or competitive data that could put them out of business did you? Nope, for the most part, the data being sold is pedestrian fare.

But even when the data being sold is unique, market prices are often far less than new-comer data sellers expect. According to a June 12, 2013 report in the *Financial Times*:

> *The average person's data often retails for less than a dollar. General information about a person, such as their age, gender, and location is worth a mere $0.0005 per person, or $0.50 per 1,000 people. A person who is shopping for a car, a financial product, or a vacation is slightly more valuable to companies eager to pitch those goods. Some of the most personal and secretive troves of data rank as the most expensive. For $0.26 per person, buyers can access lists of people with specific health conditions or taking certain prescriptions.*

That report also included a calculator for readers to determine the market value of their personal data. It's a sobering revelation to find treasured and private personal details sold for so little. It's also a grievous discovery for companies dreaming of a financial windfall from selling their customers' data.

EVEN HACKERS ARE HAVING TROUBLE MAKING MONEY ON DATA

Even hackers have trouble making much money off of stolen identities and banking and credit card numbers, although occasionally they make off with a jackpot representing high profits. One example of hackers hitting the jackpot is the case of the Target data breach in December 2013. Brian Krebs, a former *Washington Post* investigative reporter, broke the story on his cyber-security blog called Krebs on Security. He reported that an analyst at a major bank discovered the breach long before the retailing giant confirmed it on December 19th—during the height of the Christmas buying season. Target estimated some 40 million credit and debit card accounts were likely affected.

The bank security analyst found early evidence of the breach in cards for sale on an underground online "card shop." There are hundreds if not thousands of such online stores where stolen information is sold on the black market. But one card shop in particular was promising "a huge new batch of more than a million quality dumps" says Krebs. The bank bought back some of the cards and traced where they had been used. The store they all had in common was Target.

The screenshots Krebs provided in his post showed info on specific cards going for $26.60 to $44.80 per individual's card. Obviously selling millions of collective cards at this cost per unit represents a very large payoff for the hackers. But to realize that sum, the hackers would have to sell the information quickly, since affected banks rapidly nullify stolen cards. In other words, there is a specific shelf life for the usefulness of the Target breach data, as there is on most data sets.

As a result, if you are a data buyer, you need to verify the accuracy, collection age, and shelf life of the data you intend to purchase from a data broker. You will also need to consider the source, that is, take into account the credibility and reliability of the source feeds.

EVALUATING THE SOURCE

While some data brokers are (and always were) data-driven companies in their own right, such as credit bureaus and over-the-top (OTT) TV services of the Netflix and Hulu ilk, many new data brokers are jumping into the mix. Of course, they are not all created equal. Nevertheless, we are now officially in a new data economy wherein data is a new currency and many are rushing to cash in. Remember always "caveat emptor"—let the buyer beware.

But even traditional data companies can and should be suspect. Far too many of them use outdated models for analysis and some are even sloppy about who they sell their data to, thus poisoning their own well. Since data buyers want the best and most sophisticated of analysis, outdated models are not in demand. Further, no one wants to buy financial, bank, or other data that is already compromised by hacker-buyers as that data will quickly become either vulnerable or useless.

Consider credit reporting bureaus, for example. Historically they have provided the underlying data analysis that drove lending decisions in the financial industry. While none has fully disclosed their proprietary algorithms (and apparently the big three—Equifax, Experian, and TransUnion—each have their own methodologies as an individual's credit ratings are not identical among them), there is little evidence that they have added sufficient inputs to refine their risk assessments. For example, a review of credit reports on individuals shows no easy way for lenders to discern whether a late payment history is due to poor paying habits or an impact of the recent global recession. This is an important piece of information for lenders to know since the former depicts a high credit risk while the latter is barely meaningful.

But beyond the apparent use of outdated risk models and a lack of pertinent information, the underlying quality of the data may also be questionable. In July 2013, a federal court awarded $18.6 million dollars to a woman in Oregon who had asked Equifax on eight different occasions over the span of three years to correct errors in their reporting on her payment activities. It took a court decision to get Equifax to correct their records. In the absence of a strong and proactive data hygiene program, data from any source, not just credit bureaus, can be and probably is dirty, which means it's faulty and error-prone, and therefore of no or little use to data buyers.

Further muddying the question of monetary value of data from traditional sources was the discovery in October 2013 that Experian sold data—including social security numbers, driver license numbers, bank accounts, and credit card information—to identity thieves through its newly acquired Court Ventures division. The buyer, an identity theft service known as Superget.info, posed as a private investigative firm to fool the agency. However, many wondered why a monthly cash wire transfer payment for over a year didn't tip off Experian. Keep in mind that Experian has positioned itself in the market as data breach experts. The effect was a poisoning of the well for legitimate buyers, since the data being sold to the thieves was rapidly corrupted from the moment the identity thieves received their data dumps.

OUTDATED MODELS INVITE DISRUPTORS

Of course, the credit rating industry is as subject to disruption as any other industry. Once considered sacrosanct, its entire business model and reasons for existence have been radically questioned and rapidly challenged in today's fast-moving digital economy. This may beneficially stimulate change on how the industry conducts its business going forward. Indeed, PayPal has launched a 0% interest business loan program called PayPal Working Capital that may disrupt both the credit rating and banking industries, at least in part. Other startups, such as peer-to-peer lender Prosper, are beginning to emerge that make capital available to borrowers outside of traditional banks while diminishing risk to lenders through the use of more sophisticated models.

Another example of an emerging disruptor for the credit bureau industry is the Collaborative Economy Customer Score. You can learn more about the collaborative economy in Chapter 8. But for now consider just this new scoring system which combines, among other things, customer ratings (the reverse of customers rating businesses), local transaction data, loyalty data, credit scores and net worth to compute an entirely new and far more comprehensive score. As Jeremiah Owyang, founder of Crowd Companies Council puts it in his June 9, 2014 blog post, this new score reveals, "what really matters: finding out the metrics of behaviors and peer-to-peer trust, backed with factual financial data."

Because of the impact of disruptors and other market forces, credit bureau data may rise or fall in value in the future. The point is that data buyers cannot assume that data is valuable simply because the source has been around for a good long while, nor can they safely assume a new data source is any better or worse than any others.

WHAT TO LOOK FOR WHEN BUYING DATA

In any case, a data seller's reputation for providing quality data must be considered before a purchase is made but that reputation must also be reassessed often and never assumed. The buyer must also seek hard assurances that the data is regularly cleaned and protected from corruption.

Further, since most data bought and sold today isn't raw data, but an analysis of that data, buyers need to examine and evaluate the algorithm(s) the seller uses. It is no longer acceptable for algorithms to be complete trade secrets, as they are within credit bureaus. Data buyers need to know the modeling is sound in order to gauge the value of the data they are buying. Transparency is everything in determining data value.

IDENTIFYING WHAT OUTSIDE DATA YOU NEED

Choosing which data brokers to buy data from is easier when you know what data you need before starting to shop. In most big data projects, at least those that companies tend to undertake first, you will be adding information to existing data sets and algorithms. For example, you may have traditionally used a formula to successfully calculate fuel costs, pricing, or inventory control. The key to using big data to enhance any existing analysis projects is not in merely adding more data behind each of the variables you already use but in adding more variables to the equation.

"The number of inputs is changing for the same output now," explains Sunil Kakade, IT Director at Sears. "The computing is more intensive and more frequent to arrive at a more accurate and actionable output on a quickly recurring basis."

This being the case, for enhancements of existing data projects you must first identify what additional variables could refine or improve your results. Once you pinpoint what those variables are or could be, determining what data may address them in an analysis should, in theory, be straightforward. By understanding what kind of data you need, you can locate the data brokers who offer that data. This begins the process of evaluating which ones you'll select as external sources.

For projects where no formula already exists, such as in exploratory data mining efforts or in developing new questions to pose, you must first define the problem and then determine what variables and information are pertinent to solving it. The result should be a viable algorithm. Reality-check the variables you have selected to ensure that you have enough inputs and that all the inputs are relevant to the question. From there, you can determine what data you need and whether such data sets exist internally or are readily available externally.

One word of caution here. A considerable amount of data is available free. Most of it is public data provided by government agencies and nonprofits. Some if it is even available through commercial sources. The point here is that you should check first to see if the data you need is available from a free source before you purchase it. It is not uncommon for public data to be sold by commercial interests. Be careful that you don't buy that which is free for the taking. For example, New York City offers free access to more than 1,100 data sets in ten broad categories (business, education, environment, health, housing, public safety, recreation, social services, transportation, and city government) at https://data.cityofnewyork.us/ along with associated access APIs. See Figure 4.1.

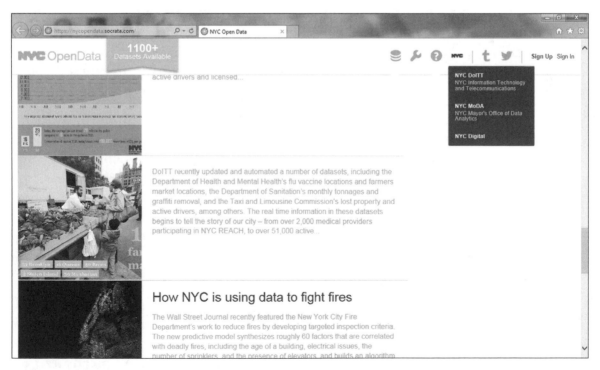

Figure 4.1
New York City's Open Data website offers 1100+ free, publicly available data sets.
Source: NYC Open Data website.

The data science team will be responsible for developing the algorithm and taking care of the technical aspects of the actual analysis. However, business leaders and users have an important role in refining and developing the project strategy. They define the problems that need solving, help identify what external data is useful or needed, and most importantly, develop and execute an action plan once the answers come in. The action plan may, and probably will, require iterative tweaking as time progresses and circumstances change. But the bottom line is that if no action results following an analysis, the entire exercise was for naught. Of course, this is not true with projects of an exploratory nature only.

This means that in order to transition to an agile and data-driven company, data literacy, critical thinking, and strategic skills must exist throughout the organization. A company's ability to leverage data depends on a prevalence of such skills and is proportionally increased or decreased accordingly.

A Word About Structured vs. Unstructured Data

While the form data comes in is of more importance on the technical side of things than the business end at the moment, it is important for business users to have at least a basic understanding of the difference between "structured" and "unstructured" data. With efforts underway to "democratize" data—by developing more user friendly analytical tools—knowing what form of data you're working with will help you use these tools as they evolve. It will also help you understand the complexity of the work that must be done.

As you might infer from the words structured and unstructured, the terms apply to the degree of formal organization of the data. Structured data is highly organized data with, for example, standardized fields, and is relatively straightforward to use. It can basically be seamlessly imported into an existing relational database. Using unstructured data is more complicated since it is frequently a mess. Unstructured information may not be easily searchable, is typically not easy to add to preexisting databases, and more often than not, can completely foul the works. Unstructured data is far more expensive to sort out and generally takes far more time and effort to incorporate as well.

So what makes data ultimately messy or unstructured? Humans do. Machines speak and record information in precise manners and therefore data originating from machines is overwhelmingly structured. Humans speak, record, and create data partly in a precise manner but more often than not in disjointed and scattered ways. A spreadsheet, for example, holds structured data that's neatly organized and portrayed in a consistent language (see Figure 4.2). Figuratively speaking, apples are in the apple column and oranges in the orange column—or should be. There are no lemons anywhere on the sheet, unless of course there is a distinct column for lemons.

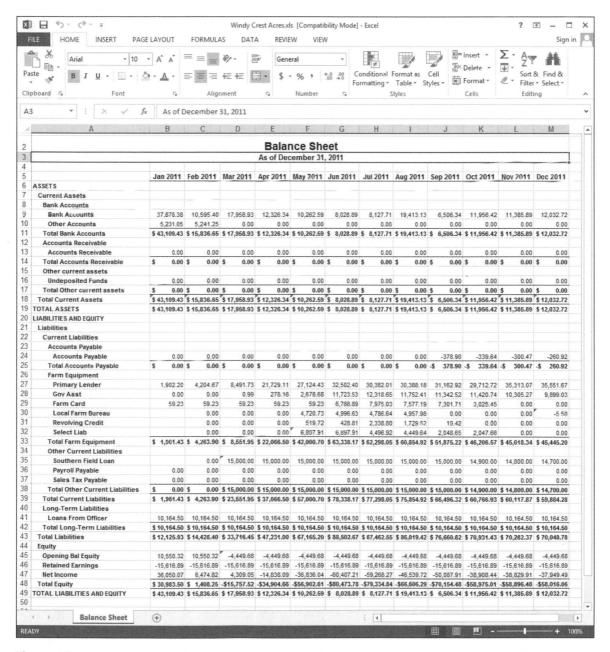

Figure 4.2
Spreadsheet example showing organized, structured data.
Source: Pam Baker.

Humans rarely work precisely. Unstructured data includes virtually anything that represents human-to-human communications. Everything from email and memos to social media posts (and quite a bit in between) falls into this category. So imagine that you are trying to figure out from all these different forms of communiqués which discussions are about oranges and which are about lemons, even though in many of them the oranges and lemons are called something else such as fruit, citrus, citrus fruit, or any number of other descriptors such as navel, tangerine, or in the case of lemons, bush or finger citron. Now think of all the alternative words in a dozen or more human languages. Add to that the number of occurrences of the words orange in conversation that refer to the color and not the actual fruit.

This means sorting this data out using keywords such as yellow or orange would be iffy at best and keywords such as "peel" or "round" would be totally useless. I'm sure you see the inherent problem here. How are you to add information about oranges to your spreadsheet example (structured data), when oranges are referred to in such vastly different ways in the email example (unstructured data) and lemons and colors are thrown into the mix as well?

While data-driven decision making is imperative to maintaining profits and a competitive edge these days, it is not an easy task to incorporate enough variety of data to get the job done properly and make it all work together.

PREVENTING HUMAN BIAS IN DATA SELECTION

You might think that cold, hard data at least is free of human bias. But that would be wrong. Human bias affects the data that's collected, which sources are used, which is mined, and which is ignored, what variables are included, what questions are prioritized, what preexisting practices are ingrained in a company, and the final formation of the algorithm. In other words, there are numerous places in the analysis process that human bias can pollute, divert, or corrupt a project. When bias is injected, the results are often disastrous.

One example that comes to mind is Mitt Romney's U.S. presidential campaign in 2012. By all accounts, many on the GOP side of things—from the candidate and workers on his campaign to conservative pollsters and Fox News commentators—were genuinely shocked at the election outcome. Polls and predictions on the GOP side all but guaranteed a win for the candidate. Unfortunately, the polls, predictions, and analysis the campaign relied on were showing the exact opposite of every other poll and analysis done at the time by other noted and non-partisan firms. Instead of questioning whether human bias had affected their polling and analysis, the campaign insisted their analysis was correct and everyone else was wrong. Hence their universal shock at the results.

This example is not meant to examine the politics of the time but rather to illustrate the dangers of human bias in data analysis. Be very careful that the data you gather, use, or buy is free of human bias. Be extra diligent in your analysis. Call in unaffiliated "reality checkers" to provide a viewpoint without axes to grind or turf to protect. If you don't, calamity can readily ensue. The only thing worse than not having data to drive your decisions is having the wrong data or analysis drive you down the wrong path.

The Danger of Data Silos

Data silos are isolated stores of data throughout the organization that can take digital and non-digital forms. They may be data trapped in a particular program such as customer relationship management (CRM) software, inventory management programs, or any number of software programs used across an organization. Data silos are especially prevalent in large organizations as it is common practice for them to use several copies of the same software—and often several versions as well—and each of these create data silos. Another type of data silo is in the form of paper files and notes. Yet another data silo may be email or software in the cloud that employees frequently use without company knowledge or permission, such as Dropbox and other file sharing tools.

Despite the obvious problems in collecting and integrating all of this data for company use, when data is trapped in silos it creates other problems too. Companies can come to believe they don't have data that they need because they can't see it hidden in silos. Therefore they buy that data from a third party or go to the expense of collecting it again. Further, when data is updated, corrected or deleted in one silo, the change is likely not recorded on the same data in other silos. This mix of duplicate info and/or a mix of versions of the same data can wreak havoc on a big data project.

Taking an inventory of what data resides where, actively reconciling versions of the same data, and otherwise cleaning company data so that its reliability is high are keys to making big data projects successful. The old computing adage of "garbage in, garbage out" still applies, in other words.

In short, then, before you go to the effort and expense of analyzing data, be it internal or external data, take steps to ensure it is *clean*—current, reconciled, and accurate.

STEPS TO TAKE TO ENSURE YOU'RE USING ALL THE DATA SOURCES YOU NEED

The most important thing you can do to identify what data and sources you'll need for modifying or extending an ongoing analysis project is to take a good, hard look at your list of current inputs. It is common for companies to stuff more data into the specific inputs of existing algorithms rather than update or change the algorithm itself. Yes, you most likely will be looking for the same outputs on many occasions, but don't let that lull you into believing the inputs should remain the same too.

If all you do is run the same algorithms with more data, then very little or nothing at all in your business will improve as a result of your data analysis. The entire point of big data is to provide methods to learn what you don't know using existing data analysis efforts—not to repeat existing exercises in a bigger fashion.

To this end, revisit your existing and potential algorithms and discover what new or additional inputs can be added to refine your results. If you do it right, you'll discover much about the data you need and you'll be able to more easily identify where that data might reside.

Meanwhile, here are initial steps you can take to ensure you are using all needed data sources:

■ What "view" do you need to solve the problem? Do you need a 360-degree view of the customer? Or, do you need to view activities occurring in a particular slice of time, under particular conditions, or in response to a specific campaign? Determine what view you need and then bring that view into focus by adding details to the picture desired. Now ask yourself who is likely to have those details? Bingo, you now know what data you need and where you might shop for it.

For example, in the case of a marketing campaign at a specific store or restaurant, you might want to add details about the weather, local events competing for attention, road work obstructing access to the establishment, competitor activities, level of expertise of staff working in the establishment on those days, local flu rates, and your own customer loyalty program data to better understand which customers came in during that period. By looking at this list, you can quickly determine what data sources are required. You'll need data from a weather service; an event calendar from one or more local organizations such as the Chamber of Commerce or a Visitors Bureau; data from local government agencies overseeing road construction; data from the local or state health department; company data on worker skill levels and performance; and data from your customer loyalty, customer relationship management (CRM), and/or customer experience management (CEM) programs.

Of course, you may think of even more details to add to understand what really happened (and why) during that marketing campaign. And that's the point: The more information you have, the better you will understand and the better you can predict what may happen next time. Figuring out what details you need first will point you to what data sources you will need as well.

■ Beware of correlations and seek causation. There will be many correlations in your data analysis. Those might be helpful but they may actually derail your efforts. Correlations are merely statistical links between how strongly pairs of variables are related. For example, height and weight are correlated in that taller people tend to be heavier than shorter people. But that doesn't mean that a shorter person will not be heavier than a taller person or that being "taller" is the "cause" of someone being heavier. Ask yourself what data points you toward or defines causation behind your findings. Again, once you know what to look for, you'll know where to look for it.

■ Probe the "why" behind processes. Just knowing the processes your company uses isn't enough, although it is a very good start. You need to know why these processes were designed as they are. Do the processes reflect former limitations in technology? Former problems in logistics or vendor/partner capabilities? Tradition? Are they based on an assumption that once was true but now is not? Find the why behind the processes and you'll soon learn what needs to be changed. From there you can identify what data you need to make a meaningful change. That is turn will indicate where that data can be found.

■ Reexamine how people in the organization work. This will be similar to your examination of processes, but this time you look at "humans" and the way they work within processes. In the context of your organization, why do they do what they do in the manner they do it? If you can determine what it is they truly seek to achieve, rather than the steps actually taken, you can fairly easily determine what additional inputs might get to those "factual truths" faster and more efficiently. Again, once you can understand what data is needed, you can determine where to find it.

■ Look for black holes in the existing knowledge base. That is those areas of current "unknowability." Black holes can be hard to find but if you look closely and ask questions in reverse, you can find many of them. Take pricing as an example. Most retailers can determine why a product at any given price sold well. But, frequently they can't determine why a product at a given price didn't sell well or at all. That's a black hole. And that particular black hole eats a lot of profits in everyday commerce because the typical retailer reaction is to slash the price further. But what if unit price wasn't the reason the product didn't sell well? What if that product didn't move because of weather or market timing or some controversy of the day? Find the applicable black holes and shed light on them. Determine what data you need in order to determine why the product didn't sell and then go get that data, wherever it exists. In turn, once you know the answer, profits could appear to magically increase simply because they are no longer being drained away through unnecessary price discounts or other reactions.

Creative and critical thinking are imperative in ensuring you have the right inputs and enough data sources to provide the variety you need. Successful big data projects are the result of a masterful blend of human and machine computing.

Summary

In this chapter you learned that unstructured data is a technical challenge but data source is more of a business challenge. You learned that variety in data almost always trumps volume (size) because more is not always better but variety in data adds dimensions to your understanding. You learned that traditional third-party data sources are often flawed but that the age of the data vendor (traditional or new) is no indication of the value or trustworthiness of their offerings. You learned what to look for before buying data and how to determine its value. You also learned several pitfalls to avoid in the process, including avoiding buying data you already have or buying data when it's available for free.

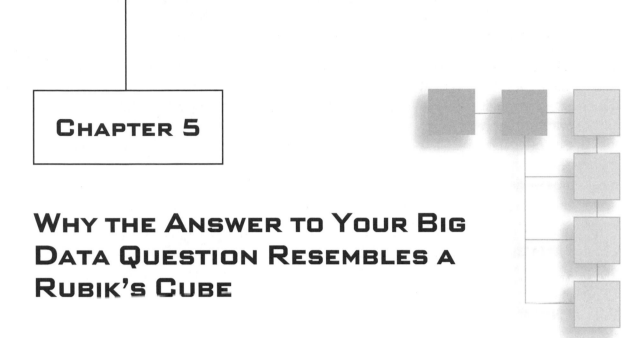

CHAPTER 5

WHY THE ANSWER TO YOUR BIG DATA QUESTION RESEMBLES A RUBIK'S CUBE

Let's pause for a second to discuss what big data results are and are not. It's important to understand what to expect and what you'll need to do next from a business perspective.

The key thing to remember is that a "data-driven decision-making" process does not mean that analytics actually make decisions for you. They don't. But using analytics means you have better and faster information on which you or others in your company can base decisions. In particular, real-time analytics, but high-frequency runs of other analytics too, will send computed data results to you rapidly and frequently. What you do with that information is entirely up to you and completely beyond the scope of a machine. In other words, you still have to make the "To Do" list and activate the troops before the results from your analytics can have a real impact on your organization.

Further, not all questions asked of data tender straightforward results. Many questions will have to be refined, often repeatedly, before you can ultimately learn what it is that you are seeking. Sometimes you'll need to combine the results from two or more questions to obtain a clear answer. And often you'll need to consider several outputs (answers) on your own. This is a bit like working a Rubik's Cube, where you need to make sure you align everything correctly to solve the puzzle. Even if you enable another algorithm to work the puzzle out for you, you still have to figure out how to weigh each of those results. In other words, you're still working to correctly align everything, whether you do so with your own mind or another algorithm.

On still other occasions, the results received will be so bizarre that you will feel compelled to test them and any associated algorithms to make sure they are correct. Testing and double-checking is important, as is making sure the data being used is clean, accurate, and relevant. However, it is usually a grave mistake to second-guess results simply because they are counter-intuitive. It is quite common for human instinct, gut-feelings, biases, and even past experience to be dead wrong. If you suspect the results are incorrect, by all means review and test the data and the algorithm, but don't just discard them and do what you "think" is the right thing. It may very well be the wrong thing to do!

Ultimately, the point of conducting big data analytics is to take that information, make a decision, and then act on that decision. Actionable data is your friend. And that leads us to…

WHAT IS ACTIONABLE DATA ANYWAY?

If you've read anything on the subject of big data at all, or attended one or more conferences on the subject, you've heard the words "actionable data" used repeatedly. In essence, it means data a user can take real action on. A simple example of this is any mobile app that offers the user information that the user can then act upon in the virtual or physical worlds, or both.

For example, consider the Expedia travel app. The user can see comparative pricing on airlines and hotels, decide which to use based on their needs, and then take action by booking one or both based on that personal decision. Thus Expedia's analytics delivered *actionable data.*

For the purposes of this discussion, actionable data is data that's delivered to business users that's meaningful to the problem at hand and that then enables users to act and change circumstances or outcomes. See Figure 5.1 for examples.

Examples of Actionable Data

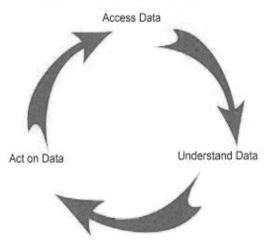

1) *Hospital scenario:*
Analytics predict the hospital will be short 50 beds in the upcoming flu season. Action: The hospital converts storage space to add 50 beds.

2) *Retail store scenario:*
Analytics reveal that consumers are buying product featured in the current ad campaign faster than expected and, at this consumption rate, inventory will run dry before the campaign ends. Action: Retailer decides to proactively order more of the product from the vendor well ahead of inventory depletion.

Access Data

Act on Data

Understand Data

3) *Corporate scenario:*
Analytics reveal that a work project in progress will require an additional 40 full-time employees to meet deadline. Action: Corporation decides to a) begin hiring process to gain 40 new employees in order to finish the project on time, b) outsource part of the work to make up for the short-fall, or c) extend the project deadline to a more realistic completion date.

4) Manufacturing scenario:
Analytics reveal that Product X has a recurring part failure putting consumers at risk. Action: Manufacturer decides a) to voluntarily recall the item, b) to offer safer replacement part or repair to affected consumers, c) to replace part in production line to limit future liability, or d) wait and see if any litigation happens first.

Figure 5.1
Examples of actionable data.
Source: Pam Baker. Illustration by Steven Duffey.

Most of your big data projects should be clearly aimed at delivering actionable data. Knowledge is most useful when it is applied. However, there is a definite business case for exploratory data analysis as well. See Figure 5.2 for examples. Exploratory analysis aids in learning the heretofore unknown. Mining data for new information is a good way to find a path to innovation, identify new market forces potentially reshaping or disrupting your industry, and any number of other valuable insights that your current algorithms do not currently reveal.

Examples of non-actionable and/or exploratory data analysis:

1) **Competitor analysis scenario:**
Analytics reveal Competitor X has received four times the amount of press coverage as your company has in the last three months. Action: None indicated. Additional analysis required.

2) **Disruptor analysis scenario:**
Analytics reveal disruptor's products are being consumed at four times the rate over last quarter. Action: None indicated. Further analysis is required.

3) **Industry analysis scenario:**
Analytics reveal four separate competitors have created partnerships with different leading entities in the emerging collaborative economy sector. Action: None indicated.

4) **Market analysis scenario for auto dealer:** Analytics reveal peer-to-peer car sharing is negatively impacting car rentals and taxi services but not impacting new car sales as of June 1, 2014. Action: None indicated. Additional analysis is required to discern future impact.

Figure 5.2
Examples of non-actionable and/or exploratory data analysis.
Source: Pam Baker. Illustration by Steven Duffey.

As discussed in Chapter 2, your big data project list should contain a majority of projects that result in immediately actionable data, along with a few projects meant to be exploratory, learning exercises. This way, return on investment (ROI) is realized as soon as possible, without jeopardizing innovation or long-term planning in the process. Far too many companies focus solely on immediate actionable data at the expense of their future. Conversely, many companies are confused over which data is actionable and waste valuable time and money floundering around in a never-ending learning exercise.

Balance between the two is key to big data success. You achieve that balance by purposefully and mindfully building a roster of mixed big data projects so that you are always running some projects meant to address current business problems and some that are designed as exploratory and future-looking. Without such a clear, planned project list to follow, you will quickly find your projects limited to your present situation and/or to an overly limited scope.

For example, if you are busy improving your processes in building widgets and ignore that the market is steadily moving away from widgets, you may soon find your company highly efficient at making widgets that no one will buy. You have to make sure you are always looking ahead even while you are working hard at addressing whatever is happening now.

THE DIFFERENCE AMONG DESCRIPTIVE, PREDICTIVE, AND PRESCRIPTIVE ANALYTICS

It is also important to understand the differences between descriptive, predictive, and prescriptive analytics in order to understand their use from a business perspective. The following sections discuss each type in further detail, but Figure 5.3 can serve as a quick overview.

The Three Types of Analytics

Descriptive analytics depict what has already happened. Real-time or near real-time descriptive analytics depict what is happening now.

Predictive analytics predict future outcomes if current events and circumstances remain on the current course. Any changes that occur in the meantime may change or negate these findings.

Prescriptive analytics deliver results accompanied with automated recommendations and/or actions.

Figure 5.3
The three types of analytics.
Source: Pam Baker. Illustration by Steven Duffey.

Descriptive Analytics

Descriptive analytics depict what has already happened. Until the advent of new big data tools, descriptive analytics were all we had. Think of every spreadsheet you've ever seen, every accounting report or financial statement, every inventory report, and so on. All of these were descriptive analytics that enabled you to look back and evaluate what has already transpired. What is new via big data in descriptive analytics is that you now have the capability to consider more information about what happened earlier. In this way, it is possible to gain more insights to evaluate what has transpired.

This is valuable for a number of reasons. For one thing, such analysis can shed light on past influencing factors that you can understand but can't control, such as a bad weather event, but that are unlikely to happen with any regularity. In such a case, you can conclude that you need not change your processes, reprimand employees for poor performance, or discard an otherwise effective marketing campaign. On the other hand, you can also use new inputs to see things you can control, but that were formerly invisible, and in turn take meaningful action. This is why modern descriptive analysis should not be seen as just a new way to do the same old thing. Existing algorithms should be reworked to include an array of new factors so that you can have more granular insights.

Real-time or near real-time descriptive analytics depict what is happening now. These are new variations of the analytics that came to be with the advent of big data capabilities. With these, you can still see more granular detail than ever before, but you can also see them while they are happening or soon after they occur, and take immediate action to leverage good events and/or reduce the impact of bad events.

Predictive Analytics

Predictive analytics, as you might expect, look forward. For example, banks use predictive analytics to predict an individual's likelihood to default on a loan before the bank issues the note and assumes the risk. Banks can also use predictive analytics to review a large group of people with common characteristics to aid in establishing meaningful criteria of default potential on the individual level. While this is good news for banks who must keep loan defaults low in order to protect their profit margins, it can result in discriminatory practices that then prove detrimental to the company in terms of regulatory and public relations issues. Predictive analytics therefore must be used with a broader view beyond simply obtaining actionable data. The results must also be viewed in terms of potential external repercussions from courts, regulatory bodies, and public backlash before action is taken.

Predictive analytics existed in earlier forms as businesses have always sought to discern the future to prepare for it or to leverage a new insight. But today's predictive analytics are far more accurate and are generally available in mere minutes. Decision-making thus becomes less reactive and more proactive as companies suddenly become more confident of what lies ahead. Unfortunately, as of this writing, very few companies are actually using the new predictive analytical tools as many are currently focused on mastering descriptive analytics in their newer, faster forms. That is expected to change in the short term, as more companies become adept at using big data.

Prescriptive Analytics

Prescriptive analytics are the new frontier. In this class of analytics, results are accompanied with automated actions or a list of recommended actions with a likely outcome for each action. The user or business may then pick one of the choices and implement it.

For example, grocery stores commonly issue coupons to customers at check-out for that customer's favorite brands. The selection of those coupons is automated as prescriptive analytics have discerned both what that customer's favorite items and brands are and when the consumer is likely to make those particular purchases again. It then sends the print command to the receipt printer to issue the appropriate coupons accordingly. The analytics prescribe the action and implement it.

Another example can be found in Facebook, which uses prescriptive analytics to determine who to recommend to you as a friend on Facebook. For example, if you and Jim have many friends in common, you are likely to have more friends in common than those you have already befriended. When Facebook cross-references all your friends' friend lists, the prescriptive analytics can determine with a high degree of accuracy which of those people are likely to be your friends too even though you haven't friended them yet. Then you receive automated suggestions of whom to friend. However, it is up to you, the Facebook user, to implement the action of friending. The prescriptive analytics in this case do not automatically connect friends for you.

Prescriptive analytics are used in much the same way by other entities such as Netflix, which uses it to recommend movies and TV shows to you based on your tastes, and Amazon, which uses prescriptive analytics to automatically offer you other items you might want to purchase. In both these cases, the prescriptive analytics automatically issue the offers and suggestions.

Not all prescribed actions are automated however. Take for example, prescriptive analytics used in the maintenance of large systems such as road, water and cable TV systems. Prescriptive analytics can determine when a road will need widening or a stoplight should be added at an intersection based upon actual and expected traffic flows and other factors.

The analytics can then prescribe an action, or a list of recommended actions, to the persons charged with maintaining good traffic flow.

In a city water system, prescriptive analytics can determine when parts should be replaced based on wear-and-tear brought about by actual usage rates or when overflow systems are likely to overpower the water purification system and prescribe the action needed to maintain the system in top form. Prescriptive analytics can do similarly with a cable TV system and prescribe actions, from replacement schedules for components to the reporting of signal bottlenecks with a recommended fix, to the people charged with keeping the system running at peak performance. In these cases, the prescribed action is not automated, rather it is issued to people who can then implement it.

In this and previous chapters, emphasis has been placed on the need for talented humans to interpret and act on big data results (output). That assertion remains true despite the advent of prescriptive analytics, because prescriptive analytics are nowhere near sophisticated enough to work well on more complex business problems. At least not yet.

To date, the questions posed to prescriptive analytics are fairly rudimentary. They are largely elementary efforts at applying prescriptive analytics to scenarios, wherein traditional "fixes" or logical actions are easily identifiable and can be readily applied. In short, prescriptive analytics are not a matter of a machine cooking up some new innovative or creative solution. Not yet anyway.

Further examples of current applications of prescriptive analytics are traffic and smart grids. In these scenarios, the analytics can determine what has happened in the past and what is likely to happen in the future, and then offer a list of solutions likely to improve the problem based on historical (previously used) fixes that turned out well.

In the case of resolving heavy traffic patterns, prescriptive analytics may tender a list of recommended actions, including installing a traffic light, charging a higher toll to encourage a route change, increasing the minimum required number of occupants per vehicle for certain lanes, expanding the number of lanes, or building a new road. These actions are logical, familiar, and not creative in the least.

By comparison, a human might create a solution list that includes more creative solutions such as building cars that do not touch the road surface at all and may even fly in air lanes; building magnetic cars that can travel "roads" up the side of buildings or glide between rooftops; self-driving cars that use the roadways more efficiently; or some new invention that replaces the use of cars entirely. Because predictive analytics as we know them today offer logical solutions based on the success of past actions rather than creative solutions entailing something never before tried, they can sometimes put you at a competitive disadvantage. Particularly if your competitors are developing more creative innovations. The same scenario and shortfall can be applied across industries when it comes to the use of prescriptive analytics as we know them today.

At this big data moment in time, prescriptive analytics are confined largely to maintenance, logistics, couponing, pricing decisions, customer upselling recommendations, and other mundane issues, where a company wishes to spend little time and effort in overseeing (and verifying) such decisions and desires a consistency in decision choices. In other words, it's a good way to speed and standardize human decision-making on issues not directly related to building or maintaining a competitive edge. In the future, it's expected that prescriptive analytics will be able to handle more complex problems, but we're a long way from that now.

No matter which class of analytics you are currently exploring, using, or planning to use, results from that analysis can be delivered in a variety of ways, requiring different human actions (and reactions) to see the project through to the end goal. Let's take a look at those now.

TYPES OF QUESTIONS THAT GET STRAIGHT ANSWERS

For some questions, the results will be pretty straightforward. For example, if a health agency wants to know the rate of infectious disease hospitalizations or the rate of spread for a particular disease in any given time frame, the answer will be clear—no human interpretation is needed. Similarly, if a hospital wants to know the potential impact of said outbreak on its beds, that too can be clearly spit out of a well-crafted algorithm. In this way, a hospital can know with a high degree of certainty when precisely it will incur a bed or staff shortage and plan accordingly.

A great number of questions can be answered succinctly with big data analysis, provided the data is clean and there are a sufficient number of relevant inputs in the equation. Even so, there is no benefit unless an action is taken. Therefore, straightforward answers still require some human planning and implementation. But at least these types of data scenarios don't require any additional human interpretation once things are set in motion.

An oversimplified way of thinking about these types of questions is to think of them as definitive in nature. Essentially, you are asking the algorithm to define or measure something specific or to measure two or more specifics against one another to calculate the impact on one. Staying with the example of hospitals, measuring infectious spread and the percentage currently resulting in hospitalizations versus available hospital beds and current bed turns, which is how quickly patients leave and are replaced by another, will quickly *define* the likely impact on the hospital as the current scenario continues on its present course. However, such a measurement analysis does not take into account "unpredicted" actions. A sudden surge in public use of a flu vaccine, say, could slow the momentum of disease and change the expected need for hospital beds. This is why you should not think of a straightforward definitive answer as the "final" answer, but instead run the analytics repeatedly and add new inputs as you go along to account for new and emerging factors.

When Questions Lead to More Questions

The point to remember is that the most useful analytics are dynamic, not static. It generally is nonsensical to run analytics once and stop, unless of course you are looking at a one-time event, such as a marketing campaign, that had a definite beginning and ending. Not only is the work dynamic, but so is the algorithm. A common mistake is to continue using the same algorithm as it is—which is *not* to say that that same algorithm cannot be reused. But in concert you should revisit and revise algorithms often (and conceivably run different iterations of algorithms on the same inputs) or you face the likelihood of missing information your company sorely needs.

In any event, analytics often spawn as many new questions as they do answers. Or at least they should, because you should be learning continuously and the new knowledge should spark more questions. Data analysis is all about learning—machine and human learning. In terms of human learning, you must become comfortable with potentially not knowing or not realizing what you do not yet know. Be eager to learn more with each new analysis. Let your intellectual curiosity guide you to ask more from your data every day. Above all, do not fear the results or the need to fit them together. In this way, you hone your own business and analytical skills and you get more from your company's big data investments.

Types of Questions That Require Interpretation— The Rubik's Cube

Other questions posed to data are not as clear cut as those in the definitive category. Questions in this realm are complex and not wholly definitive, at least not on their own. Typically, they will contain many variables, and those variables are subject to change at any time. Also, the question itself can be but one variable in a much larger question.

Often analysis of such questions calls for additional algorithms to compute the combined results to produce an answer to a much a bigger problem or they might lead to a bigger question. Either way, this process is similar to putting puzzle pieces together to see the final picture or aligning the colors on a Rubik's Cube to solve the puzzle.

Why do data scientists simplify formulas? For one thing, a model that is too complex poses a fundamental computing problem. Simpler models, although still not simple by any conventional stretch of the imagination, are more robust and (potentially) trustworthy and correspondingly less often fouled by changes in the data (all else being equal). For another, data scientists may not understand the bigger question or how to formulate it until they discover answers to a set of smaller related questions. In such a case, the difficulty is not in the computing per se, but in the discovery process.

Using Data Visualizations to Aid the Discovery Process

Often, a strong business analyst can be of great help in simplifying or streamlining the discovery process. For example, a business analyst may look at a spreadsheet containing several measurements or variables and glean an answer to a separate question not specifically addressed there. In other words, they may detect a pattern within the information that is beyond the intended purpose of the spreadsheet. Or, the information may spark a new question in the analyst's mind. Of course, it's much harder for humans to do this when there are many measurements and interrelated variables. It is at this point that visualizations are frequently used to depict massive amounts of information in a human-readable form.

The art of data visualization is a unique endeavor to enhance human perceptions with graphic representations of the information. The best visualizations reveal relationships and meanings in almost a glance. The most powerful also enable viewers to drill down within the visualization for granular views of underlying components or specific data points.

The natural talents and work performance of any given business user can be better leveraged by presenting data in a visualized form that matches how that person learns and thinks. The business user will grasp and intuit more from the information if the visualization form is either very familiar to them or closely matches the manner in which they naturally absorb information or typically perform their work.

For example, if you are presenting data to workers who work on airplane maintenance, a visualization depicting the plane that allows for easy one-click drill downs to part specifications or maintance schedules may be better understood and more helpful than, say, a word cloud depiction with the same one-click drill down capabilities.

An executive who prefers working with spreadsheets, bar graphs, and pie charts may find more traditional data visualizations, or their close cousins, to be more easily understandable and useful, at least initially. However, another executive may be more visually oriented, or she may work often on devices with small screens and find stylized graphics, such as those in Figures 5.4 and 5.5, easier and faster to use.

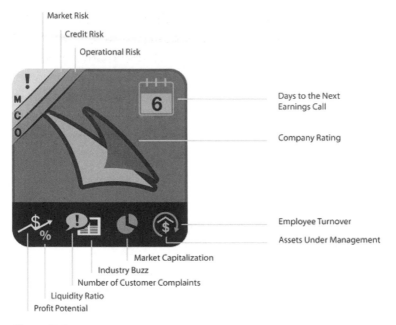

Market Risk
Credit Risk
Operational Risk

Days to the Next Earnings Call

Company Rating

Employee Turnover
Assets Under Management

Market Capitalization
Industry Buzz
Number of Customer Complaints
Liquidity Ratio
Profit Potential

Figure 5.4
An example of VisualCue's "tile" format in visualizations where you can understand numerous organizations at a glance leveraging scorecard colors (red, yellow, and green) and intuitive pictures. Here, you see one organization's relevant financial market data.

Source: VisualCue™ Technologies LLC. Used with permission.

Figure 5.5
An augmented reality visualization by VisualCue designed for ease of use on mobile devices and wearable technologies. It helps a waste management company understand the frequency, usage, and utility of their dump stations.

Source: VisualCue™ Technologies LLC. Used with permission.

Remember that when you're selecting visualizations for a presentation. If you are sending the same data to different decision makers, personalizing the visualizations is fairly simple and will result in better gains from individual interpretations and actions. If you're presenting to a group of people gathered at the same event, personalization is obviously not possible, but clarity remains the goal. Choose the simplest and cleanest visualization form that you can that still represents the findings well. You will probably find using multiple, simpler models to be more productive than attempting to generate one huge, complex, and muddied visualization.

In any case, human interpretation must be aided in a way that leverages the data, rather than strays or distracts from it.

Summary

In this chapter you learned about actionable data and how it differs from exploratory exercises. The important thing to remember is that you need to have both. You also learned the differences among descriptive, predictive, and prescriptive analytics and what each can deliver. Further, you learned the importance of presenting visualizations that match how the viewer learns and thinks.

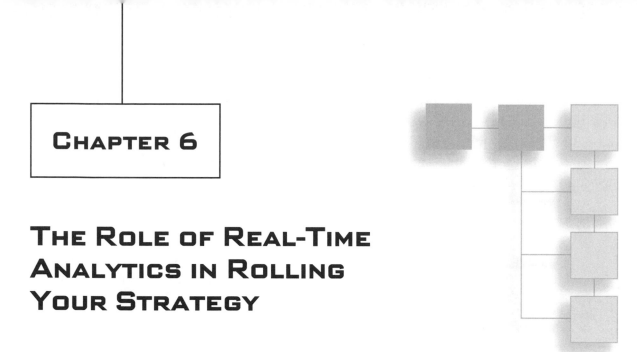

CHAPTER 6

THE ROLE OF REAL-TIME ANALYTICS IN ROLLING YOUR STRATEGY

In much the same way that filing cabinets soon overflow with paper, so too does digital data overrun available storage. In both cases, the overflow doesn't happen overnight, although it often seems that way. The growth of data in any form happens gradually over time until one day someone recognizes the mess and then wonders what to do with it all. This is how big data came to be. Company files and databases began as manageable sizes and then grew at ever-increasing rates. However, it wasn't until recently that companies purposely sought to grow data, further compounding the problem.

Of course, data analysis was taking place all along. Companies had all the ingredients to analyze data—from database administrators (DBAs), math wizards, code writers, and statisticians to functional algorithms. Everything was whizzing along more or less without any problems, although certainly with limitations, until eventually the sheer volume of data got too big to shoehorn into existing setups. Or, the data itself grew so big that shoehorning it in existing data center storage (even with the plummeting price in hard drives over the last few years) became just too expensive for most budgets to bear.

In an effort to cope, companies and other organizations tried running analysis on select data samples, rather than on entire data sets. While this tactic worked on occasion, depending on the data set and analysis, just about everyone agreed it usually wasn't good enough. So when arrays of big data tools arrived, those charged with data analysis tasks welcomed them as ways to cheaply analyze vast amounts of data. Efforts to improve big data tools in terms of costs, efficiencies, speed, and ease of use are now nearly continuous and will both ease the workload in data analysis and spur new uses of data.

One of the most widely hailed advances of our time is real-time analytics. The very idea that on-the-fly analysis of large data sets is even possible is tremendously exciting! For the first time, companies can see exactly what is happening in the here and now and respond accordingly in real-time. But like all tech applications, real-time analytics isn't a panacea. Figure 6.1 shows real-time analytics coupled with real-time collaboration for maximum decision-making agility.

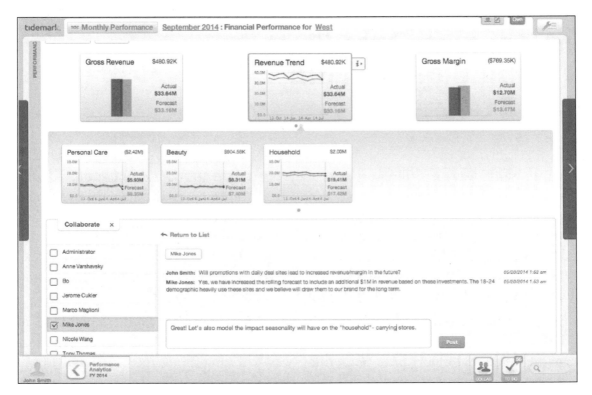

Figure 6.1
An example of real-time analytics used with real-time collaboration.

Source: Tidemark Systems, Inc. Used with permission.

Granted, real-time analytics have an important role in the new data economy and in data-driven decision making, but there are also times when a company should refrain from using them. The answer to when they should be used is an individual case-by-case call made by every company based on its specific overall strategy, market, and customers. Let's take a look then at the advantages and shortcomings in real-time analytics in order to determine where they might best fit into any particular big data strategy.

Examining Real-Time Delusions and Time Capsules

The problem with anything real-time is that, often in less time than it takes to blink, it becomes a moment in the past. Indeed, the moment you finished reading that last sentence it became a past event. Yet you're still reading this book which means you're reading it in real-time and if we could log your facial expressions while you read it we could do a real-time analysis of your reactions. However, this book was written some time ago so for all involved in its publication, it represents one or more past events and the data within it cannot be technically considered as real-time, yet the reading of it can. Confused yet? That's okay. Time is relative and hard to pin down and harder still to frame with definitive meaning in terms of "real-time" data analysis.

Chief among the many concerns in any real-time analysis is the speed in which the data is collected and whether the data itself is current enough to be considered truly real-time. With direct streaming of social media, for example, the speed and immediacy is readily evident. Not so with other data. In all likelihood some amount of time will have to be spent, no matter how nominal, to determine the immediacy of the data and to prepare it for querying, especially if it is unstructured data. The more the clock ticks while all that is happening, the less real-time analysis is possible.

In addition to the speed and immediacy of incoming data, one must consider reaction time on the other end of things as well. If, for example, marketing can do a real-time analysis on customer reactions to a marketing campaign but cannot act on the analysis for days, weeks, or perhaps even months, then they are in effect reacting to a past event and not to a real-time analysis.

In short, it's only real-time if the entire process happens nearly instantaneously. Now that's a daunting thought, isn't it?

The point here is that you must be selective in determining what information you need in real-time and how fast your company can react to it before you go to the effort and expense of analyzing it in real-time. In other words, sometimes the slower and cheaper past-time analytics work just as well and are far more practical, given what reactions are to be based on the analysis.

Nevertheless, there are many instances where real-time analytics are preferred to past-time analytics. Take, for example, fuel costs for an airline. Knowing fluctuations in fuel costs in real-time is extremely helpful in immediately adjusting ticket prices, plane utilization, and routes accordingly to ensure profitably. Such real-time information allows airlines to route planes to refuel in places where fuel is cheaper—provided of course that more fuel isn't used getting to and from those fueling destinations. Real-time analytics can determine all of that in seconds.

The same holds true for a mobile app or a GPS system that provides users with fuel costs at gas stations close by to the driver's current location. Real-time information in such cases is essential. But there are many other scenarios where real-time analytics are not only desired but vital.

Now, you've surely noticed that real-time readings must be fairly continuous in order to update information regularly enough to be considered in real-time. And that is indeed the case. Real-time readings and analysis must be rolling, that is one after another in a continuous stream of updates, in order for the information to remain in real-time status. But even when they are rolling, they may really be near-time rather than real-time per se.

Near-time means almost real-time. Sticking with the airline example, an airline may discover that is just as efficient and more cost effective to analyze data every 15 minutes, every 30 minutes, or once an hour. Anything close to but other than directly looking at what is happening right now is considered near-time. In many cases, companies are actually using near-time, believing it to be real-time. However, these often amount to the same thing in practical terms.

It is prudent to consider just how timely or "real-time" you need any given information to be. If you use real-time analysis too freely, you're burning up resources needlessly. Conversely, if you skip using them where truly needed, you are hobbling the enterprise and putting it at a potentially huge competitive disadvantage. Find the timing sweet spot for any given information collection and analysis and adjust your tactics and strategies accordingly.

Finally, take a look at your processes to ensure they are flexible enough to immediately respond to true real-time analysis. It is almost never the case that existing processes were built with enough flexibility to readily respond in real-time. Too often many companies try to fit the analysis to the process rather than adapt the process to fit the analysis. So ask yourself, if I have this information in real-time, can I react to it quick enough for it to matter? If not, change the process as needed to achieve true agility.

Whatever you choose to do with real-time analytics, make sure your motivation is *not* to relieve real or perceived pressures to hurry things along.

"What CTO today wants to stand up in front of a crowd and proclaim 'we use past-time analytics' or 'we work in an eventually-we'll-analyze-our-data' approach? Oh, the crickets we would hear," says Elise Neel, vice president, Data and Insights at PlaceIQ, a mobile data analytics company. "Real-time seems to be the catch-all answer to most analytic systems, but few organizations capitalize on the capability effectively."

USING STATIC VERSUS ROLLING STRATEGIES

Real-time analysis is not the only thing that can roll. Strategies can too. Problems quickly surface when the current strategy is static and stale but the information coming in is fluid and changing. It's more effective to have a rolling or "living" strategy that can itself be quickly adapted according to incoming information.

In the past, business strategies were static step-by-step master plans that largely reflected the opinion of the ranking executive, which was only sometimes supported by past-time analytics. If and when static strategies were changed, it was only in response to information learned after the fact. Implementation of the changes was typically slow and arduous. In other words, agility was essentially just an idea. Only small companies (or small divisions given relative autonomy within larger companies) truly had the capability to turn on a dime. They used their agility to great advantage when competing against much larger and better funded companies that changed direction with the speed and grace of a lumbering oil tanker.

By contrast, modern big data tools, such as real-time and in-memory analytics, make it possible for any organization of any size to become truly agile. However, actually doing it often requires a significant change in mindset and culture. It can be unsettling for many people to work in an environment wherein everything is fluid and nothing concrete. But fluidity is key to reshaping a company into a massively successful enterprise.

So which comes first—the data that drives change or a company culture that permits change in response to data analysis? In most cases the two are interwoven and happen in staggered steps.

A WORD ABOUT CHANGE MANAGEMENT IN MOVING TO A ROLLING STRATEGY

Usually someone within the company has to take the initiative to demonstrate how big data can be used for real company benefit. Typically they have to make a case for a process change or a new initiative to seize a data-driven advantage. At some point, top executives take interest and begin to look for confirmation and evidence that this whole big data thing is more than the latest buzzword-laden trend and is indeed an actual, useable, and trustworthy business tool. Most executives will be highly skeptical although some will embrace it fairly quickly; it all depends on how open to change any given executive is. Once there is top-level adoption, data-driven decision making becomes an accepted part of the business strategy and trickles into the culture.

Generally speaking it is an agonizingly slow and tedious process to move a larger organization forward to a more sophisticated use of data, not to mention moving it from a static business strategy approach to a rolling, data-driven one. Even if the top executive orders the transition, there will likely be resistance to the change throughout the organization. People take comfort in established routines and some won't take kindly to their disruption. See Chapter 2 on how to formulate a winning big data strategy and for more details on how and where such resistance is likely to lurk.

Your big data strategy needs to include steps to increase acceptance and adoption of data-driven decision making throughout the organization to offset this resistance to change and speed transformation. But those steps must also be flexible and subject to frequent revisions as you encounter less or more resistance along the way. In other words, you'll be using a rolling rather than a static strategy to achieve these ends too.

Your Choices in Analytics

As mentioned, real-time analytics have their place in your overall data strategy. A very important place, to be sure, but they are not right for every business problem. Further, while we touched on the fundamental differences between descriptive, predictive, and prescriptive analytics in Chapter 5, this is a good time to explain that the last two can be in real-time or not. Descriptive analytics are almost always in past-time.

Not all analytics software of any given type is created equal, nor do they all work in the same way. If you are in charge of evaluating and selecting analytics products, be sure that you understand precisely how they work and what their limitations are before you buy. Be particularly wary of the label "real-time," as some analytics are run in-memory or during streaming and some are not and there are notable time and other differences between them.

The traditional way is to query data residing on physical storage disks. There's nothing especially wrong with this method other than there are some limitations in scope and flexibility and it is too slow for real-time analysis. By contrast, in-memory analytics query data in the server's random access memory (RAM) for faster processing, providing it is a 64-bit and not a 32-bit architecture. There are other advantages to using in-memory analytics as well, such as a reduction in IT involvement. Even so, some movement of the data is required to get it from the source to RAM.

By contrast, streaming analytics are real-time analytics conducted on streaming data. They completely circumvent the need to move information between storage and in-memory thereby speeding algorithms, to as much as 100 times faster some users and vendors claim, beyond in-memory speeds. Streaming analytics also handle bigger data loads than in-memory analytics. Most batch processing systems are either already offering or steadily working towards providing this capability in response to the growing demand for real-time analytics for massive quantities of data. This category of analytics continuously monitors data streams and often automates actions, but not always.

Figure 6.2 shows Google's BigQuery web page for developers, which is found online at https://developers.google.com/bigquery/.

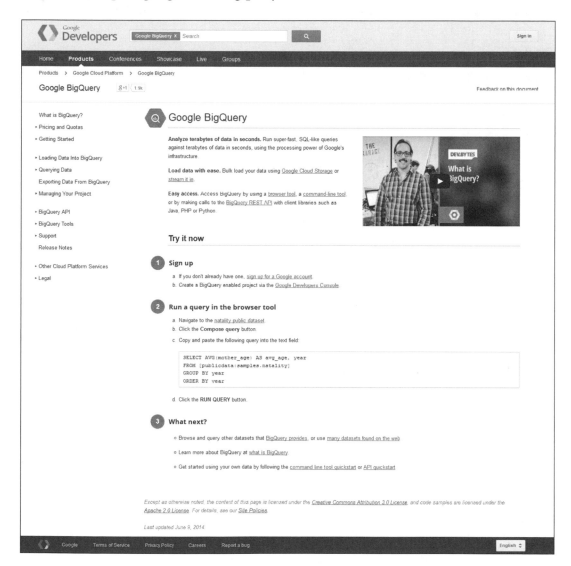

Figure 6.2
Google's BigQuery web page for developers explains how to use this streaming analytics tool. Notice that Google provides data sets and points to other data sets available on the web for product testing or developer use.
Source: Google, Inc.

As this book is written to address business strategies and use cases, deeper technical issues are left for another day (or perhaps another book). However, Figure 6.3 is an attempt to provide you with at least a glimpse of the many advantages to streaming analytics. It shows a post on Massive Online Analysis (MOA), an open source data mining tool, concerning using the R language despite the tool being written in Java. It is not the language challenges that are of concern here. Notice instead the three advantages in streaming analytics listed at the top of Figure 6.3.

Figure 6.3

A post on Massive Online Analysis (MOA) showing three advantages in using streaming analytics.

Source: MOA and Center for Open Software Innovation. Screenshot taken from http://moa.cms.waikato.ac.nz/2014/05/19/rmoa-massive-online-data-stream-classifications-with-r-moa/.

You'll need to fully understand just how real-time you need the analytics product to deliver, and how well it actually does that, before you commit.

USING DATA FROM HUMAN EXPERTS' BRAINS TO SPEED ANALYTICS

As mentioned previously, a simpler model, although still not simplistic, works better with fast and frequent analytics than a more complex model. But that is not to say that once the algorithm is written, it is done. Models and algorithms must be frequently updated and adapted to account for new factors. Inputs should never be set in place and forgotten.

For many readers this advice may seem too esoteric as you will not be doing the modeling or writing algorithms yourself. If that's the case, just remember that creative and strong business minds can and should contribute to the general model building even if they don't have the math and technical skills to write the formula. Not only is your expertise important to the model-building process, it can actually be an input in the algorithm. Don't let the technical side of things make you discount the value of the data in your own head. And that's what it is—data. Specifically, it is unstructured data in a silo. Take it out of your head, the silo, and add it to the algorithm as an input or at least use it to help shape the model.

As an example of how adding human input to the algorithm greatly enhances the outcome, consider how the U.S. military is doing that as reported by Colin Wood in a January 6, 2014 article in *Emergency Management*:

> *Collecting, correlating, and making sense of big data into a single, cohesive image is called creating a common operating picture (COP). Another problem with creating a useful COP, [Dr. Eric Little, vice president and chief scientist for a company making big data software for the military called Modus Operandi] pointed out, is that oftentimes the most valuable information isn't found anywhere in military intelligence files—it's in the expert's head. The expert's experience, knowledge and intuition often play a key role in how data is filtered and interpreted to create a COP.*
>
> *"With big data tools, however, it's possible to put the expert's knowledge into the software so everyone can use it," Little said.*
>
> *The Marine Corps, for instance, is now testing Modus Operandi's BLADE technology for use in the field. The product generates a semantic wiki from the COP that is built from the original data inputs. If, for instance, a soldier discovers some information about a person of interest who happened to have been involved in a bombing, he can update the COP with that new piece of information. Additionally, the wiki pages for that person and that bombing event would both be updated, as would any other relevant pages. Other soldiers in the field also would have access to that new information in near-real time. There's no waiting for reports to come in and connecting dots to figure things out—it's all in the system and can be found in the wiki pages.*

A semantic wiki is just one output that can be generated from a COP. Once the data has been built into an underlying graph structure, that data can be traversed with complex queries to find different kinds of patterns and output different types of visualizations. For instance, a user interested in spatial data could submit a query that generates a map from the underlying common graph. A user primarily interested in dates could generate a timeline, and so on.

"This allows the war fighters much better situational awareness," Little said, "and it gives them a much broader understanding of things that could be related to the specific items that they're looking at in their data that they otherwise might not have found or seen."

Other experts in other industries can contribute knowledge to be added to algorithms in this same way and in other ways too. Think about it for a moment. When you collect and use data from email, social media, and other unstructured sources, you are actually adding human input to your algorithms, are you not? Adding human expert knowledge and observations is a matter of deliberately doing so in a digital form that can then be used in algorithms as needed.

WHEN REAL-TIME IS TOO LATE, THEN WHAT?

Even real-time analytics can reveal past events or decisions already made, so you may discover that damage is already done or opportunity is already lost. For example, you may find yourself staring at a large number of social media posts bashing your product or your CEO's political remarks. Or, you may find that a competing product is now all the rage and too far ahead in market share for your company to make a comeback or any serious headway. Maybe you'll find that a startup has produced a wildly popular product similar to the one you were planning to introduce six months from now or that completely disrupts your industry. In other words, the analysis you do in real-time may result in bad news that is difficult to influence or change to any significant degree.

Such news may be discouraging, but it is also helpful. It is better to know what is happening now than to proceed blindly on your course, only to discover this same bad news down the road when it will have cost the company considerably more in expenditures, lost profits, customer backlash, or public ridicule.

With real-time analytics you can pivot mid-stride. If you find one product is a lost cause, you can shift your focus to another that is not. If you're facing a PR crisis, you can immediately address it before the negative impressions set into unyielding concrete. If you see a disruptor emerge, you can change your strategy or product development path accordingly. Whatever you find in real-time analysis, you can find a way to cope with it and even profit from it despite the obstacles because you are now aware of the situation.

So, yes, there is a time when real-time analytics produce results that are too late in the sense that something—good or bad—has transpired and it either hit you or you totally missed it. However, the analysis may not be too late for you to still find a way out or a way in, as the case may be. The important thing to remember is that knowledge at the right time and with the means to take advantage of it truly is power and you are powerless without it. This is why real-time analytics, properly applied, can be so crucial to your overall business strategy and why they should be a big part of your big data strategy.

SUMMARY

In this chapter you learned that real-time analytics deliver many great business advantages but they are not the best choice for every business case. You learned about the different types of real-time analytics and that not every product branded as "real-time" actually is. Although speed is of utmost importance in real-time analytics, you learned that one of the best ways to hasten your results is to add data currently trapped in experts' heads as an input in your algorithms. You saw an example of how to do that in how the U.S. military is doing it and learned other ways to add human expert data too. Last but not least, you learned that even real-time analytics can deliver results to you too late—and what to do when that happens.

CHAPTER 7

THE BIG DATA VALUE PROPOSITION AND MONETIZATION

Ask the question of where precisely there is bankable value in using big data and you'll almost always be answered with vague generalizations or an anecdote or two. Is this merely a vendor tactic to evade answering and still make the sale? No, not generally. It isn't that there is no answer, but that there are too many answers, each of which is dependent on too many variables, for there to be one short, concise response to such a question. Nonetheless, there are answers to be had and hard formulas to follow for definitive quantification and we'll look at those in this chapter.

DETERMINING ROI IN UNCHARTED TERRITORY

First, let's consider why answering the ROI question appears to be so difficult for so many. Imagine for a moment that you were in the early days of the telephone and you were asking the all important ROI question before installing this newfangled contraption in your business.

How, pray tell, would you go about determining the business value of a device that can convey voice conversations over distances? It must have appeared to be little more than a novelty to many business owners. After all, most businesses were chugging along perfectly well in the same way they always had, and that their competitors also had, for many years.

Why then should a business go to the expense of buying expensive desk phones and paying a new monthly service?

"So customers can call you or you them and your sales might increase and happen faster," the phone company rep might say.

"But they may not buy as much if they aren't in my store to see other things they might buy on impulse," the store owner might reply. "Sales could actually fall and adding to that loss is the cost of having the phone."

"Well, if you offer customers product suggestions while you're on the phone with them, the impulse buys may still happen and sales could go up," the phone company rep might respond.

"Oh, so the customers in my store are ignored while my clerk talks to the customer on the phone! Or, I have to pay someone to just talk to customers on the phone? That means I have to pay even more for the use of the phone than I planned," the store owner might wail.

"Get to the bottom line; what do I get out of spending all this money on a thing that just might prove to be a passing fad?" the store owner would undoubtedly ask.

"It depends on how well you use the phone to promote and operate your business. The possibilities are endless and new uses we haven't even thought of yet will soon appear. Also, the telephone will forever change how business is done and if your competitor has phones and you do not, you could lose a lot of sales and may even go bankrupt," the phone rep might reply.

"You're just using scare tactics to try to make me buy that thing. Why won't you just answer the question and tell me what minimum returns on my investment you can guarantee?" the store owner would reply.

Do you see the absurdity in that demand for a definite, much less a guaranteed, ROI for something that depends so much on how the user uses it, and has no history or past data to compare to?

Now, substitute "big data" for "telephone" and you see the same exact conversation happening everywhere today. Disrupting technologies are hard to explain and quantify in the beginning, but looking back, with the benefit of 20-20 hindsight, it is incredulous that so many failed to grasp what was happening at the time.

"It is no simple matter to calculate the value of the use cases you haven't yet imagined, and it usually takes a while to imagine and realize all the applications of a new technology," said David Gibson, vice president at Varonis. "Did anyone quantify the value of the Internet and TCP/IP in 1982?"

Make no mistake, big data is a disruptor and like the telephone and the Internet and other disruptors that came before it, big data is shaking the very foundation on which your business was built. It does not matter whether you acknowledge or agree that the big data-induced quake is here, your company walls could crumble and fall just the same.

The Lesson in the Skill of the Painter versus the Value of the Paintbrush

How can just a pile of data have such tremendous effect on your business? Paradoxically it doesn't. It isn't the data or the technology but how both are used for and against you that delivers the punch. Most of the power is in the hands and skills of the user and not in the tools.

Wait! You might say. Didn't we just discuss how valuable and powerful big data analytics are in the previous chapters? Why, yes, we did. However, no matter how capable and useful the tool, its actual use and the resulting outcome of its use depends heavily on the skills and talent of the user. Just as a house painter and an artist use paintbrushes differently, companies also use big data tools differently. There is nothing wrong with a house painter using paintbrushes as he does to paint a house or for an artist to use paintbrushes as she does to paint a masterpiece to hang in a museum. However, strategy and skill matter in both cases.

The house painter's strategy may be to paint quickly in order to make more profit from the job and so he uses his skill and mastery of the tools to execute his strategy to achieve the desired outcome. The artist's strategy may be to wait for inspiration rather than to rush ahead. When inspiration comes, she looks with a talented eye for detail in light and structure. Then she uses all of her skill to produce a final painting worthy of the label "masterpiece." Thus the success of both the house painter and the artist rests on their own strategy and skill more so than the ownership of paint and brushes. However, neither of them could paint anything without the paint and the brushes.

To be successful with big data, you must also have all three: strategy, skill, and tools.

Divining the value proposition of big data therefore depends considerably on how well your company wields it and how well it protects itself from other entities that are using it. Therefore it is exceedingly difficult for a big data vendor to specifically answer your questions pertaining to ROI. It is not difficult, however, for you to calculate ROI for your company as presumably you do know the rest of the equation: how well your company strategizes and implements internal, market, and customer intelligence.

The flipside to the ROI question is how your data can be monetized. You might think these two things are actually on the same side of the "show me the money" issue, and in some ways they are. In other significant ways, however, they are indeed separate issues.

Funny Money and Fuzzy ROI

While many companies today have made the leap, most big data projects are still in the early discovery stages. Very few projects have moved on to more advanced analyses and even those have yet to come anywhere close to discovering the ultimate payoffs possible from using big data.

"We are still in the discovery phase of Big Data, meaning that we don't know what jewel retailers, hospitals, and manufacturers will find there," said John Joseph, vice president of product marketing at Lavastorm Analytics. "Those discoveries haven't been made yet. As with any discovery effort, trial and error is an important part of the process. To deliver a ROI, organizations must put in light infrastructure so they can experiment, tolerate dead ends, and react quickly to ultimately find pay dirt."

Experimentation is the rule of the day but that is not to say that returns have not already been found and counted. Typically those returns have been found in improving efficiencies, primarily through cutting costs and streamlining processes.

For example, giant chip-maker Intel reports that it has developed "more than a dozen" big data projects over the past two years to improve both its operational efficiency and its bottom line. "In 2012, we had between 12 and 14 projects that together represented well over $100 million dollars in value to Intel, either in cost savings or cost avoidance," said Ron Kasabian, general manager of big data solutions for Intel's data center group.

Unfortunately, increases in efficiencies seldom excite and elicit the support of shareholders and members of the C-suite. However, when such efforts pay off to the tune of millions of dollars, everyone gets excited. But can that $100 million figure in cost savings and cost avoidance be applied universally? No, it can't. Again, how much is gained from big data use depends in large part on the soundness of the underlying strategy and the willingness and ability of the company to execute appropriate actions on the findings. One company's $100 million in savings may amount to $10 million for another company or more than a half billion for yet another.

Further, internal cost savings often feel more like funny money than real dollars to more than a few company heads. But this is a mistake in reasoning.

"Money in the bank is money in the bank. It does not matter where each dollar came from; it's all equally spendable," said Mario Faria, chief data officer (CDO) at ServiceSource and a big data advisor to the Bill & Melinda Gates Foundation, while he was on a panel of experts at the 2013 Big Data Summit held in Arizona. ServiceSource is a recurring revenue management software firm.

What he means is that every dollar saved can be spent elsewhere. In that regard there is no difference between a dollar that is received from a sale or investment and a dollar retained by a savings. It is the same as the old adage "a penny saved is a penny earned."

Indeed, that is true. Cost savings and cost avoidance do equate to hard dollars in the bank and not to soft dollars, as many fear. Still, the inability to say with complete confidence that X expenditure on big data will definitely result in Y dollars in return leaves many a big data supporter without the means to convince the powers-that-be that the company needs to make the investment or continue the big data experiments.

Hence, those who are charged with making the business case for big data expenditures commonly fall back on anecdotes, vague generalizations, and competitor studies and practices to drive the effort forward. This tactic fails as often as it succeeds. The more successful approach is to include the value proposition from the outset, complete with hard calculations. The way you do that is to tie projects to specific business problems where the answer is both actionable and measurable. For example, calculating the ROI on a big data project aimed at decreasing fraud in debit card usage online is far easier to do than trying to calculate the ROI for a big data project designed to reveal who your best customers are. While it's true that once you know who your best customers are, you can likely take action to increase the size of their average purchases, just knowing who they are is not in itself an actionable and measurable outcome.

Once you have calculated and delivered ROI in this way, the pressure to do so on exploratory and discovery projects lessens considerably as the value of big data overall has already been established.

"Most big data engagements are currently deployed either as proof of concepts (POCs) or as stand-alone projects with a defined purpose, for example, fraud detection or customer sentiment analysis," said Dr. Avinash Kulkarni, senior project manager at Infosys.

"The output in big data projects are insights that address different audiences and hence have different value," he continued. "For example, one project would look to improve fraud detection in bank transactions and hence minimize risk, while another project looks to present telecommunications companies with predictive analytics to reduce network failure. Since the goal for each project varies, it is difficult to put a definite formula to define ROI."

However, Kulkarni says as a general rule of thumb the following formula can be used:

Return on Investment = (Profit/Savings from Investment − Cost of Investment) / Cost of Investment

Later, you'll look at other, more specific formulas. For now, let's look at putting big data costs in perspective.

THE CONFUSION IN COST

A significant problem in calculating ROI for big data is that people tend to confuse returns with new revenue streams. What they really want to hear is that more or new money will be flowing into the business if they use a new technology. As discussed, hearing that they will simply gain from new efficiencies often isn't sexy enough to sway shareholders and members of the C-suite, unless of course those gains are substantial. Plus, such claims often carry the stigma of earlier, similar promises attached to previous buzzword technologies that ultimately failed to deliver. Being told that preparation for some nebulous future will require the company to purchase any given technology isn't a motivator for budget overseers to sign a check either as they tend to focus on returns in the here and now.

But make no mistake, price alone is never the defining issue for any technology—overall value is. That's why several vendors are having trouble selling big data tools. Many of them mistakenly believe price is the deal maker or breaker. When sellers have trouble answering the ROI question, they almost always fall back on discounting the price in the hope that buyers won't worry so much over returns if the initial investment is correspondingly low enough. That is not a very good tactic, as reduced prices also frequently denote little value—the opposite of what buyers are actually seeking. If the actual or perceived value to the buyer is unknown, then any price, no matter how steeply discounted, is too much. However, if the value is known and appreciable, price is merely relative and of little determinative significance.

That is not to say that vendors and brokers can demand high prices, however. The costs for big data storage and tools are already low compared to their conventional counterparts and are expected to dip even lower as the industry matures and finds its own efficiency gains. Since costs are so reasonable, big data is accessible and affordable to just about everyone, which means vendors and brokers must double their efforts to deliver value if they are to differentiate their offering and realize a profit.

All of this is exceedingly good news for big data users and buyers, however.

WHY COST ISN'T AN ISSUE

"The reality is the costs of initial investments are now extremely low: a simple big data experiment costs less than a small piece of 'conventional' market research or commercial industry report," said Rob Souza, partner and managing director at Boston Consulting Group. "Some experiments can even be done for free, such as on Google Correlate and Google Predict. Worrying about the business case for investment is a waste of management time and is often missing the point. These investments are low cost with very high potential upside."

"The price of storage is relatively cheap," agrees Anant Jhingran, vice president of data at Apigee and former CTO of IBM's information management division where he worked on the now famous Watson supercomputer. "On Amazon, for example, 1GB will cost less than $1 per year, so a 100TB data collection would be under $100K/year, which is not significant."

It's important to note at this point that the business case often isn't an argument for additional costs via new data tools and storage—but rather to reduce existing costs in data management and analytics. After all, companies have been collecting and analyzing digital data for decades and the resulting storage issues and costs have been an ongoing money drain. Further, much of that data was unusable from an analysis perspective if for no other reason than to do analysis was cost prohibitive and/or the tools needed to analyze all of it were unavailable. Unused data is opportunity lost and an ongoing money drain. But that situation can be changed.

"Collecting large amounts of data before Hadoop was expensive and only reserved for a few companies," explained Bruno Aziza, chief marketing officer at Alpine Data Labs. "The cost of storage has simply plummeted over the last 30 years: In 1980, one Terabyte of disk storage could cost up to $14 million. Today, one TB can be bought for $30. In fact, we'll soon be able to buy two Terabytes disk drive and they will fit on a 3.5-inch platter. If you do the math, you'll find that the cost of storage has gone down by 500,000 times over the last three decades. If your company is not figuring out a way to store every piece of data you can put your hands on, you're behind."

Putting the Project Before the Business Case

Indeed, because costs are so low and sometimes even free, some professionals advise running a few big data projects *before* attempting to make an official business case for them.

"The key is to change the culture to encourage experimentation, test and learn, and to avoid trying to value initial business cases," said Souza. "Once you have done the experimentation and understand the true potential it's fairly straightforward to build a business case for scaling up and making it operational."

So where are the costs an actual consideration and potentially a money pit in big data projects?

"The challenge is the computation, analytics, and insights one gains, and that is expensive—not in the traditional infrastructure cost sense, but more in the 'people' sense," said Apigee's Jhingran.

But what exactly are those costs?

CALCULATING ACTUAL COST

"In short, there are two or three costs associated with big data," explains Joel Freimuth, CEO of Blue Pearl Consulting. "The question becomes does your organization have the infrastructure and expertise to respond to what the petabytes of data tell you, so as to off-set those costs? The costs are in obtaining the data; interpreting the data; and, implementing changes in your organization to respond to what the data tells you."

And that's the bottom-line: costs are determined not by the infrastructure expenditures but in the talent needed to strategize the effort and the resources needed to implement the findings. But even that is not really an issue, for what could it cost your company *not* to have top talent and/or fail to take action? See Figure 7.1.

Total Costs of Big Data Projects

Infrastructure Costs + Human Expertise Costs + Implementation Costs =

Total Big Data Projects Costs

Figure 7.1
Total cost of big data projects.
Source: Pam Baker.

Focus on costs only in regard to keeping big data projects highly focused on actionable business intelligence, both in the short and long terms. Ensure your company has both the will and the resources to take action on the analysis, for lack of action is the greatest cost associated with big data.

WHERE VALUE ACTUALLY RESIDES

The value in big data is always found in the outcome.

"The value of Big Data is not in the 'bigness'—it is always the insights that come from the ability to spot trends and patterns when all data is assembled," said Jhingran. "So the emphasis when making the case for investment in big data should always be on what is discovered, not what is collected."

Unfortunately, that poses a problem for big data champions trying to make a business case for big data investment long before projects are started, much less completed. Hence the recommendations by some experts to run small or pilot projects first and then make the case to scale that particular project, or to use the value found in the small test case as evidence that value does exist in other big data projects by extension.

However, this tactic of starting small often does not answer the need to present significant ROI justification and predictions. For this reason, many big data champions pin their business case on resolving existing data problems and on increasing efficiencies in processes.

How to Make the Business Case from an IT Perspective

"If your organization is not as tech-savvy as the Facebook, Netflix, and Googles of the world, chances are you will find a very steep learning curve that can make it harder to sell your idea even to your own management," says Jorge Lopez, director of Product Marketing at Syncsort. "So, how can you justify a Big Data investment? For most 'mainstream' organizations the answer is: look at ways to enhance your existing architecture and reduce costs."

In this way you can derive value through comparative costs between what the company is spending now on data storage and analysis versus how much it can save with new big data fueled techniques and tools.

How and where should you start in making this case? Lopez says those in IT can do it in one of two ways:

- "First, it is no secret that most enterprise data warehouses are experiencing severe capacity and scalability constraints. Most of this capacity is ELT-driven [ELT refers to the data process known as "extract, load, and then transform"]. Batch workloads collecting and blending huge disparate data sets from multiple sources are driving up to 80% of database resources. Hadoop can become the perfect staging area to store data and process ELT workloads at a much lower price and with virtually unlimited scalability. In turn, you will free up much needed database capacity, i.e. defer or at least reduce additional database expenses, enrich your existing reports with more historical data, and improve service level agreements. [Hadoop is an open-source software framework that can be used on commodity hardware for the storing and large-scale processing of large data sets.]

■ Second, over 70% of Fortune 500 organizations still rely on mainframes to process over 30 billion transactions per day. Needless to say, mainframes generate some of the largest data volumes in the enterprise. However, most of this data goes untapped or remains on tape, which means organizations are paying millions of dollars every year just to make this data unavailable. Well, many mainframe organizations are finding that by offloading mainframe data and batch workloads to Hadoop, they not only save millions a year, but gain new insights.

Let's be clear, neither the data warehouse or the mainframe are going away anytime soon, but by rationalizing these precious resources organizations can easily justify a big data investment, build their big data skills, and deliver real savings in very short time, so when the right time comes, they are ready for their next big data analytics or research project."

How to Make the Business Case from a Non-IT Perspective

But what if you are not working in IT and you still need to quantify the value of big data before you can move ahead? You can use a similar argument.

Take for example, an attorney seeking to win a big case in court. Attorneys and their staffs spend a lot of time gathering facts and analyzing information to build their case. Big data analysis used well accomplishes the same things only faster, cheaper, and in more detail. Therefore, comparing costs of these functions done in the traditional manner with the costs of doing them with big data tools renders a well-defined and measured ROI and a reasonable expectation of benefit to both the client's case in particular and the firm in general.

Further, one of the oldest tactics in the practice of law is to overwhelm the other side with mounds of files, particularly in discovery. Big data tools can possibly make such tactics null and void, as lawyers using these tools can parse and analyze large amounts of data in record time. Given big data tools are so inexpensive it is foolhardy, if not professionally irresponsible, to practice law without the ability to thwart this and similar tactics, and to accurately and thoroughly examine all the facts at hand.

Another example is in marketing, where data use is a matter of routine in the practice.

"For example, the improvement in customer targeting from big data based segmentation, or the ability to identify failure further ahead, can be estimated from many previous analyses [using tools other than big data]," explains Rob Souza, partner and managing director at Boston Consulting Group. "Where such data analysis is familiar, this [price comparison] course works well."

The same exercise—comparing traditional costs versus big data costs to accomplish the same things only better and faster—can be applied to virtually any discipline or industry. This is why improvement in efficiencies is usually the first route taken when making a business case for big data investment. In this way, value is fairly easily quantified prior to the investment being made. Then, once the investment is made, adding to the range of big data projects becomes a much simpler task as you are no longer battling the "to do or not to do" question but instead are focused on what to do that produces actionable business outcomes for each project.

Of course, defining what to do can prove problematic, too.

"The problem is in unfamiliar cases, i.e. new uses, that you have to follow [with no previous analysis from other tools to compare it to for ROI calculation purposes]," says Souza. "You risk others getting an unassailable lead by transforming your industry, as happened in Google vs. Yahoo! in the search space, while you're waiting to get your business case signed off on. The value of a big data investment is its option value, not calculable ROI."

FORMULAS FOR CALCULATING PROJECT RETURNS

Nonetheless, establishing ROI is a familiar business mandate written in stone in many organizations. Calculations are therefore a threshold prerequisite. As mentioned previously, outputs are intended for different audiences with different goals and the values of each are therefore determined differently. In other words, there is no one ROI calculation, but many. You will have to choose the formula that fits your expected business outcome. To help you determine the best means of doing so for your project, consider the following examples of formulas designed to determine a variety of ROI values.

First, there are the basic formulas that can be used "as is," or easily tailored to fit almost any big data project, particularly if you are just beginning to use big data. One of those was mentioned earlier in this chapter:

Return on Investment = (Profit/Savings from Investment − Cost of Investment) / Cost of Investment

Here is another way to calculate big data ROI in general.

"Model the KPI [key performance indicator] you're hoping to influence. Measure the BI [business intelligence] cost of analysis. Track cost of the modifications you're implementing as surfaced by the BI. Measure the delta between your expected model and results of the modifications. Find your ROI," advised Dane Atkinson, serial entrepreneur and Founder & CEO of data analytics tool, SumAll.com.

Here is the formula Atkinson is using:

$Improvement = (Delta - Mod - BI)/KPI$

$ROI = (Delta - (Mod + BI)) / BI$

"With this formula, it's a fairly sure bet you will hit a 20% + improvement and 300% + ROI on your first pass through," he said, though, of course, your results are likely to vary.

Other professionals advocate using valuation methods other than standard ROI calculations.

"Making a business case for the investment in big data analytics comes down to a Heuristic method rather than a pure ROI play," said Steve Riegel, director of Strategy and Insights at Siteworx. Heuristics refer to techniques used in problem solving that favor speed over accuracy and precision and aim for a "good enough" solution instead. It is often used when classic problem solving techniques are too slow or fail to find a precise solution.

"The Heuristic approach would consider investing in systems that are believed to have the greatest effect on providing the insights that impact one of the primary purposes [increasing revenue or decreasing costs]."

One such Heuristic formula, he says, could be:

$Estimated\ ROI = Valuation\ of\ Purpose + Estimated\ Gain\ (Revenue + Efficiency) - Estimated\ Hard\ Costs$ $(Platform + Practice)$

But don't think estimating the "hard costs" will be the easy part in this formula.

"Estimating the hard costs—the cost of software, hardware, implementation, and training—would appear to be straightforward, but it has its challenges," explained Riegel. "IBM has classified the makeup of big data into four dimensions of volume, velocity, variety, and veracity. Hard platform costs are most impacted by volume and velocity, but these tend to be predictable. Hard practice costs are also impacted by exploring the variety and veracity of data, but this is where we also find the most gain in discovering hidden data connections across channels, systems, segments, and voices."

But even such careful calculations often fall short in delivering a complete ROI answer.

"What most hard ROI calculations will miss is attributing a valuation on purpose, which could include soft benefits such as experience, satisfaction, productivity, and brand impact," explained Riegel.

Where the ROI Math Gets Simpler

Thankfully, when it comes to calculating ROI on specialized big data projects, the math becomes somewhat simpler. Take risk assessment, for example, which requires relatively simple arithmetic.

David Gibson, vice president at Varonis, says the formula should look something like this:

ALE (Annualized Loss Expectancy) = SLE (Single Loss Expectancy) * % Chance Loss Will Happen in a Given Year

The formula for annualized loss expectancy (ALE) is:

ALE = ARO (Annual Rate of Occurrence) * SLE

Gibson offered this as a theoretical example: "Say you use big data analytics to reduce the likelihood of a data breach from once every five years (20% per year) to once every 10 years (10% per year) and the average data breach costs one million dollars. Then you'd reduce your ALE from 200,000 per year to 100,000 per year. If the big data investment is 100,000 up front and then 20,000 per year thereafter, the first year is a wash and you save 80,000 every year forward."

Compare that to marketing, which uses a wide array of data types and seeks widely varying values, thus requiring several calculations ranging from simple to complex.

"For example, Company A has a simple database of nothing more than 20 million email addresses but is considering purchasing a 'data append' to add what they feel could be more valuable information from another company that they can use to personalize their email messages and thus drive higher average conversion rates and greater sales," said Randy Malluk, vice president of Strategy & Analytics at RevTrax. "In particular, they are going to purchase a first name at a cost of 1/1,000th of one cent (0.001) per record, for every record, for a total of $20,000. If we suspect that addressing consumers by their first name will increase the likelihood of conversions, and increase the conversion rate by even 1/10th of one percent, the $20,000 investment will yield a $20,000 profit. If we think it will move the needle one full percent, it could potentially yield a return of almost $6 million dollars."

Figure 7.2 shows how a simple opportunity analysis can be used to calculate estimated sales impact.

Pro Forma Opportunity Analysis

0.1% Assumed Lift

	Current Data	Proposed Data
# of Emails in Database	20,000,000	20,000,000
Average Conversion Rate %	3.00%	3.01%
Total Conversions	600,000	602,000
Average value per Conversion	$30.00	$30.00
Average Sales per Full File Blast	$18,000,000	$18,060,000
Cost of Data Investment	$0.00	$20,000.00
TOTAL SALES	$18,000,000	$18,040,000
EXPECTED ROI		$20,000

1.0% Assumed Lift

	Current Data	Proposed Data
# of Emails in Database	20,000,000	20,000,000
Average Conversion Rate %	3.00%	4.00%
Total Conversions	600,000	800,000
Average Value per Conversion	$30.00	$30.00
Average Sales per Full File Blast	$18,000,000	$24,000,000
Cost of Data Investment	$0.00	$20,000.00
TOTAL SALES	$18,000,000	$23,980,000
EXPECTED ROI		$5,960,000

Figure 7.2
Using opportunity analysis to calculate estimated sales impact.
Source: Randy Malluk, Vice President of Strategy and Analytics, RevTrax.

"While this is an extremely simple example, companies can elect to use increasingly detailed data sets for highly targeted marketing, and virtually none of them come without their own associated costs," he said. "Using a simple model to understand how the investment moves the needle, you can quickly calculate if the results are worth the investment."

THE BIG QUESTION: SHOULD YOU SELL YOUR DATA?

Inevitably the question of data monetization surfaces in the ROI discussion. There is always particular interest in selling company data once the massive stores come under the spotlight. Surely someone would pay good money for all this "valuable" data, right?

Not really, no. Data has already become a fungible commodity and the prices are now so low that it is doubtful that selling your data would be worth the effort. But wait, you might say. There are data brokers out there making a fortune selling data! Everyone is buying, leasing, and collecting data, so someone will surely pay us for ours.

The problem is that the data most data buyers want is the very data you would most likely exclude or anonymize in order to protect your company's competitive edge, trade secrets, and profitability. What is left after you apply all that redacting is worth little to anyone in the markets your intact data would interest. Further, the overly-sterilized data you are offering is likely to be repetitive of information data buyers already own or could easily and cheaply obtain elsewhere.

Selling Insights

Raw data then is rarely of much value. Insights, however, are another story. There is a thriving market for big data insights, particularly those that big data users cannot arrive at on their own.

This is why data brokers and would-be data brokers go to such great lengths to collect data not easily collected by other entities and then sell their insights of it.

For example, some smart TV manufacturers load their products with what amounts to "spyware" to collect data on how consumers are using the TVs and what they watch, including the capturing of personal videos such as those of weddings or children's birthday parties. This activity is usually done without the consumer's knowledge. Any information on the collection and use of personal data or an opt-out capability is carefully buried deep within the system, where only the most tech-savvy consumers can find it. The information is collected, parsed, and analyzed and the results sold to whoever is willing to write a check for it. The value to buyers is in the uniqueness of the study and analysis.

That is not to say that smart TV manufacturers are the sole source of such data, however. A cable TV company or even a game console manufacturer, indeed any company that provides an Internet connected set-top box or even a TV smartphone app, can capture this same information from their customer base. But therein lies the differentiator. The size and demographics of the customer base affects the desirability of the data and analysis.

Therefore, a single data buyer may buy or lease data from multiple TV data brokers for a variety of reasons. For example, a buyer may get data from multiple TV data brokers in order to get a more sweeping view of consumer behaviors on a national scale. Many cable TV companies operate in only a few regions, therefore cobbling together their data becomes necessary if the buyer is interested in national TV viewing patterns. No one smart TV manufacturer owns the entire TV viewing market, nor does any one game console or set-top manufacturer so their data and/or analysis may also be purchased and cobbled together with other data. The point is that each of the sources delivers unique information not readily available through other data sources. Hence, the value is high.

Rarity Equals Cha-Ching!

The same concept is true in other industries. Specialized data and analysis without readily available duplication has value across the board. Take for example, smartphone manufacturers and telecoms. It's not that most data buyers want the full fire hose stream of raw data on where smartphone users go everyday throughout their entire day, nor do they want a minute-by-minute account of what consumers are doing on their mobile devices at say 1:21pm on the second Tuesday of each month. The majority of data buyers do, however, want to know the relevant insights that can be gleaned from that data.

That's why Google and other mobile device and services entities are working to connect consumer behavior in both the virtual and physical worlds by tracking online activity as well as brick-and-mortar store visits and analyzing relationships between the two. In this way, Google or a telecom or a device-maker can determine, among other things, whether and how online activity is related to in-store visits and purchases in consumers' behavior and, in turn, whether that's "actionable" for the specific parties. It is this type of unique information and analysis that data buyers seek, and not data for data's sake.

So, can you monetize your data by selling it? Yes, if you create unique value, i.e. specialized data cooked to offer unique insights that are so fresh that they are a hot attraction. And no, in general, if you serve it like sushi: raw and cold.

Otherwise, another route to monetize your data is through packaging actionable insights that can be used to improve your own internal processes, innovate, increase sales, disrupt an industry, prevent fraud, increase profit margins, and other business objectives.

Summary

In this chapter you learned that costs are not the issue in big data investments as big data storage and tools are very cheap compared to their conventional counterparts that you are likely using now. Further, the costs of storage and big data tools are continuing to fall. However, there are other costs that must be considered, such as the costs of human expertise in big data management and analysis and in the expenses involved in implementing the results of the analysis. You learned several formulas that are used to calculate ROI for big data use in general and for specific types of projects. You also learned that sometimes it's better to run a small project or two before you make a business case for further investment in order to show that returns are possible.

Last but not least, you learned that raw data rarely has much value, especially if some of the information is redacted to protect the data sellers' competitive edge, trade secrets, and its own profitability. Such overly sterilized data is likely to be repetitive of information that data buyers already own or could easily and cheaply obtain elsewhere. However, unique insights gleaned from data are very valuable and easily sold.

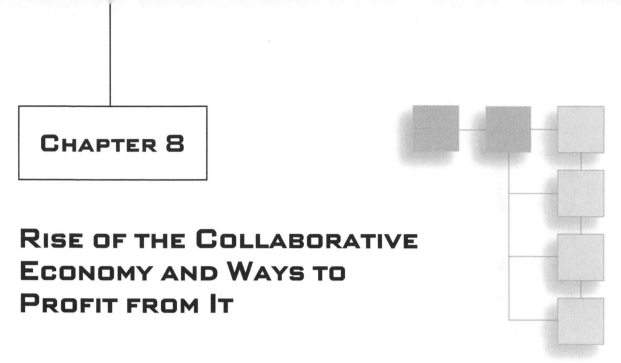

CHAPTER 8

RISE OF THE COLLABORATIVE ECONOMY AND WAYS TO PROFIT FROM IT

Big data is not only changing how business is done, it is changing the economy as well. As previously discussed, a new data economy is emerging wherein data is exchanged for money or used in lieu of currency. Data is steadily becoming a valued resource and a bankable asset. However, data in and of itself is not currently shown as a line item on a balance sheet and doesn't appear as an asset to be depreciated on an IRS form. Nor can a company borrow money using data as collateral. At first glance this appears to be an anomaly, for how can an asset be an asset if it cannot be fully treated as one?

DATA IS KNOWLEDGE AND AN ASSET

Think of data as knowledge. Knowledge can be and is sold. For example, a college graduate sells her knowledge and potential performance based on this knowledge in a job interview. The company buys her knowledge by hiring her. The same happens with every job candidate who possesses knowledge gained through years of experience in a field. Again, the hiring company "buys" this knowledge by hiring this job applicant, too. Thus, knowledge is an asset for employees and employers alike.

But it is not something that can be listed on a register as a taxable and depreciable, hard asset or used as collateral in borrowing money. Why? For one thing, it is almost impossible to affix a set value on the knowledge bought and sold because there are too many unknown variables. While several college graduates earn the same degree, they don't typically perform at the same level on the same job. The same is true of employees who gain knowledge through experience. Several candidates may possess the same number of years in the same or equivalent jobs, yet their actual performances on the new job will vary.

Without the ability to brain map, that is, to objectively quantify the amount and usefulness of knowledge held in the brain and to assess the individual's ability to use and adapt that knowledge to future situations, a specific value cannot be determined. The same holds true for data, i.e. knowledge, which a company possesses. Few companies have mapped their data holdings, much less their applications and their current and future market value. Without such defined and certain measurements, it is impossible to affix an asset value. Therefore, data is thought of in terms of a strategic asset rather than a hard one.

Gartner Inc., an information technology research and advisory firm, explains the concept of data as an asset this way in a June 5, 2013 statement to the press:

> Cloud computing was first positioned as a way of turning capital expenses into operational expenses, while saving on cost of ownership and helping to grow a more scalable and agile information infrastructure. Then cloud started to support other styles of working, such as multi-tenancy which appeals to public sector organizations which are not competitive. They can use the same applications and information creating business processes and information sharing across organizational borders. Now, there are also examples of "information as a service," where applications can call other applications in the cloud to perform a task or deliver a crucial bit of information.
>
> Turning that principle around, and allowing information to flow—albeit under certain conditions—cloud would turn into a "Bank of Information." "If we allow others to access some of our information, we receive interest," said Frank Buytendijk, research vice president at Gartner, "We get other information back, or more metadata on the use of our information by others. If we use information we don't own, we pay interest in the same way. In this way, exchange rates could develop, based on exchanging information."
>
> The underlying message of all these examples is that information is an asset in its own right. "It has value," said Mr. Buytendijk. Gartner calls this emerging discipline of valuing information "infonomics." It is not something of the far future; in fact, this is happening today in various industries, in commerce and public sector, in large and small enterprises.
>
> Just as the finance organization manages money, and HR is responsible for intellectual capital, a new information organization may emerge, outside of IT, led by the Chief Data Officer (CDO).

Gartner estimates that there are currently about 100 established CDOs out there already, more than double the number in 2012, and expects this to grow to 25% of enterprises worldwide by 2015. Further, Gartner found 65% of CDOs are in the United States, while 20% are in the U.K., and there are CDOs currently in over a dozen countries. In addition, the research giant found that over 25% of CDOs are women, almost twice as high as for CIOs (13%) and the position is most common in heavily regulated industries, media, and government.

As time progresses, we will likely see companies become more proficient at accounting for their data assets. However, for the near future at least, it is unlikely that these assets will be thought of as anything more than strategic assets.

Meanwhile, as counterintuitive as it may seem, the data economy will continue to grow in value and at an accelerating rate. As it does so, business models will be ruptured and new ones will rise, and the market itself will also radically change. All of this will happen due to the rapidly changing nature of knowledge exchange.

One example of this is the emerging "collaborative economy," wherein things, ideas, and information are shared rather than bought.

BIG DATA'S BIGGEST IMPACT: MODEL SHATTERING

While big business and big government are busy collecting and analyzing information on individuals, consumers are busy finding new and creative ways to reduce costs and circumvent vendor and brand lock-in. In other words, consumers are showing increasing interest in reducing cost of ownership in everything they use. Many are also motivated to side-step purchasing from organizations that load consumer devices with spyware thereby forcing the consumer to subsidize the very spying activities that are used against them. Some seek to avoid corporations that track consumer data in leasing, renting, and services use too.

For example, when consumers share a car through a peer-to-peer service, the data collected from the car by the manufacturer and dealer are no longer solely attributable to a single individual or family, whether or not that was the user's intent. Car sharing makes much of that data from those vehicles effectively worthless. With no means—yet—of tracking who is actually driving the vehicle, the data gatherers cannot accurately parse the data and assign data points to specific people. Worse still, manufacturers and dealers have no way of discerning which vehicles are being shared and which are not. If car sharing continues to gain momentum, as most industry watchers believe it will, then vehicle data will increasingly become of less value in determining or predicting driver behaviors, at least until there is some reliable way to identify specific drivers.

Even if individuals aren't trying to escape the ceaseless data collection, they do enjoy access to things like cars without the need to absorb ownership and maintance costs. Further, they save money by using cheaper peer-to-peer services such as FlightCar and RelayRides instead of the higher rental fees charged by traditional car rental companies.

Sharing assets such as cars is a cornerstone of the rising collaborative economy and it is already wreaking havoc on corporate big data projects and negatively affecting traditional business models. In the case of car sharing it is the rental car and airport businesses that suffer.

A July 29, 2013 *Forbes* article explains the impact this way:

> The stakes are high, since rental car companies generate much of their income–estimates of up to half of the $25 billion per year–at airports, making them a major next battleground in the sharing economy. Airports are also highly regulated, often by city, state and federal agencies, making them complicated for startups to enter.

> When car owners leave their car at the airport with FlightCar and catch a flight, the company rents it to another person who is arriving at the airport. Instead of paying for parking while the car sits idle, the car owner gets paid from the traveler who rents the car (the owner gets about $10 to $20 per day; FlightCar takes a cut). The car owner gets $1 million in insurance coverage in case of damages and a free car wash before returning to claim the car. Meanwhile, the traveler looking for a rental car gets a cheaper rental than from traditional services.

Traditional car rental companies and airports are fighting to hold their ground but the collaborative economy is exceedingly difficult to hold at bay. Consider this situation reported in that same *Forbes* article:

> SFO [San Francisco airport] says FlightCar is a rental car company and should pay its off-airport rental car fees of $20 for each airport visit plus 10% of all revenue. Besides saying FlightCar isn't a rental car service, Zaparde [Rajul Zaparde, 19, cofounder of FlightCar] says other rental car services get advertising rights on the vehicles that travel to the airport, which FlightCar doesn't have.

> Zaparde also says San Francisco officials' claim that FlightCar undercuts other rental car services isn't accurate. That's because FlightCar's services is 30% to 60% cheaper because it doesn't maintain or own any cars. In other words it isn't undercutting rental car companies, because it has a totally different business (and business model).

Consumers are also demonstrating increased interest in faster and cheaper innovation than that demonstrated by most corporations. This newfound common-man interest in innovation is borne from necessity more so than for a craving for something new.

"The collaborative economy is a powerful, if nascent, movement in which people are getting the things they need and want from each other, it's a combination of trends like the sharing economy, maker movement, and co-innovation," explains Jeremiah Owyang, founder of Crowd Companies, a consultancy specializing in the commercial exploitation of the collaborative economy. "In the growing Collaborative Economy, people fund, make, and share things with each other, rather than buy from inefficient corporations."

To understand the larger collaborative economy, it is important to first understand its basic components: the sharing economy, the maker movement and co-innovation. Each of these is discussed in the following sections.

The Sharing Economy

The "sharing economy" is not an exchangeable term for the collaborative economy, but instead is one element of it. The term refers to the sharing of things in lieu of purchasing or leasing these items. Essentially it is a peer-to-peer model wherein people pay to temporarily use things owned by other people, such as renting a room or home accommodations through new services such as Airbnb, which is a peer-to-peer lodging service (see Figure 8.1)—instead of booking a hotel room.

This should not be confused with the existing bed-and-breakfast or timeshare models, as this new peer-to-peer model does not require that the accommodations always be available for rent, or that the owner be in the full- or part-time business of renting accommodations. Also, peer-to-peer sharing service companies do not own anything. They merely facilitate the sharing of information on what's available for rent and matching owners with renters via websites and mobile apps. Further, peer-to-peer sharing is done on a much larger scale than either the timeshare or bed-and-breakfast models, thanks mostly to the ease and widespread availability of Internet-based communications and the subsequent readily available data on what's available to be shared.

Figure 8.1
The Airbnb website showing peer-to-peer lodging locations in over 34,000 cities in 190 countries and counting. Users rent accommodations from private individuals in lieu of staying at a hotel or bed-and-breakfast.

Source: Airbnb website.

But peer-to-peer sharing, also known as peer-to-peer renting, is not limited to room accommodations. More and more goods and services are being shared, including boats, cars, private jets and other things. As a March 9, 2013 article in *The Economist* describes it:

> *Just as peer-to-peer businesses like eBay allow anyone to become a retailer, sharing sites let individuals act as an ad hoc taxi service, car-hire firm, or boutique hotel as and when it suits them. Just go online or download an app. The model works for items that are expensive to buy and are widely owned by people who do not make full use of them. Bedrooms and cars are the most obvious examples, but you can also rent camping spaces in Sweden, fields in Australia, and washing machines in France. As proponents of the sharing economy like to put it, access trumps ownership.*

> *Rachel Botsman, the author of a book on the subject, says the consumer peer-to-peer rental market alone is worth $26 billion. Broader definitions of the sharing economy include peer-to-peer lending (though cash is hardly a spare fixed asset) or putting a solar panel on your roof and selling power back to the grid (though that looks a bit like becoming a utility). And it is not just individuals: the web makes it easier for companies to rent out spare offices and idle machines, too. But the core of the sharing economy is people renting things from each other.*

As peer-to-peer sharing grows, many companies in various industries from hospitality to car, boat, and aircraft and fine jewelry dealers, as well as many others, will be negatively impacted and their models disrupted if not entirely shattered. In this new rising marketplace, consumers will become the new competitors of corporations. In other words, the same consumers that corporations rely on for revenue will also be their competitors or potential competitors and therefore a threat to revenue.

The Maker Movement

The second component, the maker movement, is another thing entirely. Think of it as an extension of the Do-it-Yourself (DIY) model. Earlier DIY activities were largely done as a means to save money on such mundane but necessary actions as installing carpet, home painting, and car repairs. Consumers learned how to do some things themselves in order to avoid paying professionals for the service. Some consumers also enjoyed DIY projects as a matter of pride or as a hobby.

But the maker movement has gone beyond that simple premise to include the creation of products and services in a much broader scope and on a bigger scale. In other words, DIY has evolved from simple improvement projects to the making, designing, or enhancement of things. The goal is no longer limited to simply maintaining or upgrading things we already own. Creation and innovation of anything and everything is the order of the day in this movement.

"What exactly does DIY mean these days? Traditionally, it's been related to 'how-to' content, including things like 'how to change a tire,' but over the past couple of years, it's been coined much more broadly to describe any activity that uses an element of creative skills to make or design something on your own," wrote Brit Morin, founder and CEO, Brit + Co, an online community and e-commerce platform, in her May 2013 *Huffington Post* blog post.

"Using this definition, DIY can stand for everything from baking a cake, to decorating a bedroom, to creating handmade products like jewelry," she continued. "Some also use DIY in a more technical context as it relates to making gadgets like robots, printers, and other programmable devices hacked together using free software and tools found across the web. Finally, I know people who would even claim that they 'made' products such as their custom Nike iD sneakers, even if that meant they personalized the colors and design online and had the production take place elsewhere. In essence, the very word 'making' or the act of being a 'maker' or 'DIYer' is rapidly changing and is affecting more people than ever before."

What's the big deal about a few independent artisans designing and making stuff? Haven't individuals been doing this sort of thing since forever? For one thing, the movement has more than a few members and it's growing. Further, the market trend is moving away from mass manufactured goods and towards more personalized items. Consumers are increasingly in search of unique items that are distinctive because of the limited number made, some identifiable tie-in to personal interest and style, or the backstory of the item or its maker.

Some big brands can already see the writing on the wall and are testing different methods of embracing the maker movement before being destroyed by it. A March 17, 2014 article in *AdWeek* explains how that works:

To pack more wallop among the denim-and-leather set, Levi's is turning to people like Alice Saunders, a 29-year-old designer and history buff in Boston with a fetish for World War II duffel bags. Saunders, ironically, could care less about mainstream fashion, preferring vintage felt hats and rustic jewelry. What Levi's likes is her passion and the $165 one-of-a-kind tote bags she creates for her Forestbound brand using old, salvaged military fabrics. "My ultimate find is an old Navy duffle bag that the sailor had hand painted with pictures of pinup girls or palm trees," Saunders says. "I can make it into a tote that tells the history of that time."

Makers tap into an American admiration for self-reliance and combine that with open-source learning, contemporary design, and powerful personal technology like 3D printers. The creations, born in cluttered local workshops and bedroom offices, stir the imaginations of consumers numbed by generic, mass-produced, made-in-China merchandise.

Sensing potency, Levi's and other big-ticket marketers such as General Electric, Home Depot, and Best Buy are tapping into the maker movement to infuse their brand identities and product lineups with a whiff of individuality. For brands, "it's all about the emotional tug of the maker movement," says Tom Bernthal, CEO of Kelton, a brand strategy consultancy. "Even if a maker product is not better than a mass-produced version, people have a more positive feeling about it because the makers' stories are personal."

With the advent of 3D printers and other production means now coming within the grasp of individuals, the maker movement will also include coding the designs for new products that can be easily downloaded and produced in the buyer's home. This shift will deeply impact several industries including manufacturing, retailing, and shipping.

An additional threat will be found in a sharp uptick in counterfeit goods. The consumer's ability to reverse-engineer corporate-made products and exactly reproduce them at home, or add touches of their own, will dramatically increase and substantially impact corporate bottom lines.

Co-Innovation

Co-innovation is the third element of the collaborative economy. We can easily see examples of this in action today in cars, trucks, SUVs, and other vehicles wherein manufacturers partner with technology, Internet, and mobile industries to co-innovate new products and services and embed them in vehicles. From these co-innovation tactics come a number of new businesses such as OnStar and other commercially available emergency and convenience services. As products and services become more complex in order to offer more benefits and features to the user, co-innovation increasingly becomes a necessity in business.

However, individuals can co-innovate as well. For example, biohackers often co-innovate in order to improve outcomes or home lab tools. In one example of biohacking, which we'll get to in a moment, the biohacker designed a new head to enable other hackers to easily convert a simple and readily available Dremel tool into a cheap but efficient centrifuge. Improvements on biohacking tools happen rapidly as the biohacker community works collectively and independently to improve them much as is done in the open source code community. Because such co-innovation happens rapidly and cheaply, it will increasingly put corporations that rely on expensive talent and equipment to do the same thing at a distinct competitive disadvantage.

Further, it has been the traditional practice that anything an employee discovers, innovates, or invents belongs to the employer rather than the creator. That model will be quickly shredded as more and more innovating talent turns to co-innovating outside the employer sphere to both increase profit to the creator and bring the innovation to market quicker. Indeed, disruptive products and services will appear so rapidly that it will be extremely difficult for many corporations to regain their footing.

Taken together, these three elements comprise the collaborative economy. How much this market shift will affect your company depends entirely on your particular market segment's potential for collaborative economic disruption and how well you respond to it. That means you will have to use big data to predict impact but also to deduce possible means of competing in an ever-changing environment. Those means will be in revised or new business models, often put into effect on the fly.

EXAMPLES OF NEW MODELS EMERGING IN THE NEW COLLABORATIVE ECONOMY

In his 2014 report titled "Sharing Is the New Buying: How to Win in the Collaborative Economy," Jeremiah Owyang describes how this rising new economy is disrupting our current economy and indeed unraveling the industrial revolution entirely.

"That means that people go to a site like LendingClub to get funding for their new project, rather than a traditional bank," he said. "Or, they may go to a site like Etsy or Shapeways to get custom made goods, or go to a site like eBay to buy pre-owned goods, instead of buying new products from retailers. In each of these cases, the crowd is self-empowered to get what they need from each other."

Figure 8.2 is a visualization of the data collected by Vision Critical, a leading cloud-based software company that specializes in customer communities, and Jeremiah Owyang of Crowd Companies, an association for large brands in the Collaborative Economy. You can access the complete report at http://bit.ly/1eVInFA, if you want. However, Figure 8.2 shows you at a glance how the collaborative economy is shaping up and examples of the major players in the space.

Figure 8.2
A taxonomy of the collaborative economy: categories and examples.

Source: Reprinted with permission from Crowd Companies and Vision Critical, who jointly created and own this visualization. For data collected by Vision Critical, a leading cloud-based software company that specializes in customer communities and Jeremiah Owyang of Crowd Companies, an association for large brands in the Collaborative Economy, please access the complete report at http://bit.ly/1eVInFA.

But the collaborative economy is shaping itself in ways beyond those that Owyang and Vision Critical describe in that report. For example, biohackers are disrupting the giant pharmaceutical and genetic industries. One example of how they are doing this includes home or field DNA extractions with little more than a couple household chemicals such as dishwashing detergent and a simple homemade centrifuge using a common and inexpensive Dremel tool. Another example is field producing cheap or for-free antibiotics.

If you want to learn more about what white-hat biohackers are doing and how they are doing it, you might want to read my post "Biohacking 101: Tools of the Biopunk Trade" on the Genome Alberta website: http://genomealberta.ca/blogs/biohacking-101-tools-of-the-biopunk-trade.aspx You'll want to take particular note of the video embedded in that post, wherein a biohacker demonstrates how he extracts DNA from fruit.

Further, the rise of 3D printers and their steady subsequent reduction in costs makes it possible for people to share data to feed to these printers to fabricate items themselves rather than purchase them already assembled from commercial companies. As public adoption of 3D printers rises, sales of preformed or preassembled products by manufacturers and retailers will dramatically fall. In addition, traditional sales will decrease even more sharply as devices come on the market that enable consumers to recycle materials and reform them in 3D printers for new uses.

All told, this is a massive movement that will forever redefine business and the marketplace. This is why your big data strategy must be far broader than just improving how you do business now. It must also include a focus on how to change your business model as necessary to survive and capitalize on changes brought about by ever-evolving industry and market disruptors.

AGILE IS OUT, FLUID IS IN

For decades now, the business cry has been "agile." The goal was to create sufficient agility in big companies, and governments too, to enable fast, efficient, and effective responses to opportunities and challenges in the market. However, traditionally that meant changes in products and services and perhaps a business process or two, but not generally to the underlying business model. This definition of agile is quickly becoming antiquated. The new goal will be to become *fluid*, that is, to change the shape of the entire organization as needed to fit an ever-evolving market.

A few companies are already demonstrating signs of fluidity:

- Owyang cited existing examples of early business models in this new collaborative economy in an interview with *Silicon Prairie News*, including BMW renting cars in San Francisco instead of selling them, and to the U-Haul Investors Club, which gives consumers a cut of the revenues.

- The aforementioned example of custom Nike iD sneakers' appeal to the maker's movement is an example of Nike's early attempt at fluidity.

Other companies want to take those first steps too, but are unsure where to start. Big data can quickly enable you to identify where your company has the best chances of adapting to leverage emerging trends, so that is the first place to start. Still there are some common areas where companies can first begin their journey toward a fluid business model. They are:

- **Find ways to proactively include consumer participation in design and production of products and innovation in services.** For example, do as Nike did and let consumers customize the product or look to crowd-sourcing for product and service innovation or co-innovation. Think hive mind instead of walled R&D gardens.

- **Reexamine your distribution models.** Don't assume that build-and-ship will remain the mainstay of the business world. Prepare now to ship code and raw material requirements to home and other third-party 3D printers. That capability is not widespread yet, but it will be. It's highly probable that commercial 3D print centers will appear, which means that companies can produce goods on such printers in their own 3D centers in a variety of locales or on 3D printers owned and operated by the likes of Kinko's, FedEx, UPS, and similar ilk. This shift will radically change production and shipping models as well as the overall distribution model. Retailers, for example, will be hard pressed to justify their margins when goods can be distributed directly to the consumer or to a 3D printing service center. Figure 8.3 shows an example of a desktop 3D printer.

- **Proactively seek ways to leverage the sharing economy,** as BMW is now doing by testing the idea of renting cars rather than selling them. But don't think in terms of existing rental service models. For example, in the automotive industry, think in terms of renting cars by various increments such as by the hour and even by the year. Remember that many of the vehicles sold will ultimately be used in peer-to-peer sharing—that is your new true competition. Consider offering a service that enables owners to share their vehicle after purchase to grab a piece of this market similar to the way Airbnb has done in the hospitality industry. This tactic will likely work in moving all expensive and luxury goods. Alternately, look at new ways to deliver value to actual ownership and to reduce total cost of ownership (TCO) to make ownership ultimately more appealing than sharing. This will buoy product sales.

- **Look at automation with an eye toward enabling sharing and maker movements.** Most companies today look to automation solely to cut costs. Indeed, cutting costs will continue to be a pressing issue as the collaborative economy forces costs down and mercilessly destroys margins in the process. But now you need to look to automation as a means to change your distribution model, to quickly adapt to product innovation in production, and to enable customers to customize products on the fly.

■ **Broaden your opportunities for co-innovation**. Proactively seek to co-innovate with individuals rather than just with corporate partners. In exchange, offer something tangible such as pay, co-ownership of patents, and/or intellectual property protection.

■ **Work at co-owning data rather than sneaking and taking it.** Besides being transparent in your big data collection efforts, the best way to reassure customers that you are not spying on them, but rather you are eager to serve, is ask customers and prospects to help you do the project. You leave people feeling empowered when they can volunteer information and willingly clean their data too. Further, it you ask them to actually help you with a big data project, they feel pride and a degree of ownership in the outcome. Tactics such as these will go a long way in improving your analysis and public acceptance of your work. Further, such an effort can easily prove to be a brand differentiator and actually improve brand loyalty.

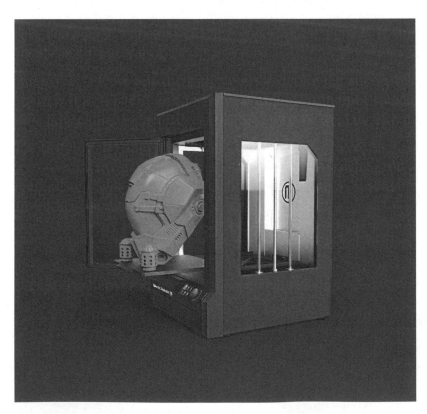

Figure 8.3
An example of a desktop 3D printer. This is the MakerBot Replicator Z18 3D printer.
Source: MakerBot.

Using Big Data to Strategize New Models

It isn't enough, however, to simply tag along by experimenting with new models already being tested by other companies. If you only do that, you'll always be behind.

Instead of focusing almost exclusively on what ROI you can get out of your big data efforts today, make it routine to check the road ahead often. Look specifically for signs that the market is changing and proactively look for profitable ways to tap into those movements early. Big data tools are highly efficient at pulling and analyzing information from external sources whenever you need it. Leverage that capability to the hilt. For example, instead of just pulling in social media data to learn what people are saying about your product or to learn more about your own customers, look to see what people are talking about and trying that may eventually affect your business or industry too.

But don't stop there. Look to the foundational trends as well and find ways to leverage that too. For years now, everything has been moving toward consolidation and everything is being connected to the Internet. You need to divine what changes these cracks in the foundation of the business world will likely bring about in the future.

For example, where distinctly defined organizations once stood now stand companies with blended purposes. Cable companies now offer phone services and phone companies now offer TV services. In the consumers' eyes, they are the same. That underlying trend in blending and service blurring will continue. Look to big data to show you where and how you can capture new revenues and new market share through a similar consolidation or blending of new offerings.

Further, while the "Internet of Things" offers you unprecedented and increasing access to information, don't overlook the other inherent advantages that may be lurking there. Consider ways to use this trend to change your organization to a more fluid state. Just as companies once had all employees ensconced onsite and now those huge commercial buildings are mostly empty as many employees work remotely, the "Internet of Things" will change how businesses are physically structured and organizationally organized. Consider what is becoming possible as more things come online and either transmit or receive data. Using big data can help you discover unchartered opportunities and threats lurking within an Internet populated by things.

In short, the overall movement is trending toward personalized services and products and peer-to-peer services and away from structured, huge organizations and mass produced products. Recognize this trend now and seek ways to relate and partner with consumers rather than focusing exclusively on new ways to throw customized ads at them. Expand your marketing efforts to include recruiting enthusiastic individuals as co-innovators, or perhaps paying or otherwise rewarding customers in exchange for their data. Other innovative ways to create and expand customer relationships that exceed mere transactions and advertising should also be constantly explored. The result will be to reshape your organization so that it can function and profit in a world that increasingly favors the consumer over corporate interests.

In the end, the companies that ultimately survive and profit will be those who master big data to the point that they can successfully use predictive analytics to change their overall company, processes, services, and products rapidly and snare fast moving opportunities. This is why you must use big data for more than just short-term goals. This is why ROI should not be your main focus or motivation in using big data. Make absolutely sure that your big data strategy is big enough to do all that must be done.

SUMMARY

In this chapter you learned that multiple disruptors are shaking up individual industries and the market as a whole. You saw specific real-world examples of current rising trends. Chief among those is the emerging collaborative economy, which is vastly enabled by Internet communications, mobile apps, and 3D printers. You learned that this new economy has three major components: the sharing economy, the maker movement, and co-innovation. But the big lesson learned here is that you must use big data to find and react to emerging disruptors and trends, not only in your own industry but in the market as a whole, as diligently as you use it to improve your business as it now stands. It is imperative to always be looking ahead.

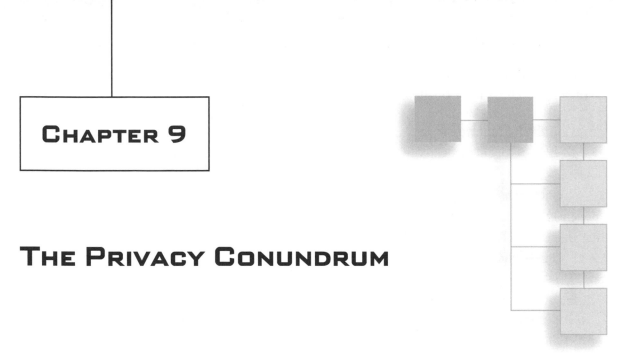

CHAPTER 9

THE PRIVACY CONUNDRUM

Data analysis is not a new tactic in either government or corporate work. For centuries, data in all its forms has been collected, analyzed, traded, and sold. Sometimes entities were forthright in their data collection and use, but that was often the exception rather than the rule. During all that time there were no widespread public objections to these practices, in part because many were hidden—and even with the transparency of the Internet, many remain so.

For example, throughout history, organized governments made records of everything from land, business, and patent ownership to voter registrations, individual and business incomes, professional and marriage licenses, births, deaths, and census headcounts. They also observed and recorded the actions of people they suspected were a threat to the public (or to their own power) in some way. This is true across many government agencies, but especially with those charged with law enforcement or national defense.

Businesses also collected a considerable amount of data on everything related to customers and prospects but also in fraud detection, products and warranties, production, inventory, shipping, competitors, and myriad other business functions.

The names, addresses, and phone numbers of millions of people were sold and traded regularly, most often in the recent past as mailing and prospecting lists. Nearly every mailbox and email inbox—until U.S. federal legislation was passed in 2003 in the form of the rather dubiously named CAN-SPAM Act—overflowed with "junk" mail. Home phones also rang incessantly at the demand of telemarketers up until the Telephone Consumer Protection Act (TCPA) passed in 1991. Although most consumers found these activities annoying and welcomed the legislative protections, again there was no public outcry against the collection and sale of private data.

The CAN-SPAM and TCPA Acts

CAN-SPAM is an acronym for the "Controlling the Assault of Non-Solicited Pornography and Marketing" act. It became Public Law 108-187 when the 108th Congress passed it in December 2003. The intention as specified in the law is "to regulate interstate commerce by imposing limitations and penalties on the transmission of unsolicited commercial electronic mail via the Internet." Penalties for entities sending emails without consent from the recipient and/or for sending fraudulent emails range from fines and a loss of proceeds and computing assets to imprisonment according to specific guidelines set forth in the law.

After the law passed, "spam" became a new word in the public lexicon and came to mean any unwanted email.

Congress enacted the Telephone Consumer Protection Act (TCPA) in 1991 to restrict telemarketing and "robocalls," that is, the automated dialing systems with pre-recorded phone messages. In 1992, the Federal Communications Commission (FCC) adopted rules to implement the act including establishing a requirement for entities making such calls to maintain an up-to-date and company-specific Do Not Call list, which consisted of phone numbers of people who requested they not be called. In 2003, the FCC and the Federal Trade Commission (FTC) coordinated to create a national Do Not Call list for citizens and businesses to list phone numbers they didn't want to receive telemarketing calls or robocalls on from any entities.

In 2012, the FCC revised its TCPA rules to include these requirements of telemarketers:

- To obtain prior express written consent from consumers before robocalling them.
- To no longer allow telemarketers to use an "established business relationship" to avoid getting consent from consumers when calling their home phones.
- To require telemarketers to provide an automated, interactive "opt-out" mechanism during each robocall so consumers can immediately tell the telemarketer to stop calling.

But now the public *is* alarmed and outraged over data collection and its use, which begs the question: why? What has changed?

Four major shifts in how data is collected and used have caused this newfound public ire. The first is that data collection tactics are far more invasive than in years past. Secondly, more and a larger variety of comprehensive data is collected, correlated, and deduced, which reveals far more telling details than most people are comfortable with others knowing. Thirdly, the protection previously found by data trapped in silos has crumbled, leaving the average person more exposed and vulnerable to data integration. Last, but not least, companies and governments are gathering data far beyond the scope of traditional business or governmental efforts and frequently doing so through surreptitious means.

This chapter discusses those shifts in more detail. First, let's examine when the public became aware of these shifts and whether that knowledge helped them.

THE DAY THE WHISTLE BLEW AND KILLED THE MYTH OF INDIVIDUAL PRIVACY

The general public was unaware of these shifts in data use until the now-infamous Edward Snowden, a former NSA contractor, blew the whistle on how extensive the government's data-collection efforts have been. The world held its breath as he subsequently backed up his claims with a slew of classified documents and other official evidence. It was then, on June 5, 2013—when the first of many exposes was published by *The Guardian* and *The Washington Post* at Snowden's behest—that "big data" became a household word. The public, for the very first time, saw what could be and was done with their data. To say it was shocking to discover that information they once thought completely private was for all practical purposes public and being sifted through by the government, is the understatement of the year.

Of course, Snowden himself became the epitome of the dangers in collecting and storing big data for governments and businesses alike. One employee or one contractor with the desire to steal or expose information can easily do so and big data often offers the best of pickings. Hackers, be they lone criminals, corporate spies, or in the employ of governments, also find big data the richest of mines. But this side of the story worried only those in the government and corporate worlds, at least initially.

The U.S. public meanwhile stood collectively agape at just how much their government knew about them. Americans learned about heretofore secret data programs such as PRISM and XKeyscore. They came to understand that the government collected metadata on phone calls and texts, gathered emails and social media posts, and even collected browsing history and other data far beyond the communication basics on millions of citizens—all without notice, permission, or benefit of a traditional warrant.

Note

PRISM is a system the NSA uses to gain access to previously considered private communications from, to, and/or between users on nine different Internet services. According to a PowerPoint presentation leaked by Edward Snowden and reported by *The Washington Post,* those nine services include Google, Microsoft, Yahoo!, and Facebook although all four companies hotly denied giving the NSA "direct access to the servers." Whether or not such a specific denial indicates the NSA accesses this information either without the services' knowledge or by another means remains under debate. James R. Clapper, Director of National Intelligence, shed little light on the technicalities but did say in a press release that the program is duly authorized by the courts and that the system does not target U.S. citizens.

Shortly thereafter, leaders and citizens in other countries joined the Americans in slack-jawed shock as Snowden's seemingly endless parade of disclosures revealed an all-encompassing dragnet of the most intimate of private details. No information, it seemed, was beyond the grasp of the U.S. government.

What almost got lost in the Snowden story was the fact that the U.S. government is not the only government busily gathering data on its own citizens and those of other countries too. Eventually those details came out, although the reactionary fanfare was more subdued, presumably because people all over the world were numbed by then to the endless deluge of offenses against their privacy.

Note

XKeyscore is a system the NSA uses to collect "nearly everything a user does on the Internet," according to NSA training materials for XKeyscore released by Edward Snowden to the press. In the first video interview that Snowden did with *The Guardian,* Snowden said that sitting at his desk he could "wiretap anyone, from you or your accountant, to a federal judge or even the president, if I had a personal email." The claim was vehemently denied by U.S. officials. Not long afterwards, Snowden released the training materials that showed that NSA analysts could easily do so by filling in a simple form including a broad or vague reasoning for the action and continue without the need of NSA management oversight or permission or court review.

For example, *The Guardian* reported on February 27, 2014 that Britain's surveillance agency GCHQ collected millions of webcam images of people using Yahoo! 1.8 million people were targeted at random in a six-month period alone. Some of those people were U.K. citizens and some were American. Many of the images captured were sexually explicit. All of the images were stored in U.K. government data centers.

"GCHQ files dating between 2008 and 2010 explicitly state that a surveillance program codenamed Optic Nerve collected still images of Yahoo! webcam chats in bulk and saved them to agency databases, regardless of whether individual users were an intelligence target or not," reported Spencer Ackerman and James Ball at *The Guardian*.

Yahoo! reacted furiously to the webcam interception when approached by *The Guardian*. The company denied any prior knowledge of the program, accusing the agencies of "a whole new level of violation of our users' privacy."

Dangers in the Aggregate

Although it is no surprise that governments spy on one another, friend and foe, big data techniques and tools allow them to do so with a broader sweep and in a more granular fashion than in past eras. Governments can now cheaply and easily gather enormous volumes of digital data on millions of people geographically located anywhere, store the data indefinitely, and analyze it at will—now or in the future—on specific individuals or on huge groups. None of this was possible, or at least not practical, before the advent of cheap storage and big data tools. But now that such is possible, governments around the globe are greatly and rapidly increasing the scope of their surveillance activities.

The Phone Call Heard Around the World

Take for example Vodafone's voluntary revelations on governments around the world eavesdropping on its customers. Vodafone is headquartered in the U.K. and is the world's second largest mobile phone carrier. The giant telecom released a report in June 2014 summarizing government surveillance actions worldwide as the company experienced them in the course of conducting its business in 29 countries. Among other things, the report reveals that the governments in at least six countries are directly hardwired into the carrier's infrastructure. However, the company stopped short of reporting the names of those six countries for fear of government retaliations:

In some of our countries of operation, we are prohibited in law from disclosing aggregate statistics relating to the total number of demands received over a 12 month period. In others, the law may expressly prohibit the disclosure that law enforcement demands are issued at all. In a number of countries where the law on aggregate disclosure is unclear, the relevant authorities have told us that we must not publish any form of aggregate demand information. We believe that defying those instructions could lead to some form of sanction against our local business and—in some countries—would also present an unacceptable level of risk for individual employees, to whom Vodafone owes a duty of care.

A June 6, 2014 Reuters report analyzed and summarized the Vodafone report this way:

Vodafone did not name the six [nation-state governments directly connected to the carrier's infrastructure] for legal reasons. It added that in Albania, Egypt, Hungary, India, Malta, Qatar, Romania, South Africa and Turkey it could not disclose any information related to wiretapping or interception.

The Vodafone report, which is incomplete because many governments will not allow it to disclose requests, also linked to already-published national data which showed Britain and Australia making hundreds of thousands of requests. It showed that of the countries in which it operates, EU member Italy made the most requests for communication data.

Vodafone received no requests from the government of the United States because it does not have an operating license there. It exited a joint mobile venture with Verizon last year.

In the cases of the six countries, the company said government agencies had inserted their own equipment into the Vodafone network, or diverted Vodafone's data traffic through government systems, to enable them to listen into calls, and determine where they were made.

"For governments to access phone calls at the flick of a switch is unprecedented and terrifying," said Shami Chakrabarti, Director of the human rights group Liberty.

Figure 9.1 lists some of the highlights from the Vodafone report for easy reference. These same highlights are also noted by Reuters in the article quote.

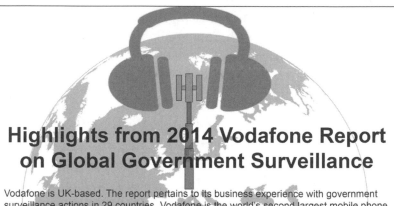

Highlights from 2014 Vodafone Report on Global Government Surveillance

Vodafone is UK-based. The report pertains to its business experience with government surveillance actions in 29 countries. Vodafone is the world's second largest mobile phone carrier.

A minimum of six nations are directly connected to Vodafone's infrastructure for the purpose of eavesdropping on users. The six nations were not identified in the report to protect Vodafone employees and its business in those countries.

Albania, Egypt, Hungary, India, Malta, Qatar, Romania, South Africa, and Turkey governments' activities in regards to wiretapping or call interception were not revealed in the report because those countries expressively forbid such disclosures.
Of European Union members, Italy made the most requests for communication data.

Vodafone received no requests from the U.S. government of the United States because it does not operate there given it exited a joint mobile venture with Verizon in 2013.

Britain and Australia made hundreds of thousands of requests for communication data.

Figure 9.1
Highlights from the 2014 Vodafone report on Global Government Surveillance.
Source: Vodafone and Reuters reports. Graphic by Pam Baker. Illustration by Steven Duffey.

Vodafone's report might not have been inspired by the Snowden revelations or perhaps it was simply a response to public pressure that followed thereafter. Whatever the company's motivation, it was the first in its industry to dare report even as much as it did. That in turn either pressured or encouraged other mobile carriers to follow suit.

The Guardian reported on June 6, 2014 that "a spokeswoman for Deutsche Telekom, [a telecom that owns half of Britain's EE mobile network and operates in 14 countries including the US, Spain and Poland] which has 140 million customers worldwide, said: "Deutsche Telekom has initially focused on Germany when it comes to disclosure of government requests. We are currently checking if and to what extent our national companies can disclose information. We intend to publish something similar to Vodafone."

But even if all mobile carriers were to come forth with reports, the value of such would be limited. The Vodafone report noted that "inconsistent publication of statistical information by individual operators amounts to an inadequate and unsustainable foundation for true transparency and public insight" and "it is not possible to draw any meaningful conclusions from a comparison of one country's statistical information with that disclosed for another." Therefore, it is unlikely that the true extent of government surveillance actions of this type can be known in the immediate future.

The Vodafone report made one other notable point that should be considered here:

> Vodafone's networks are designed and configured to ensure that agencies and authorities can only access customer communications within the boundaries of the country in question. They cannot access customer communications on other Vodafone networks in other countries.

While this statement is important in that it provides some protection for customers in other countries, it does not completely protect them as any calls made to or received from someone in the affected country are accessible to that nation's surveillance practices with or without cause. "A number of governments have legal powers to order an operator to enable lawful interception of communications that leave or enter a country without targeting a specific individual or set of premises," said the Vodafone report.

Despite our inability at the moment to get a precise handle on just how much mobile phone data the world's governments are collecting, we now know enough to understand that communications over the Internet and over cellular networks are heavily compromised. Big data tools have given every government the means to spy on anyone, and any business, anywhere.

How John Q. Public's and Veterans' Data Help Other Nations Plan Attacks

The government in one country no longer has to restrain their snooping to leaders of another government or the workings of key infrastructure entities in that nation. Now governments can take a hard and in-depth look at citizens of that country too, or subsets of it, in order to find that nation's vulnerabilities.

Jerry Davis, a Marine Gulf War veteran who served as the VA [Veterans Administration] CISO from August 2010 until February 2013, said that shortly after he took the VA job, [Stephen] Warren [acting VA chief information officer] told him, "We have uninvited visitors in the network," according to a report in NextGov.com on testimonies before an open Congressional hearing on nation-sponsored attacks against the VA. Davis said after an investigation he determined that "these attackers were a nation-state sponsored cyber espionage unit and that no less than eight different nation-state sponsored organizations had successfully compromised VA networks and data or were actively attacking VA networks."

VA databases contain highly detailed information on millions of U.S. military veterans, including health records, social security numbers, and email and home addresses. Further, some DNA records and medical studies results are also stored there.

While many veterans and the public at large perceived these attacks as privacy invasions and potential identity theft schemes, these efforts are likely far more nefarious and dangerous than that, because it is the aggregate and not the individual data that reveals the most damaging information. The ability to infer additional conclusions adds significant peril.

For example, it is conceivable that a nation-state could learn from VA data a common susceptibility to specific diseases that would help the nation-state develop bio-weapons not only against the U.S. military but the American public at large. Further, a study of common injuries in U.S. military personnel could enable a nation-state to infer flaws in training and/or protective gear design. This information could then be used to adjust or perfect military tactics and weapons to take advantage of U.S. military vulnerabilities.

Figure 9.2 shows the Veteran Population information from the National Center for Veterans Analysis and Statistics available on the VA website at http://www.va.gov/vetdata/ Veteran_Population.asp. Other information on military veterans can be found there as well, as can links to additional outside data sets that contain information about veterans. While this information is made available as part of a government transparency effort on the workings of the VA, medical data on individuals is not released for public view. To access that data, the nation-states had to attack the network unlawfully.

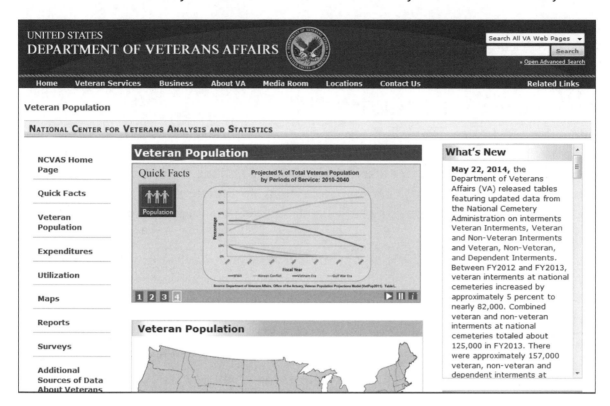

Figure 9.2
Sample data and statistics available online from the National Center for Veterans Analysis and Statistics.
Source: U.S. Department of Veterans Affairs website http://www.va.gov/vetdata/index.asp.

Although it is not unheard of for nation-state sponsored attacks to involve identity and monetary theft, such attacks are more often for the attempted purpose of damaging or disabling the country's overall financial infrastructure, rather than raiding individual accounts for simple monetary gain. However, big data tactics easily enhance both.

In any case, the widespread invasive and aggressive use of big data by so many nations makes it nearly impossible for any one of them to unilaterally cease using it, if for no other reason than as a means to thwart big data-fueled attacks aimed in their direction. It is the modern-day version of the nuclear arms race. Only this time, there are no production facilities and weapon silos for satellites overhead to spot or the U.N. to find and inspect in order to eventually curb or stop the proliferation.

Big data real-time analysis can quite literally be done on the fly, thereby making it increasingly challenging to detect it, much less to stop it. Revelations of attacks are almost always after the fact. However, this is slowly changing as security professionals are improving their own use of big data to uncover attacks in real time. Eventually, predictive analytics should consistently enable the prevention of many such attacks. For now, the best that can be done is to detect them in progress, though successful efforts remain relatively few.

Data Proliferation Escalates

Against this big data backdrop, individual privacy could be argued as a casualty of war if not already a moot point. If citizens in any given country are successful in curbing their government's data collection and use practices via regulations, what have they gained if governments in other countries can continue doing so unfettered? Further, it could be argued that hobbling one's own country's big data efforts drastically diminishes its ability to protect its citizens.

Of course, that was the exact same argument used in favor of nuclear proliferation. Bombs were built to stop bombs from being used, even though everyone knew that these bombs posed a threat to all of mankind. Still, once any technical genie is out of the bottle, it is difficult for humanity to cork it in again. And in truth, we didn't completely back away, as obviously nuclear bombs still exist in large numbers today. They have yet to be eliminated from the threat-scape and probably never will be. The same is true of big data use, except it is more widespread and even less likely to be abandoned.

The privacy conundrum is further complicated by the private sector's unfettered use of data. If future regulation focuses exclusively on governments' collection of data, then the private sector's big data works will likely continue on unabated, thereby guaranteeing individual privacy will erode further. In addition, it's conceivable that the private sector could profit from regulations that forbid or restrain governments in collecting data as the corporate world may collect that information and sell it, or sell the analysis of it on demand, to governments. Further, even if the private sector cannot profit from this, it can still be required to make the information available to various governments.

In addition, numerous corporate entities such as Facebook and Google have already collected sufficient information on individuals and businesses to infer behaviors for decades to come. It is also likely that the United States and foreign federal governments have as well. There is no realistic way to ensure data is permanently erased in any of these collections. Therefore, any new privacy regulations that may be forthcoming to curtail big data collection and use are, for all practical purposes, too late to do much good.

Lastly, there is no clear definition of who owns what data, making the argument to delete data on individuals harder to make and win. We'll get to that issue in more detail momentarily.

Drawing the Line on Individual Privacy

For now, suffice it to say that the issue of individual privacy in not as clear-cut as it first appears. Resolving this conundrum, while not impossible, is not an easy or quick task.

Did Snowden's and Vodafone's revelations help the public in the end? Yes and no. The public cannot address issues it does not know exists. But that knowledge may lead to privacy protections via regulations that sound good, but in operation are ineffectual or even increase the problems.

Also, a privacy protection industry is now evolving to thwart data collection. These tools mask information or make the tracking of its origin difficult. That industry will cut both ways. Many of these new tools will help individuals keep their information private—to some degree—but those same tools will also enable terrorists and criminals to hide before and after they strike.

One example of such a privacy enhancing tool is the DuckDuckGo search engine, which has a no-tracking policy and leaves no trace of users' activities online. Figure 9.3 shows the DuckDuckGo search engine interface.

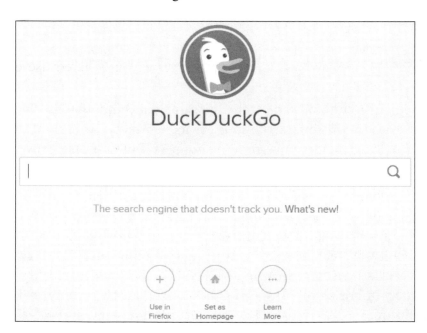

Figure 9.3
DuckDuckGo is a search engine with a no-tracking policy designed to protect users' privacy while online.
Source: DuckDuckGo at https://duckduckgo.com/.

Another example of a privacy enhancement tool is Switzerland-based ProtonMail, an email service designed by a group of Harvard and MIT students who met while working at the European Organization for Nuclear Research (aka CERN) in Switzerland. Their goal was to build an email service that surpassed even Snowden's professed favorite encrypted email service, Lavabit. Not so coincidentally, Lavabit has since shutdown. The owner explained why in a May 2014 interview with *The Guardian*:

> My legal saga started last summer with a knock at the door, behind which stood two federal agents ready to serve me with a court order requiring the installation of surveillance equipment on my company's network.

> My company, Lavabit, provided email services to 410,000 people—including Edward Snowden, according to news reports—and thrived by offering features specifically designed to protect the privacy and security of its customers. I had no choice but to consent to the installation of their device, which would hand the U.S. government access to all of the messages, to and from all of my customers as they travelled between their email accounts other providers on the Internet.

> But that wasn't enough. The federal agents then claimed that their court order required me to surrender my company's private encryption keys, and I balked. What they said they needed were customer passwords, which were sent securely, so that they could access the plain-text versions of messages from customers using my company's encrypted storage feature. (The government would later claim they only made this demand because of my "noncompliance.")

> Bothered by what the agents were saying, I informed them that I would first need to read the order they had just delivered and then consult with an attorney. The feds seemed surprised by my hesitation.

> What ensued was a flurry of legal proceedings that would last 38 days, ending not only my startup but also destroying, bit by bit, the very principle upon which I founded it—that we all have a right to personal privacy.

It remains to be seen as to whether ProtonMail can escape the same fate. Undoubtedly the founders thought basing the service in Switzerland, famous for its neutrality, would put it beyond the jurisdictions of various and sundry government snoopers. But that may prove not to be the case.

In an April 2014 U.S. court case, Judge James Francis in New York ruled that Microsoft would have to deliver data on one of its users even though that data was stored on a server in Ireland. "Anyone issued with a subpoena by the United States must provide the information sought, no matter where it was held, he said," according to a report in BBC. That decision puts Microsoft in a very bad position because if the company complies with the U.S. court order, it is immediately in breach of European data transfer laws. Conversely, if Microsoft complies with the European data transfer laws, it will fail in complying with a court order. But the consequences of this decision could go far beyond Microsoft's plight.

"This startling ruling could have a significant impact on not only the use of free email services like Hotmail and Gmail, but also all cloud-based services like Office 365, Google Apps, and even cloud providers like Amazon," writes Drinker Biddle attorneys Bennett B. Borden, Andrea L. D'Ambra, and Edward James Beale in their post in the *National Law*

Review. "If this ruling stands and is widely adopted, U.S. service providers may be compelled to produce customer data regardless of the jurisdiction in which it physically resides."

The consequences may go even further than that if other countries decide to do the same.

"What could be interesting—if by interesting we actually mean 'scary and really bad'—is if other countries decide that, given this as a precedent, their various laws about data—such as the recent 'right to be forgotten'—should also apply to the United States. Ultimately, it could mean a hodgepodge of data control Balkanization that could result, as the saying goes, in the end of the Internet as we know it," writes Sharon Fisher in her post in TechTarget.

However, Microsoft's Corporate Vice President & Deputy General Counsel David Howard wrote in a blog post not only the company's plans to appeal the decision but he also says his company had planned to do so all along in order to have the issue decided once and for all.

From this one example you can detect how easily privacy regulations can make a mess of things even though they are well-intentioned. Solving the privacy conundrum is an exceedingly difficult thing to do. But back to the narrower point, ProtonMail's fate and success as a secure email service rests on the outcome of this and other events (see Figure 9.4).

Figure 9.4
ProtonMail is an encrypted service designed to ensure user privacy and to be outside the jurisdictions of governments most prone to prying.
Source: ProtonMail at https://protonmail.ch/.

Meanwhile, many individuals attempt to stymie big data collection efforts by routinely offering false information, whether that's giving the wrong ZIP code to a store clerk, using a "for spam purposes only" email address online, using mobile apps to report incorrect GPS coordinates for the user's location, or other means.

Figure 9.5 shows the GPS shifting option in the privacy settings on the SinglesAroundMe mobile phone app. Although the app is designed to help singles find other singles to meet and date that are close by, the app "allows people to shift their public geolocation for the sake of their mobile privacy and security while on a smartphone or social network," according to the company's press release.

Figure 9.5
The privacy settings on the SinglesAroundMe mobile phone app showing the GPS Shift option based on the company's patent pending Position-Shift invention. By selecting this option, the user's location is reported as somewhere other than where the user actually is.

Source: SinglesAroundMe press release http://globenewswire.com/news-release/2014/01/08/601158/10063479/en/The-Next-Big-Thing-in-2014-Shifting-your-GPS-location-on-a-smart-phone-for-the-sake-of-your-mobile-location-Privacy-and-Security.html.

Such efforts in deliberately masking or falsifying information will work initially in protecting privacy, at least partially, as it is currently difficult for most big data efforts to reconcile records and purge incorrect information. However, that will become less of a problem in the future as big data tools become more sophisticated and able to detect such data manipulations.

There is also a commonly overlooked threat buried in providing false information as a privacy protection tactic. It can ultimately paint an incorrect picture of that person which could harm him or her in many ways, including in obtaining credit, getting a job, or proving innocence of a crime before a court. Wrong information, in other words, can sometimes be more harmful to the individual than correct information. Further, correcting wrong information can prove to be a near impossible task as the information is sold and traded and thus stored on many servers, making the location and ownership of such records unknown to the person trying to correct their record.

The Business Side of the Privacy Conundrum

Obviously, there is no panacea for individual privacy protection. The correct answer to the privacy conundrum, if one exists, will likely consist of multiple solutions implemented on many fronts. Even then, like all other security threats in existence today, any privacy protection solutions we develop will likely only work temporarily. In other words, humankind will be seeking ways to protect individual privacy for eternity, or at least as long as computers exist.

For the purposes of this book, the focus is on privacy issues from the business perspective. While each of us is an individual and the wrongs businesses may afflict are also afflicted upon us, we must incorporate the advantages and repercussions of collecting private data on individuals within our corporate big data strategies and primarily in terms of business value.

To that end, it is important to understand where and what lines have been crossed so far and which tactics are likely to go astray.

The Four Big Shifts in Data Collection

To recap, four major shifts in how data is collected and used have occurred, specifically in invasiveness, variety, integration, and scope.

Historically, data on individuals was largely generated by transactions initiated by individuals. In other words, customer data was collected when a customer bought or leased a product or service. Similarly, prospect data was collected when an individual who was not a customer requested information or filled out a form such as a contest or prize drawing entry form. The individual was arguably in control of disseminating their information by virtue of the fact that they had to initiate the transfer of information to a particular entity. Further, they could in most cases elect to conduct the transaction without conveying any information about themselves, such as by paying in cash and by not establishing a customer relationship with the vendor.

While it is true that companies, primarily merchants, often sold the information to other companies, primarily in the form of mailing or sales prospecting lists, the information about the individual was largely confined to data the individual initially divulged and/or to the most basic of transactional data points generated by his or her purchase. Further, this information often "aged out," meaning that it became invalid over time. It was rare for a company to keep records older than seven years, and they usually did not keep up with periodic changes in any given individual's data, such as a change in address, phone number, credit status, or employment.

Some data on individuals was also exchanged in the regular course of business, such as the release of payment records to a credit bureau or as a credit reference. But even this data aged out over time. The concept of a "permanent record" did not exist in the private sector or in the public mind.

Figure 9.6 summarizes the four big shifts in data collection for easy reference. Each is discussed in finer detail in the following sections.

The Four Big Shifts in Data Collection

I.   **Invasiveness** – Governments and businesses collect far more information than they have traditionally and they tend to do so surreptitiously. Data is typically passively submitted, meaning the consumer does not actively, knowingly or intentionally offer or surrender the information. Nor do consumers understand how much is inferred from their information. Governments and businesses do not acknowledge or respect previously and widely accepted privacy boundaries.

II.   **Variety** -- Data collections are now routinely augmented with data from other sources. Such augmentation may come from nearly any data source: adding social media data, machine data or, of course, data from other business and government databases. It is this greater variety of data that reveals details about individuals that were impossible to obtain to any appreciable degree in earlier years.

III.   **Integration** -- The widespread existence of data silos provided considerable cover for individuals in regard to privacy. If a company has data but cannot use it, on one level it is the same as not having the information at all. But that too has changed. Companies and governments are working to swiftly eliminate silos and integrate the data, not only within their own organizations but in pooled data resources with other entities. Individuals then are left exposed and vulnerable to all. No longer can the details of their lives remain in the shadows of mountains of data silos. Instead, they find themselves standing naked on a flat data landscape that is too brightly lit.

IV.   **Scope** -- While companies and governments are quick to justify their use of privacy invading tools in the name of security, marketing, better customer service, and other business or mission aims, the truth is that they have increased their scope beyond standard data uses to include gathering knowledge for knowledge's sake. They have collectively stepped over clearly marked privacy lines with no real excusable and acceptable reason for doing so.

Figure 9.6
The four shifts in data collection.
Source: Pam Baker. Illustration by Steven Duffey.

Data Invasiveness Changes

The situation is radically different today. While some information is still offered freely by individuals to a business entity, until recently it was rarely shared with the understanding it would be thoroughly sliced, diced, and analyzed down to the last intimate detail and that both the raw data and the analysis would remain stored in datacenters for perpetuity. Neither did consumers realize how much other information could be inferred from the little data they willingly provided.

By the time consumers understood this, it was effectively too late. Their information was already captured, analyzed, and on its way to predictive analytics where corporations would seek to accurately predict consumer behaviors in future years.

However, most data today is passively submitted, meaning the consumer does not actively, knowingly or intentionally offer or surrender the information. This is the part where invasiveness comes in to play.

Certainly no one agreed to allow all the world's governments to track their every phone call, text, and email or to take pictures of them through their own webcam. Neither did anyone give permission to cable and satellite TV companies to track their TV viewing habits or smart TV manufacturers to capture and analyze their home videos of children's birthday parties, weddings, family unions, and otherwise private affairs.

The Case of the Out-Smarted Smart TV

Here is one example of that. In a blog post that quickly went viral, Jason Huntley, a U.K.-based ICT consultant, detailed his shocking discovery that his LG smart TV was sending extensive information about his viewing habits to the Korea-based manufacturer. Specifically, he learned that the television was logging USB filenames and viewing info to LG servers. He was shocked again when he opted-out of LG's data collection efforts, after finally finding the means to do so buried deep in the settings menu, only to find that the data collection did not stop.

"This information appears to be sent back unencrypted and in the clear to LG every time you change channel, even if you have gone to the trouble of changing the setting above to switch collection of viewing information off," he wrote in his November 18, 2013 Doctor-Beet's Blog post.

"It was at this point, I made an even more disturbing find within the packet data dumps," he explained in that post. "I noticed filenames were being posted to LG's servers and that these filenames were ones stored on my external USB hard drive. To demonstrate this, I created a mock AVI file and copied it to a USB stick."

"My wife was shocked to see our children's names being transmitted in the name of a Christmas video file that we had watched from USB," he added.

But televisions are not the only devices turned against their owners. Smartphones, cars, tablets, and even smart kitchen appliances, smart meters that measure electrical usage, and other devices, most with the prefix "smart" but not all, can be spying devices unknowingly subsidized by the spied upon. Such practices add insult to injury and are typically met with strong consumer outrage and backlash when such comes to light.

LG, for example, was publicly embarrassed by the disclosure and its accompanying and rather creepy corporate video promising advertisers that "LG Smart Ad offers useful and various advertising performance reports that live broadcasting ads cannot, in order to accurately identify actual advertising effectiveness." The video pitch to advertisers was taken offline as soon as Huntley's post went viral but you can still see it on *LiveLeak*. The company admitted that the opt-out command did not actually allow users to opt out and promised to provide a firmware update to rectify the problem. It is unclear whether all LG smart TV owners got the update and/or understood that they still had to hunt for the opt-out option buried in the Settings menu and actively set it in order to stop the data collection. In all probability enough of them don't know to do that and enough new buyers have not heard of the problem at all, that LG's data collection program will continue in some form.

The Spreading Spy Net

Further, consider that line in LG's corporate video again. How can a TV maker possibly "accurately identify actual advertising effectiveness" from just a consumer's TV viewing habits? The answer is that it can't. To be able to confirm an ad's effectiveness, one would need to see actual purchases made after viewing the ad and in direct response to the ad. To make such an immediate purchase, consumers would have to purchase the product through the TV or online using a different device. But in order to see such buying response in action, LG would have to be able to snoop the user's entire network and not just the TV. It is theoretically conceivable that LG and other smart TV manufactures can do exactly that since their devices are connected to the users' home networks.

It's a mistake to believe that LG is the only TV manufacturer or TV-related product or service engaging in surreptitious and invasive data collection. Almost every set-top box and gaming system sold today does something similar or is capable of doing so. It is also not far-fetched to imagine that TV attachments such as Google's Chromecast and Apple TV can at some point, if they aren't already, combine smartphone location, sound and camera snooping with TV viewing in order to present ads pertinent to the user's activity at the time (no matter how intimate) on the TV or mobile device.

It is also naïve to believe that such activities are limited to entertainment and communication devices. Every device connected to the Internet presents potential snooping capabilities for manufacturers and service providers.

Big Brother 'R Us

All companies are aware of this, of course, which means the race is on to be the most invasive in order to win at the big data game. Except this isn't a game. Real people can be and are hurt by all these spying-for-profit activities. Nonetheless, with the advent of the "Internet of Things," wherein every device of every kind from lighting fixtures in airports and boardrooms, to cameras and sensors on cars and street corners, and on farm machinery and in nightclubs, to devices that can read your fingerprints from afar, to things we've not yet imagined are connected to the Internet—everything anyone does can and will be one day recorded and analyzed.

This is Big Brother incarnate and Big Brother is us.

Further, any data the private sector captures can be used by governments as well, either through the governments' legal purchase of the data, secret capturing of it, or by legal mandate, either governmental or in litigation through the nearly all-encompassing (and aptly named) "discovery" process.

This is the important point that businesses and consumers most often miss. Whatever data is collected can be taken by governments or others. Unfortunately, no one is read the Miranda Rights prior to the data collection or the government's taking possession of it. That is, no one says to the consumer if you buy this TV, phone, tablet, refrigerator, car, or whatever, everything you do in, with, or around it can and will be used against you. And if this doesn't worry company leaders, it should since CEOs, R&D scientists, and other business leaders in possession of company secrets also own and use these same devices. And it's not just government surveillance that business leaders and key personnel have to worry about; corporate espionage works much the same way.

So, yes, invasiveness in data gathering has not only increased, it is increasing with each passing day.

Data Variety Changes

And that brings us to the second major shift: data variety.

Historically, companies and governments had a very limited view of individuals confined to a thin slice of the individual. Typically, the data any given company or government agency held was confined to what it had gathered on its own. Further, the data was directly related to a business or mission goal, such as to customer service, sales, or in the case of governments, lists of narrowly defined citizen activities such as tax collection, births, marriages, and licensed business owners.

That is no longer the case. With the advent of big data tools and techniques, these data collections could and are augmented with data from other sources. Such augmentation may come from nearly any data source: adding social media data, machine data, or, of course, data from other business and government databases. It is this greater variety of data that reveals details about individuals that were impossible to obtain to any appreciable degree in earlier years.

Yes, entities obviously shared data in previous years and, yes, that data was sometimes merged with existing data. The difference is that in years past, such compilations were typically done in order to better achieve a single and well-defined business or government purpose, whereas now data augmentation is more often done specifically to discover more about individuals, whether or not such has an immediate or direct business or mission implication.

The result is that increased data variety today means entities learn far more about individuals than they necessarily need to know to conduct their existing business. Entities today also deliberately seek additional knowledge about individuals not necessarily to improve their business as it is today, but for information they can sell to other entities or leverage for future profit even if they have no idea how they might accomplish that now. This is not an environment that favors individual privacy. Quite the contrary; this environment fosters a rabid search for increasingly private details.

Data Integration Changes

And that brings us to data integration as a threat to individual privacy.

Traditionally, any data gathered by an entity remained in that entity's data center or filing cabinets. Further, companies and governments often could not consider all of their data in a single view, since much of it was trapped in silos, which were in different locations, different storage formats, and in different departments such as billing, shipping, and customer service. This data was largely unusable and unreadable outside that department.

The widespread existence of data silos provided considerable cover for individuals in regard to privacy. If a company has data but cannot use it, on one level it is the same as not having the information at all. But that too has changed. Companies and governments are working to swiftly eliminate silos and integrate the data, not only within their own organizations but in pooled data resources with other entities.

Individuals then are left exposed and vulnerable to all. No longer can the details of their lives remain in the shadows of mountains of data silos. Instead, they find themselves standing naked on a flat data landscape that is too brightly lit.

Data Scope Changes

This brings us to the fourth major shift in data collection: scope.

Even though we've touched on this aspect a bit already, it is important to more fully comprehend just how much scope has broadened in data collection in order to better see just how far companies and governments are willing to cross the lines into creepitude in privacy invasion. Keep in mind that governments and businesses once restrained data collection to what was needed to complete a specific business purpose or mission. Now the focus has flipped from completing the business at hand to tracking and defining individuals to the nth degree whether or not such details are necessary or relevant to the normal course of business.

But it's equally important to understand that many big data efforts are not designed to be huge dragnets capturing all the data in reach in an effort to know all that can be known, and yet their scope often increases anyway. This is the same phenomena that afflicts projects of every type, even those that are not digital in nature. It's called "scope creep," which refers to uncontrolled changes that happen throughout a project that then result in growth or spread of the project's scope. The changes "creep" into the project and the scope swells.

When big data projects, like all other types of projects, are not managed properly, scope creep sets in. But sometimes the scope creep comes not from within but from other parties building on the original intent of a technology or project so that its uses become bigger, more varied, or redirected from what was intended.

One example of this can be found in biometric data, which is collected and used as a means to provide secure access to data or physical assets, such as hardware and buildings.

"Biometric data is the only way that we currently know of to approach the ideal of being able to identify anyone anywhere with 100% certainty," says Jim Cantrell, CEO of IDair, a producer of touchless biometric sensors for identity verification. "Technologies are developing for facial recognition, electronic fingerprinting, voice recognition, and even ear recognition."

But biometric information including retina and fingerprint scans can also become "coat hangers," as Lee Tien, a senior staff attorney at the Electronic Frontier Foundation (EFF) calls them. So like everything else in the digital world, biometric data can be used for purposes beyond or even opposite to the initial goal.

"In other words," writes Lee Roop in a blog post at AL.com, "with a Social Security number, you can find out many other things about someone. Fingerprints could be same way," he said, and "someone else could use it to pretend to be me."

While biometrics presents great opportunities in security, that is, in positively identifying the authorized user, they also provide the means to connect more information about an individual than may be possible without such precise identification measures.

"The real challenge for safeguarding data, facilities, or valuables with biometric data will really be in protecting the biometric source data that will be used to validate users," explains Cantrell. "Right now biometric data is not considered to have a high value on the identity black market. That will surely change in a future where biometric authentication is used regularly."

But it isn't just criminals who are likely to value biometric data in the future. Companies and governments intent on discovering every detail about individuals are likely to abuse this information too.

Fingerprints Plucked from the Air

IDair is one example of a company producing biometric sensors for security purposes. The company produces, among other things, a product called AIRprint that can scan and identify a person's fingerprints from as far away as three to six feet (one to two meters). See Figure 9.7. "Since users don't have to touch a fingerprint scanner, there's no problem with the imaging surface becoming fouled," explains Clay Dillow in his article about the product in *Popular Science*. "And of course, additional layers of security like facial recognition can be piled on to make up a more robust, complete biometric profile of a person that provides that individual with access without the need for a key or passcode, either of which can be lost, stolen, or shared without authorization."

"The technology works much the same way satellites process terrain imagery, using a lot of edge detection and image sharpening to turn a fingerprint captured at a distance into a usable and identifiable image," continues Dillow.

Figure 9.7
The AIRprint product. Note that the device is small and can be used just about anywhere unobtrusively.
Source: IDair LLC. Used with permission.

A basic AIRprint fingerprint scanner reportedly costs about $2,000, making it attractive to many companies in the private and public sector. Employers and other organizations with a specific membership, such as gyms and country clubs, might use it to ensure only authorized persons have access to the premises. Retailers looking to identify who is in their stores and tie that information with other data to better track shoppers will likely also be interested. And, of course, biometric authentication will eventually become the prime means retailers will use to verify credit and debit card purchases to help thwart fraud and theft.

But in order to use biometrics, retailers, credit card processors, banks, and other entities cannot avoid building a fingerprint database of their own. Hackers, law enforcement, and government agencies will be highly interested in this data.

"Given recent events such as the Target data breach and the NSA spy scandals, the thought of having a highly valuable biometric database that can be breached will surely be of great concern in the future," says Cantrell. "Rather than building a 'Fort Know' for biometric data that is 'impenetrable,' the industry needs to take steps to make biometric data easily replaced as this will go a long way towards making biometric data a more universally accepted and useful tool for user authentication."

At the moment IDair's system is not connected to fingerprint databases such as at the FBI, the company says, and that relieves fear that employers and companies can access more information than one would want to reveal. But it's foolish to think that someone, somewhere will not figure out how to connect this data to other identifying data in the future.

"It's the security of the fingerprint database that concerns privacy experts such as Lee Tien, a senior staff attorney at the Electronic Frontier Foundation," writes Lee Roop about the AIRprint product in a blog post at AL.com. "There are so many steps where a (digital) fingerprint can leak," Tien said.

"Yes, it can be abused," [Joel] Burcham, president of IDair, agreed in a comment in Roop's post. "Anything can be abused. The point is, are there restrictions in place to not abuse it?" The answer with IDair is yes, he said. "But what it's going to come down to is: Do you want to go through that door? Do you want to buy something with Amazon?"

There's the rub isn't it? Individuals cannot opt out of many data collection efforts like this one, but instead will be forced to consent in order to enter and/or buy anything, including life necessities. How then can privacy be protected when it must be surrendered at every turn and in increasingly intimate detail?

Retailers Increase Their Creepitude Scope

People can't easily protect their privacy from new surveillance tools by wearing gloves, shoving their hands in their pockets, or pulling a scarf across their face as they walk in the door, walk down the street or walk through a mall's common areas because imaging technologies already exist that can "see" through fabrics and grab information anyway.

Although few companies are using products of the body and face-recognition ilk today, adoption will increase over time. How do we know this? Because retailers are already using other kinds of in-store spying technologies and it is no great leap in logic to assume companies in other industries are too.

Regulatory agencies are making the same assumption. For example, the FTC, in attempting to get ahead of the privacy issues posed by facial recognition, held a workshop in late 2011 on the technology and issued a staff report in late 2012 recommending best practices on its use.

It's no secret that many retailers are using tiny cameras in their stores to track how long customers look at specific merchandise. It's also no secret that certain stores tap into customers' cell phones to track who entered the store, how long they stayed, and what they looked at.

"Nordstrom's experiment [with tracking customers' movements by following the WiFi signals from their smartphones] is part of a movement by retailers to gather data about in-store shoppers' behavior and moods, using video surveillance and signals from their cell phones and apps to learn information as varied as their sex, how many minutes they spent in the candy aisle, and how long they look at merchandise before buying it," wrote Stephanie Clifford and Quentin Hardy in their July 14, 2013 article in *The New York Times*.

"All sorts of retailers—including national chains, like Family Dollar, Cabela's, and Mothercare, a British company, and specialty stores like Benetton and Warby Parker—are testing these technologies and using them to decide on matters like changing store layouts and offering customized coupons," the article continues.

That article goes on to say that retailers can also use smartphone WiFi signals to detect how many people walk past the store without entering. However, snooping on shoppers in the real world via their own phones is not limited to these arguably innocuous uses.

According to a November 6, 2013 report in *Digiday*:

> Google is beta-testing a program that uses smartphone location data to determine when consumers visit stores, according to agency executives briefed on the program by Google employees. Google then connects these store visits to Google searches conducted on smartphones in an attempt to prove that its mobile ads do, in fact, work.
>
> Google declined multiple requests for comment.
>
> If someone conducts a Google mobile search for screwdrivers, for instance, a local hardware store could bid to have its store listing served to that user. By pairing that person's location data with its database of store listings, Google can see if the person who saw that ad subsequently visited the store.
>
> It's common for Google, mobile app developers, and other business entities to justify such actions by claiming users gave consent by virtue of opting-in. However, as the Digiday report makes clear, users rarely understand what they are actually opting-in on.
>
> Google's ability to make this connection is predicated on users opting in to location services on their smartphones and thus, in some cases, being subject to constant location monitoring.
>
> Dan Auerbach, staff technologist at the Electronic Frontier Foundation, said that users might not realize they've opted in to constant location tracking when they opt in to location services.
>
> "The disclosure mechanism for these apps are pretty weak," he said. "I think there's a gap between user expectations and what apps are really doing."

Further, according to that same *Digiday* report, Google can track a user's location even when the user is not using a Google app. It is doubtful that very many consumers realize that.

"Google hinted that it would start measuring store-visit conversions in an Oct. 1, 2013 blog post. But that is already happening, whether consumers know it or not," wrote John McDermott in that *Digiday* report.

Retailers use other surreptitious means to identify and spy on customers as well.

"Tesco, a UK-based supermarket giant, is installing hundreds of screens that will scan shoppers' faces while they wait in line at its gas stations," reports David Vranicar in a blog post in *TechNewsWorld*. "The camera leers at customers and estimates their ages, sex, and how long they looked at a displayed ad. The information gathered from the shoppers will then be dished to advertisers."

As retailers and those who cater to advertisers increasingly gather data from facial recognition and fingerprints, to video cameras and mood detectors, individual privacy is systematically destroyed. Further individual security is ultimately compromised as all data can be breached by criminal elements and obtained by governments, both at home and abroad.

Light Fixtures as Data Collectors

There are so many ways companies and governments can spy on customers and citizens that it is no longer possible for individuals to protect their privacy. For example, Newark Liberty International Airport installed 171 new LED light fixtures in Terminal B that continuously collect data on everyone coming and going, according to a report in *The New York Times*. "Using an array of sensors and eight video cameras around the terminal, the light fixtures are part of a new wireless network that collects and feeds data into software that can spot long lines, recognize license plates, and even identify suspicious activity, sending alerts to the appropriate staff."

"What began as a way to help governments and businesses save energy by automatically turning lights on and off has become an expanding market for lights, sensors, and software capable of capturing and analyzing vast amounts of data about the habits of ordinary citizens," continues *The New York Times* article.

It's just a matter of time before light fixtures and other innocuous looking devices and accoutrements are in use everywhere to collect data on everyone. Indeed, there may be such a device over your head or close by as you are reading this. But maybe not. These devices are just beginning to appear in our world now. Just give it a little more time though and they will be commonplace. These and other seemingly mundane products are fast becoming the backbone of the larger "Internet of Things" (IoT) movement.

Scope Unjustified

While companies and governments are quick to justify their use of such privacy invading tools in the name of security, marketing, better customer service, and other business or mission aims, the truth is that they have increased their scope beyond standard data uses to include gathering knowledge for knowledge's sake. They have collectively stepped over clearly marked privacy lines with no real excusable and acceptable reason for doing so.

It has yet to be shown that privacy invasion on a large scale has any meaningful advantage to either businesses or governments. For example, despite the NSA and other federal agencies' massive data collection efforts, and even clear warnings from the Russian government about one of the Tsarnaev brothers, the 2013 Boston Marathon terrorist bombing wasn't stopped. However, after the bombing occurred the government started probing sales of pressure cookers like the ones used in the bombing.

THE BUSINESS QUESTION YOU MUST ASK

This brings us to an important aspect in developing big data strategies for your organization: are your data collection processes and uses respectful of individual privacy? If not, is your organization prepared to cope with the repercussions that are sure to come?

Most organizations try to sidestep this important self-examination by rationalizing that every organization is doing the same so they must do so too in order to remain competitive. But this is no justification for despicable acts. If it were, every child would be able to skirt punishment by saying "well, Johnny did the same thing" and no criminal would ever be convicted since the defense would be "others are doing it too."

Another common rationalization is found in the widespread confusion over who owns data, and by extension, who has the right to disclose, use, sell, or share the data.

WHO REALLY OWNS THE DATA?

Data ownership essentially boils down to this one question: Is the owner the entity that created the data, or is the owner the subject of the data? Or both?

To clarify the innate complexities in these questions, consider it reformed in the context of real scenarios. A telecom routinely gathers and analyzes data from users in order to connect calls and invoice customers correctly. To do so requires the tracking of cell phone use by every customer. Does the telecom own this data since they created it in the natural course of business—or do individual customers own the parts of the data (data points) that pertain to their generally presumed private actions? At this point, it is prudent to also remember that, at least in the United States, possession of such "business records" can mean that they are excluded from Constitutional Fourth Amendment search-and-seizure protections.

But back to the original question: does the data creator or the subject "own" the data? If the answer is the creator, then who is the creator: the telecom company or the customer? The former had to generate these activity reports and thus, arguably, created the data. However, the latter had to take actions before the former had anything with which to create a report.

Now apply that question to other industries and you see the same complexities come into play. In banking, is the owner of the data the bank that must by necessity create it internally to keep track of money deposited and spent by customers? Or does that data belong to the customer since financial data is widely presumed to be (and pursuant to numerous federal and state laws is defined as) private information?

In healthcare, does the patient own his or her medical data? After all, medical information is arguably the most sensitive personal data of all. Or, does the provider who performed the medical tests own the data? At least medical data ownership is a little clearer—it's protected as private data in most countries. In the United States, it is protected primarily by two acts—the Health Insurance Portability and Accountability Act of 1996 (HIPAA) and Health Information Technology for Economic and Clinical Health Act of 2009 (HITECH)—along with amendments and rules applicable to each.

HIPAA and HITECH

The Health Insurance Portability and Accountability Act of 1996 (HIPAA). HIPAA provides for both the privacy and security of personally identifiable health information through the enforcement of data reporting and sharing standards provided in the law. Penalties for noncompliance are substantial. The HIPAA Privacy Rule specifically addresses protecting individual privacy in personally identifiable data in any form. The HIPAA Security Rule specifically addresses securing electronic health information. You can find more information on both on the U.S. Department of Health and Human Services website.

Health Information Technology for Economic and Clinical Health Act of 2009 (HITECH). The Centers for Disease Control (CDC) succinctly explains this complex law as follows: "The HITECH Act supports the concept of electronic health records—meaningful use [EHR-MU], an effort led by Centers for Medicare & Medicaid Services (CMS) and the Office of the National Coordinator for Health IT (ONC). HITECH proposes the meaningful use of interoperable electronic health records throughout the U.S. healthcare delivery system as a critical national goal. Meaningful use is defined by the use of certified EHR technology in a meaningful manner (for example electronic prescribing); ensuring that the certified EHR technology is connected in a manner that provides for the electronic exchange of health information to improve the quality of care; and that in using certified EHR technology the provider must submit to the Secretary of Health & Human Services (HHS) information on quality of care and other measures.

The concept of meaningful use rested on the five pillars of health outcomes policy priorities, namely:

- Improving quality, safety, efficiency, and reducing health disparities
- Engaging patients and families in their health

- ■ Improving care coordination
- ■ Improving population and public health
- ■ Ensuring adequate privacy and security protection for personal health information

You can find more details on HITECH and meaningful use on the CDC website at www.cdc.gov.

THE ROLE OF EXISTING LAWS AND ACTIONS IN SETTING PRECEDENT

Do HIPAA/HITECH and similar laws in other countries set a precedent that the subject of data, and not necessarily the creator of data, owns the information? Perhaps. When and if that case is made, it will undoubtedly crash headlong into the longstanding decision that U.S. copyrights belong to the creator and not the subject of the work, although copyright case law since the Supreme Court's 1991 opinion in *Feist Publications, Inc., v. Rural Telephone Service Co.* has excluded mere "compilations" such as phonebooks from copyright's protections.

Certainly many countries, most notably in Europe, have gone to considerable effort to protect private data and to define what data is considered legally private. But those efforts often fall short as many of those same governments routinely cross the privacy line in data collection, most often in the name of public security. Remember the case mentioned earlier of the U.K. government taking pictures of its own citizens and those of American citizens through privately owned webcams and by misusing a private company's service? In that case, the company so misused was Yahoo!, an American-owned company. By what logic or rights then does the U.K. government contend it has ownership of that data? Is this data considered "created" by the government or was it simply stolen from private individuals and from Yahoo!?

Of course, the U.K. is not the only country deploying such privacy invasive tactics. The point here is that it is difficult to provide any meaningful protection of individual privacy when the government itself disregards the spirit of the law, if not the letter.

But that is not to say that one branch or agency of government will not continue in their quests to redress privacy grievances against others branches and agencies. And as they do so, organizations will be affected for better or worse, as undoubtedly data ownership will remain in flux for the duration.

The Snowden Effect on Privacy Policy

Currently several new efforts are underway in the United States, some driven by the White House, others by Congress, and more are likely to follow. One example is the White House's recent efforts to study and presumably address privacy issues in the wake of the Snowden revelations.

"The Obama administration aims to gain a more holistic view of Big Data, including the ways in which it's 'altering the landscape of how data is conventionally used' and the impact such use may have on traditional notions of privacy given its 'immense volume, velocity and potential value,'" said John Podesta according to a post by Angelique Carson in the International Association of Privacy Professionals (IAPP)'s newsletter, *The Privacy Advisor*. She is quoting Obama administration White House Counselor John Podesta during his keynote address at the "Big Data Privacy: Advancing the State of the Art in Technology and Practice" MIT event in March 2014.

Podesta's keynote address is available online on the MIT website.

"We need to be conscious of the implications for individuals" said Podesta. "Big Data reveals things about them they didn't even know about themselves. We want to explore the capabilities of Big Data analytics but also the social and policy implications of that." He remained vague, however, on whether national regulation is a possibility.

As of this writing, President Obama was seeking feedback from stakeholders and the general public via the White House website on whether or not the existing U.S. privacy framework is sufficient for big data use or if some additional privacy protection actions are needed.

Obama also tasked the National Institute of Standards and Technology (NIST) with developing a "cybersecurity framework" that includes some focus on individual privacy, albeit in the scope of cybersecurity big data projects. Specifically, much attention in the initial NIST discussions and participant feedback focused on the proposed addition of Appendix B and its "privacy methodology" to the framework.

"The now released 'voluntary' framework is substantively changed from the earlier drafts and preliminary framework," wrote attorney Richard Santalesa in his post in IAAP's *The Privacy Advisor*. Santalesa is attorney and founding member at the Sm@rtEdgeLaw Group and co-chair of the IAPP's KnowledgeNet in Stamford, CT.

Santalesa continued to explain the actions on that front to-date:

> For starters, NIST repeatedly stresses that the framework will be considered a "living document" to be "updated and improved as industry provides feedback" and, more significantly, NIST, acknowledging it was

swimming against the consensus current, eliminated the prior privacy-focused Appendix B. While the frame-work still contains an Appendix B, proper, it's essentially the previous preliminary framework's Appendix E, Glossary, with the notable deletion of a definition for personally identifiable information.

In lieu of an in-line privacy methodology replete with "shalls" and "should," NIST added a new Section 3.5, which lays out a diffuse methodology to address individual privacy that is "intended to be a general set of considerations and processes since privacy and civil liberties implications may differ by sector or over time and organizations may address these considerations and processes with a range of technical implementations.

This marks a welcome change privacy professionals should embrace… the new Section 3.5 offers a litany of "processes and activities" that "may be considered" in addressing privacy implications inherent in framework-driven cybersecurity efforts.

Given this is a living document subject to frequent changes, and that several privacy advocates and numerous privacy professionals are ensuring all such efforts do not lose momentum, it is imperative for organizations to stay abreast of all such developments and regularly change their big data strategies accordingly.

The Fallacies of Consent

The question of data ownership does not end there. It becomes even more muddied in cases where the subject seemingly gave "consent" for its collection and use by another party.

Take for example smartphone data. Most smartphone users want to use mobile apps of one kind or another to do any number of tasks, or perhaps just to stay in touch via social media. Generally speaking, users feel safe selecting an app from the device-related app store, such as Google Play for Android phones and iTunes for Apple iPhones. Typically users select familiar branded apps first, such as Facebook and Gmail, and then add apps of interest that have high user ratings. Why do consumers follow this pattern in app selection? It boils down to user trust in the brand or developer.

As part of the app download and updates, a set of permissions are required from the user. Multiple studies have found that most users either don't read that list of permissions or do not fully understand them, yet the majority of users will grant those permissions anyway. Once those permissions are granted, the apps begin collecting data in ways users fail to understand or imagine, and that data is then often sold to all and sundry.

Further, many apps continue to collect data even when the user is not using the app by quietly running in the background and performing functions beyond what the user would expect them to do.

As of this writing, Google was going a huge step further than many data-hungry app developers. "This is an exciting first step to give marketers more insight into how AdWords drives conversions for your business by showing you both the conversions you see today, like online sales, as well as an estimate of conversions that take multiple devices to complete," reads the official Google blog post explaining its new *Estimated Total Conversions* service for AdWords. "Over time, we'll be adding other conversion types like phone calls and store visits as well as conversions from ads on our search and display network."

Implied in that last statement is that Google will track consumer visits to stores, and presumably their purchases there as well (by combining data from stores), plus track phone orders. How else could Google deliver on its promise to estimate or show actual conversions in these venues and channels?

It is safe to say that most consumers will be caught unaware by this tracking and reporting of their whereabouts, purchases, and phone calls. Advertisers, on the other hand, will be elated to be able to see and study customers and missed prospects in such detail.

While Google may be the first to pull off this level of consumer tracking, it will not be the last. Meanwhile, Google will enjoy the fruits of its labors. The rewards of its accomplishments will be considered by many in business circles as well earned.

But this brings us full circle. Who owns the data Google, and soon many of its contemporaries, will create? Or to put it another way: Who owns the information, the spy or the spied upon?

That is the burning question of our age.

The answer, if we ever arrive at one, will impact your business strategy; therefore, it is crucial to stay abreast of public debate and regulatory actions and to react accordingly.

VALUES IN PERSONAL VERSUS POOLED DATA

To further cloud privacy issues, pooled or converged data lends significant public benefit. For example, using big data to spot emerging public health or security threats can avert disasters. By using massive amounts of data, researchers can conceivably find links that lead to cures for previously incurable diseases; develop vaccines against emerging or current health threats; find and thwart terrorists and cyber-criminals; correctly predict and detect weather-related and other natural disasters; find and rescue victims of natural or manmade disasters; find abducted children; dramatically improve government services;

build more sustainable cities; find and improve new energy sources; and, thousands of other beneficial efforts both imagined and unimagined at this time.

If data is choked off in order to protect individual privacy, these beneficial efforts will be slowed or even stalled. This brings us to another tough question that begs an answer. Is it better to protect the individual's privacy or the individual's well being?

Many in the Western world will immediately answer privacy since it is fundamental to freedom and democracy. However, these same people would likely answer differently if their life or the lives of their loved ones were in immediate danger from disease, a natural disaster, or a terrorist act. This is not to say that safety should by default trump freedom, rather this observation is offered to illustrate the difference perspective makes in finding an answer.

Varying perspectives complicate the process of setting priorities in benefits vs privacy, yet it must be done before a consensus can be reached on what constitutes truly private information and where and when that information can be legitimately used for the public good. In all likelihood, the accepted answer will also vary among countries. See Figure 9.8.

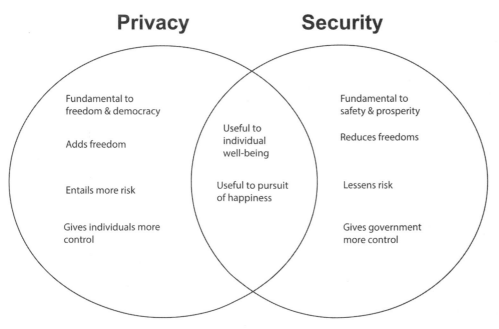

Figure 9.8
A Venn diagram of privacy versus security.
Source: Pam Baker. Illustration by Steven Duffey.

The Fallacy in Anonymizing Data

The notion of anonymizing data as a cure for privacy concerns needs to be dispelled at this point. In most cases, re-identifying the information is simply too easy. Indeed, the ability to re-identify anonymous data has existed for years now and techniques have been perfected over time.

Meyer Michelle gave an early example of this in practice; indeed he cited the very event that led to the creation of HIPAA, in a 2013 Harvard Law blog post titled "Online Symposium on the Law, Ethics & Science of Re-identification Demonstrations."

> In the mid-1990s, the Massachusetts Group Insurance Commission (GIC) released data on individual hospital visits by state employees in order to aid important research. As Massachusetts Governor Bill Weld assured employees, their data had been "anonymized," with all obvious identifiers, such as name, address, and Social Security number, removed. But Latanya Sweeney, then an MIT graduate student, wasn't buying it. When, in 1996, Weld collapsed at a local event and was admitted to the hospital, she set out to show that she could re-identify his GIC entry. For $20, she purchased the full roll of Cambridge voter-registration records, and by linking the two data sets, which individually were innocuous enough, she was able to re-identify his GIC entry.

As privacy law scholar Paul Ohm put it, 'In a theatrical flourish, Dr. Sweeney sent the Governor's health records (which included diagnoses and prescriptions) to his office." Sweeney's demonstration led to important changes in privacy law, especially under HIPAA. But that demonstration was just the beginning.'"

While HIPAA protects patient privacy in medical data, few laws protect anonymized data in general from re-identification efforts. If such existed they would prove troublesome if not impossible to enforce. It is so common for anonymized data to be re-identified these days, that it is a wonder that anyone bothers to anonymize it in the first place. At most, correct identification of persons represented in the data is merely slowed for those willing to exert the time and effort. Therefore, we must understand that for all practical purposes, privacy cannot be guaranteed to the individual via anonymizing the data.

Balancing Individual Privacy with Individual Benefit

However, it is equally true that there is significant benefit to individuals when converged data is used to discover an avoidable or treatable problem or to develop some beneficial advantage that can then be delivered to the individual.

These two truths deliver another conundrum for both the public and private sectors: how to balance individual privacy with individual benefit and find business/mission value?

The most common mistake businesses make is in failing to ask that question prior to embarking on big data projects. Indeed, ethical considerations regarding privacy were almost universally ignored in the early days of big data use.

As mentioned in Chapter 2, "How to Formulate a Winning Big Data Strategy," formal ethics rules are only recently evolving for the big data practitioner. Some reputable organizations with a list of ethics rules you can follow now include the American Statistical Association (ASA); The National Science Foundation (NSF) supported Council for Big Data, Ethics, and Society; and the Data Science Association.

To prevent consumer backlash and liability, you need to make a hard set of ethical rules a significant part of your big data strategy. Simply rationalizing that individual benefit is sufficient excuse to disregard privacy will not suffice, particularly when said benefit has dubious value to the individual and substantive value to the big data user, such as a personalized ad. If the underlying value is to you in selling something then the right to individual privacy trumps your need to know.

The key is to find balance in individual and company or agency benefit and to implement your actions in a way that will be acceptable to your customers and to regulatory bodies.

WHEN DATA COLLECTION COULD MAKE YOU OR YOUR COMPANY LIABLE

Certainly liability issues should be forefront on your mind in determining what data to collect, how you collect it, and what you infer. However, few companies understand that they can also potentially be liable on other counts *because* of their efforts to protect individual privacy.

Take for example, Ford Motor Company and its efforts to maintain individual privacy despite its highly detailed collection of data from sold and leased vehicles.

"We know everyone who breaks the law; we know when you're doing it. We have GPS in your car, so we know what you're doing," said Jim Farley, executive vice president of global marketing at Ford, during the 2014 Consumer Electronics Show (CES). "By the way, we don't supply that data to anyone."

But Ford's CEO, Alan Mulally, was quick to counter Farley's statement on the sidelines at CES and in Bloomberg and other media interviews. He said Ford does not collect data on drivers and does not share data with any entity without expressed consumer consent. Presumably he means that Ford does not share vehicle data such as information on wear and tear that could be used to infer driving habits since he specifically said that the company does not collect actual driver behavior data. In any case, there appears to be data that could be used to learn some potentially damaging things about individual drivers, such as a tendency to drive fast or recklessly, somewhere in the mix.

The giant vehicle maker's intent is not at question here. If anything, Ford's efforts in supporting legal privacy protections are to be commended. Rather Ford's situation serves as an illustration of how potentially the best of intents can be used against a company.

The potential problem here is that Ford does know, at least to some extent, what drivers are doing by virtue of the fact that it is collecting data on the vehicles. That means it has the capability to "see" a crime, after the fact or in progress, if the execution of that crime involves a Ford vehicle. Even if the company does not actively look for this information within its data, the fact remains that it could. Although it sounds far-fetched at this time, the question then becomes whether the company could be held legally liable by some future court for either not proactively searching for such information of crimes or in not reporting such information since they do, in theory, possess such information in its raw form? The answer is unknown at the moment as to date no one has tested this theory in the courts. However, given the creativity of the plaintiff's bar, concern remains that victims of a crime may one day attempt to sue companies for not proactively assisting law enforcement intervention.

Imagine what this could potentially mean if, say, a terrorist bomber used a Ford vehicle and Ford found itself liable for damages and human suffering because it did not detect and report driver behavior indicative of such a threat, assuming such a pattern could be identified? Or, if Ford can detect erratic driving that could indicate a drunk driver at the wheel, but did not report such to law enforcement and that driver ends up killing people, what might the liability cost be to Ford, especially when multiplied by several such incidents over a period of many years? Combined, such potential losses could be huge even for a company as large and financially strong as Ford.

Of course Ford is not the only vehicle manufacturer potentially facing such a risk—all collected vehicle data conceivably poses some danger of future legal liabilities. It is doubtful that such issues have escaped their internal debates. It is even probable that their efforts to ensure individual privacy internally and externally through the support of privacy protecting regulations, are at least partially motivated by the need to limit or eradicate such future liability scenarios. However, it should be made clear that this is merely logical conjecture. If liability avoidance is partly a motivation for supporting privacy protections, it simply underscores their business acumen and dovetails nicely with the needs and desires of their customers.

Organizations in other industries should take note and seriously contemplate the vast number of ways they could potentially be found liable after the fact simply by virtue of owning data on individuals. A very good way to help limit this exposure is to make absolutely sure you collect no more data than is necessary to conduct your business. But then does that conflict with big data efforts? Another good approach is in supporting the development and implementation of sensible privacy regulations and guidelines, so you know better how to proceed within accepted parameters and practices.

"It's just really important that we have boundaries and guidelines to operate," *Bloomberg News* reported Mulally told reporters on the sidelines of the show. "Our homes, the cars, everything is going to be on the Internet. Everything's going to be connected. And so what are the guidelines? What do we want?"

That's a very important question that deserves a well-defined answer, not just for consumer benefit but for companies and governments too.

The Business Value of Transparency

The trend has been to collect data on individuals surreptitiously. The default is nearly always set as an opt-in. Opt-out options, on the few occasions such are offered, are too often buried to make it difficult for the average consumer to find, and are far too often disabled by the data collector.

The fear that individuals will not grant permission for such intrusive and intense data collection is well founded. But the notion that asking for forgiveness after being caught at the dirty deed is more productive than asking for permission in advance is a heavily flawed business premise. As previously discussed, such tactics can lead to consumer backlash, a stifling regulatory environment, potentially hefty legal fines and liabilities, a poisoning of your data well by consumers providing wrong information in order to protect their privacy, and the rise of privacy protection tools designed to totally foul your data collection and analysis efforts. If this trend of favoring surreptitious means in data collection and analysis continues, ultimately businesses and governments will find the fruits of their efforts rotten and unusable. What is the business value then in continuing in this fashion?

Switching to a transparency model provides better business value in the end because it negates most if not all of the negative impacts incurred from the surreptitious model. But that is not to say that it is an easy path to follow. Given that people worldwide currently feel the burn of betrayal from device manufacturers, businesses and their own governments too, the number of opt-outs in transparent data collection efforts will initially be extraordinarily high. The amount and variety of data collected will immediately plummet and some big data efforts will stumble and fail as a result. In other words, everything businesses and governments fear will happen will likely come to be. Much of what they have already accomplished through big data will be shattered and destroyed as thousands if not millions of people express their fear, doubts, and rage by clicking on the opt-out button or otherwise refusing permission.

Revelations in the Transparency Model

A truly transparent model reveals the following:

- Precisely what personal data is gathered—where, when, and how
- Why the entity is asking for the data, that is, what the gatherer intends to do with this data
- What the entity and its partners are likely or capable of inferring from this data—when used alone or layered with other data—in clear language and a "what this means to you" format
- Where that data is stored or moved to and how long the entity plans to store it
- Who the data gatherer plans to share or sell the data with or to
- What the expected benefits are to the individual in return for the data
- How the data is protected, both from hackers and from too much data sharing with other entities
- How the individual can view and correct erroneous information now and in the future

As devastating as that will first appear, it will actually lead to access of more and better data. In the first place, while many people will opt out or otherwise refuse permission in a transparent data collection model, not everyone will. There will still be some data available for analysis throughout this conversion process and the data will be "cleaner" as a result. Further, once public anger subsides and people can easily see what data you want to collect, how you'll use it, and specifically how that will benefit them, then opt-ins will actually increase. One need only look at the rising number of Facebook and Google service users to see that a user's awareness that data gathering is taking place does not necessarily deter the use of the service. Although Facebook and Google did not necessarily intend for users to be aware of their data collection, the fact remains that the majority of users now know of it, at least in a general way. Yet remarkably few have withdrawn from using either.

The same use patterns will apply, only more so, for entities that become openly transparent about their data collection and use. Consumer acceptance will actually rise. Further, if given the means to view and correct their data, many consumers will do that too, thus greatly improving the company's or government agency's data quality and analytical outcomes. There are other benefits to transparency, such as a notable brand differentiator and in increased public relations value, increased brand loyalty, decreased liability, decreased costs in data collection and data cleaning, and increased public support for government actions, as well as others.

THE ONE TRUTH THAT DATA PRACTITIONERS MUST NEVER FORGET

The one truth all data practitioners should hold fast is this: Big Brother is us and we are the individual. It is our data practices and the practices of others like us that collectively give life to the once fictional Big Brother concept. But each of us is also an individual and whatever data use horrors we allow to exist will haunt each of us in turn.

Together we know privacy or none of us do.

SUMMARY

In this chapter, you learned about the complexities in determining data ownership and in developing meaningful privacy laws and rules. You learned the four shifts in data collection that are courting serious repercussions for businesses and governments alike. But you also learned from real-world examples how companies can find themselves legally liable or otherwise penalized even if they do respect personal privacy and privacy laws, and that some companies are proactively seeking updated privacy laws to protect themselves from liability. Finally, you learned the business value of a transparency model over a surreptitious one.

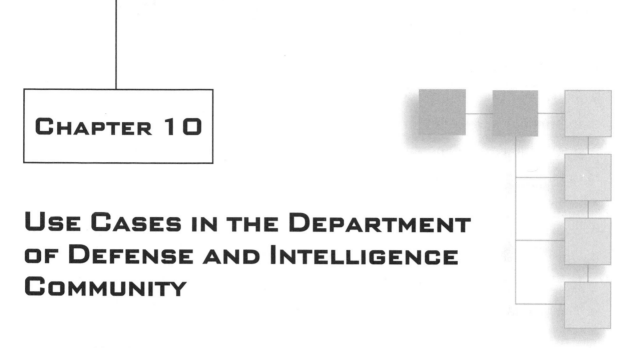

CHAPTER 10

USE CASES IN THE DEPARTMENT OF DEFENSE AND INTELLIGENCE COMMUNITY

During public debates on privacy rights, the use of big data by governments takes center stage. There is nothing more frightening to the public psyche than an all-seeing, all-knowing Big Brother government that's collecting and scanning everything from email to phone call info to what you posted on Twitter last week. The recent and ongoing leaks from Edward Snowden, a former Central Intelligence Agency (CIA) employee and a former contractor for the National Security Agency (NSA) turned whistle-blower, continue to feed that fear. Many of the resulting concerns are covered in Chapter 9 on the privacy conundrum. Here we'll look at the other side of those issues, from the governmental perspective. But first let's look at actual use cases the government deploys.

Given their urgent and important national security mission needs, it is no surprise that technologists in the Department of Defense (DoD) and Intelligence Community (IC) have sought out new approaches to analyzing and using data. After all, big data is uniquely suited to quickly and efficiently searching mega-sized data for markers that could indicate criminal and terrorist activity. Big data tools also make it possible to see and note personal relationships between criminals and terrorists that might otherwise remain hidden. Modern data analysis can even accurately predict rising nation aggressors and impending war. Big data tools can also make it easier to find and respond to cyber attacks in progress. Further, big data can power artificial intelligence and drive automated war machines to attack faster and more precisely than their human counterparts. Indeed, there are so many ways to use big data in national defense that it boggles the mind. Even more uses for it will appear as mastery of big data improves.

Currently these are the types of big data solutions being fielded in these domains:

- Situational awareness and visualization
- Information correlation for problem solving
- Information search and discovery in overwhelming amounts of data
- Enterprise data management for cyber security
- Logistical information including asset catalogs
- Enhanced healthcare and public health analysis
- Open source information: analysis and integration
- In-memory data modernization
- The enterprise data hub: optimizing it and operations
- Big data in weaponry and war

It's important to understand some of the goals government pursues and the challenges it faces in order to understand why the federal government does what it does with data.

SITUATIONAL AWARENESS AND VISUALIZATION

This topic is of such importance to the DoD and the IC that entire disciplines developed around it. Key among them is the construct of Geospatial Intelligence or GEOINT. GEOINT is the exploitation and analysis of geospatial information to enhance situational awareness and decision-making. It includes the use of imagery, terrain data, and real-time data sources.

There is even a government agency specifically focused on this form of intelligence. It is called the National Geospatial-Intelligence Agency (NGA); their slogan is "Know the Earth… Show the way… Understand the World." Its mission is massive, ranging from warfighter intelligence in the heat of battle and humanitarian and disaster relief in the thick of the crisis anywhere in the world to domestic counterterrorism, counternarcotics, and border, special events, and transportation security efforts at home.

Part of that mission is fulfilled using two Domestic Mobile Integrated Geospatial-Intelligence System vehicles (DMIGS), which are self-contained, specialized RV-looking vehicles for use in domestic crises, natural disasters and special events requiring intense security. Figure 10.1 is a screenshot of the DMIGS fact sheet found on the NGA website.

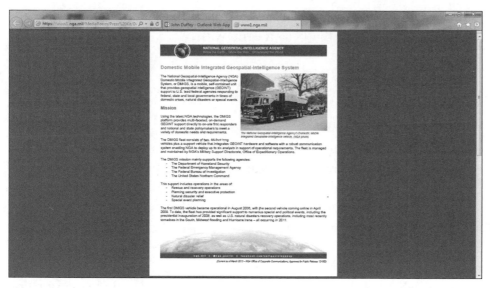

Figure 10.1
Domestic Mobile Integrated Geospatial-Intelligence System vehicles (DMIGS) fact sheet.
Source: National Geospatial-Intelligence Agency (NGA).

The NGA also "defends the nation against cyber threats by supporting other intelligence agencies with in-depth analysis of cyber networks." The agency supports all other agencies in the DoD and IC community. See Figure 10.2 for a screenshot of an NGA fact sheet describing the agency's mission, from the NGA's official website.

Figure 10.2
NGA fact sheet describing the agency's mission.
Source: National Geospatial-Intelligence Agency (NGA).

Data collection and the on-the-fly, real-time analysis needs for this agency alone are massive. Big data tools and techniques are the best means with which to achieve its many missions.

In a DoD and IC context, GEOINT usually involves tracking and analyzing subjects of special interest, such as adversary locations as well as "own force" location, the locations of friendlies and neutrals, plus information on current weather and other environmental factors.

This information is almost always displayed on screens for analysts and decision-makers, some of which can be highly interactive. Analysts and operators increasingly demand dynamic displays that can respond to questions of any sort on-the-fly, including questions no one has asked or potentially considered before. This means old static intelligence approaches (such as reviewing satellite pictures taken hours or days before) are not conducive to the enhanced situation-awareness demands of the DoD or the IC. Situational awareness is not always visual; sometimes the data solution being fielded will be a push of text-based information or even audio clues, but regardless of the approach, big data infrastructure and applications are key.

With the immediacy of information available through big data, national defense agencies and military forces can be in a position to more effectively respond to imminent threats as well as predict where and how those threats are likely to emerge. The importance of immediate, high-quality intelligence cannot be overstated in terms of saving lives and winning the day.

INFORMATION CORRELATION FOR PROBLEM SOLVING (THE "CONNECT THE DOTS" PROBLEM)

The intelligence community has continuously struggled for years with information correlation challenges, including correlating information between agencies and between data sets. With the ever-increasing amounts of data, these challenges have grown significantly. The 9/11 Commission report highlighted these problems by underscoring that the community "failed to connect the dots" and thus failed to prevent the infamous 9/11 terrorist attack. Since the 9/11 tragedy, the community has certainly revisited processes and enhanced technical capabilities. In short, the IC has made significant progress in better seeing the big picture and then disseminating appropriate pieces of that vision to its various agencies so that appropriate action can be taken. And all of this came to be as directed by two U.S. Presidents, several Congresses, and the Commission report, seemingly with the full backing of the American public.

Following those directives, the Department of Homeland Security (DHS) openly makes the point that it shares information on all government levels and with myriad law enforcement agencies on its website, stating that "Homeland Security is Hometown Security." Specifically, it reads:

> In the ten years since 9/11, the federal government has strengthened the connection between collection and analysis on transnational organizations and threats. Terrorism-related information sharing across the intelligence community has greatly improved. Moreover, we have strengthened the ability to convey intelligence on threats to the homeland in a context that is useful and relevant to law enforcement and homeland security officials at the state and local level.

> DHS, working closely with the FBI, has re-focused its information sharing and production efforts to better address the needs of state and local governments and private sector partners. In addition, DHS continues to improve and expand the information-sharing mechanisms by which officers are made aware of the threat picture, vulnerabilities, and what it means for their local communities.

There are four key elements that comprise the architecture for sharing information among all homeland security partners, that is, state and local governments and private sector partners. Those, too, are generally described on the DHS website and links are provided to web pages on each of the four elements to provide more detailed information:

- **National Network of Fusion Centers:** Fusion centers serve as focal points within the state and local environment for the receipt, analysis, gathering, and sharing of threat-related information between the federal government and state, local, tribal, territorial (SLTT) and private sector partners.

- **Nationwide Suspicious Activity Reporting Initiative:** The Nationwide Suspicious Activity Reporting (SAR) Initiative (NSI) is a joint collaborative effort by the U.S. Department of Homeland Security, the Federal Bureau of Investigation, and state, local, tribal, and territorial law enforcement partners. This initiative provides law enforcement with another tool to help prevent terrorism and other related criminal activity by establishing a national capacity for gathering, documenting, processing, analyzing, and sharing SAR information.

- **National Terrorism Advisory System (NTAS):** The NTAS replaces the color-coded Homeland Security Advisory System (HSAS). The NTAS alerts are based on the nature of the threat. In some cases, alerts are sent directly to law enforcement or affected areas of the private sector, while in others, alerts are issued more broadly to the American people through both official and media channels.

  These alerts include a clear statement that there is an imminent threat or elevated threat. An imminent threat warns of a credible, specific, and impending terrorist threat against the United States. An elevated threat warns of a credible terrorist threat against the United States.

NTAS alerts contain a sunset provision indicating a specific date when the alert expires—there will not be a constant NTAS alert or blanket warning that there is an overarching threat. If threat information changes for an alert, the Secretary of Homeland Security may announce an updated NTAS alert. All changes, including the announcement that cancels an NTAS alert, will be distributed the same way as the original alert.

This system will more effectively communicate information about terrorist threats by providing timely, detailed information to the public, government agencies, first responders, airports and other transportation hubs, and the private sector.

■ **If You See Something, Say Something:** The Department's nation-wide public awareness campaign—a simple and effective program to raise public awareness of indicators of terrorism and violent crime, and to emphasize the importance of reporting suspicious activity to the proper state and local law enforcement authorities. While this is not a big data application per se, it is a collaborative intelligence, or crowd-sourcing intelligence, effort the results of which can then be vetted and/or enhanced by big data techniques and tools.

After 9/11, the public was almost unanimous in agreement that the ability to connect the dots within and between agencies was critical to preventing terrorist attacks and keeping the public safe. Indeed, the American public was highly critical of its government in its failure to do so earlier. But now that the data silo-busting practice has been in place for years and people are more aware of the extent of data collection by the government and how big data works, more than a few are worried that such surveillance will be turned against them rather than used in their behalf.

"Very soon, the cop on the corner, through his handheld device, is going to have access to all of this data, and he will because we'll be presented with scenarios where if he had had it, it would've stopped this crime or stopped this attack, and the restrictions will be blamed. And, you know, Pandora's Box is going to be opened," said Ben Wizner, director of the ACLU Speech, Privacy and Technology Project, and a legal advisor to Edward Snowden in an interview with Michael Winship, senior writer at Moyers & Company. Wizner made those comments shortly before he travelled to the 2014 SXSW tech event to moderate a session in which Edward Snowden made a speech via teleconference.

But that is what elected officials, the 9/11 Commission report, and the Patriot Act mandated that the agencies do, precisely with the intent of preventing terrorist and criminal events.

The amount of data the IC now needs to sort through has increased in ways hard to fathom by outsiders and requires the use of big data tools and techniques, the very things the public is now wary about. Nevertheless, the deluge of incoming information means that connecting the dots regarding clues to adversary action remains a formidable challenge. History indicates it may never really be "solved," but with new big data approaches and highly trained analysts, it can certainly be optimized.

That is not to say however, that government efforts in this regard have been perfected. To date the DoD and IC still struggles with technical issues in achieving its mission.

"The existing architecture of the Department of Homeland Security's (DHS) myriad databases—known as the DHS Data Framework—which are crucial for the department's many disparate components to perform their primary mission were found to not be conducive to effective implementation of the 'One DHS' policy," reports Anthony Kimery in his article in *Homeland Security Today*. "This policy was implemented to provide DHS personnel timely access to the relevant and necessary homeland security information they need to successfully perform their duties in protecting the homeland. The disclosure appeared in the annual *2013 Data Mining Report to Congress* by DHS's Privacy Office."

> *The goal of the DHS Data Framework is to provide a user the ability to search an amalgamation of data extracted from multiple DHS systems for a specific purpose and to view the information in a clear and accessible format. The DHS Data Framework is supposed to "enable efficient and cost-effective searches across DHS databases in both classified and unclassified domains."*

Despite these items and goals, vexing technical issues pale in the face of the continued public controversy over privacy, despite the existence of numerous privacy protection directives and behavioral mandates in each agency. This is not to say that the public is wrong in its concerns over privacy, but merely to underscore the confusion government agencies face in trying to meet conflicting directives and concerns.

On the one hand, such governmental agencies are required to aggressively seek intel, correlate it efficiently and effectively, and share that information between all potentially interested agencies on the federal, state, and local levels—and sometimes beyond our borders. To this day the American public demands that threats be prevented and scary scenarios, such as the mysterious disappearance of Malaysian Flight MH370, be solved instantly or at least within a few days. Flight MH370 disappeared on March 8, 2014 while en route to Beijing and carrying American citizens. Whether or not its fate is discovered after the publication of this book, the fact remains that the American public was genuinely surprised that the U.S. government (nor any other international organization or foreign government) did not know immediately where the plane was located or what happened to it.

The NSA in particular caught the brunt of public criticism for the plane's disappearance—even though the NSA is not, and never has been, charged with tracking flight data. The Federal Aviation Administration (FAA), under the Department of Transportation, is the United States' aviation authority. One might conceivably expect the NGA to have at least some knowledge of the plane's fate given that one of its missions, as outlined in Figure 10.2, is to ensure "safety of navigation in the air and on the seas by maintaining the most current information and highest quality services for U.S. military forces and global transport networks."

Yet many people, including some members of the media, blamed the NSA based on nothing other than the belief that the NSA is omnipotent in its data-gathering capabilities and omniscient in its analytic abilities, myths generated in part from the Snowden revelations (as well as numerous television shows and movies that depict intelligence agencies as able to perform near-miraculous data manipulation).

But even when some people learned that the NSA is not charged with flight data tracking, most countered with the argument that by "NSA" they meant the entire U.S. government and that, since agencies were required to correlate information and cooperate in data sharing, all agencies possessed the same knowledge. This is not the case, yet the myth persists in the public mind.

On the other hand, the public, some members of Congress, and even the White House are now saying that the agencies should severely curtail their data collection efforts in order to preserve individual privacy rights.

It is a "damned if you do, damned if you don't" situation for the agencies. No matter which way they turn, criticism will be harsh and immediate.

This environment makes it exceedingly difficult for analysts to know how to proceed. Stress levels are exceedingly high in agency workers and morale is low. Obviously, something needs to be done to clearly define big data limits in government use and the degree of risk the public is willing to assume as a result. That will prove a prickly quandary for everyone. But government agencies, like all other enterprises, cannot function effectively without a clear directive. Therefore, they have no choice but to continue in keeping with the directives currently in place.

They do so, by and large, to the best of their abilities and within the limits of current technologies and policies, while also continuing to search for new tools and methods with which they can connect more dots.

Changes in their directives will come, if they ever do, only at the behest and enactment of duly elected officials and not by the agency's own accord.

The point here is that the DoD and IC's work with big data is more complex by nature, and far more complicated in terms of privacy concerns and shifting political winds than that of their private sector counterparts.

INFORMATION SEARCH AND DISCOVERY IN OVERWHELMING AMOUNTS OF DATA (THE "NEEDLE IN HAYSTACK" PROBLEM)

The rapidly increasing amounts of stored data in DoD and the IC complicate the ability to find information they know they have within those stores. This challenge is often referred to as finding a "needle in a haystack" because the metaphor underscores the potential difficulty and the need to look at everything to decide whether the data pertains to that which is sought. In a computer science context, this means any search across data needs to (in some fashion) check everything in the database to see if there is a match. The larger the database the longer it takes. Some databases became so voluminous that searches can take hours, days, or even longer to return results. This problem exists in all enterprises and is one of the reasons for the dramatic adoption of Apache Hadoop based solutions. This is especially true in the DoD and IC. Once Apache Hadoop was able to demonstrate solutions to this critical challenge the DoD and IC began running to this approach to enhance search and discovery. Apache Hadoop, if you've not heard of it before, is an open-source software framework for storage and large-scale processing of data sets for distributed computing.

Even so, the DoD and IC data collections are arguably the largest in the world. The challenges inherent with exceptional size are far from resolved with existing big data tools.

"We're looking for needles within haystacks while trying to define what the needle is, in an era of declining resources and increasing threats," said David Shedd, deputy director of the Defense Intelligence Agency, at a conference and reported by Ray Locker at *USA Today*.

It is for this reason, as well as others, that the IC continues to seek commercial and public assistance in perfecting code, tools, and analytics on several fronts.

For example, the Defense Advanced Research Projects Agency (DARPA) is developing a program called Mining and Understanding Software Enclaves (MUSE) in which it hopes to develop new and better coding which the agency calls "big code." The reason for this effort, according to DARPA's own notice, attached to its solicitation for individuals and commercial vendor participation, number DARPA-SN-14-21, is "to realize foundational advances in the way software is built, debugged, verified, maintained, and understood." In part, DARPA seeks to avoid distorting or collapsing data in the process of analyzing it and wants to substantially increase data security in the process. The goal is to keep data intact during analysis without diminishing the speed of analysis.

Many hard-won IC advances in big data science are shared back with the public and commercial interests, as are advances from other government agencies such as NASA.

For example, DARPA has made its Open Catalog available on a public website at http://www.darpa.mil/OpenCatalog/. It lists DARPA-sponsored software and peer-reviewed publications for interested parties to see and review (see Figure 10.3). On that website is this proclamation:

> *DARPA is interested in building communities around government-funded software and research. If the R&D community shows sufficient interest, DARPA will continue to make available information generated by DARPA programs, including software, publications, data, and experimental results.*

"Making our open source catalog available increases the number of experts who can help quickly develop relevant software for the government," said Chris White, DARPA program manager in a DARPA issued press release. "Our hope is that the computer science community will test and evaluate elements of our software and afterward adopt them as either standalone offerings or as components of their products."

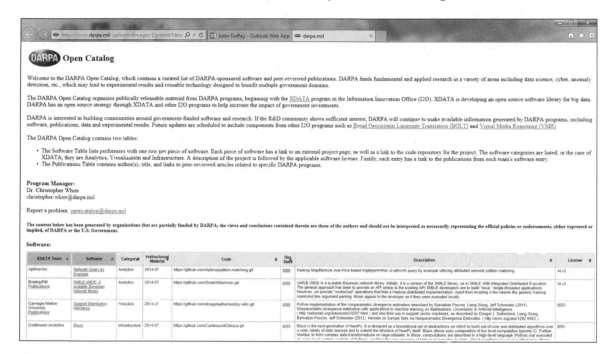

Figure 10.3
Sample of DARPA Open Catalog listing.
Source: Defense Advanced Research Projects Agency (DARPA).

But DARPA isn't the only member of this community offering open data accessible to the public and researchers. Many others are too.

Take for example the DoD's Open Data website, shown in Figure 10.4. It offers 55 raw data sets, 277 data extraction tools and widgets, 68 legal data sets, and eight web APIs, as of this writing. More are sure to follow over time.

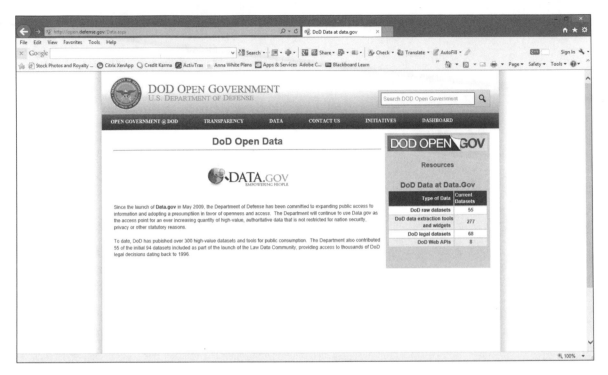

Figure 10.4
Screenshot of DoD's Open Data website.
Source: Department of Defense (DoD).

Obviously, such openness could lead to efforts designed to thwart DARPA's and other agencies' work as easily as it could enlist aid. Just as obviously, agencies don't list anything overly sensitive in their open data collections for precisely that reason.

Government workers have to walk a very thin line between sharing info publicly and keeping it quiet to ensure national security. Even so, DARPA and other agencies in the DoD and IC communities do routinely solicit aid from highly skilled experts outside the agency and from commercial vendors. They also often open information for wide review and use afterwards. Such is not typical of a government that would accurately be labeled as "big brother." Indeed, as covered in Chapter 11, "Use Cases in Governments," the U.S. government, overall, shows a tendency to share open data. Further, it is trending towards increased collaborative efforts.

ENTERPRISE CYBER SECURITY DATA MANAGEMENT

Even though we touched upon the NGA's work in cyber security, data challenges for cyber security uses deserve special and further mention. To distinguish computer attacks and data theft from normal computer activity and normal network traffic is a continuing challenge since attackers go to great lengths to hide their activities and actively modify behavior in response to new detection methods.

The only way to approach and tackle challenges like this is to "instrument" the technology in the enterprise, including all PCs, servers, and communications equipment, and have those devices report back when they have indications of strange behavior. This is the case in both the public and private sectors.

The problem is that every device can report back a huge amount of information even when everything is working okay. Finding adversary activity across a large enterprise means data from across the enterprise must be looked at, but attempts to put in place architectures that span the entire enterprise in a coherent way have all failed until new "big data" approaches came to be and could be brought to bear. Now enterprises have an ability to bring far more data together, not just from their own computer error logs and network attack information, but also data from vulnerability reports and from other organizations that have been attacked. This is allowing new enhancements in the ability to detect quicker and react faster to adversary behavior against enterprise IT across agencies.

Through growing collaborative efforts, the public and private sector can benefit from comparing their big data fueled security efforts and thereby collectively identify and foil attacks and attackers at a higher and faster rate. This type of cyber security related information sharing is one of the goals of the Whitehouse's Executive Order 13636, issued in February of 2013. Further, as mentioned above and shown in Figure 10.2, the NGA does in-depth analysis of cyber networks to diminish and thwart cyber threats against the nation.

LOGISTICAL INFORMATION, INCLUDING ASSET CATALOGS ACROSS EXTENSIVE/DYNAMIC ENTERPRISES

Logistics, the management of the movement of resources from where they are to where they need to be, has always been an important discipline in military matters. Churchill put it this way: "Victory is the beautiful, bright-coloured flower. Transport is the stem without which it could never have blossomed."

In today's DoD, where fielding high-tech forces and where others must be ready to respond on very short notice, logistics takes on increased urgency. Where forces go, their supply chain must follow. Big data use cases in support of DoD logistics are being informed by best practices in the industry. Solutions are being fielded that allow for increased understanding of what supplies exist and what supplies are needed and how to get supplies from one place to another.

These differ from traditional supply chain management tools as big data enables the consideration of more factors important to mission success than those previously available. Such additional factors include weather and terrain obstacles; enemy presence and live fire obstacles; supply sources available locally and regionally as well as from afar; the absence or availability of electricity, refrigerants and other supply storage and transport needs (such as foods and medicines that need refrigeration); and real-time tracking of troop movement so supplies are delivered to the right place even though that place may not have a postal or street address.

ENHANCED HEALTHCARE

The Military Healthcare System exists to ensure the Department of Defense (DoD) is always in a position to ensure the country's sovereignty and do everything possible to treat those wounded on the battlefield. It also means doing whatever is necessary to proactively safeguard the health of all individuals in the ready forces, that is, the active service personnel. In addition, the Military Healthcare System delivers healthcare to many DoD dependents.

Big data solutions are being explored in military healthcare to enhance patient outcomes and speed recovery times. There is no advantage to the DoD, American taxpayers, active personnel or their families in embracing the traditional private sector healthcare model wherein focus is on number of treatments and tests performed rather than on patient outcome. The Military Healthcare System is strictly focused on achieving best possible patient outcomes by the most direct and efficient means. In this way, active personnel remain at optimum health levels and ready for action at all times. Those members who are stricken by disease or wounds can be restored to fully functioning levels quickly to ensure the force stays strong and ready. Those that cannot be restored to previous health levels are given the fastest possible relief and the best outcome that American medicine can muster.

Healthcare is further administered to veterans through the Veterans Health Administration, which is also using big data to better patient outcome although with mixed success. While the VA is currently being heavily criticized for slow to no medical delivery for some veterans, such is largely attributable to management failings and the meanderings of bureaucracy. As long as a substantial backlog of veteran medical files, treatment records, and treatment access exists, big data efforts to enhance healthcare for these individuals will be hampered or stalled outright. Untenable bureaucracy and management practices also thwart big data gains in both the public and private sectors.

Entering false or erroneous data erodes and even destroys the value of big and small data analysis alike, yet this appears to be exactly what happened at the VA.

Minutes before offering his resignation Friday [May 30, 2014], Veterans Affairs Secretary Eric Shinseki presented President Barack Obama with a damning audit that paints the VA healthcare system as bound by unrealistic expectations and a culture that pressures appointment schedulers to falsify data tied to performance bonuses, according to a May 30, 2014 article by Paul Giblin and Rebekah L. Sanders in The Republic, Arizona Central, a Gwinnett company.

The reviews and the resulting firestorm that has spread from Phoenix to Washington was sparked in April by a whistle-blower, Dr. Sam Foote, a former Phoenix VA physician, continues that article. He described to The Arizona Republic and congressional leaders improper scheduling schemes and secret lists that caused veterans to wait months for medical appointments. Foote said at least 40 patients may have died while waiting for care.

Despite these worrisome events, the VA healthcare system has been found by multiple studies to deliver on par or superior care compared to healthcare delivered in the private sector. A 2004 RAND study found that "the VA system delivered higher-quality care than the national sample of private hospitals on all measures except acute care (on which the two samples performed comparably). In nearly every other respect, VA patients received consistently better care across the board, including screening, diagnosis, treatment, and access to follow-up."

Subsequent RAND studies have found much the same. This is neatly summarized in an August 8, 2012 RAND blog post by Arthur L. Kellermann:

[Rand] published a second systematic review, this time focusing on how well VA and non-VA facilities deliver medical and non-surgical care. After examining 36 high-quality studies, the team concluded that the VA almost always came out on top when the study examined how well health systems follow recommended processes of care. When the study compared mortality rates, VA and non-VA facilities generally achieved similar outcomes.

The nonpartisan Congressional Budget Office (CBO) found in its 2007 report that the VA also did a much better job in controlling healthcare costs than its private counterparts.

Kellermann summarized the CBO's findings and their meanings in his aforementioned blog post:

"Government healthcare" is often characterized as wasteful and inefficient. But here too the VA's experience suggests otherwise. In 2007, the nonpartisan Congressional Budget Office (CBO) released a report that concluded that the VA is doing a much better job of controlling healthcare costs than the private sector. After adjusting for a changing case mix as younger veterans return from Iraq and Afghanistan, the CBO calculated that the VA's average healthcare cost per enrollee grew by roughly 1.7% from 1999 to 2005, an annual growth rate of 0.3%. During the same time period, Medicare's per capita costs grew by 29.4%, an annual growth rate of 4.4%. In the private insurance market, premiums for family coverage jumped by more than 70%, according to the Kaiser Family Foundation.

Every health system has its faults, and the VA is no exception. In recent years, it has been challenged by severe budgetary constraints and a surge in demand, as large numbers of injured and ill veterans return from the wars in Iraq and Afghanistan. Its Vietnam-era veterans are aging rapidly and the agency must contend with growing case complexity. When a system as big as the VA falls short, anecdotes about shortcomings get more play than reams of data.

While the VA's focus is on better patient outcome, a task big data greatly aids, obstacles to delivering healthcare, namely severe budgetary constraints and a surge in demand, are also best overcome by big data in both streamlining effective treatments and adding efficiencies to business and treatment processes.

The strategic plan for the Military Healthcare System IT system, which is separate from the VA healthcare system, articulates a goal of enhancing the use of data to provide enterprise-wide awareness and enterprise intelligence in a way that makes information visible, accessible, understandable and trusted, as well as secure. This is all geared to enhancing outcomes for patients and the overall DoD. Use cases toward this end can, for instance, include the automated prediction of best treatment for particular patients based on their history and genetics, or the prediction of medical supply needs, or the optimization of preventive treatments based on region or unit.

Another use case is in studying battle injuries and disease incidents in active duty personnel and veterans in order to strategically devise better protective battle gear and disease preventatives including vaccines, new medicines, and improved field tactics.

Open Source Information

The term "open source information" is used in a special way in the DoD and IC. This should not be confused with open source computer code or open source data. In this context, the term refers to information that is not from the DoD or IC. It is not collected in secret; it is from the press or from publicly available Internet-based sources.

Open source information might include information on the weather or other environmentals, or sourced from the news media, social media, or even research into foreign government leaders. The DoD and IC have always relied on this publicly open information as a baseline of reporting, but with the overwhelming amount of data available via this source new challenges arise in its analysis and integration into overall DoD and IC assessments.

How can the entire vastness of the Internet be queried and the right nuggets brought forward for correlation with internal DoD and IC information? This type of use case requires a blended approach of solutions leveraging existing search and retrieval technologies on the Internet, plus new ways to correlate and search and fuse information with internal holdings. This is clearly a big data challenge.

In-Memory Data Modernization

With the drop in cost of dynamic random access memory (RAM), very large quantities of data can now be held entirely in RAM, which can be accessed magnitudes faster than data stored on slow hard disks, and new software-based solutions are enabling the use of these large quantities of RAM in analysis. This is changing the ability of IT to support operational missions with dynamic data. Since RAM is faster, analysis of data can be faster in theory as well. In DoD and many IC missions, the need for speed can be a big force multiplier and can contribute to success on the battlefield by enabling forces to act and react quicker than an adversary's slower and more traditional communications, command, and control structures permit. This is a growing and increasingly important use case and driver of architectural changes in the DoD and IC.

The Enterprise Data Hub

This use case is focused on enhancing the ability of technology to support enterprise missions while providing enhanced security and agility and more economical use of resources. The enterprise data hub is a place to store all data, both structured and unstructured, for a very economical cost. This alone is a fantastic, highly desired capability.

The enterprise data hub construct has far more capability and features, as you would expect from a well-engineered solution, including enhancements that simplify processing, analysis, and the ability to manage data. Most every enterprise in DoD and the IC today leverages a wide variety of systems to support their diverse data hub goals. These include data warehouses for operational reporting, storage systems to keep data available and safe, specialized massively-parallel databases for large-scale analytics, and search systems for finding and exploring documents.

These separate systems support different workloads, but are not equipped to handle today's exponential growth in data volume and variety, or the range of users who now seek insights from that data. Because each system is purpose-built for a particular class of data and workload, no single system can provide unified access to all relevant information. An enterprise data hub, however, can provide this by meeting a simple objective: Acquire and combine any amount or type of data in its original fidelity, in one place, for as long as necessary, and deliver insights to all kinds of users, as fast as possible. And do so for an efficient cost. An enterprise data hub approach does this in a way that supports a variety of workloads, including batch, interactive SQL, enterprise search, and advanced analytics, together with linkages to existing applications and systems. The DoD movement to this approach holds great promise in enhancing overall agility across multiple mission areas.

BIG DATA USE CASES IN WEAPONRY AND WAR

While the agencies concerned with the development and deployment of wartime weaponry and decision-making are understandably silent on advances in those areas, the necessity of using big data to improve both is readily evident. It is therefore logical that the IC is moving ahead in using big data for these efforts as well.

In some cases, big data is used to supplement the decision-making of human operatives. For example, satellite imagery on screen monitors can often appear more like vague shapes than distinctive markers. A human operative has to interpret those images and make an on-the-fly decision before initiating a drone strike. This poses a two-fold problem: not all human operatives are equally skilled and none of them are likely to come to the correct decision 100% of the time. By using big data in conjunction with current methods and additional operative training, the military can improve outcomes and reduce unnecessary casualties and property destruction.

Indeed, any precision-guided munition, be it automated or human-assisted, benefits greatly from big data as an added element. Even small improvements in targeting accuracy and weapons selection can have substantial impact on successful outcomes in the use of smart weapons. Big data, when done correctly, delivers far more than small improvements in accuracy. For example, the single most important development in targeting over the last 40 years has been GPS enabled munitions. However, GPS alone has limitations. Big data augments accuracy by adding other factors, such as wind speeds, most effective target strike zones for target disablement or destruction, on-the-fly threat identification, and target verification, as well as other influencing factors, along with GPS to more finely tune targeting.

However, the use of human operatives tends to slow reaction time. As a result, many governments around the world are testing the use of autonomous war machines. In these cases, the machine, rather than a human, decides when, where, and whom to strike. The earliest such automated fire-control systems date back to naval guns in the early 1900s, but obviously use of big data today, with improvements in artificial intelligence overall, can mean significant increases in accuracy and predictability. If the quality of either is even a little off, the results could be permanently devastating. Because of potential bad outcomes, this strategy is highly controversial worldwide and not likely to see any wide-scale use without a human being present in the command chain, even if their role is only to keep tabs on what such systems are doing and put a stop to an engagement gone awry.

"Equally important, opponents must point out the threat to peace and security posed by the prospect of a global arms race toward robotic arsenals that are increasingly out of human control," writes Mark Gubrud, a postdoctoral research associate in the Program on Science and Global Security at Princeton University and a member of the International Committee for Robotic Arms Control, in his report titled "Stopping Killer Robots" in the January/February 2014 issue of the *Bulletin of the Atomic Scientists*.

These are the use cases most often used in the DoD and the IC and by their counterparts in several other countries. However, other big data use cases are being explored as tools and techniques continue to improve. Look for use cases to evolve accordingly.

SUMMARY

In this chapter you learned about the many ways the Department of Defense and Intelligence Community use big data and to what effect. Namely, these communities currently use big data for:

- Situational awareness and visualization
- Information correlation for problem solving
- Information search and discovery in overwhelming amounts of data
- Enterprise data management for cyber security
- Logistical information including asset catalogs
- Enhanced healthcare and public health analysis
- Open source information: analysis and integration
- In-memory data modernization
- The enterprise data hub: optimizing it and operations
- Big data in weaponry and war

While their ambitious goals have yet to be fully realized, big data has already proven to be invaluable to their missions. Challenges in big data use in the public defense and security sector mirror those in the overall private sector with a couple of notable exceptions: data stores in these communities are the largest in the world thereby adding infinite complexities in its use, and the privacy conundrum is exacerbated by the multiple national security challenges that require detailed, often personal information to succeed.

CHAPTER 11

USE CASES IN GOVERNMENTS

Big data has myriad uses in governing on all levels, from the intergovernmental level in the United Nations to the local level in cities, small provinces, and townships all over the world. For the first time, governments can analyze data in real-time rather than rely on past and often outdated traditional reports to make decisions that affect today and tomorrow. Such information enables a government to make its services and processes more efficient, but it also closes the gap between immediate public needs and lagging government response. It is one of the best means to put government in sync with its constituents' needs and concerns, in other words.

This chapter covers multiple use cases at several different government levels. However, use cases in the Department of Defense (DoD) and Intelligence Community (IC) are detailed in Chapter 10, as they require special mention and treatment that can distract from the focus here on general governance and citizen services. Folding those use cases into this chapter would also not do the DoD's and IC's herculean and often controversial data efforts justice.

Other government use cases such as those at the Department of Energy, Centers for Disease Control (CDC), and the United Nations Global Pulse are also touched upon in other chapters. This is because governments do not work in a vacuum. Public-private partnerships are common. Often government agencies share information in order to spur positive development throughout the entire community and thereby broaden the benefits to all constituents. In order to show this interplay as it applies to big data use, some government efforts are highlighted in several other chapters according to the industry each such effort aligns with. For example, you'll find note of the Department of Energy's big data efforts in Chapter 16 on energy and the CDC's work noted in Chapter 13 on healthcare, and so on. However, the big data works of any given government agency are not necessarily contained in any one chapter, so you are likely to find mentions of them in several chapters, although none of the mentions are repetitive.

Indeed, two of the most notable trends that big data tends to accelerate are collaboration and a collapse or consolidation of industry divisions. In the commercial world, this phenomenon is clearly evident. One example is in the consolidation of the telecom and cable TV industries. Cable TV companies now routinely offer telecom services from home phones to mobile apps. Conversely, telecom companies offer TV services. Both are Internet Service Providers (ISPs). Because of this model convergence, industry outsiders and consumers tend to see the two very differently regulated industries as one.

EFFECTS OF BIG DATA TRENDS ON GOVERNMENTAL DATA

In the case of government work in big data, it is becoming increasingly difficult to point to a dividing line between what data belongs to the government and which belongs to a private concern because a primary third-party data source for enterprises and individuals is governmental data sets. Some of that data has always been public record and therefore available. However, before the advent of the Internet, this data was difficult to access due to the need to locally request it and the inability to easily find related data squirreled away in various government agency silos. Even after widespread access to the Internet, it was years before governments focused on providing data on the web to the public. It took years longer for the effort to become comprehensive. Now that data is widely available, plus data sets are continuously being provided by nearly every agency. Efforts such as the White House's Project Open Data are also broadening the data resources available from the federal government.

On the other hand, the government needs and collects data from commercial sources and private individuals in order to develop comprehensive data sets before they can share them back again. One example of this is the government's access to disease occurrences and health issues in individuals in order to generate reports on current and predicted disease epidemics or to discover a cause in an environmental health hazard.

Another example is social media. For instance, all posts on Twitter are now actively archived in the U.S. Library of Congress dating back to Twitter's inception in 2006 and going forward presumably for at least the life of Twitter. At the time the archival efforts were announced, Twitter had already exceeded 200 million users. Most of them were U.S. citizens but certainly not all. Most users did not complain about the government collecting the information as it was a public forum by nature, except where users made their Twitter accounts private. Tweets that were deleted or locked are not collected by the Library. It is an immense data set that uniquely reflects the culture overall and the prevailing immediate thoughts of the day.

A 2013 Library of Congress whitepaper explains why the LOC was interested in adding the entirety of Twitter's posts to its archives:

> As society turns to social media as a primary method of communication and creative expression, social media is supplementing and in some cases supplanting letters, journals, serial publications and other sources routinely collected by research libraries.

> Archiving and preserving outlets such as Twitter will enable future researchers access to a fuller picture of today's cultural norms, dialogue, trends and events to inform scholarship, the legislative process, new works of authorship, education and other purposes.

According to a January 4, 2013 post by Erin Allen on the Library of Congress (LOC) blog, the most recent of LOC published updates, this is where the LOC's efforts stand in regard to Twitter:

> The Library's first objectives were to acquire and preserve the 2006–2010 archive; to establish a secure, sustainable process for receiving and preserving a daily, ongoing stream of tweets through the present day; and to create a structure for organizing the entire archive by date.

> This month, all those objectives will be completed. We now have an archive of approximately 170 billion tweets and growing. The volume of tweets the Library receives each day has grown from 140 million beginning in February 2011 to nearly half a billion tweets each day as of October 2012...

> Although the Library has been building and stabilizing the archive and has not yet offered researchers access, we have nevertheless received approximately 400 inquiries from researchers all over the world. Some broad topics of interest expressed by researchers run from patterns in the rise of citizen journalism and elected officials' communications to tracking vaccination rates and predicting stock market activity.

The size of the Twitter data set has undoubtedly grown since that report given the LOC reported it receives "nearly half a billion tweets each day as of October 2012." However, according to the LOC whitepaper, the size of the data set at that time was as follows:

> On February 28, 2012, the Library received the 2006–2010 archive through Gnip in three compressed files totaling 2.3 terabytes. When uncompressed the files total 20 terabytes. The files contained approximately 21 billion tweets, each with more than 50 accompanying metadata fields, such as place and description.

> As of December 1, 2012, the Library has received more than 150 billion additional tweets and corresponding metadata, for a total including the 2006-2010 archive of approximately 170 billion tweets totaling 133.2 terabytes for two compressed copies.

Additional examples of the government collecting data on individuals include the census count mandated by Article I of the U.S. Constitution and unemployment reports by the Department of Labor, as well as many others. Other efforts are more controversial, such as those exposed by the Snowden revelations. Those are detailed in Chapter 9, which covers privacy and highlighted in Chapter 10, which includes use cases in the DoD and IC community.

In short, data is one big circle where all parties, be they individuals, non-profits, commercial interests, or government agencies, give and take data and collectively generate it. In many cases data ownership is a matter yet to be clearly defined because of this collective generation and distribution and the resulting confusion over who "created" what specific data or data elements. Additional data ownership issues are covered in earlier chapters. For the purposes of this chapter, we will look solely at use cases at all government levels without regard to data ownership issues, except to note where such concerns interfere with the effort.

UNITED NATIONS GLOBAL PULSE USE CASES

While the United Nations has always used data in the course of developing and executing its many missions, the development of Global Pulse, online at http://www.unglobalpulse.org/, signaled a new direction for the Executive Office of the United Nations Secretary-General. Global Pulse focuses exclusively on proactively harnessing big data specifically for economic development and humanitarian aid in poor and underdeveloped nations through policy advisement and action. Now, this is no easy task, as usually there are no sophisticated data brokers or commercial data collectors in many countries from which to buy or extract the data—big or otherwise. Therefore, collecting relevant data is largely a piecemeal affair.

Instead of doing big data in traditional ways, Global Pulse describes its data efforts as looking for "digital smoke signals of distress" and "digital exhaust" for telling clues, according to Robert Kirkpatrick, director of Global Pulse in the Executive Office of the Secretary-General United Nations in New York. An example of digital smoke signals are Twitter posts on job losses, spikes in food prices, natural disaster occurrences, disease outbreak, or other indicators of emerging or changing economic and humanitarian needs.

Figure 11.1 shows an online interactive visualization depicting which countries have the most people talking on Twitter about the list of development topics depicted. According to the 2013 Global Pulse Annual Report, through a partnership with DataSift, Global Pulse filtered 500 million Twitter posts every day looking for Tweets on these topics. This visualization depicts the end analysis. The interactive visualization can be found online at http://post2015.unglobalpulse.net/#.

Figure 11.1
An online interactive visualization depicting Twitter conversations on development topics of interest to Global Pulse.
Source: Global Pulse.

An example of digital exhaust is mobile phone metadata. Sometimes whiffs of digital exhaust can be caught wafting in public view but often Global Pulse has to resort to begging telecoms to share the information. The begging has resulted in meager offerings. "Telecoms don't like to share the information for fear of user privacy concerns and feeding competitive intelligence," said Kirkpatrick when he spoke as a member of a 2013 Strata NY panel for a media-only audience. "Sometimes they'll give it to us if it's been scrubbed, that is heavily anonymized, so competitors can't see who their customers are." The trouble with that of course is that the process of heavily anonymizing data can strip it of any useful information or limit inference from the aggregate. The second difficulty with that plan is that anonymized data can be reidentified by any number of entities motivated to do so. In essence, anonymization of the data does little to protect the information from prying eyes but it does sometimes impede Global Pulse and others in the development community in their humanitarian and economic development efforts.

Even so, Global Pulse continues on in its never-ending search of data from myriad sources that can help pin down emerging troubles anywhere in the world. In recognition that Global Pulse is not the only good willed entity in search of this information and dedicated to this cause, the unit shared its hard learned lessons with the global development community through several published guides. One example is its "Big Data for Development Primer," which includes key terms, concepts, common obstacles, and real world case studies.

Another example is its guide titled "Mobile Phone Network Data for Development," which contains research on mobile phone analysis. Global Pulse describes this guide's usefulness this way:

> For example, de-identified CDRs [call detail records] have allowed researchers to see aggregate geographic trends such as the flow of mass populations during and after natural disasters, how malaria can spread via human movement, or the passage of commuters through a city at peak times.

> The document explains three types of indicators that can be extracted through analysis of CDRs (mobility, social interaction, and economic activity) [and] includes a synthesis of several research examples and a summary of privacy protection considerations.

Perhaps the most informative base concept found in Global Pulse's "Big Data for Development Primer" is the redefining of the term *big data* for the development community's purposes and the clarification in its use.

> "Big Data for Development" is a concept that refers to the identification of sources of big data relevant to policy and planning of development programs. It differs from both traditional development data and what the private sector and mainstream media call big data... Big data analytics is not a panacea for age-old development challenges, and real-time information does not replace the quantitative statistical evidence governments traditionally use for decision-making. However, it does have the potential to inform whether further targeted investigation is necessary, or to prompt immediate response.

In other words, Global Pulse uses the immediacy of the information as an important element to support UN policy development and response. It does not, however, use big data as a replacement for traditional data analysis methods. This demonstrates a level of sophistication in big data use that is commonly missing in many private sector endeavors.

FEDERAL GOVERNMENT (NON-DoD OR IC) USE CASES

The U.S. government has made substantial strides in making more government data available to citizens, commercial and non-profit interests, and even to some foreign governments. That effort is continuing so you can expect to see more repositories and additional data sets made available over time.

Data.gov is the central site for U.S. government data and is part of the Open Government Initiative. The Obama administration's stated goal is to make the government more transparent and accountable. But the data provided also often proves to be an invaluable resource for researchers and commercial interests. The Data.gov Data Catalog contains 90,925 data sets as of this writing. You can expect that count to steadily climb higher over time and for the data sets to individually grow as well.

In order to illustrate the ease in accessing this information, Figure 11.2 shows sample Data.gov Data Catalog listings (although not the entire listing of course) and Figure 11.3 shows the alternate, which is interactive data sets. Both can easily be filtered according to your specific needs. The interactive data sets enable you to search, filter, discover, and make charts and maps right in your web browser. There are also APIs available for use by developers. Further, anyone can download the full list of Open Data Sites in either CSV or Excel formats.

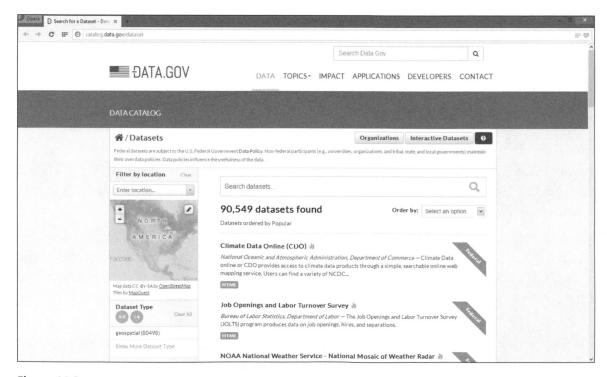

Figure 11.2
Data.gov federal Data Catalog sampling.
Source: Data.gov.

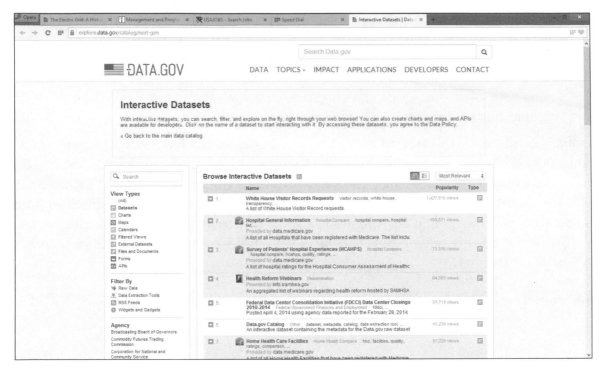

Figure 11.3
Data.gov interactive data sets.
Source: Data.gov.

Beyond these data sets are international open data sets accessible through the Data.gov site. The full list of international open data sites can be downloaded from http://www .data.gov/open-gov/ in CSV and Excel formats.

The second U.S. Open Government National Plan, announced in December 2013, added 23 new or expanded open government commitments to the previous data release plan announced in September 2011, containing 26 commitments total. The commitments address many areas pertinent to forming a more open government, but only a few pertain to data set releases.

In terms of usefulness to media, civic watchdogs, and researchers, the modernization of the Freedom of Information Act (FOIA) and the transformation of the Security Classification System are notable in the second plan. In the case of the modernization of FOIA, the official federal plan calls for, among other things, a consolidated request portal so that requesters need not search for the right agency nor its protocols in order to make a request. It also calls for improved internal processes to speed the release of information once a request is made.

In regard to the second plan's intended transformation of the Security Classification System, efforts are underway to prevent overclassification of government documents and thus drastically reduce the number and types of documents so protected from inception. Further, efforts are underway to declassify documents faster once the need for security classification has passed. These two efforts will lead to more government data coming available for public or commercial use.

There is a third new source of data made available under the second plan. This one is sure to attract a lot of attention given the widespread American public and international concern after Snowden's revelations on the NSA's data-collection activities. As of this writing 2,000 pages of documents about certain sensitive intelligence collection programs conducted under the authority of the Foreign Intelligence Surveillance Act (FISA) were posted online at "IC on the Record" at this url: http://icontherecord.tumblr.com/tagged/declassified. Presumably more declassified documents are to come.

Figure 11.4 illustrates what declassified listings look like on that site and shows a sample document summary with updates and live links to the data.

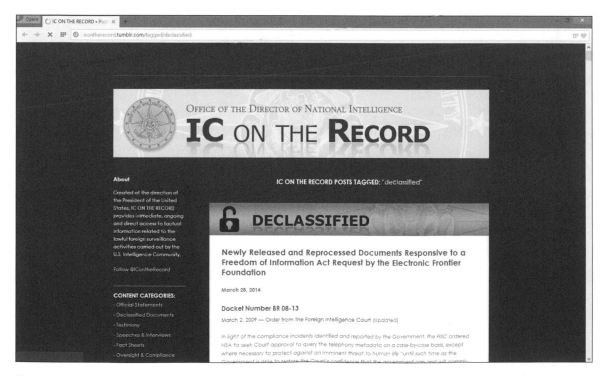

Figure 11.4
The federal declassified documents page.
Source: Office of the Director of National Intelligence "IC on the Record" web page.

Specifically, "The Open Government Partnership: Second Open Government National Action Plan for the United States of America" issued by the White House, states:

> As information is declassified, the U.S. Intelligence Community is posting online materials and other information relevant to FISA, the FISA Court, and oversight and compliance efforts. The Administration has further committed to:
>
> **Share Data on the Use of National Security Legal Authorities.** The Administration will release annual public reports on the U.S. government's use of certain national security authorities. These reports will include the total number of orders issued during the prior twelve-month period and the number of targets affected by them.
>
> **Review and Declassify Information Regarding Foreign Intelligence Surveillance.** The Director of National Intelligence will continue to review and, where appropriate, declassify information related to foreign intelligence surveillance programs.
>
> **Consult with Stakeholders.** The Administration will continue to engage with a broad group of stakeholders and seek input from the Privacy and Civil Liberties Oversight Board to ensure the Government appropriately protects privacy and civil liberties while simultaneously safeguarding national security.

All of these initiatives combined demonstrate that the federal government is using big data to inform its decisions but is also sharing data as a means of fueling or aiding private and commercial efforts as well as a public relations initiative.

STATE GOVERNMENT USE CASES

State governments vary greatly in their use of big data. Sophistication in the use of advanced analytics also varies from state to state. Some states rely on a mix of their own existing data and that which they pull from the federal government or is pushed to them. Other states are busy integrating data from cities, townships, counties, and federal agencies as well as integrating data across state agencies. Of the states most involved with multilevel data integration and advanced analytics, most are focusing on increasing efficiencies in internal processes, public services, and tax collections. A few have branched out into other big data uses, but most of those are at fledgling stages.

Most states are making at least public records data readily available online but you usually have to find that information in a state-by-state online search. Some state agencies also offer mobile apps that contain specialized data.

Figure 11.5 shows sample mobile applications displayed on the federal Data.gov site. These three are all Missouri state apps but plenty of other states offer apps, especially on tourism. At the moment, finding such apps requires a search of app stores by individual state and interest.

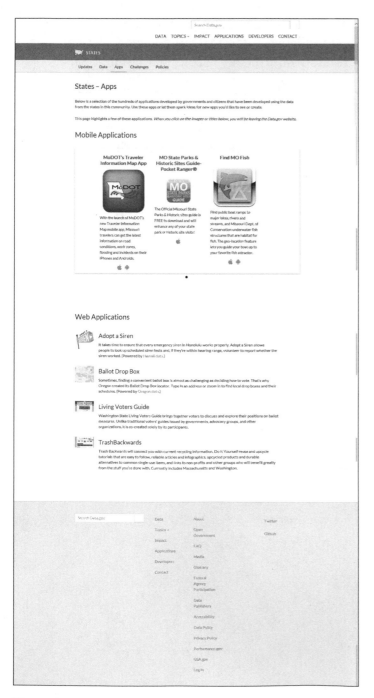

Figure 11.5
Missouri state mobile apps found on federal Data.gov website.
Source: Data.gov.

Most states have yet to build a central portal for data access as the federal government has done. Generally speaking, data is widely available at the state level but still requires the searcher to know which agency to go to or spend time and effort searching for it.

Figure 11.6 shows the Georgia Department of Public Health as an illustration of how some states are offering data at the state level but also pointing users to data available on the federal level that has not yet been incorporated in the state's data set. Such measures are taken in an effort to make as much data as possible available, while the state works to digitalize their records and make them more easily accessible.

Some state data is also not made public because of privacy or regulatory concerns. The more geographically narrow the data set, the easier it becomes to reidentify individuals. Therefore, state and local governments must always be conscious of the potential threat to individual privacy and the potential failure in complying with regulations such as the Health Insurance Portability and Accountability Act of 1996 (HIPAA).

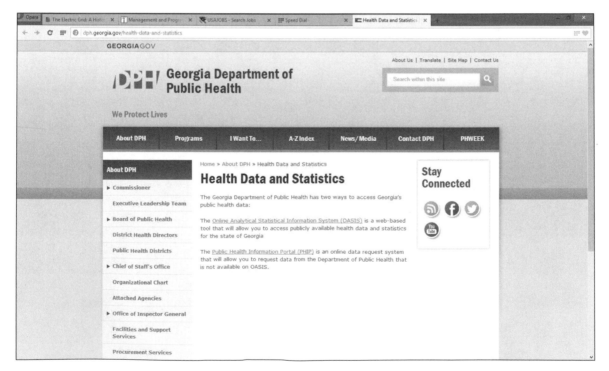

Figure 11.6
The state of Georgia's health data and statistics.
Source: Georgia Department of Public Health.

As of this writing, no multistate data set groupings have been created by state governments that are voluntarily combining their data for the benefit of their region—at least none that I have found. Inevitably, regional data sets will come available. It is already common for states in a region to work together on several fronts from economic development to law enforcement. Combining their data regionally will only bolster those efforts.

There are a few websites available that provide data on state-to-state comparisons, such as is found on StateData.info, a website supported by the National Institute on Disability and Rehabilitation Research (NIDRR), The Institute for Community Inclusion (ICI), the Administration on Intellectual and Developmental Disabilities, and University of Massachusetts, Boston. Such websites tend to share data focused within a special interest. In the case of StateData.info, and readily evident from the site's list of supporters, the specific interest is state services made available to persons with disabilities. Other sites with other special interests exist as well.

See Figure 11.7, which shows a sampling of how StateData.info combines federal and state data to do its analysis. Most sites with special interests do the same or something similar. This is another reason why open federal data is so valuable to other entities besides government agencies. Note on the left upper side of Figure 11.7 that the site allows and enables downloading of its raw data, as well as quick views of the group's analysis on state trends and state comparisons. This is yet another example of how data is so broadly shared that ownership of the data is almost impossible to determine. It is the openness of data, however, that enables the greatest advancements in both the public and private sectors.

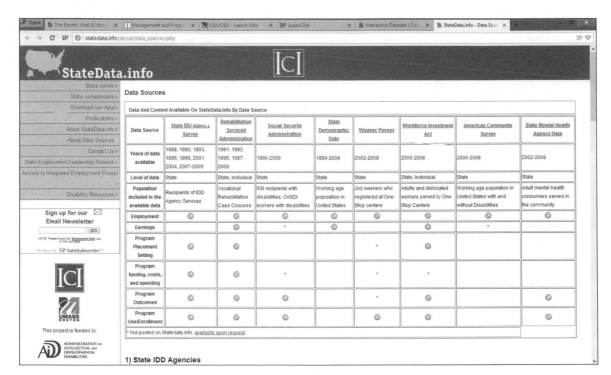

Figure 11.7
Sampling of how StateData.info combines federal and state data to do its analysis.
Source: StateData.info.

State governments are using big data to varying degrees to guide their decisions, but also sharing data publicly and with private partners too. Much of the effort is focused on improving internal processes and on marketing public attractions and services. Few states are experimenting with much beyond these basics at this point. But this will change as state governments begin to understand big data tools better and acquire the talent needed to initiate new data projects.

LOCAL GOVERNMENT USE CASES

Very few local governments are working in big data now, due largely to funding cutbacks and a lack of talent capable of doing big data projects. For the most part, local governments are using traditional data collection and analysis methods largely confined to their own databases and local and state sources. An example of a local outside source is data from utility companies.

Large cities tend to be far ahead of the curve. See Figure 11.8, which shows New York City's Open Data portal found at https://nycopendata.socrata.com. There the city provides over 1,100 data sets and several stories about how the city is using data. Figure 11.9 shows an NYC Open Data pullout detailing some of the efforts New York City is accomplishing through the use of all this data.

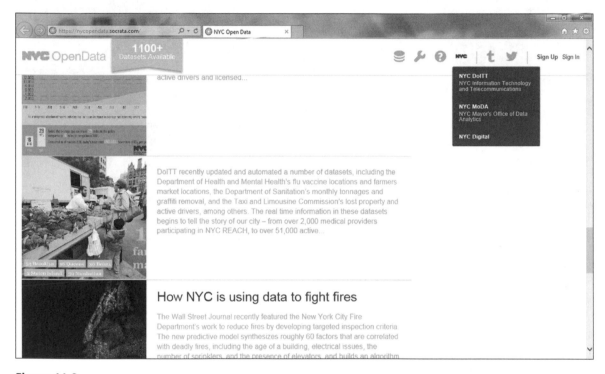

Figure 11.8
New York City's Open Data portal.
Source: New York City website https://nycopendata.socrata.com.

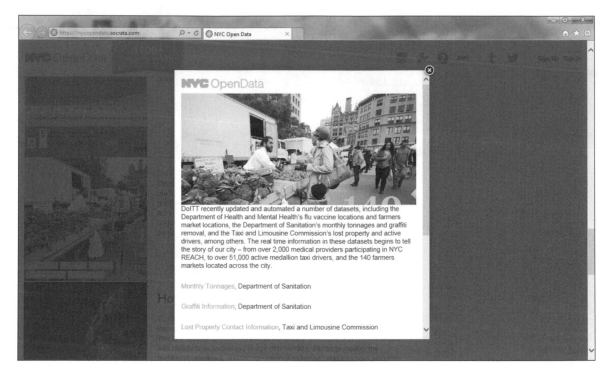

Figure 11.9
NYC Open Data pullout detailing some of the efforts New York City is accomplishing through the use of big data.
Source: New York City website https://nycopendata.socrata.com.

However, interest in big data solutions at the local level is high in many towns, cities and counties, particularly those that are focused on cost savings, process efficiencies, and improving tax and fee collections. The Center for Disease Control (CDC) said that there is high interest in localized health data as well. Such requests are not surprising, for it is typical of budget-strapped local governments to turn to the federal and state governments for aid in obtaining localized data and analysis.

Local governments will eventually benefit from the growing spread of data from myriad sources and simpler analytics that can then be more easily used at the local level.

LAW ENFORCEMENT USE CASES

Of the few things that are truly certain in this life, growth in human population seems to top the list. Equally certain is the fact that government services and resources are typically stretched thinner with population increases. Law enforcement agencies on every level are repeatedly hit with budget cuts and manpower shortages and yet must find a way to perform to the public's unwavering expectations.

For some time now, law enforcement agencies have incorporated a number of technologies to help them detect and fight crime. The array of tools currently at their fingertips is quite impressive. They include things like gun shot audio sensors, license plate readers, face recognition technology, GPS location tracking, in-car cameras, wireless graffiti cameras, and thermal imaging for area searches complete with corresponding police car monitors.

There are other tools more innovative than the standard fare of cameras and sensors too. One example is IDair's system that can read fingerprints of people passing by up to 20 feet away from the device. As of this writing, IDair was already moving its product beyond military use and into the commercial realm. That means law enforcement and private companies can both buy it. Like security cameras on commercial property, police will likely be able to access data on commercially owned IDair systems too. The device is about the size of a flashlight and can be placed anywhere.

Another example is smart lighting systems for public places such as airports and shopping malls.

"Visitors to Terminal B at Newark Liberty International Airport may notice the bright, clean lighting that now blankets the cavernous interior, courtesy of 171 recently installed LED fixtures," writes Diane Cardwell in her article in The New York Times. *"But they probably will not realize that the light fixtures are the backbone of a system that is watching them."*

"Using an array of sensors and eight video cameras around the terminal, the light fixtures are part of a new wireless network that collects and feeds data into software that can spot long lines, recognize license plates and even identify suspicious activity, sending alerts to the appropriate staff."

Other examples in innovative law enforcement technologies include diagramming systems, crime mapping, evidence collection systems, police pursuit reduction technologies, and cameras for police dogs.

Paul D. Schultz, Chief of Police in Lafayette, Colorado described those technologies in his post in *The Police Chief* magazine this way:

Evidence and deterrence: *Crime scene investigations are also aided by these systems in scanning for physical evidence. Imagers can detect disturbed surfaces for graves or other areas that have been dug up in an attempt to conceal bodies, evidence, and objects. The device can also scan roadways for tire tracks or other marks that are not visible to the naked eye.*

Proactive imager surveillance enables officers to scan public parks, public streets, alleys and parking lots, public buildings, transportation corridors, and other areas where individuals do not have an expectation of privacy.

Diagramming systems: *Thanks to improvements in computer technology, crime scenes and collisions can now be diagrammed in a matter of minutes, as compared with hours just a few years ago. The systems that make this possible are highly accurate and easy to use, and they create extremely professional-looking images for use in court or for further analysis.*

The high end of diagramming technology is the state-of-the-art forensic three-dimensional scanner that uses a high-speed laser and a built-in digital camera to photograph and measure rapidly a scene in the exact state in which the first responder secured it.

Crime mapping: *The ability to depict graphically where crime has occurred and to some extent predict future crime locations enables field commanders to direct patrols through intelligence-led policing. The days when officers patrolled random areas hoping to catch the bad guys are giving way to a new era in which agencies use crime maps of every patrol district to assign officers to patrols in a reasonable and logical manner.*

Reducing police pursuits: *New systems that integrate the ability to track a suspect vehicle through a Global Positioning System (GPS) device that attaches to the suspect vehicle are reducing the need for police pursuits. This technology enables officers to apprehend a dangerous suspect at a later date when the safety of the community can be maximized.*

Cameras for K-9 units: *In the near future, agencies will be able to equip their K-9 units with cameras and two-way radio systems that will allow a K-9 handler to stay a safe distance from a dangerous event while at the same time providing command and control of a police dog. This technology will be useful for search-and-rescue operations as well as dangerous-building searches. Testing of a prototype system is supposed to begin this year [2014].*

While all these tools help law enforcement and security forces cover more ground and collect more evidence, they also generate a continuous stream of data. For that data to be helpful, agencies and security personnel must be able to parse and analyze it quickly. Big data tools are essential in making the data useful.

However, it is not only machine data that is useful to law enforcement, but social media and other unstructured data as well. Again, big data tools are useful in collecting, parsing, and analyzing this data, too.

While the majority of big data use cases in law enforcement pertain to actively fighting crime, collecting evidence and preventing crime in the agency's jurisdiction, big data tools and techniques are increasingly also used to share and integrate crime data between local districts and between agencies at all government levels. Further, big data is now being actively considered as an aid for internal needs such as for operational compliance and process improvements.

Summary

In this chapter you learned how governments from the federal to the local level are using big data. You learned that a handful of big cities are well ahead of the curve in both using and sharing big data. Smaller cities, townships, and county governments tend to be woefully behind largely due to budget and talent constraints. The majority of those strive to at least make data from public records available, but many are hoping that the federal and state governments will eventually provide them with more granular data useable on the local level.

State governments vary widely in both commitment to using big data and in proficiency. However, the goal is almost universal: to make data, big data tools, APIs, and mobile apps widely available to the public. In the interim, some states and state agencies are providing what data they have now, while also pointing users to federal data in an attempt to make as much data as possible.

As of this writing, no multistate data set groupings have been created by state governments that are voluntarily combining their data for the benefit of their region. However, there are a few websites available that provide data on state-to-state comparisons, such as is found on StateData.info. Those tend to address special interest issues rather than broader comparisons.

You also learned that the U.S. government has made substantial strides in making more government data available to citizens, commercial entities, and non-profit interests, and even to some foreign governments. That effort is continuing so you can expect to see more repositories and additional data sets made available over time. Data.gov is the central site for U.S. government data and is part of the Open Government Initiative.

You also learned that international and foreign data sets are also available on Data.gov/open-gov. Indeed, international sharing of data is commonplace to a degree. Even the United Nations is interested in obtaining and using big data from a variety of countries.

While the United Nations has always used data in the course of developing and executing its many missions, the development of Global Pulse, online at http://www.unglobalpulse.org/, signaled a new direction for the Executive Office of the United Nations Secretary-General. Global Pulse focuses exclusively on proactively harnessing big data specifically for economic development and humanitarian aid in poor and underdeveloped nations through policy advisement and action. Now, this is no easy task, as usually there are no sophisticated data brokers or commercial data collectors in many countries from which to buy or extract the data.

Instead of doing big data in traditional ways, Global Pulse describes its data efforts as looking for "digital smoke signals of distress" and "digital exhaust" for telling clues. An example of digital smoke signals are Twitter posts on job losses, spikes in food prices, natural disaster occurrences, disease outbreak, or other indicators of emerging or changing economic and humanitarian needs.

In short, governments at every level are seeking to use and share big data to better serve their constituents, spur innovative economic development, and to provide humanitarian aid.

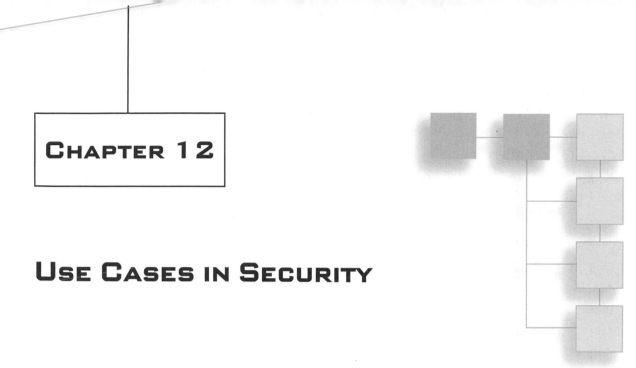

CHAPTER 12

USE CASES IN SECURITY

For the purposes of this chapter, we will look at use cases, opportunities, and challenges in the general security industry, making no distinction between the cyber-security and physical/facility security subsectors. This is because the subsectors are less distinct with each passing day. Indeed, for all practical purposes, the entire security industry has blended into one already, given the digitalization of devices and sensors and the advent of the Internet of Things.

EVERYTHING IS ON THE INTERNET

The term "Internet of Things" refers to all things being connected to the Internet. That's not an exaggeration. Literally everything—from smart refrigerators and digitalized toilets inside the home and smart utility meters outside; to lighting fixtures in public spaces and sensors of all kinds; mobile, wearable computing, and implanted medical devices; vehicles from planes, trains, cars, and trucks to golf carts and farm tractors; TVs, set-top boxes, gaming consoles and even baby monitors; manufacturing, home health and hospital equipment—everything is being connected to the Internet.

Every single one of those things is producing digitalized information at a phenomenal rate. In other words, they are making big data non-stop. This form of data is called *machine data,* that is, data created by machines rather than by humans. It is arguably the easiest of all data forms to parse and analyze because of its tendency toward standardized output. For the most part, it is structured data. It's not messy like social media data is, wherein human expression is unstructured. Humans can say or mean the same thing using a variety of words, sentiments, and emoticons. Something as simple as a pun or sarcasm can warp the final interpretation in analysis. Wherever conformity exists in data, analysis is far more accurate and faster.

Not only are all of those devices producing data that is easy for analysts—in security or otherwise—to use, they are potentially recording every detail of our individual and collective lives. Nothing, no matter how mundane or esoteric, escapes the machine collective's notice. Databases everywhere are brimming with the stories of our lives.

It is in this context that security experts must now work, whether they are charged with cyber-security (protecting data) or with physical security (protecting facilities, events, and persons). Very little in security work relies on direct human observation anymore.

"It's not in the hands of the security pro on the ground anymore," a security professional, who asked to remain anonymous, lamented at a professional conference. "Everything is being pushed to the network guys."

But that is not to say that security work has gotten any easier. Despite all this data, all these additional mechanical eyes, and all the other extensions of the security expert's manifested presence, the exponential growth of threats and the steady rise in the sophistication of the attacks are still outpacing security efforts.

Compounding the problem is the need to preserve individual privacy. Whenever privacy is given priority, risk increases. Wherever security is given priority, individual privacy is breached and rarely can it return to its previous setup. This privacy conundrum remains the biggest challenge of our day. See Chapter 9, "The Privacy Conundrum," for more details on that dilemma.

Indeed, recognizing the effects on privacy and security, the Federal Trade Commission, in an effort to get ahead of the Internet of Things curve, held a workshop in November 2013. Called "Internet of Things—Privacy and Security in a Connected World," the idea was to begin to explore the issues and "focus on privacy and security issues related to increased connectivity for consumers, both in the home (including home automation, smart home appliances, and connected devices), and when consumers are on the move (including health and fitness devices, personal devices, and cars)." See http://www.ftc.gov/news-events/events-calendar/2013/11/internet-things-privacy-security-connected-world for more information on that event.

With that backdrop in mind, this chapter focuses on big data's role and discusses use cases in the security industry.

DATA AS FRIEND AND FOE

People tend to think of big data in black or white terms, as good or evil, with nary a shred of gray in between. But data is only information; the good, bad, and the ugly parts grow out of how it is used.

Privacy issues often arise when data is collected for one purpose but then stored where it can be used for entirely different purposes later. In other words, the data is gathered and stored, but it becomes impossible for that information to be retrieved, deleted, or otherwise guarded by the person that information is about. This leaves the door wide open for future abuse, even when the original purpose was benign.

On the other hand, security professionals can only do so much in identifying immediate threats in real time. It is often the case that they need to backtrack through data to find the trail of evildoers and predict what they are likely to do next. In other words, once security professionals are aware of suspicious or malevolent activity or intent, they often need to examine more data than just the data presented in the moment. That means looking at past data, including data collected and stored earlier before anything or anyone was suspected. Hence, there is value in collecting and storing massive amounts of data over time.

And therein lies the rub. Policies that are good for privacy are bad for security and vice versa. Yet those who seek privacy also want to be safe and those who seek to provide security also want privacy for themselves. Data, then, is both friend and foe in both causes.

The challenge is in finding the right balance between privacy and security, but that is easier said than done.

Take antivirus software for example. In order for the software to identify and eliminate computer viruses in your email, downloads, files, and apps on your computer, the software must be able to "see" what is there. That means your email, downloads, and files on your computer are not technically private. But neither would your email and computer files be private if there were no antivirus programs as many cyber-criminals would then be watching and stealing your information.

Unfortunately, antivirus software and cyber-security efforts in the past were limited to detecting computer threats after they occurred. There really wasn't a way to predict or detect cyber-threats any earlier. That means no matter how diligent a user was in using the protective software, viruses, Trojans, worms, and other cyber-threats still got through the defenses.

Further complicating this problem is the fact that no two antivirus/malware software products work the same way or catch the same threats. This means that a cyber-threat can slide past some protective software and not others. But even if a user were to use two or more anti-malware programs, it is unlikely that all threats would be caught or blocked. Indeed, there are plenty of cyber-threats that are not detected by *any* security software.

This is largely due to the fact that threats are caught after attacks happen. Until that point, security software and security pros do not know they exist and therefore can't block or otherwise thwart them. Further, some cyber-attacks are so sophisticated that they can disable or "blind" antivirus/malware software to their presence. Other malware can instantly replicate itself the moment after being eradicated by antivirus software. The level of sophistication being displayed by some cyber-attacks and cyber-spying cannot be overstated. Further, the level of sophistication in cyber-crimes radically increases with the passing of every day. Indeed, big data is itself a target, as cyber-criminals find it relatively easy to hide their tools within the massive amounts of data now encumbering companies everywhere.

However, there is real hope that this paradigm can be upended through the use of big data. Massive amounts of data enable information security (InfoSec) professionals to see emerging threats and patterns earlier and even to predict impending attacks. Big data also aids in identifying the source of the attack, which can lead to attackers ending up behind bars instead of hovering over keyboards. Obviously, this is a huge win for the good guys.

Use Cases in Antivirus/Malware Efforts

One antivirus-related example is how Kaspersky Lab uses big data in the development and ongoing refinement of its Internet security and InfoSec products. Kaspersky Lab is headquartered in Moscow, Russia but its holding company is registered in the UK. It is an international group operating in nearly 200 countries and territories around the world. It produces products for individuals, small and mid-sized businesses, and huge corporations and governments.

The company uses its cloud-assisted Kaspersky Security Network (KSN) to collect data on new threats and vulnerabilities, such as viruses, malware, and phishing websites, from millions of voluntary participants.

"It's important to have a global view of new threats that may appear in one region and quickly spread to other regions," said Vladimir Zapolyansky, director of Global Product & Technology Intelligence at Kaspersky Lab.

This information is sent quickly to its security experts and then warnings are sent to its global customer base in response. Much of this process is automated to further speed communications. The company claims that when a new threat is detected, the new threat intelligence spreads to its customer base in as little as 60 seconds.

Big data-fueled antivirus/malware efforts, particularly when coupled with crowd-sourcing, produce faster detections and responses than were previously possible. In general, big data driven security programs take minutes rather than hours to detect the problem and send a warning to vulnerable clients.

Returning to the example, KSN is a complex distributed infrastructure. It is a hybrid model using both traditional protection tools and new tools such as big data and cloud technologies. This enables Kaspersky to quickly identify previously unknown threats and move rapidly to block or eliminate them. It also helps them blacklist online attack sources and provide reputational data for applications and websites.

Even so, this is no easy task. According to Kaspersky Lab's internal data, "about 315,000 new samples of malware appear 'in the wild' every day."

Privacy issues get even trickier when a security company relies essentially on crowdsourcing to help catch the bad guys. Eliciting the help of millions of voluntary participants means respecting their privacy in the process or else volunteers will fall from the program in quick succession. In other words, trust is everything.

According to "Kaspersky Security Network," a Kaspersky whitepaper, "KSN's working mechanism includes several key processes such as the continuous, geographically-distributed monitoring of real-life threats to users' computers, analysis of that data, and the delivery of relevant intelligence and countermeasures to protected endpoints."

In other words, Kaspersky is collecting data from each volunteer's computer on an entirely automated basis. So how does it do that and still protect each volunteer's privacy? The company explains in its KSN whitepaper:

> All the information obtained is depersonalized. Kaspersky Lab organizes the information it receives in large chunks according to data type, and nobody can trace which data was received from any one individual. Kaspersky Lab protects all the information collected by KSN in accordance with current legal and security statutory requirements.

While it is true that anonymized data can be reidentified by experts, the data KSN collects appears to be contained within Kaspersky's databases rather than shared or sold in the raw, which greatly reduces the risk that such would occur. Of course Kaspersky could do so internally, but that is unlikely as well since frankly there's little to no benefit in the company doing so.

In essence, any program launched by a user is evaluated by several factors, including the vendor's digital signature and control hash, source verification, and program integrity. If the computer program is found to be legitimate, it's added to a whitelist. If not, it's added to a blacklist. KSN ensures a constant update of both lists. According to Kaspersky, here's the internal process on the handling of newfound malware:

> As soon as a program is defined as malware, it is reported to Kaspersky Lab's Urgent Detection System and the information becomes available through Kaspersky Security Network. Therefore, even before the signature for that piece of malware is created and downloaded to secured endpoints, they receive a corresponding measure of protection. In that way Kaspersky Lab's clients receive prompt information about new threats—including a basis to stop unknown ones—minutes after the launch of a cyber-attack. A traditional signature database update takes hours to do the same thing.

The company uses other technologies such as a reputational technology they call "Wisdom of the Crowd," which notes popularity and reputation of a program based on KSN user input, and cloud-assisted anti-spam technology. The cloud portion detects and blocks spam without the need for an anti-spam filter to be placed on the computer.

Figure 12.1 shows the basic principles used in Kaspersky Lab's products' interaction with KSN.

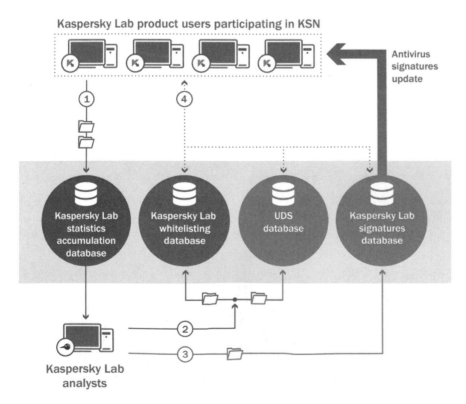

Figure 12.1
The basic principles used in Kaspersky Lab's products' interaction with KSN.
Source: Reprinted with permission. Copyright Kaspersky Lab.

While each provider's processes are different in building and maintaining their antivirus/malware programs, most readily see the advantages of using big data in their mix. Some providers excel at wielding big data and others not so much, just as is the case in other industries.

In general, use cases for this sector are in detecting emerging threats, predicting upcoming threats, speeding the response to same, blocking and eliminating threats, arresting and prosecuting criminals by both identifying the source and providing a data trail of their activities as evidence, and in general, improving the mix and strength of defenses.

How Target Got Hit in the Bull's Eye

It's important to note that many companies that provide antivirus/malware programs for individuals also provide enterprise-grade, that is, corporate-level, data protection. In this section, the focus is on the obstacles and opportunities encountered in a standard enterprise where IT labors specifically to protect the company's proprietary and sensitive data, including but not limited to payment processing and personal data. It's an ongoing and exceedingly difficult challenge fraught with many liabilities.

One example of how failure to protect data can lead to chaos and huge losses, both in immediate and future monies, is the infamous Target breach of 2013. For a snapshot of what happened, consider this excerpt from a January 10, 2014 report in *The Washington Post* by Jia Lynn Yang and Amrita Jayakumar:

> *The Target breach already ranks as one of the worst ever. During the peak of holiday shopping last month, Target said that up to 40 million customers' credit and debit card information had been stolen from people who shopped in stores from Nov. 27 to Dec. 15. On Friday, the company said a new group of 70 million customers—some of whom might also have had their card data stolen—have had their personal information compromised, as well.*

> *The growing scandal has triggered at least two class-action lawsuits, drawn state and federal investigations, and damaged Target's bottom line. The company on Friday cut its fourth-quarter earnings forecast and said it expects sales to decline by 2.5%.*

> *"All the costs are going to eat up their profits," said John Kindervag, an analyst with Forrester. "There's going to be shareholder revolts. There's going to be prosecutions. They've stepped in quicksand. It's not going to be fun."*

Protecting data is essential for as you can see from this report, the implications of not doing so effectively can be devastating.

So how did the Target breach happen? Brian Krebs, former investigative reporter for *The Washington Post* and now a noted and highly respected, independent cyber-security blogger, was the person who first broke the Target breach story. He continued to investigate the situation and periodically post his findings on his blog called *KrebsOnSecurity*. On February 14, 2014, he posted details on the cause of the breach:

> The breach at Target Corp. that exposed credit card and personal data on more than 110 million consumers appears to have begun with a malware-laced email phishing attack sent to employees at an HVAC firm that did business with the nationwide retailer, according to sources close to the investigation.
>
> Last week, KrebsOnSecurity reported that investigators believe the source of the Target intrusion traces back to network credentials that Target had issued to Fazio Mechanical, a heating, air conditioning and refrigeration firm in Sharpsburg, Pa. Multiple sources close to the investigation now tell this reporter that those credentials were stolen in an email malware attack at Fazio that began at least two months before thieves started stealing card data from thousands of Target cash registers.
>
> Two of those sources said the malware in question was Citadel—a password-stealing bot program that is a derivative of the ZeuS banking Trojan—but that information could not be confirmed. Through a PR firm, Fazio declined to answer direct questions for this story, and Target has declined to comment, citing an active investigation.
>
> There is no question that, like Target, Fazio Mechanical was the victim of cyber-crime. But investigators close to the case took issue with Fazio's claim that it was in full compliance with industry practices, and offered another explanation of why it took the Fazio so long to detect the email malware infection: The company's primary method of detecting malicious software on its internal systems was the free version of Malwarebytes Anti-Malware.
>
> To be clear, Malwarebytes Anti-Malware (MBAM) free is quite good at what it's designed to do – scan for and eliminate threats from host machines. However, there are two problems with an organization relying solely on the free version of MBAM for anti-malware protection: Firstly, the free version is an on-demand scanner that does not offer real-time protection against threats (the Pro version of MBAM does include a real-time protection component). Secondly, the free version is made explicitly for individual users and its license prohibits corporate use.

The giant retailer had security practices in place but it failed to find and protect against vulnerabilities and poor practices presented by its vendor/contractor base. Krebs explained how that group was plugged into Target's systems:

> Fazio's statement also clarified that its data connection to Target was exclusively for electronic billing, contract submission and project management. The company did not specify which component(s) of Target's online operations that Fazio accessed externally, but a former employee at Target said nearly all Target contractors access an external billing system called Ariba, as well as a Target project management and contract submissions portal called Partners Online. The source said Fazio also would have had access to Target's Property Development Zone portal.

The malware connected and spread from there.

A Senate staff report titled "A 'Kill Chain' Analysis of the 2013 Target Data Breach" produced on March 26, 2014 for Chairman Rockefeller, Committee on Commerce, Science and Transportation, notes numerous failures that perhaps a big data approach might have thwarted.

Among the failures the Senate report notes is this: "Target appears to have failed to respond to multiple automated warnings from the company's anti-intrusion software that the attackers were installing malware on Target's system." Further the report says that Target "appears to have failed to respond to multiple warnings from the company's anti-intrusion software regarding the escape routes the attackers planned to use to exfiltrate data from Target's network."

We'll get to the common problems in security alerts and how big data can help with that later in this chapter. For now, consider Figure 12.2 from the Senate report for a quick view of events in the Target breach displayed in a timeline.

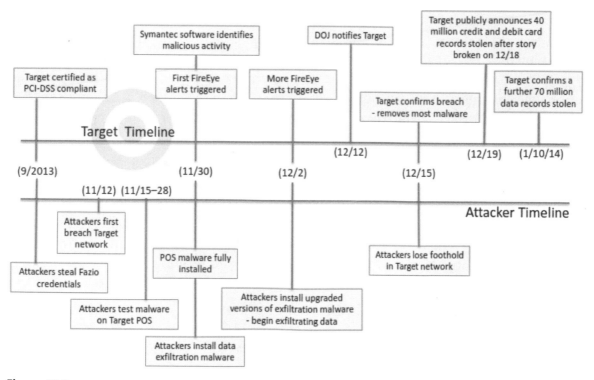

Figure 12.2

Timeline chart of events in the 2013 Target breach.

Source: Senate staff report titled "A 'Kill Chain' Analysis of the 2013 Target Data Breach" produced on March 26, 2014 for Chairman Rockefeller, Committee on Commerce, Science and Transportation.

Big Data as Both Challenge and Benefit to Businesses

Companies, both big and small and in every industry, face similar difficulties and unexpected vulnerabilities. Both are growing exponentially.

"We have seen complex enterprises struggle with both the benefits and challenges of big data," said Kristine Briggs, vice president of Operations at Neohapsis, a security, compliance, and risk management consulting company based in Chicago. "From data classification, to identity and access management, IP protection, storage, and compliance, our clients have what seem to be ever-growing challenges in effectively securing, and most importantly, getting value out of, their data. Add the challenges and opportunities presented by cloud computing, and the situation becomes even more complicated."

But most enterprises are not only interested in protecting data and reducing their risks, they also want to see return on investment (ROI) from the security data they glean in the process.

"In addition to the imperative of securing their most critical data, many enterprises want to get value out of their cyber-security data if possible; most global enterprises have implemented Security Information/Event Management systems (SIEMs) and Governance Risk and Compliance (GRC) systems to try to achieve this, very few with stellar results," said Briggs. "SIEMs can help manage the volume of security and event data, but rarely provide the intelligence needed to react quickly, and more importantly they are rarely tuned to be able to correlate the data from different sources to come to intelligent, actionable conclusions."

"Put more simply, you get lots of data, and can generate dashboards on things like unpatched systems and other tactical points, but they rarely provide what you need to actually improve your security posture on a strategic level. GRC systems, though conceptually attractive, are very complex to implement and customize, and generally take a team of people to get a commensurate amount of value to balance out the cost. Neither type of system effectively supports the constant organizational and technological change we see in global enterprises today."

Figure 12.3 shows a Neohapsis NeoX user interface used to manage vulnerabilities across an entire company. The figure shows a highly filterable list page of vulnerabilities aggregated together from many different providers. Complex searches can be accomplished by drilling down through any of the facets. Reduced time managing vulnerabilities generally equates to more time available to prioritize, remediate, and retest.

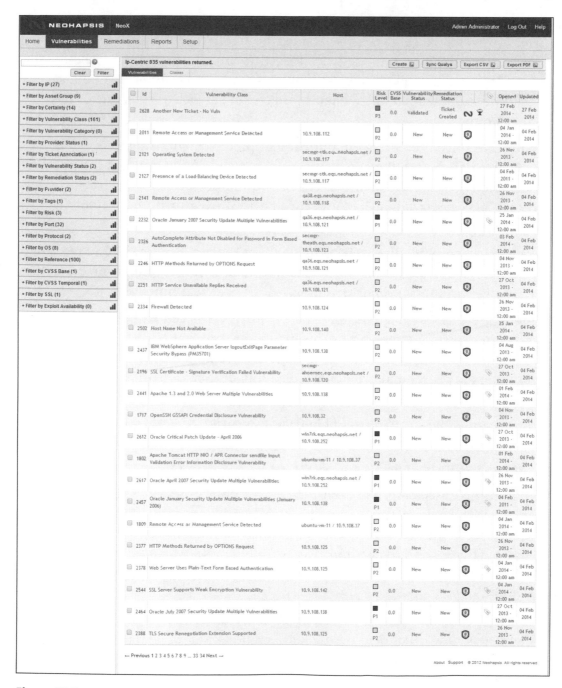

Figure 12.3

This is a Neohapsis NeoX user interface used to manage vulnerabilities across an entire company. The figure shows a highly filterable list page of vulnerabilities aggregated together from many different providers.

Source: Reprinted with permission. Copyright © Neohapsis.

It should also be noted that the security community faces potential liabilities. For example, security firm Trustwave faced two lawsuits filed by Green Bank and Trustmark Bank claiming the firm was negligent, along with Target, for the Target breach. These banks and others lost millions of dollars since by law they, rather than their customers, must absorb the costs of fraudulent credit and debit card charges as well as the costs of reissuing new cards to customers.

Those lawsuits have since been dropped, but without prejudice, meaning they can be filed again at some later date before the applicable statutes of limitation run out. The security industry is completely unnerved by the lawsuits, and the potential for future such suits, that could cost them everything. They are flocking in droves to big data tools to help protect them against such liabilities.

Big data analytics, when used effectively, provide the means to use data from a variety of sources, add inputs in the algorithm to include new and/or more factors for evaluation, and analyze massive amounts of information in real or near real time.

There are many use cases for big data in cyber-security. As noted in the earlier section, namely they are in detecting emerging threats, predicting upcoming threats, speeding the response to threats, blocking and eliminating threats, arresting and prosecuting criminals by both identifying the source and providing a data trail of their activities as evidence, and generally improving the mix and strength of defenses.

But that is only part of the story in using big data in security.

WHERE VIRTUAL AND REAL WORLDS COLLIDE

Up to this point, this discussion has been focused on pure cyber-attacks. But given the ongoing convergence between the real and virtual worlds, security personnel have to broaden their scope to include threats that cross that rather tenuous line. For example, cyber-criminals, activists, and cyber-terrorists are not limited to stealing, blocking, or manipulating digitalized data. They can cause havoc, damage, and even human casualties in the real world too.

Given the Internet of Things and the fact that almost all critical infrastructure in any developed country is now dependent on digital operations, the potential for highly damaging cyber-attacks in the real world cannot be overstated. Power grids, water systems, and entire economies are just a few of the things that can be crashed by sophisticated cyber-attacks. People can also be attacked and even assassinated by cyber-attacks on medicine delivery systems and implanted medical devices such as pacemakers, as well as through other devices.

In response, the Whitehouse issued an Executive Order (13636) in February of 2013 calling for a "cyber-security framework" to protect critical infrastructure. The Executive Order tasked various governmental agencies with developing a cyber-security framework and identifying critical infrastructure in need of security. Subsequently, on February 12, 2014, the Commerce Department's National Institute of Standards and Technology (NIST) released a framework for improving critical infrastructure cybersecurity.

> *"The framework provides a consensus description of what's needed for a comprehensive cybersecurity program," said Under Secretary of Commerce for Standards and Technology and NIST Director Patrick D. Gallagher. "It reflects the efforts of a broad range of industries that see the value of and need for improving cybersecurity and lowering risk. It will help companies prove to themselves and their stakeholders that good cybersecurity is good business."*

NIST also released an accompanying roadmap document and stressed that the framework "is expected to be a first step in a continuous process to improve the nation's cybersecurity." In others words, this effort will never end.

Life in the modern world is fragile. A country's entire banking and financial system can be completely wiped out without a single bank vault being cracked. Security is no longer limited to vaults, locks, and body guards or border guards. Attacks can come from far away, absent the physical presence of the perpetrators and without sound or any other warning.

While most citizens of every country are completely unaware of the fragility of their reality, security professionals suffer no such illusion. Despite their instincts, experience, and diligence, security pros cannot be everywhere at once nor can they personally observe everything that may indicate a looming threat. Big data tools are quite frankly their only hope in evening the odds. Even so, as it has been said before, an attacker needs only to succeed once whereas a protector must succeed in every case and on every front.

Use cases for big data in this category include those in any other cyber-security effort as well as in the development of innovative protective measures. This includes but is not limited to offline overrides in medical equipment that react to unauthorized changes in commands or performance and offline secondary and compartmentalized or containerized emergency and backup systems such as for electric grids, water, and banking systems.

Indeed, one of the biggest benefits of big data in security is its ability to predict likely threats and afford the means to design both prevention and response.

MACHINE DATA MAYHEM

InfoSec used to focus on endpoints, such as computers and mobile devices. When that proved no longer effective, the industry shifted to focus on protecting the network. That was followed by an intense focus on protecting the data. Eventually keeping everything behind a firewall became impossible as more data flowed in and out, from and to various sources and devices. In other words, as more of everything became connected, from employees bringing their own malware laden devices to work, in what is now called Bring Your Own Device (BYOD) programs, and data moved to and from the cloud and between sources, the notion of a firewall and company security was forced to change too.

The Farmer's Security Dilemma

Along comes the Internet of Things to infuse even more data from more sources into any given business and the general data pool. For example, a farmer might buy a tractor that can deliver more data to him on the condition of his farm. But that same tractor likely also reports data to the manufacturer about how the tractor is performing. It could also report to the dealer so the dealer can start marketing more parts, accessories, services, and new models to the farmer. The farmer may also elect to share his tractor's data with a farming association or a mega-vendor, such as Monsanto. Or, the tractor manufacturer may share that farmer's tractor data with a whole slew of other entities unbeknownst to the farmer.

All told, that one farm tractor is reporting an awful lot of data in various directions, and only some of it with the farmer's expressed knowledge and consent. The rest is likely harvested and shared without his direct knowledge.

Some uses of that data are helpful to the farmer and to other farmers, but a good bit of it is really used to help the collaborators peddle their wares to farmers. It is not necessarily helpful to the farmer for a vendor to know so much about his business—particularly not if he also must rely on the vendor to sell him products on credit. The vendor could easily look at the farm data and withhold the sale considering the farm a bad credit risk before a single plant in the field broke ground.

There are other ways that data can be used against farmers too. Early in 2014 the American Farm Bureau Federation warned farmers that danger lurked in all that data sharing. In a January 22, 2014 report in NPR, Dan Charles summed up the Bureau's concerns this way:

"Mary Kay Thatcher, the farm bureau's senior director for congressional relations, says farmers should understand that when data move into the cloud, they can go anywhere.

For instance: Your local seed salesman might get the data, and he may also be a farmer—and thus your competitor, bidding against you for land that you both want to rent. 'All of a sudden he's got a whole lot of information about your capabilities,' Thatcher says.

Or consider this: Companies that are collecting these data may be able to see how much grain is being harvested, minute by minute, from tens of thousands of fields. That's valuable information, Thatcher says. "They could actually manipulate the market with it. They only have to know the information about what is actually happening with harvest minutes before somebody else knows it. I'm not saying they will," says Thatcher. "Just a concern."

Now imagine smack in the middle of all that, the growing complexities in securing that data. It's moving in multiple directions and it is unclear whether anyone, least of all the farmer, knows where it all resides much less how well protected this data is. The data then becomes exponentially vulnerable, i.e. the risk expands with the number of locations in which this data resides and is subject to the security weaknesses in each company that is holding the data.

Further, because the farmer (the data source) has little to no idea on what information is being reported to whom, there is no real way for him to protect his data. Even if the farmer had exceptional computer and security skills, it is doubtful that he could sufficiently protect his data or detect intrusions because too much of the data gathering mechanisms are deliberately hidden from him on the equipment. With so little security protection at the source, the data harvesters are also at risk of a hacker entering the data stream and/or following it to the data gatherer's repository and systems. A hacker could even mimic a machine and attack Dow, John Deere, Monsanto, or any other farm machine data harvester in a way very similar to the Target data breach. In several other ways too.

The Internet of Things Repeats the Farmer's Security Dilemma Ad Infinitum

Similar concerns lurk in machine data sharing in every arena. A wearable fitness app tells the wearer important information about their own health. But it could also report that information to the manufacturer who could then sell or share it with an employer or a health insurance company to be used against the owner. A home smart refrigerator can do the same thing by reporting to others what you and your family are eating. Hackers can have a field day with all of it.

The same is true with personal car data, which follows almost exactly the tractor scenario, albeit with different players. And if you think the gadgets that car insurance companies are handing out are a great freebie designed to save you money, think again. The data from those things are marketed as a way for insurance companies to reward good drivers but in all likelihood it will be used to hike premiums on everyone one hair shy of being a driving saint. If you opt out of giving them your data, the insurance companies will probably hike your premiums as a result. Make no mistake, no company collects and analyzes big data with the intent of *decreasing* its revenues and profits.

And today's tech-equipped cars are making selling a used car a security hazard too. Twenty years ago you merely signed over your title and handed the keys to the new buyer. But today you need to "wipe" your media center's Bluetooth connection data and purge phone records or else face your personal contacts and phonebook winding up in the hands of the next driver. According to an April 16, 2014 report in *Business Insider*, Vice President Joe Biden was caught up in this when he returned his leased Cadillac without wiping his cell phone contacts. Many of his "important numbers," including that of his wife Jill, remained in the car's data stores.

In the case of enterprises, data flowing from consumer devices to field sensors, and every other type of machine, is adding tremendous amounts of data that now has to be stored, analyzed, and protected. Further, malware can be attached or fed through these machines to corrupt or breach the entire database. But this threat can also extend to damaging real company property and operations, rather than just stealing data.

Therefore, big data use cases are two-fold in this area: managing the data generated by the machines and protecting the enterprise and the machines from malicious attacks implemented through machine data.

CURRENT AND FUTURE USE OF ANALYTICS IN SECURITY

We've touched on some of the challenges in modern day security and how big data is used to offset or thwart them. Let's now take a look at how security work itself is prone to problems and what can be done to address those issues.

At the moment, security tools, whether big data driven or not, are highly segmented. The result is a cacophony of noise. There are multiple alerts on these systems signifying a dizzying array of factors and most are plagued with false reads. Security professionals encounter extreme difficulty in making sense of it all, much less in prioritizing or effectively responding to any of it.

To remedy this, Avivah Litan, a respected analyst with Gartner Research, recommends the security industry move toward context-aware analytics. Specifically in her presentation, "Seven Dimensions of Context-Aware Security Analytics," at the 2014 Gartner

BI & Analytics Summit, she wrote that "context awareness refines the behavior of intelligent systems."

And indeed it does. The reason there are too many alerts and far too many false reads is that most intelligent systems today are not as smart as they could be. Everything is being analyzed in a vacuum, that is, in a data silo. Context bursts that silo and gives meaning to the actions noted.

Figure 12.4 is a slide from Litan's presentation showing the existing processes of intelligent systems in a typical ATM withdrawal.

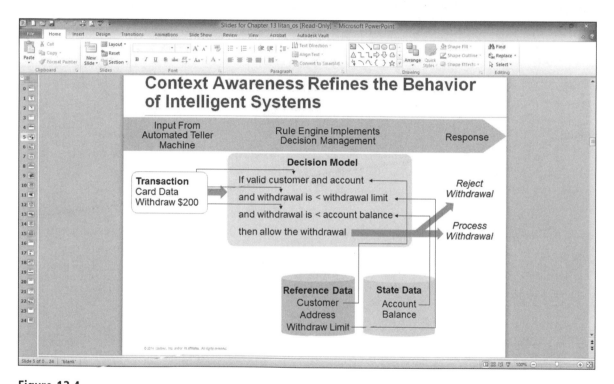

Figure 12.4
The intelligent systems in a typical ATM withdrawal.

Source: Gartner 2014 Business Intelligence & Analytics Summit Presentation, "The Seven Dimensions of Context-Aware Security Analytics," Avivah Litan, March 31–April 2, 2014.

Figure 12.5 is a slide from Litan's presentation showing that same process using context-aware security analytics.

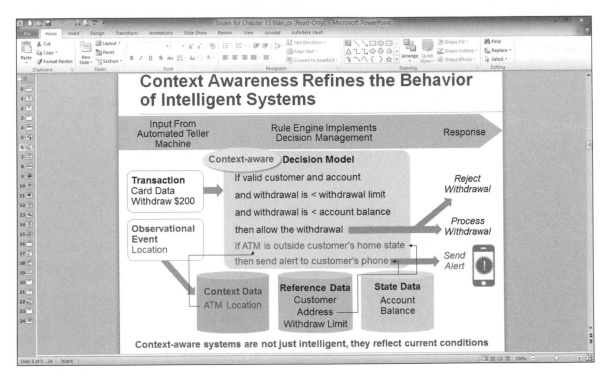

Figure 12.5
Using context-aware security analytics on the same process.
Source: Gartner 2014 Business Intelligence & Analytics Summit Presentation, "The Seven Dimensions of Context-Aware Security Analytics," Avivah Litan, March 31–April 2, 2014.

As you can tell from these two comparative slides, context-aware analytics aid both the bank's security efforts and its customer relationships. While all customers expect full security in their banking, they do not like their debit and credit cards unnecessarily blocked from use. And that happens quite regularly as bank security personnel struggle to identify legitimate purchases and withdrawals. By using context-aware analytics, as Litan suggests, customers are not unduly frustrated and bank security personnel can more efficiently direct their attention to blocking actual theft.

Litan further suggests that these context-aware analytics be applied in seven layers that collectively better inform security personnel and improve security protocols in a more comprehensive manner.

Figure 12.6 is a slide from Litan's presentation showing all seven layers.

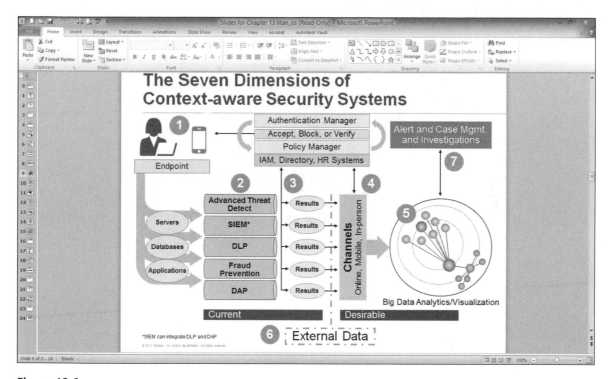

Figure 12.6

The seven layers of context-aware security systems.

Source: Gartner 2014 Business Intelligence & Analytics Summit Presentation, "The Seven Dimensions of Context-Aware Security Analytics," Avivah Litan, March 31–April 2, 2014.

Specific use cases include, but are not limited to, the following depicted in Figure 12.7, another slide from Litan's presentation.

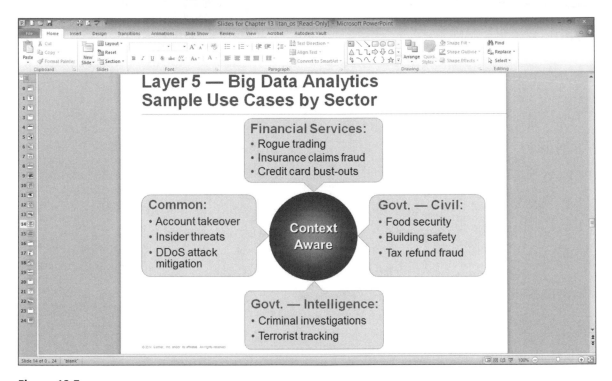

Figure 12.7

Layer 5: Big data analytics. Sample use cases by sector.

Source: Gartner 2014 Business Intelligence & Analytics Summit Presentation, "The Seven Dimensions of Context-Aware Security Analytics," Avivah Litan, March 31–April 2, 2014.

As was pointed out previously in other chapters, ROI is very high when the use case is highly defined and the output is both actionable and measurable. Litan makes that point as well, specific to context-aware security analytics. Here in Figure 12.8, she cites specific use cases that tend to render high ROI in the use of this type of analytics.

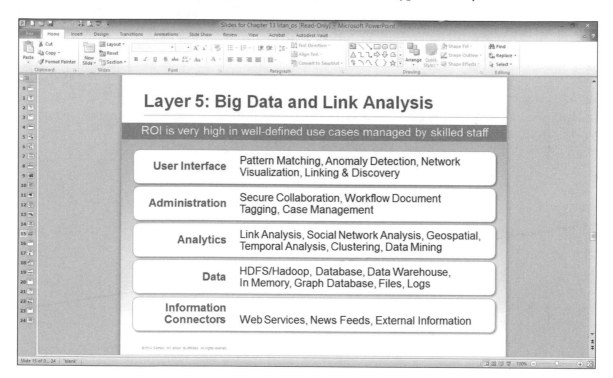

Figure 12.8
Return on investment is high with well-defined use cases.

Source: Gartner 2014 Business Intelligence & Analytics Summit Presentation, "The Seven Dimensions of Context-Aware Security Analytics," Avivah Litan, March 31–April 2, 2014.

All told, the security industry is arguably the most active in big data use and with good reason. It must protect itself as vigilantly as it protects customers and constituents. There is no margin for error in the face of increasing and more sophisticated threats and the ever-growing number of laws and regulations. Meanwhile, enterprises expect security efforts to be effective without impeding the flow of business or diminishing customer satisfaction. It's a big order that can only be fulfilled with strategic data analysis.

Summary

In this chapter you learned that for all practical purposes, both the physical and digital security sectors have blended into one, given the digitalization of devices and sensors and the advent of the Internet of Things. You discovered that as many if not more security risks reside in purposeful sharing and surreptitious data gathering by previously trusted sources, such as manufacturers and vendors, than as exist in the criminal world. Opportunities for hackers are growing and data breaches will increase. You also learned that many new security risks are popping up in unexpected places such as in the sale of a used car, the operation of a farm tractor and the use of smart home appliances. Ultimately you learned the many ways big data is both friend and foe in security efforts and a few ways to make it friendlier.

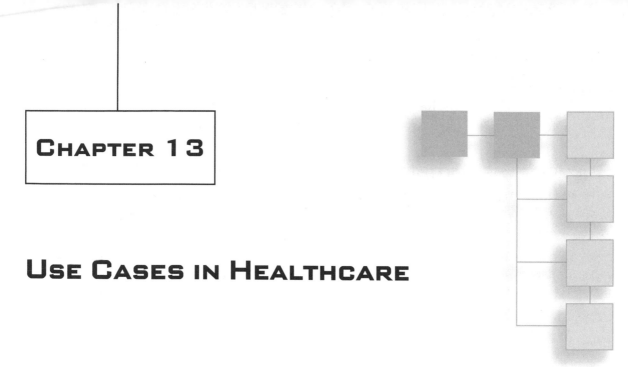

CHAPTER 13

USE CASES IN HEALTHCARE

One of the best uses for big data in terms of potential benefit for humanity is in healthcare and the medical sciences. After all, huge quantities of data have existed in this sector for quite some time. Further, these are already data-driven industries, albeit in a highly siloed and splintered fashion. It would appear that pooling data and analyzing disparate data sets for additional insights would be the next logical step. And indeed it is. It's obvious to all in this sector that medical advancements and better patient outcomes could rapidly result from such efforts.

Unfortunately, that is easier said than done. For one thing, many of the industry players are highly competitive and their information is frequently considered by the players to be highly proprietary. The very idea of sharing that information with existing and potential competitors is highly unnerving to them. For another thing, the industry is highly regulated. Revealing all their data could lead them to legal and compliance troubles they would have otherwise avoided. Topping the list of regulatory concerns is the Health Insurance Portability and Accountability Act of 1996 (HIPAA), as amended by the Health Information Technology for Economic and Clinical Health Act (HITECH), and its counterparts in other nations, which safeguard patient health information. How does one go about sharing data on thousands if not millions of patients when the barrier is so high to sharing data on just one patient?

Despite these challenges, efforts are underway to share data in order to speed cures, treatments, and vaccines; rapidly shift to models designed to improve patient outcomes; optimize the shift to genetic-based, personalized medicines to replace current antibiotics that will soon no longer be effective; find new and more effective ways to prevent health issues from developing in the first place; and innovate entire healthcare systems on a scale never before seen. But these are just a few of the goals. There are more, many more.

SOLVING THE ANTIBIOTICS CRISIS

Part of the impetus for hurrying the use of big data to achieve these ends comes from a pressing lack of time. For one thing, bacteria are evolving to the point that current common antibiotics will no longer work effectively. One widely known example of such an evolved organism is methicillin-resistant Staphylococcus aureus, or MRSA. But MRSA is not an aberration. Soon, very soon, nearly all harmful bacteria will be antibiotic resistant. Indeed, Dr. Arjun Srinivasan, an associate director at the Centers for Disease Control and Prevention, told *Frontline* in October 2013:

> *"For a long time, there have been newspaper stories and covers of magazines that talked about 'The end of antibiotics, question mark?' Well, now I would say you can change the title to 'The end of antibiotics, period.'*
>
> *We're here. We're in the post-antibiotic era. There are patients for whom we have no therapy, and we are literally in a position of having a patient in a bed who has an infection, something that five years ago even we could have treated, but now we can't. ..."*

Dr. Srinivasan rightly pointed out in that same interview that antibiotic resistance is not only dangerous on its own, but that it also renders other medical treatments that impede the patient's own immune system dangerous too. In other words, surgeries we see as minor and routine today suddenly become deadly; the same is true with other medical treatment and procedures such as organ transplants, kidney dialysis, and chemotherapy for cancer patients.

As a stop-gap measure, Dr. Srinivasan continued to say in that interview that the medical profession has reached back in its archives to find older antibiotics that haven't been used in years:

> *"What that means is that we've had to actually reach back into the archives, if you will. We've had to dust off the shelves [and revisit] some older antibiotics that we haven't used in many, many years. We stopped using them because they were very toxic, and as new antibiotics came about that weren't so toxic, we of course stopped using these older antibiotics.*
>
> *Colistin is a great example. And now we're back. We're using a lot of colistin, and we're using more of it every year. It's very toxic. We don't like to use it. It damages the kidneys. But we're forced to use it in a lot of instances.*

But what's really worrisome is that now we're seeing bacteria that are resistant even to colistin, so there are infections for which we have really nothing to offer a patient. We're in a situation where the patient will get better or the patient won't get better based on whatever the defenses the patient might have, but we have nothing to offer them to help them get better."

The Lancet, a serious and well respected medical journal, published a report by *The Lancet Infectious Diseases* Commission on November 17, 2013 titled "Antibiotic Resistance: Global Response Needed." That report clearly states the problems inherent in facing and solving the worldwide threat of antibiotic resistant organisms:

Many efforts have been made to describe the many different facets of antibiotic resistance and the interventions needed to meet the challenge. However, coordinated action is largely absent, especially at the political level, both nationally and internationally... Within just a few years, we might be faced with dire setbacks, medically, socially, and economically, unless real and unprecedented global coordinated actions are immediately taken.

Another huge obstacle to overcoming this threat is economic, both in terms of limited resources due to struggling economies and in terms of profitability for pharmaceutical companies. *The Lancet* report says this about the effects of profit-seeking on antibiotic development:

Only two new classes of antibiotic have reached the market since the 1970s; Coates and Bergstrom state a clear need exists for the development of new products. However, economic challenges around the potential profitability (and hence incentive to invest in research and development) of new antibiotics remain. Innovative funding solutions are needed to promote research in this specialty, while removing the incentive for pharmaceutical companies to attempt to maximize sales volume of any newly developed product. Figures from the Office of Health Economics show that the value of a new musculoskeletal drug to a pharmaceutical company is likely to be 20 times higher than the value of a new antibiotic, and make the scale of the funding challenge plain. New models of collaboration, including academia, research funders, and not-for-profit organizations, could restart the stalled engine of antibiotic discovery.

And there, ladies and gentlemen, lies the very serious motivation for the use of big data in solving these problems despite the challenges they present to individual privacy. Because if we don't, plenty of individuals around the world will die.

Using Big Data to Cure Diseases

Infections are not the only things claiming human lives in increasing numbers. Cancers, heart disease, diabetes, and other ills are too. Improved treatments and cures for these are too slow in coming to save the millions of people who routinely die from these around the globe.

Together this points to a dire need to share massive amounts of information with both traditional and non-traditional researchers worldwide in a massive, collaborated hunt for effective solutions. Why the focus on including non-traditional researchers too? Because often the best solutions come from minds not confined to traditional thinking, teachings, or profit oriented. For example, a 16-year-old boy named Jack Andraka recently accomplished more in his sophomore year of high school than his professional counterparts had in decades.

"I created a new way to detect pancreatic, ovarian, and lung cancer that costs three cents and takes five minutes to run," he said in a CBS Evening News interview in May 2013. "It's 168 times faster, over 26,000 times less expensive, and over 400 times more sensitive than our current methods of diagnosis. Eighty-five percent of all pancreatic cancers are diagnosed late, when someone has less than a two percent chance of survival. And our current test costs $800 per test and misses 30% of all pancreatic cancers."

To tackle problems as huge as we are incurring today, all hands must be on deck, whether they are talented high school teens, biohackers, academia, or government or commercial researchers. Time is quite literally running out both for affected individuals and mankind as a whole.

From Google to the CDC

Sixteen-year-old Jack Andraka said he used data he found on Google and simply "tinkered" in his bedroom to find a new, faster, more effective, and cheaper way to detect cancer. Think about that for a moment. Just with the amount of data that a teenage boy can find on Google, a serious medical advancement came into being. Now think about what can be accomplished if medical and patient data are pooled and made accessible to thousands if not millions of innovative minds around the world.

But why can't they just do that using Google search like the kid did, or even use existing big data tools such as Google Flu Trends, you might ask. The answer is that medical and scientific big data exists far beyond the confines of the Internet. That which is online, or collected digitally online, is too limiting. Further, for such data to be useful it must be exacting and precise. It must follow strict protocols and include traditional data collection methods and refined statistical analysis.

Consider the case of Google Flu Trends versus the CDC's traditional methods of tracking outbreaks of the flu. A paper titled "The Parable of Google Flu: Traps in Big Data Analysis" authored by David Lazer, Ryan Kennedy, Gary King, and Alessandro Vespignani and published by Harvard, explained why Google lost in comparison to the CDC:

In February 2013, Google Flu Trends (GFT) made headlines but not for a reason that Google executives or the creators of the flu tracking system would have hoped. Nature reported that GFT was predicting more than double the proportion of doctor visits for influenza-like illness (ILI) than the Centers for Disease Control and Prevention (CDC), which bases its estimates on surveillance reports from laboratories across the United States. This happened despite the fact that GFT was built to predict CDC reports.

The problems we identify are not limited to GFT. Research on whether search or social media can predict x has become commonplace and is often put in sharp contrast with traditional methods and hypotheses. Although these studies have shown the value of these data, we are far from a place where they can supplant more traditional methods or theories.

"Big data hubris" is the often implicit assumption that big data are a substitute for, rather than a supplement to, traditional data collection and analysis. We have asserted that there are enormous scientific possibilities in big data. However, quantity of data does not mean that one can ignore foundational issues of measurement, construct validity and reliability, and dependencies among data. The core challenge is that most big data that have received popular attention are not the output of instruments designed to produce valid and reliable data amenable for scientific analysis.

The initial version of GFT was a particularly problematic marriage of big and small data. Essentially, the methodology was to find the best matches among 50 million search terms to fit 1,152 data points. The odds of finding search terms that match the propensity of the flu but are structurally unrelated, and so do not predict the future, were quite high. GFT developers, in fact, report weeding out seasonal search terms unrelated to the flu but strongly correlated to the CDC data, such as those regarding high school basketball. This should have been a warning that the big data were overfitting the small number of cases, a standard concern in data analysis.

This ad hoc method of throwing out peculiar search terms failed when GFT completely missed the nonseasonal 2009 influenza A–H1N1 pandemic. In short, the initial version of GFT was part flu detector, part winter detector. GFT engineers updated the algorithm in 2009, and this model has run ever since, with a few changes announced in October 2013.

Although not widely reported until 2013, the new GFT has been persistently overestimating flu prevalence for a much longer time. GFT also missed by a very large margin in the 2011–2012 flu season and has missed high for 100 out of 108 weeks starting with August 2011. These errors are not randomly distributed. For example, last week's errors predict this week's errors (temporal autocorrelation), and the direction and magnitude of error varies with the time of year (seasonality). These patterns mean that GFT overlooks considerable information that could be extracted by traditional statistical methods.

In Figures 13.1 and 13.2 you can see screenshots of Google Flu Trends and the CDC's weekly U.S. influenza map, respectively. This is to illustrate their reporting tools only. The two figures are not directly comparable here as they are of different time periods. The Google Flu Trends screenshot was taken on April 12, 2014. The CDC screenshot is of week ending April 5, 2014.

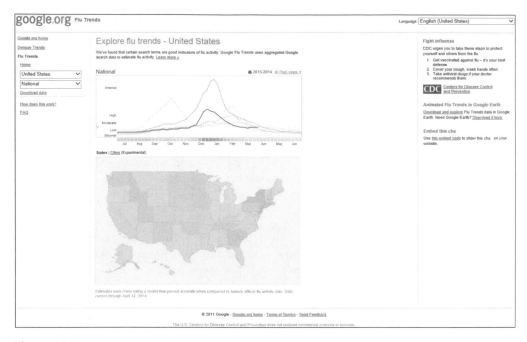

Figure 13.1
Google Flu Trends from April 12, 2014.

Source: Google Flu Trends taken from https://www.google.org/flutrends/us/#US.

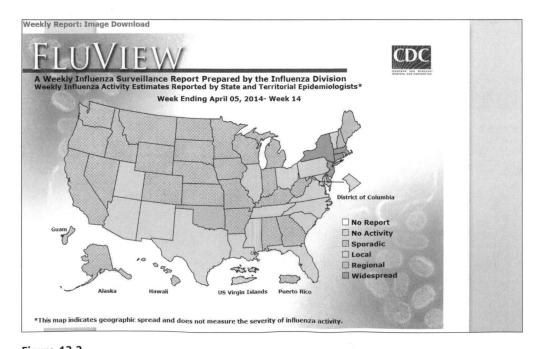

Figure 13.2
The CDC's weekly influenza map and data reporting for the week ending April 5, 2014.

Source: CDC's weekly influenza map and data reporting for the week ending April 5, 2014 taken from http://www.cdc.gov/flu/weekly/usmap.htm.

Therein lies not only the problem but the solution. It is the combination of all data—traditional data and statistical methods combined with new data inputs and new algorithms—that renders the most accurate outcomes. Even the teenaged Jack Andraka had to move beyond online research to finish his work in developing a new means to detect cancer. From the aforementioned CBS Evening News report:

"Jack requested space from research labs to pursue his work nearly 200 times," said President Obama. "200 times he asked, 200 times he was turned down. Finally, with the help of some folks at Johns Hopkins, he got the research facilities that he needed."

This is why it is important to not only add traditional medical and scientific data to the mix but to make it accessible to a wide audience and further, to enable the inclusion of new data as it becomes available, such as the results of young Andraka's work in an actual Johns Hopkins lab.

To this end, health organizations, both profit and nonprofit, and government agencies such as the CDC are now making data sets widely available for public use.

CDC's Diabetes Interactive Atlas

One example of how the CDC is doing this can be found on the agency's online Diabetes Interactive Atlas. The Atlas depicts national, state, and county data in a collection of maps, tables, graphs, and motion charts and enables the viewing of data in myriad ways simultaneously. Figure 13.3 shows the features, tutorials, FAQ, data resources, and sample visualizations on the homepage of the Atlas. The information is available for public use and is free. Users need only click on the features or data sources they want to use. Further, users can drill down from there using a variety of filters.

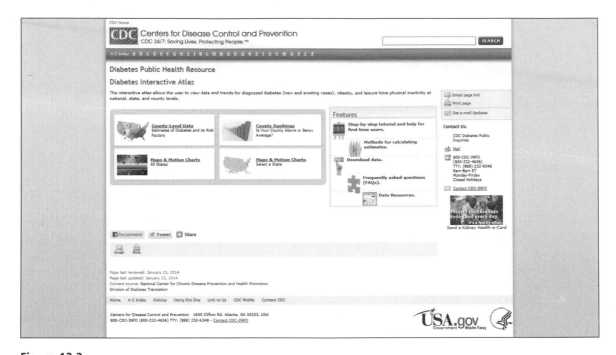

Figure 13.3
The Diabetes Interactive Atlas web page on the CDC website depicting features and data available from the CDC on diabetes.

Source: Diabetes Interactive Atlas website on the CDC website found at http://www.cdc.gov/diabetes/atlas/.

"We use data from traditional collection methods such as surveys, administrative type data such as from hospitalizations and the Agency for Healthcare Research and Quality (AHRQ), and other reliable sources," said Linda S. Geiss, Diabetes Surveillance Team Lead, Division of Diabetes Translation at the Centers for Disease Control and Prevention, in a phone interview.

"Electronic health records (EHRs) data is more about quality of care and mostly helpful to doctors," she explained. "But EHR, state hospitalization, and Veteran's Administration data, and all these different ownerships of data, will eventually be combined as there is an information revolution underway here in the United States. But right now I don't think we have really big data at least not like Great Britain has. They have a lot of encounter data."

She underscored the importance of the traditional survey data the CDC uses, something we can see for ourselves in the above mentioned comparison between Google Flu Trends and the CDC's flu data analysis.

"Surveys add stuff you can't get [solely] from medical records," she said. "We developed a method using census, behavioral risk factor surveillance systems, and we used that data to estimate risk and new diabetes incidents (new cases)."

Even so, it's slow going to get even more reliable data in the system to further aid public and private researchers, healthcare providers, and public health policy efforts.

"Any data system has a lot of privacy concerns and confidentiality issues to address," she said. "The more detailed you get, the more difficult it is to protect privacy. Further, a lot of data systems are tied to national and state regulations so there are lots of compliance issues."

This situation makes it difficult for the CDC to collect more encounter and lab data on local levels and to share that data on a granular level as well. The irony is that counties and cities and townships desperately need that data as they are closest to the people most in need of help.

"Prevention happens at that level and people need that information," said Geiss. She said county-level data is mostly used by county public health agencies at the moment and that requests for more information at that level come in regularly. "People are most excited about our county-level estimates now. But the further down the scale on the geographic level we go, the less data we have. Our samples aren't such that we can estimate everything at the county and state level."

Figure 13.4 shows county data for the state of Georgia. Users can use the slide to change to data in specific years or to watch the change in the data over the years. Rolling over the state reveals the name of each county and clicking on a county reveals that county's data on cases of diagnosed diabetes.

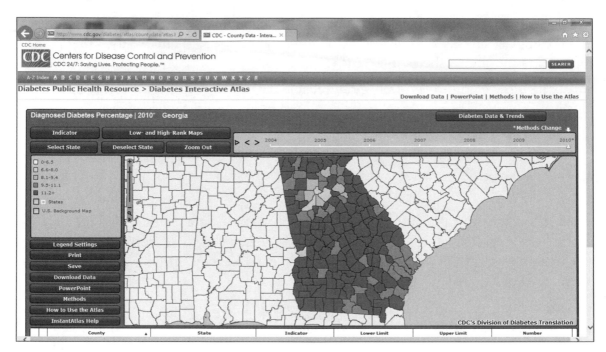

Figure 13.4
The Diabetes Interactive Atlas web page on the CDC website depicting county data for the state of Georgia.

Source: Diabetes Interactive Atlas page on the CDC website found at http://www.cdc.gov/diabetes/atlas/.

Of course the CDC offers more data than just data on diabetes. Much of it is available through its websites but if you need something else other than what you find, you can always contact the CDC to request additional information.

Also, Geiss mentioned the Agency for Healthcare Research and Quality (AHRQ) as one of the CDC's many quality data sources. It should be noted that the AHRQ possesses the largest data collection on hospital care data in the United States. That data is publicly available as well. Figure 13.5 shows the different data sets and tools available there, organized by type of inquiry.

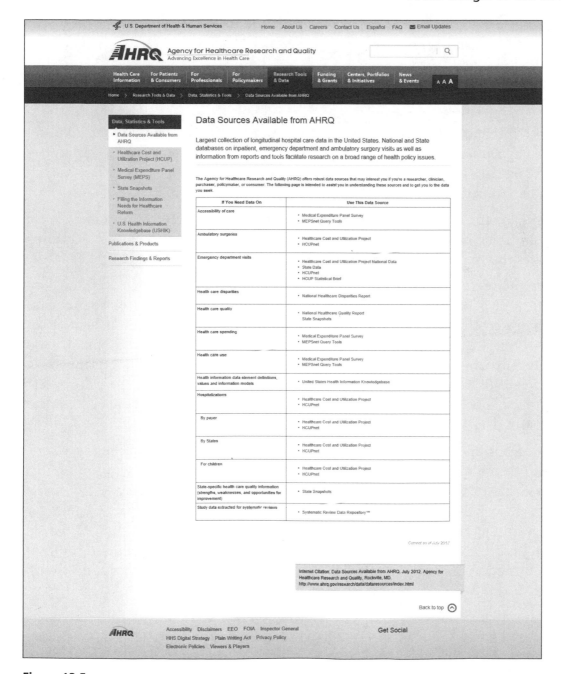

Figure 13.5

The U.S. Department of Health and Human Services Agency for Healthcare Research and Quality (AHRQ) Data Resources web page.

Source: The U.S. Department of Health and Human Services Agency for Healthcare Research and Quality (AHRQ) Data Resources web page found at http://www.ahrq.gov/research/data/dataresources/index.html.

It is nearly everyone's hope that health data will one day be widely available from all reliable sources, but in such a way that privacy is protected. There is real momentum in sharing healthcare today and that will only increase over time.

Project Data Sphere

Ironically, patients and patient advocacy groups *do* want their data added to the mix, and want that to happen fast, despite privacy concerns. The sicker patients are, the faster they want to see their data put to good use—if not for their benefit, then certainly fast enough to benefit others suffering from the same disease, disorder, or disability.

"Patients who go on trials are eager to see the results improve outcomes for others," said Nancy Roach, Chair of the patient advocacy group, Fight Colorectal Cancer. "Creating large databases that span multiple trials will help move the bar faster for patients."

And that dream of "creating large databases that span multiple [clinical] trials" is happening today. It's called Project Data Sphere. It's a non-profit effort supported by a diverse group of pharmaceutical companies, disease and medical researchers, and patient advocacy groups. Project Data Sphere is an independent initiative of the CEO Roundtable on Cancer's Life Sciences Consortium (LSC). It launched a new data sharing platform in April 2014 found online at www.ProjectDataSphere.org to "provide a single place where the community can broadly share and analyze high quality, historical patient-level cancer comparator-arm data."

In addition, organizers said at launch that the platform will also offer facilitated research networks and community research challenges intended to spark new discoveries. Initial data sets available in the Project Data Sphere platform were provided by AstraZeneca, Celgene, Pfizer, and Sanofi. These and other organizations, including the Alliance for Clinical Trials in Oncology (sponsored by the National Cancer Institute), Amgen, Bayer, Johnson & Johnson, Memorial Sloan-Kettering Cancer Center and Quintiles also committed to providing additional cancer data sets. SAS provided the data analytics at no charge to the initiative and free tools for Project participants.

Among the stated goals for the project are accelerated drug development, data standardization, improved and more efficient trial designs, and a better understanding of disease progression and endpoints. The initiative seeks expert help from legal and privacy experts, clinicians, commercial institutions, and patient advocacy groups to optimize their framework for responsible data sharing.

"We have nine data sets from different sources at launch with an additional 25 data sets in preparation," said Charles Hugh-Jones, vice president of Medical Affairs North America at Sanofi, a multinational pharmaceutical company, and a member of the CEO Roundtable on Cancer's Life Sciences Consortium (LSC) in a phone interview. "At launch, the data tends toward prostrate cancer. But value will grow as the data grows from more and more sources, all of it structured data from academic and industry phase III cancer clinical trials."

This means that data gathered in each of those trials for a single purpose, can now be repurposed for other efforts related to detecting, treating, and perhaps even curing cancers of every kind. See Figure 13.6.

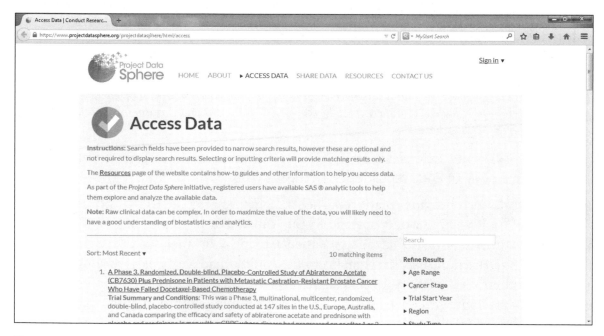

Figure 13.6
The Project Data Sphere "Access Data" web page showing instructions and data set sorting and filtering options for the nine data sets available, with an additional 25 data sets promised to be available soon.
Source: The Project Data Sphere web page found at https://www.projectdatasphere.org/projectdatasphere/html/access.

"There is a 90-95% attrition rate of moving from Phase I to final approval," said Hugh-Jones. That data is typically shelved and never looked at again since drug or treatment approval was never obtained. But just because the idea didn't work, for whatever reason, doesn't mean that the data gathered in the process isn't useful for something else. "Integrating the data sets adds considerable value," he said. "You can share and integrate data sets and analyze multiple data sets using Project Sphere." The point is to create an ecosystem where traditional and nontraditional researchers can independently and collaboratively solve problems."

To date, there are precious few such efforts underway in healthcare but there is huge interest and demand for them.

Sage Bionetworks

Another example of this type of effort is Sage Bionetworks. It defines itself and its work on its website as:

We work to redefine how complex biological data is gathered, shared and used. We challenge the traditional roles of individuals and groups, patients and researchers. Our work includes the building of platforms and services and undertaking research developing predictors relating to health. Arising in 2009 from a donation by Rosetta Inpharmatics (Merck Inc), we are a non-profit research organization based in Seattle and collaborate with a worldwide network.

We create technology platforms that facilitate collaboration on data, governance platforms that enable data sharing and reuse, run challenges to solve complex biomedical problems, and perform our own cutting-edge computational biology and research.

Sage Bionetworks' software is available in Github. Github is an open source website containing millions of open code repositories at Github.com.

Sage Bionetworks also provides platforms such as Synapse and BRIDGE, and a variety of tools, services, and creative works specific to this cause. For example, BRIDGE is a web-based, open source platform that allows patients to provide their data and insights as active research partners rather than remain in the traditional role as passive subjects. Synapse, on the other hand, is a platform designed to facilitate collaboration among scientific teams and integrations with analysis tools and programming environments.

This group too works with several large pharmaceutical companies as well as a number of biotechnology companies and international academic partners. Their projects cover a broader span of diseases than Project Sphere, however, including cardiovascular disease, cancer, metabolic disease, and neurobiology.

As the benefits of data pooling, sharing, and cross-data set analysis begin to show tangible benefits in healthcare and medical research, such efforts will become more commonplace. Just don't expect much to happen in this vein until privacy and competitive issues are better and more uniformly resolved.

THE BIOHACKER SIDE OF THE EQUATION

Now, about those "non-traditional researchers" all these new data initiatives are talking about. It's prudent to point out that they're not all gifted high school or grad students. Indeed, some of them are a different breed of talent entirely. Collectively they are called biohackers.

As is the case with computer hackers, they come in both the white hat and black hat varieties. That is, some biohackers are out to commit good deeds and others are set on doing the opposite. Like computer hackers before them, the vast majority of biohackers in these early days of the movement are indeed white hats.

One example of what biohackers are up to is creating cheap antibiotics in the field where medicines can't easily be shipped nor stored once they arrive for lack of refrigeration. They also hack DNA and experiment with creating genetic-based medicines, cures, and biological defenses. And believe it or not, they're doing all these things individually and alone in tents, at their kitchen sinks, and in garages, but also in groups at workshops and specialty gatherings, called everything from DIYbio (do-it-yourself-biology) to biohackathons. When they gather in groups, they learn from one another as well as collaborate on projects. Such gatherings happen all over the world and very frequently.

LA Biohackers is an example of such a group of amateur but highly talented scientists. Their meetings are always held on Sunday afternoons and the group has its very own lab in downtown LA. It was funded through members' fundraising efforts and open to all members for use. One of the workshops held in April 2014, to give you an idea of the types of projects they tackle, was called Backyard Brains SpikerBox Workshop—a collaborative affair hosted by Backyard Brains and the LA Biohackers. It may sound scary, but they were doing real science in that workshop.

Indeed, their science work is so respectable that the group announced on its website on March 17, 2013:

> LA Biohackers are the first non-university affiliated educational "franchise" of the Build-A-Genome course created at Johns Hopkins University. This NSF-funded project is looking to completely synthesize a significantly redesigned genome of Saccharomyces cerevisiae, more commonly known as brewer's or baker's yeast. Although normally taught to advanced undergraduates and early graduate students, we will be offering the class and the opportunity to directly contribute to a major scientific project along side prestigious universities. Adapting the course to a group that may have minimal existing biology background will be a process, but it's one that I know I am definitely looking forward to.

While most biohacker groups are strictly ad hoc, many are not. For example, classically trained biologist Ellen Jorgensen and her colleagues opened Genspace, a non-profit

DIYbio lab in Brooklyn devoted to citizen science, aka biohackers in this case. Genspace is government compliant, meaning that it meets the same government requirements as traditional labs do. She even gave a TED Talk in June 2012 called "Biohacking—You Can Do It, Too" to encourage others to build such labs and pursue biohacking.

Jorgensen's not the only one to endorse the effort; so does Microsoft founder Bill Gates. Steven Levy wrote this about Gates' thoughts on biohacking in an April 19, 2010 *Wired* article:

> *Just ask Bill Gates. If he were a teenager today, he says, he'd be hacking biology. "Creating artificial life with DNA synthesis. That's sort of the equivalent of machine-language programming," says Gates, whose work for the Bill & Melinda Gates Foundation has led him to develop his own expertise in disease and immunology. "If you want to change the world in some big way, that's where you should start—biological molecules." Which is why the hacker spirit will endure, he says, even in an era when computers are so ubiquitous and easy to control. "There are more opportunities now," he says. "But they're different opportunities. They need the same type of crazy fanaticism of youthful genius and naïveté that drove the PC industry—and can have the same impact on the human condition. In other words, hackers will be the heroes of the next revolution, too."*

There are numerous resources available to both beginner and advanced biohackers, including the OpenPCR and BioBricks projects. A polymerase chain reaction (PCR) machine is basically a copy machine for DNA. OpenPCR is a DIY kit containing everything needed to build a PCR machine—a "thermocycler designed to reliably control PCR reactions for DNA detection, sequencing, and other applications." It even ships with a Windows and Mac GUI application making it easier to use than traditional PCR machines. BioBricks Foundation provides fundamental building blocks used in synthetic biology which they call "biobricks." Being able to pick up parts like that considerably speeds the biohackers' work. Then there are virtual PCR labs such as one offered by the University of Utah and open source repositories like The Open Biohacking Project/Kit on Sourceforge.

There are also biohackers designing gear for other biohackers, such as a custom head for an ordinary Dremel motor tool which turns it into a highly effective and very cheap centrifuge. To view such a tool in action in a field tent in the hands of biohacker, Cathal Garvey, watch his Vimeo video at http://vimeo.com/23146278.

All told, biohackers are making serious headway into areas once thought as the fortified holdings of academics and giant pharmaceutical and biotech companies. Biohackers tend to produce, innovate and invent faster than many of the best funded R&D departments on the planet. In this way, they have become a threat to many incumbent industries. They are especially a threat to the pharmaceutical industry as a structure, which may, at least in part, explain why formerly bitter competitors are now open to teaming on big data projects to make discoveries faster. It may also explain why some of these companies are now bringing biohackers and other non-traditional researchers into the fold. It's simply better business to have them as part of the family than as determined and possibly agitated outside rivals.

Whatever is the case, data is being generated by citizen scientists as fast if not faster than their professional counterparts, and data analysis is extremely helpful to both the professional and citizen camps in reaching important breakthroughs at an accelerating pace. As noted in Chapter 8, on the rise of the collaborative economy, the business landscape is shifting beneath the feet of many industries. It's ordinary people working together and effectively replacing established industries that is causing much of that shift. Such disruptions call for unprecedented speed in creating new models and adapting to new circumstances. Big data analytics are ideally suited both to detecting such changes early and in helping companies respond to them.

EHRs, EMRs, and Big Data

No discussion on the role of big data in healthcare is complete without mention of the 2010 Affordable Care Act (ACA), also commonly referred to as Obamacare. While the Act has been controversial, for the purposes of this chapter we'll ignore the politics and examine its effects on healthcare data and data use instead.

Among the many technical requirements in the Act are the mandated use of electronic medical records (EMRs) and electronic health records (EHRs). To be clear, since confusion over the two terms is common, an EMR is a digital patient file created by a single healthcare provider and an EHR is a compilation of EMRs for a complete record on a single patient, parts of which come from different doctors and providers. For example, if patient Jane Doe sees Dr. Cureall, a single EMR is created of all Ms. Doe's visits to Dr. Cureall, complete with diagnosis on each visit, treatment and services rendered, drugs prescribed, tests ordered, and any referrals to other providers that might have been made. That EMR is then joined to that patient's total EHR, where other physicians and providers have also added their EMRs on that same patient plus shared data, such as X-rays and lab results within. This is helpful in that it creates a complete record of the patient's healthcare, thus helping to prevent medical mistakes and delays, and in accelerating diagnosis and the delivery of the correct treatment as well as eliminating unnecessary duplication in medical testing. For these reasons and others, patient outcome improves and healthcare costs (in theory) go down.

Geiss with the CDC mentioned earlier in her comments in this chapter that EHRs and EMRs are mostly helpful to doctors. That is true—for now. Soon though the data generated within and from those will be helpful to others as well. Chief among the beneficiaries will be the patients themselves. Patients will soon be able to view their entire medical records online and address any errors, reference instructions from their physicians as often as necessary, and in general be more in control and informed about their health and the care they are receiving. Gone are the days when a hospital or doctor could easily hide the fact that a sponge or tool was accidently left in a patient during surgery or that an infection was acquired in the hospital. This new transparency alarms many in the healthcare system, as it potentially provides the means for increased malpractice suits. However, it is hailed by many, from researchers and providers to patient advocacy groups, as a good means to partner with patients, glean more knowledge, and achieve better patient outcomes.

The ACA also requires new medical coding called ICD-10 or more specifically, ICD-10-CM for diagnosis coding and ICD-10-PCS for procedural coding. ICD-10 is far more detailed coding than the previously used and very antiquated ICD-9 coding. Once fully in effect, the new coding will provide a number of advantages, not the least of which will be highly useable structured data that can easily be searched and parsed as needed to transform all of U.S. healthcare.

As of this writing though, physicians and providers are struggling with computerized provider order entry (CPOE) and many of them have yet to master it. The result is pure havoc in many hospital environments. However, that is to be expected given the newness of ICD-10 coding and the almost overwhelming digital overhaul of the U.S. healthcare system. Add to that the shift from fee-for-service to pay based on patient outcome, and the uncertainty among providers as to how that shift will play out in terms of their pay, and things get chaotic quickly. However, things will settle down once providers become better acquainted and more accustomed to using the new technologies and codes. Like any technological shift, effective change management is key to success. Interestingly, big data tools—specifically analytics and visualizations—are helping with that too. A number of hospitals are using those tools now both to help physicians and other providers understand the changes and how to manage them and also in complying with the new mandates. In other words, with the use of big data tools, alerts can be sent to providers to urge specific actions to maintain compliance. The traditional way meant reports delivered after the fact, when it was too late to take corrective actions retroactively.

MEDICARE DATA GOES PUBLIC

Meanwhile, former Health and Human Services (HHS) Secretary Kathleen Sebelius announced in April 2014 the public release of Medicare data on services and procedures rendered, plus billing and payments to providers.

"Currently, consumers have limited information about how physicians and other healthcare professionals practice medicine," explained Sebelius in a statement to the press. "This data will help fill that gap by offering insight into the Medicare portion of a physician's practice. The data released today afford researchers, policymakers and the public a new window into healthcare spending and physician practice patterns."

The data released contained information from more than 880,000 healthcare providers who received in total $77 billion in Medicare payments in 2012, under the Medicare Part B Fee-For-Service program. Analyses can be done comparing 6,000 types of services, procedures and provider billing and payments.

The revelations on provider billing will likely be as big a help to patients, and as huge a shock to providers, as the Centers for Medicare and Medicaid Services' (CMS) earlier release of hospital charge data. That release exposed huge differences in hospital charges for the same services. For the first time ever, consumers could compare what hospitals charge for common inpatient and outpatient services across the United States. This information induced pricing pressures in the hospital industry. Until now, hospitals and providers worked hard to keep pricing a secret and to present billing information in such a way as to make it impossible for consumers to do hospital price comparisons. The public largely had assumed prices were similar or identical between hospitals. That notion was promptly dispelled. See Figures 13.7 and 13.8.

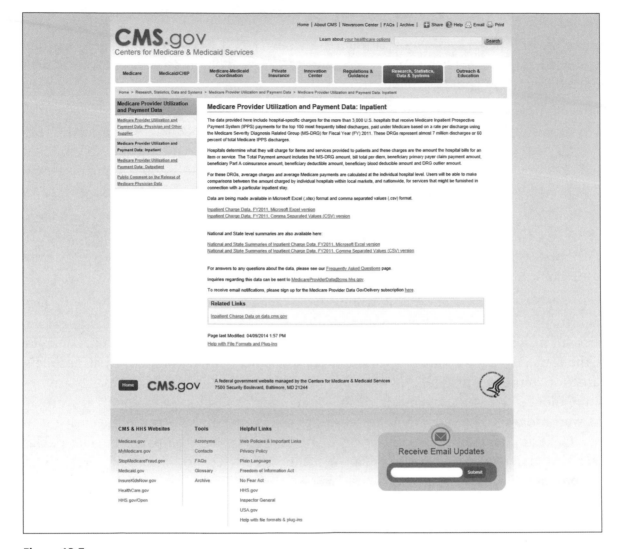

Figure 13.7
The CMS web page showing instructions and the hospital charge data set the agency calls "Medicare Provider Utilization and Payment Data: Inpatient."

Source: CMS.gov web page with access to hospital charge data found at http://www.cms.gov/Research-Statistics-Data-and-Systems/Statistics-Trends-and-Reports/Medicare-Provider-Charge-Data/Inpatient.html.

This new CMS release is the beginning of inducing pricing pressures on physicians and providers as well, making healthcare overall more competitive.

"Data transparency is a key aspect of transformation of the healthcare delivery system," said CMS Administrator Marilyn Tavenner in a statement to the press. "While there's more work ahead, this data release will help beneficiaries and consumers better understand how care is delivered through the Medicare program."

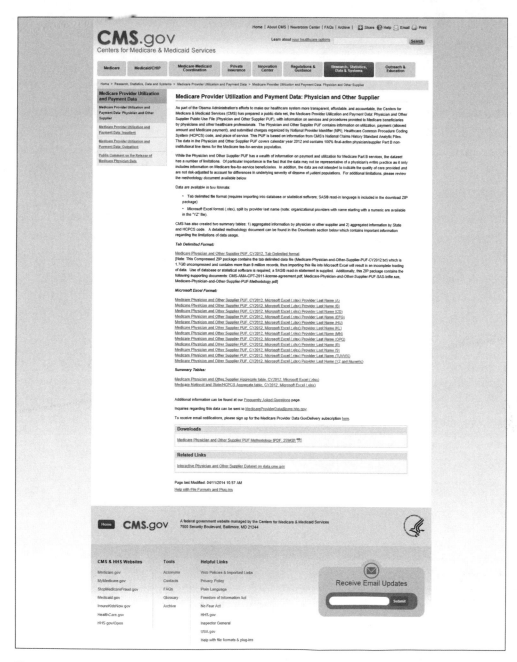

Figure 13.8

The CMS web page showing instructions and the physician data set the agency calls "Medicare Provider Utilization and Payment Data: Physician and Other Supplier."

Source: CMS.gov web page with access to physician data set found at http://www.cms.gov/Research-Statistics-Data-and-Systems/Statistics-Trends-and-Reports/Medicare-Provider-Charge-Data/Physician-and-Other-Supplier.html.

Expect more healthcare and medical research data to be released as more sources make it available for public use over the coming years.

Summary

As you can see from these use case examples, data is now center stage in healthcare on all sides of the industry. Patients are increasingly relying on it, as are researchers, developers, patient advocacy groups, clinicians, institutions, non-profits, and others. All are using data to advance their causes. Some of those efforts are broad collaborations; others are in direct conflict with one another.

Data is used in healthcare to cure humankind of what ails it and to break bottlenecks in discoveries and innovations. It is used to better patient outcomes and to battle rising costs. Big data is used to inform policymakers and to proactively warn providers of impending compliance issues on the hospital floor in real-time, as well as everything in between. Data reveals all from the drug abuser visiting multiple emergency rooms to get a fix to fraudulent insurance and Medicare/Medicaid claims to bad medical practices and price gouging by the industry.

It enlightens and improves healthcare but also illuminates and destroys healthcare as we know it. Those providers who wield data analysis well and take smart action will prosper. Those who don't, won't. The Information Age is behind us. We are now entering the Knowledge Era where facts matter and decisions are data-driven.

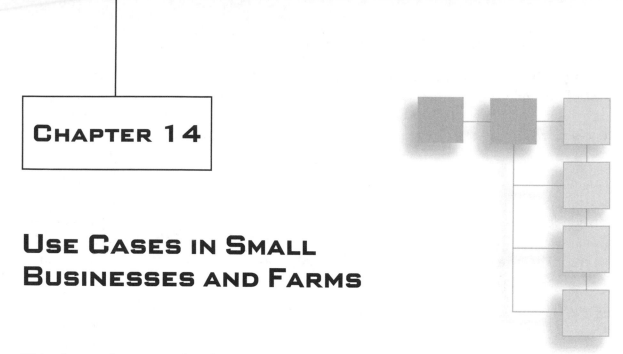

CHAPTER 14

USE CASES IN SMALL BUSINESSES AND FARMS

This chapter focuses on big data use cases in small and mid-sized enterprises of any kind. For the purpose of this chapter, family-owned and/or small farms are included in this category, as they share more in common with other small businesses in regards to data use than they do with large commercial farms.

However, given that arguably more farm equipment comes loaded with sensors, automated data gathering, and onboard analytics than say, a small bakery's, optometrist's, florist's, or restaurant chain's equipment does, and given the current push by large corporations to get farmers to add their data to a common pool, special attention is given to farms later in this chapter.

Otherwise, the general discussion of data use in small businesses is applicable to all small businesses, regardless of their industry. Certainly there are some industry-specific differences between small businesses, but core business functions, needs, and related data uses are very similar if not functionally identical in some cases.

BIG DATA APPLIES TO SMALL BUSINESS

As addressed earlier in this book, the term "big data" is unfortunate as it denotes mammoth collections of data sets when actually big data tools are more about complex computing than about data size. Small businesses sometimes misunderstand the term to mean big data tools are useful only to large businesses or useful to small businesses wrangling very large data, say in the technical or medical research industries. But this is not the case. Small businesses need neither possess large data sets nor work primarily with such in the natural course of their business in order to benefit from these tools. Nor should the idea of "complex computing" throw you off balance. Many of today's big data tools are easy to use and are getting easier every day. The crux of the effort hinges on your ability to strategize. From there, it's relatively easy to figure out which data you need and what to ask of it.

This chapter covers a number of data use cases that can aid small and mid-sized businesses (SMBs) in becoming more profitable and in growing their business, too. Conversely, it is also important to note how big data is changing the types of services now available to SMBs. A prime example of this is found in data-driven, emerging lending sources. These make capital more available and easier for most SMBs to qualify for than traditional bank loans.

In short, the overall marketplace is changing on every front. For one thing, big data gives SMBs incredible business advantages that were once only in reach of the biggest companies. But it also makes large companies more agile and innovative, and their offerings more personalized—strengths that formerly belonged to smaller businesses. This means that large companies using big data can better compete with the SMBs' legendary personalized service and innovative capabilities. This poses a new threat to SMBs.

In any case, failing to use data to drive decisions and predict your path forward not only leaves an SMB in the dark, but will eventually leave it crushed by other market forces.

THE LINE BETWEEN HYPE AND REAL-WORLD LIMITATIONS

That is not to say that big data hype is fact. Remember first and foremost, that big data is a tool and nothing more. It's a mighty powerful tool that can make all the difference in how profitable your operation will be, but a tool nonetheless. And while big data can give you important and even vital insights, it can't think for you. Indeed, it is the best strategists that win using big data, not those who own the most expensive, fanciest big data tools.

Critical thinking and analytical skills are required. So is the ability to strategize. In short, big data is no silver bullet substitute for business acumen. As is the case with any tool, it only works as well as the craftsman using it.

Remember also that knowledge is power. That is, the right knowledge at the right time, in the right place with the ability to act on it, is power. Otherwise, "knowledge" is mere trivia. And what you're after in your big data efforts is power. You want the power to know what's happening in your own business right now as well as the market at large. You want to know your customers well so you know what products or services will sell well and which need to be tweaked or discarded. You want the power to shave costs to the bone and still muscle your way forward. You want the power to see what's coming next so you can adapt and prosper no matter the circumstances. And all that, plus more, is what big data brings: the power of knowledge. It's still up to you to place it correctly and then figure out how best to use that knowledge, however.

PICKING THE RIGHT TOOL FOR THE JOB

Fortunately, many big data tools are free or available for a very minimal fee. That includes Google Analytics, Google AdWords, Google Earth, and MicroStrategy's Analytics Desktop. Others offer free trials, such as Tableau, so you can test them in your business before you buy. Still others that generally cost more are more powerful alone or added to these free tools. Although this book is not about tools per se, but about the strategic use of data, it is important to note the vast diversity in big data tools in order to illustrate how they are best used in different business strategies.

Take this example of Google Earth made by Tim Devaney and Tom Stein in their May 30, 2013 post in *Forbes' BrandVoice*:

> *Roofing contractors are not the first professionals who spring to mind when you think cutting-edge technology. But some roofers are using big data to drastically cut their costs. A contractor used to take a call, drive to look at a roof and, often, realize it was not a job he could take on. That meant time and money wasted. Smart roofing companies use big data to avoid that expense. A contractor gets a call, takes an address and inspects the roof at Google Earth. If he does the job, he can use Google Earth to check out the roofs of other homes in the neighborhood and offer the owners a deal.*

Most small businesses would not think of something so easy to use as Google Earth or Bing Maps Bird's Eye to be a big data tool. But that is precisely what they are. That's one of the most interesting things about big data, the end analysis is quite often deceptively simple to use. But this also goes back to the earlier points that:

- Big data is not just for big companies.
- The information has little to no value unless you act on it.
- It is your strategy borne out in its use that benefits or harms your company.

In the roofing example, the roofers using Google Earth to evaluate a job before they take it, and to find other homes in the area ripe for the selling of their services while they are working in the area, are great strategic uses of this big data tool. Just having Google Earth on the phone in their pocket would not have benefitted their company at all.

Figure 14.1 shows Google Earth's landing page with the choice of the free or the Pro versions. There is also an Enterprise version for companies that own large amounts of geospatial data. Many small businesses need only the free version to fulfill their needs. However, the Pro version provides more services and customer support. You can use Google Pro in a trial version for a limited amount of time to see if you need these features for your business. Figure 14.2 shows some of your choices in device modes, related products, and tools, as well as a few interesting highlights to warm up your imagination in the Google Earth free mode. You may also want to take a look at the options available to you in Bing Maps Bird's Eye.

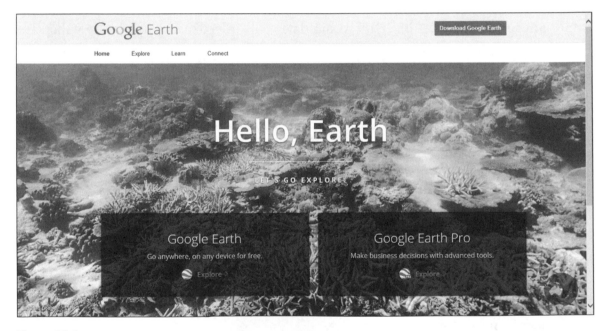

Figure 14.1
Google Earth's landing page with the choice of the free version or the Pro version. One click takes you where you need to go.
Source: Google Inc.

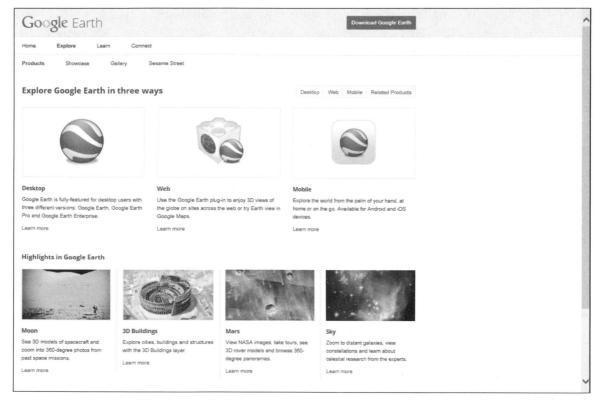

Figure 14.2
Your choices in device modes, related products, and tools, as well as a few interesting highlights to warm up your imagination in the Google Earth free mode.
Source: Google Inc.

Coming back to the issue of big data tool diversity, let's consider Google Analytics and its applications. Google Analytics reveals a great deal of information about your customers and prospects in regards to your ads, videos, company website, and mobile apps, as well as across social media, and more. It's a great set of tools to use to learn more about where your customers are, what they like, and what they're likely to buy from you. Further, you can add other apps to it to discover even more.

Figure 14.3 shows the Google Analytics Applications Gallery, including some of the apps you'll find there. Each is capable of extending Google Analytics in its own way. Notice the category listings on the left side of the page where you can choose apps according to specific tasks such as Email Marketing, Customer Relationship Management (CRM), and Business Intelligence (BI). How you choose to configure these tools depends entirely on your strategy and your specific company needs.

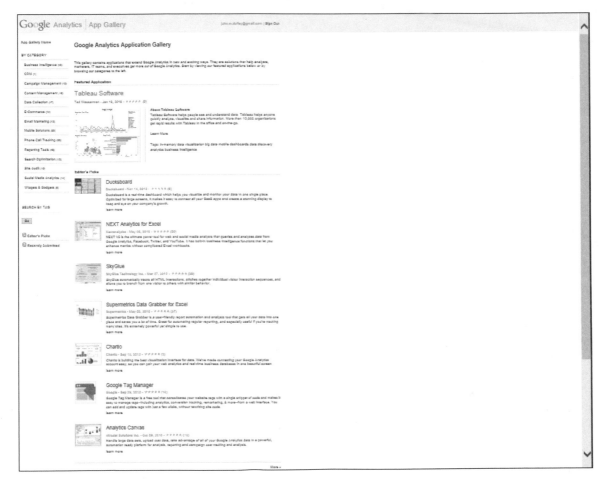

Figure 14.3
Google Analytics Application Gallery showing a sample of the available apps that can be used to extend Google Analytics.
Source: Google Inc.

However, you may find that a free tool built for easy expansion to a paid-professional version is the better choice for your company. These enable you to upgrade without any interruption or need to re-enter your data. In other words, you can upgrade on the fly with little fuss. An example of such is MicroStrategy Desktop Analytics (see Figures 14.4 and 14.5). With this tool you can convert from the free version to the more muscular professional MicroStrategy program with little more than a click. By comparison, if you use Google Analytics and maybe another app compatible with it, transferring to a larger, stronger program with more features after your company grows may prove to be a bigger pain than you bargained for. Further, MicroStrategy offers several data sets for the taking that you may find useful too. This should not be construed as an endorsement of any one product, but rather as a discussion of things you might want to consider in tool selections.

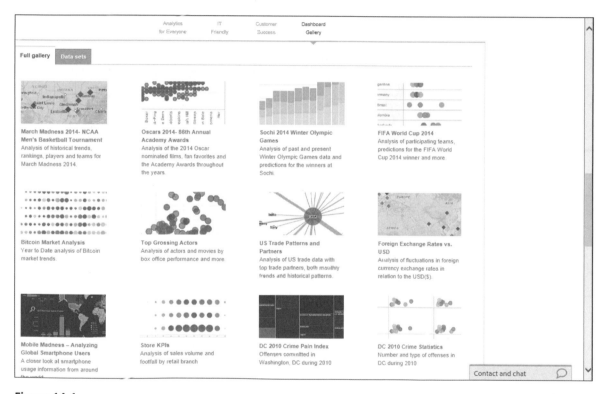

Figure 14.4

MicroStrategy's visualization gallery enables you to see which types of visualizations might be most useful to you and your company.

Source: MicroStrategy, Inc. Used with permission.

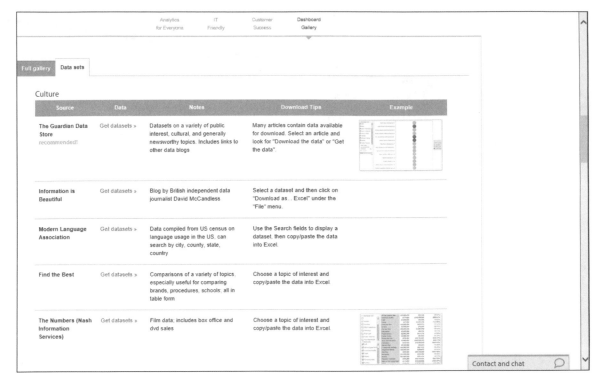

Figure 14.5
A sampling of data sets available through the MicroStrategy website, which include such categories as public interest topics, comparison data sets, and film and DVD sales data.
Source: MicroStrategy, Inc. Used with permission.

Several vendors provide big data products and services tailored to SMB use. You may want to consider selecting one of them to aid you with big data projects, particularly if your needs are beyond the scope of free tools and/or if you lack the IT skills or personnel to deploy a sophisticated big data program on your own.

"Because IT staffs are typically small, it is important to choose a trusted technology and services partner who will really invest in getting to know your business and help to evaluate which solutions will best fit your requirements and support implementation," says Judy Smolski, vice president of IBM Midmarket. "Next, consider how advances in cloud computing can help you manage the costs of solutions around big data. Finally, when it comes to selecting the right data solutions, begin by prioritizing which pieces of data are most important to your business. It may be easy to access literally petabytes of data, but the challenge is prioritizing the data and determining how to leverage it for business advantage."

None of this discussion should be construed as an endorsement or disparagement of any product listed, but rather as examples of the many differences found between products and to illustrate that there are numerous things to be considered, such as whether the tool will scale as your company grows, compatibility and integration issues, costs such as free versus fee, your IT staff's skills or limitations in their time, and others.

You can use big data tools to mine your own customer data, including loyalty card data, and data that you import from other sources, such as social media, credit report data, and other data helpful in understanding and/or qualifying your customers and prospects. In this way, you can precisely target high-value customers and prospects plus personalize sales pitches and business offers. This enables you to increase your sales and decrease the time you spend chasing after them.

Other chapters in this book will aid you in determining which data sources you need to tap to augment the data you already have, or to use in other quests for which you have no data of your own. Chapters in this book are organized by industry, but in reality, you'll likely need data from several of them in order to better understand your own market, cut costs, and leverage developments and innovations coming from other industries. For example, a florist or a small business using a fleet of vehicles will benefit from using data from both the transportation and energy sectors. You'll find data sources from each in their respective chapters. Such information may enable you to cut or predict future costs in fuel for your own fleet or cut costs in shipping if you're using third-party transportation services. There are other benefits you can realize too, such as this one plucked from the same *Forbes' BrandVoice* article:

"Another trend is the rise of sensors to track and make decisions," says Steve King, partner at Emergent Research and coauthor of the recent report The New Data Democracy: How Big Data Will Revolutionize the Lives of Small Businesses and Consumers. "Small businesses are starting to benefit from that. FedEx has a cool product called SenseAware that lets you put sensors on perishable packages. It provides a shipment's exact location, precise package temperature and information on whether a package has been opened or exposed to light or whether it was dropped, based on the recorded G forces."

So if you own, say, a flower shop, you know if your suppliers are providing you with inventory that's fresh and handled properly. You can use big data to plan better, work smarter—and make your business bloom.

Be sure to read other chapters in this book with an eye toward how you can use this information to better your own business circumstances. In this way, you won't be swayed by big data hype, but instead making decisions based on what your business needs and what you can realistically do. Whatever you do, don't assume that other sectors will not affect you, as they most certainly will. Also don't assume that your existing competitors will remain the same. With the current blending of offerings and convergence of industries currently underway, it is very likely that new competition will arise from industries you previously did not consider as competitors.

Examples of External Data Sources You Might Want to Use

As mentioned previously, one of the big advantages to using big data tools is the ability to augment your own data with data from other sources. It's quite common for SMBs to wonder where they might find such data sources and what the costs of such might be. There are many public data sets available for free and more showing up everyday. Privately owned data usually does require a fee to be paid, although it is frequently nominal. You will have to check prices with private sources individually as pricing often is not posted publicly or is subject to change without notice necessitating verification before each purchase.

Although it is not possible to include every data source in this chapter, as there are too many and more are added everyday, this section contains a few examples of the types of data sets that are available and the sources where you can find that data. It would also be prudent to read other chapters in this book to find other data sources specific to the varying needs of your business. Your goal should not be to gather all the data out there, but to find the data sets you need to discover the answer(s) you seek.

Some big data vendors will offer data sets, as mentioned earlier and shown in Figure 14.5. An example of another kind of vendor sponsored/supported data sets is Many Eyes, an experimental data sharing project by IBM Research and IBM Cognos. Many Eyes is "set up to allow the entire Internet community to upload data, visualize it, and talk about their discoveries with other people," according to its own website description. Figures 14.6 and 14.7 show the Many Eyes project website. The project's more formal explanation on the website says:

The heart of the site is a collection of data visualizations. You may want to begin by browsing through these collections—if you'd rather explore than read directions, take a look!

On Many Eyes you can:

1. *View and discuss visualizations*

2. *View and discuss data sets*

3. *Create visualizations from existing data sets*

If you register, you can also:

4. *Rate data sets and visualizations*

5. *Upload your own data*

6. *Create and participate in topic centers*

7. *Select items to watch*

8. *Track your contributions, watchlist, and topic centers*

9. *See comments that others have written to you*

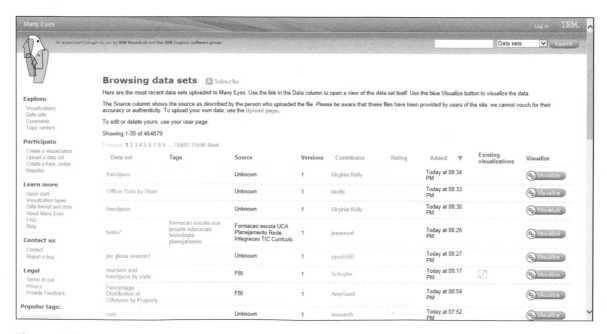

Figure 14.6
A sampling of data sets available on the Many Eyes website.
Source: Many Eyes project by IBM Research and IBM Cognos.

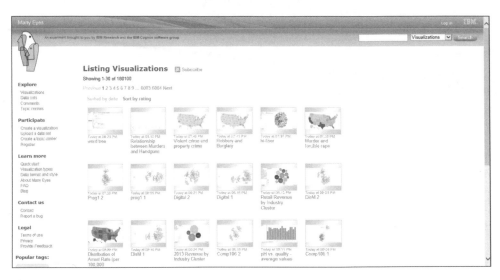

Figure 14.7
A sampling of data visualizations available on the Many Eyes website.

Source: Many Eyes project by IBM Research and IBM Cognos.

Other data sets are offered through web services companies, such as through Amazon Web Services (AWS). Figure 14.8 shows a sampling of public data sets available on the AWS website. Note the list of categories and developer resources on the left side of the page.

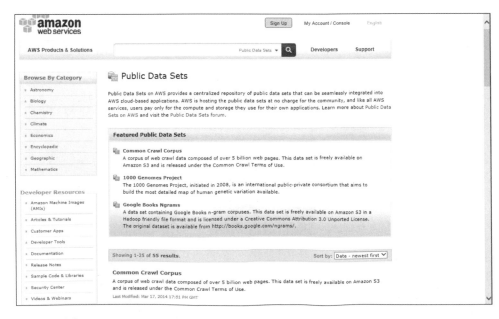

Figure 14.8
A sampling of public data sets available on the AWS website. Note the list of categories and developer resources on the left side of the page.

Source: Amazon Web Services (AWS).

There are also data sets offered by Yahoo! Figure 14.9 shows the Yahoo! Labs data set offerings.

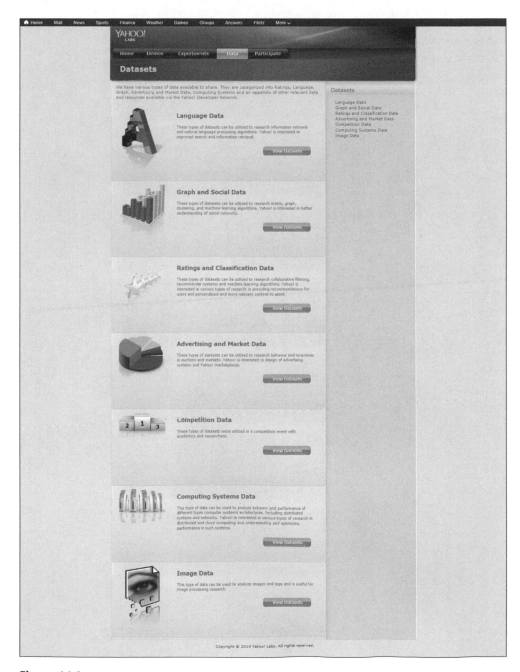

Figure 14.9
The Yahoo! Labs data set offerings.
Source: Yahoo! Labs.

Other data sets are offered on a variety of open data sites usually centered on a specific or special interest, such as the Open Science Data Cloud (OSDC). Figure 14.10 shows a sampling of data sets available on OSDC.

Figure 14.10
A sampling of data sets available on the Open Science Data Cloud (OSDC) website.

Source: Open Science Data Cloud at https://www.opensciencedatacloud.org/publicdata/.

Some of the most bountiful sources for data sets come from federal or city/county government agencies. Data.gov, shown in Figure 14.11, is the central repository of federal agencies.

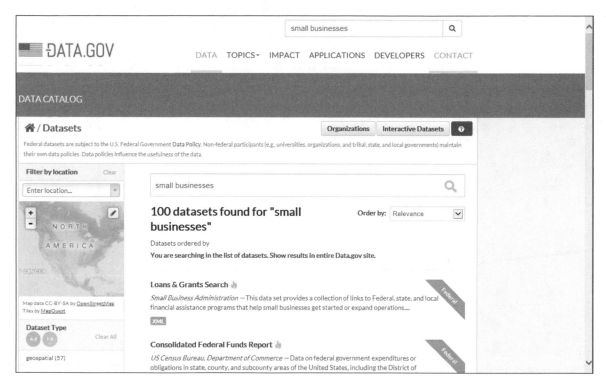

Figure 14.11
The Data.gov website with a sampling of data sets found using "small businesses" as the key in the site's search bar.
Source: U.S. federal government at Data.gov.

Due to state and local level open government, open data sets can easily be found with a simple search engine search using key phrases (state/city/county name), plus the phrase "open data" (or "data sets"). Figure 14.12 shows an example of a state government data set offering, whereas Figure 14.13 shows an example of a city government data set offering.

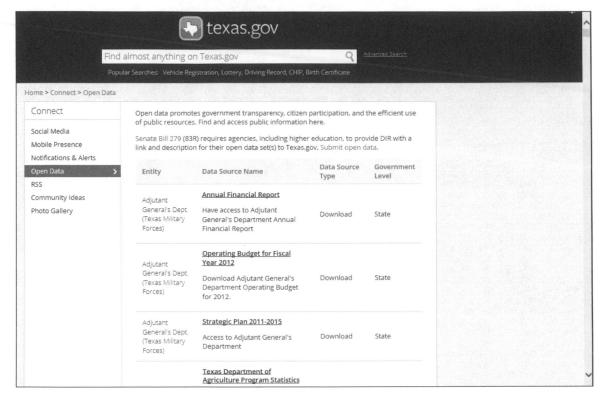

Figure 14.12
A sampling of data sets available from the Texas state government. You can find data sets offered by any state with a simple Internet search.

Source: Texas state government at http://www.texas.gov/en/connect/pages/open-data.aspx.

You can search most government data sets by categories, topics, and keywords. Small businesses can use this information for a variety of purposes, from identifying best locations for new stores to finding loans, grants, and a variety of other resources. Some of this data, such as weather, energy/fuel costs, tax incentives and costs, and regulations, are also useful in combining with a small business' existing data to compute an answer to a perplexing business problem.

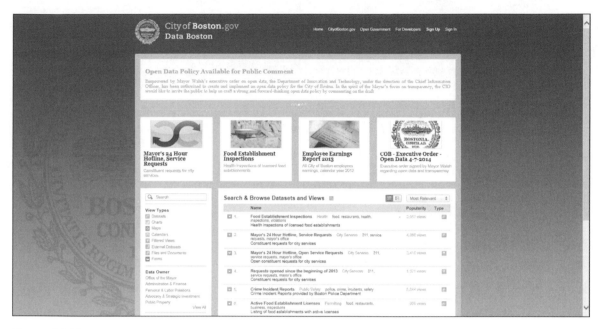

Figure 14.13
A sampling of data sets available from the city of Boston. Other cities, towns, and counties offer publicly available data sets as well.

Source: City of Boston at https://data.cityofboston.gov/.

As you can tell from these few examples, data is readily accessible and available almost everywhere. Decide what information you need first and let that guide your search for data sets.

A Word of Caution to Farmers on Pooling or Sharing Data

Although this word of caution is meant specifically for farmers, it could also be applied to other small businesses considering the purchase of smart equipment or requests from corporations to share their data. It is essential that small businesses and farms consider these issues carefully before proceeding.

As of this writing there was much debate over whether farmers should share their farm data and add it to the data pools created by such corporate giants as John Deere, Monsanto, DuPont Pioneer, and others. The American Farm Bureau Federation (AFBF), a national independent farmers' group, has repeatedly issued warnings to farmers that such data pooling could be harmful to individual farmers, farmland values and prices, and the food market. According to a April 9, 2014 *Reuters* report, the potential dangers outlined by AFBF are:

> *"Virtually every company says it will never share, sell or use the data in a market-distorting way—but we would rather verify than trust," farmer Brian Marshall of the AFBF told the U.S. House Committee on Small Business in February.*
>
> *The data would be a gold mine to traders in commodity markets and could influence farmland values.*
>
> *While there are no documented instances so far of data being misused, lengthy contracts packed with open-ended language and differing from one supplier to the next are fueling mistrust.*
>
> *But for a commodities trader or investment bank, a broad pool of real-time data about how many acres of soybeans U.S. farmers planted or whether corn yields in Iowa were above expectations could be a gold mine.*
>
> *Already, feedback from crop tours organized to inspect the harvests are keenly watched and can move markets.*
>
> *And the concern is that a company might be enticed to venture beyond agronomic services, given that a public company must put its shareholders—and therefore profits—first.*

The huge companies asking for data from farmers (some of which are harvesting data without the farmer's knowledge too) contend that the data will always belong to the farmer, that the data is used only to "help" the farmer farm more profitably, and that the farmer's data will be anonymized so that the privacy of the data is maintained and details are not tracked back to any individual farm. Here is how that same *Reuters* report explained some of those claims:

> *Companies like Monsanto, DuPont Pioneer, and tractor giant John Deere maintain that data produced on the farm by a farmer belongs to that farmer.*
>
> *But property guidelines surrounding data, which can be copied, aggregated, and transmitted at lightning speed, are not as simple as that.*
>
> *John Deere's enterprise privacy statement, tucked away on its website, shows that the company can collect data on Deere equipment or any devices connected to it such as an iPad, unless the farmer opts out.*
>
> *The list of the company's uses for that information includes customer service and marketing, but also "analytics." And data gathered by its machines can be retained by Deere indefinitely.*
>
> *DuPont Pioneer says anonymized data, including yield and products used as well as GPS location information, can be used and disclosed by the company "for any purpose."*

While it is true that the data generated by new smart farming equipment will provide the farmer with valuable information he or she can use in numerous ways to increase yields and profits, it is also true that the same information can be used against a farmer if it falls in the wrong hands or is used for other purposes. It can also be used to market goods and services to the farmer incessantly making the very machine you bought a constant annoyance to machine operators.

The next sections examine the claims made by companies urging farmers to share their data. By looking closely at each, you can more clearly detect the problems in these claims.

The Claim that the Data Belongs to the Farmer

This is an exceedingly frail claim at best. The issue of data ownership is an ongoing point of contention in all big data efforts and it has yet to be clearly defined by law. In the current environment, a corporation can truthfully say that the raw data belongs to the farmer, and still lay claim of ownership or grant itself a broad license on the aggregate and the analysis, which is in practical terms as good as ownership. Further, the loose language most corporations offer in terms of data ownership and how data will be collected and used is far too open to interpretation to offer any meaningful privacy and data ownership protection for the farmer. Concrete answers to these issues should be well-defined with clear recourse for the farmer spelled out in no uncertain terms. Indisputable, clear language over collection, usage, and data ownership should also be established prior to farmers making any such agreement. The AFBF was working on these very goals at the time of this writing, but farmers should continue to be diligent on these issues in their own behalf.

The Claim that the Data Is Used Only to "Help" the Farmer Farm More Profitably

This claim is misleading if not blatantly untrue. Yes, the data generated from smart farm equipment will most certainly be helpful to the farmer. However, its primary purpose is to aid the corporation gathering it with or without the farmer's knowledge. With this data, these corporations will learn what and how to market their products and services to you. You may find this information helpful and you may not but in any case, the focus of such efforts is to sell the corporations' goods and services and not necessarily on improving your farm. Think of it this way—do you really want vendors to know every single detail about you and your farm when you know in advance that such details will be used to sway your buying decisions?

Consider this piece of information from the previously cited *Reuters* report:

"Big agricultural companies see big profits ahead. John Deere has said precision services and its 'intelligent solutions group' would be a major piece of doubling its size from a $25 billion company in 2010 to a $50 billion company by 2018. Monsanto underscored its devotion to farm data analytics when it bought weather data-mining company the Climate Corporation in October, describing it as its 'entry ticket into a $20 billion market opportunity.'"

Certainly these corporations have the right to increase their earnings and the duty to shareholders to do just that. However, those dollars will be coming from somewhere and certainly getting data on individual farms and farmers will help them sway farmers to reach deep into their wallets for one product or service or another. The question then becomes whether it is in the farmer's best interest to help the corporations in selling him more stuff and services? Maybe. But then again, maybe not.

Consider also, this gem of information from another Reuters report published in the *Chicago Tribune* on March 20, 2014, which cites examples specific to Caterpillar's construction and mining sales efforts, but could conceivably apply to its farm equipment sales efforts too:

> *Caterpillar is the latest company to see big dollars in so-called big data. There are, by its reckoning, more than 3.5 million pieces of Caterpillar equipment in the field, many of them fitted with sensors that send out continual status updates about important mechanical systems and operator performance.*

> *Caterpillar believes dealers could be billing for billions of dollars more each year if they did a better job of thinking of those machines as smart digital devices, **constantly pinging them with sales and service opportunities**, not just dumb pieces of iron.*

> *Better exploited by the dealers, the information could immediately increase part and service sales to existing customers, Caterpillar says.*

The emphasis on "constantly pinging them with sales and service opportunities" was added here in this text in order to bring it to the attention of farmers. The question is, do farmers see any value in "constant pinging" of advertisements and pushy calls to buy goods or services—not just on the equipment but other devices such as their phones and tablets—or will farmers see such as annoyances distracting them from their work? One thing is for certain, providing even more data to these corporations on top of what they collect directly from the machinery will only serve to invite more communications/advertisements and more intense sales efforts.

The Claim that the Farmer's Data Will Remain Private

There is also a claim that the farmer's data will be anonymized so that the privacy of the data is maintained and details are not tracked back to any individual farm.

This claim too is misleading at best and blatantly untrue at worst. In the first place it has been repeatedly proven that anonymized data can be re-identified easily enough by any number of experts and entities. Anonymization, in other words, does not afford any real protection of identity or privacy—outside of heavily privacy protected data such as healthcare data, which is governed by HIPAA and other privacy regulations. Further, the motivation for these corporations to anonymize data is weak. They need to be able to associate the data with a specific farm in order to improve their pitches and sales to that farmer. Why then would they want to make it impossible for them to do so by anonymizing the data? Further, even if the corporations were to live up to this pledge, that is no guarantee that other users who may buy or hack the data would not re-identify the data. Think again about these statements from the previously cited *Reuters* report:

> *The data would be a gold mine to traders in commodity markets and could influence farmland values.*

> *But for a commodities trader or investment bank, a broad pool of real-time data about how many acres of soybeans U.S. farmers planted or whether corn yields in Iowa were above expectations could be a gold mine.*

> *Already, feedback from crop tours organized to inspect the harvests are keenly watched and can move markets.*

From these statements alone, you can easily see how strong the motivation could conceivably be to re-identify the anonymized data.

Again, it is prudent for farmers and other small businesses to carefully weigh decisions in regards to data sharing and pooling, and in regards to buying equipment outfitted to gather data and report it back to the manufacturer, before proceeding.

Note that this discussion is not meant to disparage any company or industry in any way, but rather to illuminate the issues both sides need to work at resolving. The advice here is that small businesses and farms should seek such resolution and clarity before committing to any data sharing agreement or smart machine purchase that may collect information on their business and report such to a third-party, with or without the owner's knowledge. Conflicts of interest often do exist.

Money, Money, Money: How Big Data Is Broadening Your Borrowing Power

While small businesses are busy figuring out how best to use big data and whether or not to share or pool their data and if so then with whom, other industries are busy using big data to figure out how best to serve and profit from SMB customers. In many cases, big-data-spawned disruptors arrive to change circumstances for the better for small businesses. One example is in lending. Now, thanks to innovative data uses by emerging lenders, capital is more accessible to SMBs.

In general, banks and traditional lending institutions have stuck with their age-old business and lending models. They still trudge over to the one of the big credit bureaus to get information on borrowers, dutifully ask for the small business' business plan and other information, and check off their decades-old list of stuff to know about borrowers. One wonders why they bother since it's quite common for the lending officer to pretty much chuck all that aside and make the decision based on how he or she feels about the borrower. At least that was the case up until the last recession. That's when banks came under fire for making truly horrible lending and investing decisions that took individuals and the nation to the brink of disaster. After that happened, banks froze lending for a while. Now lending is open again, but it's really hard for most small businesses to qualify for a bank loan. Traditional lending institutions are now very wary of lending money to anyone other than their best and oldest customers.

Meanwhile, small businesses suffered through every stage of that bank neurosis. To this day, it's tough for many SMBs to get a loan or find funding. Fortunately big data spurred some new lending entities that make finding capital considerably easier. Of course, this is bad news for banks and other traditional lending institutions, as these new upstarts are eating much of their lunch. But that's a story for another chapter. For now, let's look at how all this works for small businesses.

Credit bureau data is essentially useless to lenders as, among other things, it does not distinguish between which borrowers are deadbeats and which were hurt by the recession but are otherwise responsible payers. All that matters to a credit bureau is that an account was paid on time or it wasn't, and how long and how large the account is. Further, if your identity is stolen, which is a common occurrence these days, your credit history is usually compromised and it can take years to straighten that out before you can borrow again.

By comparison, the emerging new breed of lenders want to know the actual level of risk involved with lending money to you and they're willing to discount or even completely ignore credit bureau data to do so. While credit bureaus keep looking back at the past as if it is a true reflection of the future, alternative lenders use big data to calculate past and present borrower circumstances, coupled with predictive analytics to forecast the borrower's future, to design and implement new lending models.

The alternative lender's model is generally fairer to the small business borrower and is usually a more positive view as well. In other words, the new model favors the borrower more so than the old bank model does in calculating credit worthiness. However, it is important to note that debt is still debt no matter where it is incurred. Lenders will still take actions to collect and debtors may find such actions insufferable. Therefore, it is still wise to avoid carrying too much debt. It is also wise to keep close check on all fees and interest rates and other loan costs before you sign any paperwork. But if you find you need capital, here are a few examples of new lenders you might want to consider. Keep in mind that more alternative lenders will appear on the scene over time, so be sure to check all your options before every attempt to borrow to ensure you are taking the best route for your company.

Many but not all of the alternative lenders are in the lending game to support their own customers and not to broadly loan money.

PayPal Working Capital

PayPal Working Capital is one example of this new breed of lenders. A small business borrower's credit worthiness is based solely on the strength of its PayPal sales. PayPal charges no interest and has no set monthly payment dates. The borrower pays the loan back with a share of its PayPal sales as they occur. If you don't make any PayPal sales in one period, you owe no payment for that period. There is a fixed fee for getting the loan, but no interest, late, or hidden fees which banks typically charge. There is also no penalty for pre-payment.

Amazon Capital Services

Amazon Capital Services is another example, although as of this writing the loans are only available by invitation. In an October 4, 2012 article in *The Wall Street Journal* titled "Small Businesses Are Finding an Unlikely Banker: Amazon," Sarah E. Needleman and Greg Bensinger wrote this about the new lending service:

With its foray into commercial lending, 18-year-old Amazon.com Inc. is looking to help sellers obtain cash more quickly than they might otherwise from a bank or other traditional lender, an Amazon spokesman said. "Our goal is to solve a difficult problem for sellers," he said.

Merchants who spoke to The Wall Street Journal said they were offered loans ranging from $1,000 to $38,000 apiece, with interest rates from less than 1% (for one of them) to 13.9% (for most who were interviewed). Small-business credit-card interest rates typically range from 13% to 19%.

Those who received an Amazon Lending pitch also characterized themselves as heavy sellers of goods through Amazon's website.

Kabbage

Kabbage is an example of an alternative lender that offers loans to a broader base of small businesses. It lends money to online businesses who sell through sites such as eBay and Amazon but also to brick-and-mortar merchants. While traditional credit scores are part of the calculated "Kabbage score," credit bureau rankings are just one of many data points used and are thus weighed more equitably. Figure 14.14 shows the Kabbage website explaining how you can qualify for a loan. The company explains the Kabbage score on its website as:

> *The Kabbage score is the aggregation of all the data points we use to determine advance eligibility, advance limit, and your first 2 months advance rate. These data points may include, but are not limited to your average revenue per month, years in business, credit history, and the ongoing monitoring of the transactional data from the services you linked. The more services you link, the better understanding Kabbage has of your business.*

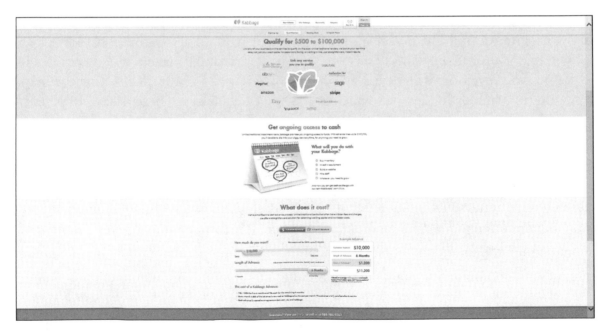

Figure 14.14
Kabbage website explains how to qualify for a loan from Kabbage.
Source: Kabbage at https://www.kabbage.com/how-it-works.

Meanwhile, the economy is recovering and traditional lenders are slowly making small business loans again. Many are also trying to modernize by using big data to qualify borrowers rather than relying solely on credit bureau data and scores. Keep an eye on future banking changes that may benefit your company as well.

Summary

Everything in this chapter is meant to show you real-world examples of the many ways big data is benefitting and sometimes potentially harming small businesses and farms. The main take-away here is that you cannot ignore big data and expect to stay in business. Big data and big data tools are not a luxury, but a necessity.

In this chapter you learned that small businesses and farms do not need to own much data in order to use big data. There are plenty of public data sets freely available and even data sets that are sold are often available for a nominal fee. You also learned that insights from big data analysis are already in your pocket on a smartphone, such as Google Earth and Bing Maps Bird's Eye, and how small businesses can use those to their benefit. You saw a number of examples of tools you might want to consider using, from Google Analytics to desktop tools like those made by Tableau and MicroStrategy. You learned some of the pros and cons involved in data sharing and pooling. And, last but not least, you learned how other businesses are using big data in order to serve SMBs better—particularly in lending.

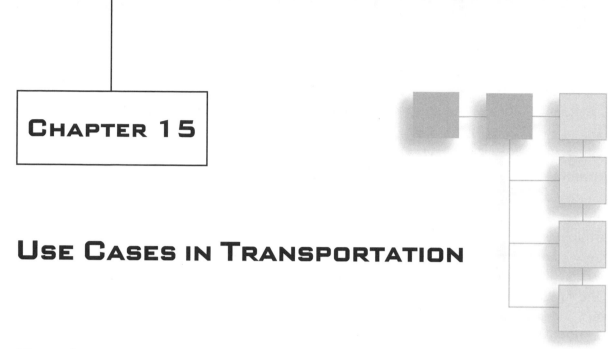

CHAPTER 15

USE CASES IN TRANSPORTATION

Many advances in transportation have been underway for years now, but they tend to surprise and delight the average person when they seemingly appear overnight on the market. Not too long ago, it was a novelty and even a status symbol to have a car phone installed in a vehicle. Now, for all practical purposes, the average new car is an extension of the phone with Bluetooth built-in and phone links right from the steering wheel in many new cars. Other features are following the same path in rapid technological advancements and convergence. Some features prove so successful, particularly if they add an element of safety, that they end up mandated in all vehicles.

Take for example, back-up cameras found today mostly on high-end vehicles but increasingly on a few mid-end vehicles as well. The National Highway Traffic Safety Administration (NHTSA) issued a mandate in March 2014 that in effect requires all vehicles weighing less than 10,000 pounds, including buses and trucks, to have back-up cameras onboard by May 1, 2018. The regulation doesn't call for back-up cameras per se, but the standards that must be met frankly can't be met with anything less. Soon there will be back-up cameras on vehicles throughout the United States and all will or can create data.

REVVING UP DATA IN A RACE FOR MONEY

Features initially make it into vehicles to either increase their allure to buyers or as a matter of driver and public safety—and sometimes both. It is only in recent years that it dawned on developers and automakers that many of these features could generate valuable data too. At first, data collection was thought of in terms of advantages to the automakers, most notably in developing new ways to help diagnose increasingly complex engine and control systems or as revenue streams from drivers, insurance and lien holder sales. For example, features that offered emergency services for drivers, those of the OnStar ilk, also provided data that was valuable to car insurance companies and vehicle repossession companies working for lien holders.

Insurance companies wanted the data specific to driving patterns to better assess their risks in covering any given driver, their risks overall, and their risks by geographic area and by demographic. Lien holders and repossession companies wanted to know where deadbeats hide the vehicles so they could snatch the collateral back. Automakers found these multiple revenue streams from the same device to be exhilarating boosts to their bottom lines. Such was particularly helpful in bad economies in offsetting sales slumps. One can hardly blame them. In the one hand there was subscription money from the drivers; in the other was cash from insurance companies, lien holders, and repossession outfits. It all presented a two-fisted reward picture reminiscent of Rich Uncle Pennybags from the game Monopoly.

Car dealers also found new data-generating, in-car features to be financially rewarding. The margins on car sales are surprisingly low for auto dealers; most of them heavily depend on their service departments to bring in the majority of revenue and to keep cash flow steady. Lo and behold they discovered that by reading data on cars they could cut costs in diagnosing the correct problem and making repairs. They also discovered that the ability to diagnose and repair or pull maintenance faster meant more service work could be performed per day, which also led to an increase in revenue. Further, the diagnostic data also could be reported to drivers, increasing the number of regular and total service department visits and orders thereby increasing revenue in the service centers. In effect, the features became highly effective marketing tools since drivers tend to view them as helpful tools and highly prefer them to advertisements. Plus, machines, at least in the consumer's mind, do not lie. The prevailing assumption is that they report vehicle diagnostic readings for what they are and without any emotion or second agendas. Never mind that humans who do have agendas do the programming. However, vehicle diagnostics appear to be reporting truth to drivers. At least for now.

The Disrupting Fly in the Data Ointment

There's a fly in that particular ointment for dealer cash ills. New vehicles have been developed that need little or no service. Tesla was first to market with such vehicles.

Here is how Tesla Motors explains the need for service, or rather the lack thereof, on its website:

Unlike gasoline cars, an electric car doesn't need oil changes, fuel filters, spark plugs, smog checks, etc., which are only needed if the mode of locomotion involves burning oil derived products. For an electric car, you don't even need to replace the brake pads, because most of the braking energy is regeneratively captured by the motor and returned to the battery.

As such, we are comfortable making the annual checkup entirely optional. There is still value to having Tesla look at the car once a year for things like tire alignment, to address a few things here & there and perform any hardware upgrades–our goal is not just to fix things, but to make the car better than it was. However, even if you never bring in the car, your warranty is still valid.

There was an immediate flurry of lobbying and political activity to stop Tesla from opening dealerships in several states in order to protect existing dealers' income generated by their service departments. However, electric cars are improving fast and soon many will be on the market that are essentially maintenance-free. Eventually traditional vehicles will all but disappear. This is the effect all disruptors have on any industry, a complete change in business models. Therefore there may potentially be a limited window of opportunity for car dealers to profit from the automated sharing of diagnostic data with drivers. Soon most vehicle maintenance and upgrades will be done remotely through software updates, much as occurs now with in-home Blu-ray DVRs and gaming systems.

But low- to no- maintenance electric vehicles aren't the only disruptors on this road; autonomous/driverless cars are coming too. While some found Google's driverless car and its early cross-country experimental trek little more than an interesting novelty, the technology is moving fast to widespread testing. In 2014, major shows, such as the International Consumer Electronics Show (CES) and the big auto show in Detroit, unveiled numerous car prototypes from several manufacturers, such as BMW and Audi, that were either driverless or contained the beginning technologies headed to that end.

Data Wins Are Not Eternal

You can see from these trends that while data lends many advantages to companies, those advantages are not forever-lasting. To remain competitive, companies must use data in ways that make sense today but also use it to prepare for a future when those techniques and models will no longer work.

However, the focus in using data from cars and in-car technologies has broadened beyond the auto manufacturers and dealers scope. Governments, from the township and county level all the way to the federal level, are also looking to this data to improve roadways, safety, and traffic flow.

Additionally, citizens are purposely generating data in transportation to improve conditions. One example is a mobile app that enables ordinary citizens to automatically report potholes and other road conditions in need of repair to government authorities. The Street Bump app uses the motion detector in a phone the driver places in the car to sense potholes. It then records the GPS location of the pothole and automatically reports it to authorities. Street Bump is the brainchild of former Boston mayor, Thomas Menino, and came to life with the help of the Mayor's Office of New Urban Mechanics. The app has been tweaked over time to eliminate false reads, but it is a great example of a government-constituent partnership and the use of in-car technologies (even though the phones aren't built-in, in this case) in crowd-sourcing and innovating solutions to traditional problems.

Data Use in Trains, Planes, and Ships

But data is changing all of transportation and not just vehicles and roads. Trains, planes, ships and other forms of transportation including everything from drones and intelligent, autonomous war machines to ferries and golf carts, are being transformed. In each case, data generation, analysis, and data-driven innovation are at the heart of the transformation. Also, increasingly the data is being publicly shared. For example, Figure 15.1 shows data on ferry operators and ferry vehicles available in the Data.gov catalog. Note that the portal is easily shared on social media through buttons on the page and that suggestions for more data sets are solicited on the page as well.

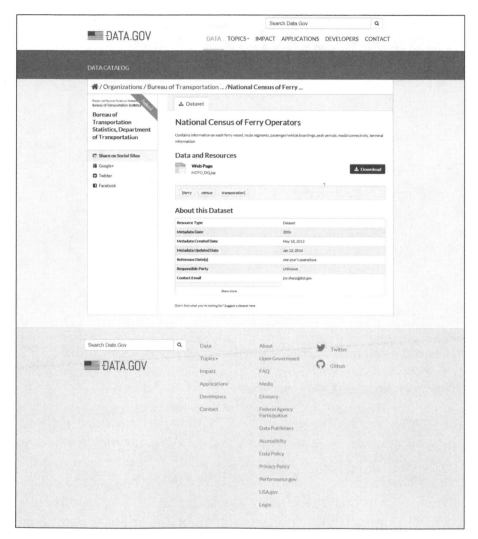

Figure 15.1
Data set on ferry operators, vehicles, and routes available in the Data.gov online data catalog. Note that the portal is easily shared on social media.

Source: Data.gov catalog Bureau of Transportation data set on ferry operators and vehicles from http://catalog.data.gov/dataset/national-census-of-ferry-operators.

Figure 15.2 shows a screenshot of the U.S. Department of Transportation's data inventory web page, with links to their digital strategy pages, developer resources, and data inventory. Whatever your interests are in transportation data, you'll likely find it freely provided by the government. If however, you don't find the data sets you need, you can request them and usually they'll be provided by the appropriate agency without difficulty.

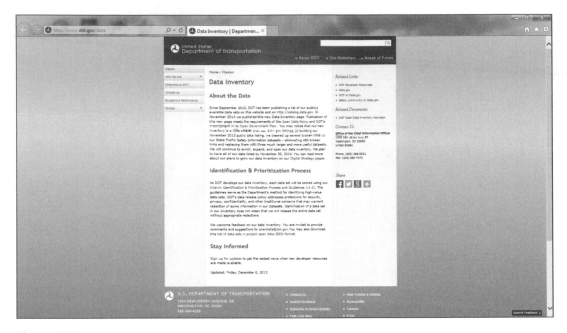

Figure 15.2
The U.S. Department of Transportation's data inventory web page, with links to their digital strategy pages, developer resources, and data inventory.

Source: U.S. Department of Transportation data inventory page from http://www.dot.gov/data.

For the purposes of this chapter in illustrating use cases in transportation, we will look specifically at automotive examples, as these are generally the easiest for most readers to relate to. These use cases are also similar to activities in other transportation sectors, although there are marked differences per sector as well. Indeed entire books can be written on the topics of each chapter in this book. The purpose here is to offer specific use cases to aid readers in formulating their own strategies. One good spark of the imagination is often all it takes to start meaningful and rewarding big data projects in any company. Hopefully, you'll find multiple sparks in the pages of this book that you can use.

CONNECTED VEHICLES: THEY'RE PROBABLY NOT WHAT YOU THINK THEY ARE

Although most people think of "connected vehicles" in terms of cars being connected to their owners' devices both in and out of the car, and connected to the Internet, the term actually has a different meaning. Connected vehicles as a specific term means connectivity between vehicles and road infrastructures, usually achieved with the aid of wireless technologies.

The U.S. Department of Transportation (DOT), Research and Innovative Technology Administration (RITA), defines connectivity in connected vehicles as:

- Among vehicles to enable crash prevention.

- Between vehicles and the infrastructure to enable safety, mobility, and environmental benefits.

- Among vehicles, infrastructure, and wireless devices to provide continuous real-time connectivity to all system users.

Some existing vehicle features point to movement in this direction already—assisted parking, driverless parking, especially in parallel parking, automated braking to avoid collision, and lane change alerting systems, to name but a few. Certainly driverless cars are connected vehicles, operating autonomously by correctly communicating with and interpreting the data from the environment in real-time. Each of these technologies generates and collects data and all do analytics on-the-fly.

In other words, the technologies involved are pretty much proving themselves already to be both useful and reliable. However, little is left to chance in this regard. RITA has done extensive work in standardization and certification of such vehicles, as well as in testing to ensure they can all communicate accurately with one another and detect and analyze changing road and weather conditions. RITA has extensive research available as a result. If you are interested in this data or have questions about RITA's research, you will find contact information for the appropriate individuals at RITA listed on each web page of specific research efforts on RITA's website. Figure 15.3 shows a sample of RITA research and how various stakeholders play a role in that research. The research depicted is on "Harmonization of International Standards and Architecture around the Vehicle Platform."

Figure 15.4 shows sample data available from The Bureau of Transportation Statistics (BTS), which is a part of RITA. According to the BTS website, "BTS brings a greater degree of coordination, comparability, and quality standards to transportation data, and facilitates in the closing of important data gaps." Further, the website explains that as a statistical agency, BTS:

- Is policy-neutral—An objective broker for the facts

- Covers all of transportation—BTS is cross-modal in nearly everything

- Does independent data collection and analysis, but BTS also serves all the other modes to help them be more effective and efficient

- Sets standards for transportation data

- Has special statutory protections (essentially the same as those for Census Bureau and Bureau of Labor Statistics) for the confidentiality of the data collected

■ Has unique competencies in statistics, economics, information technology, geographic information systems, and transportation

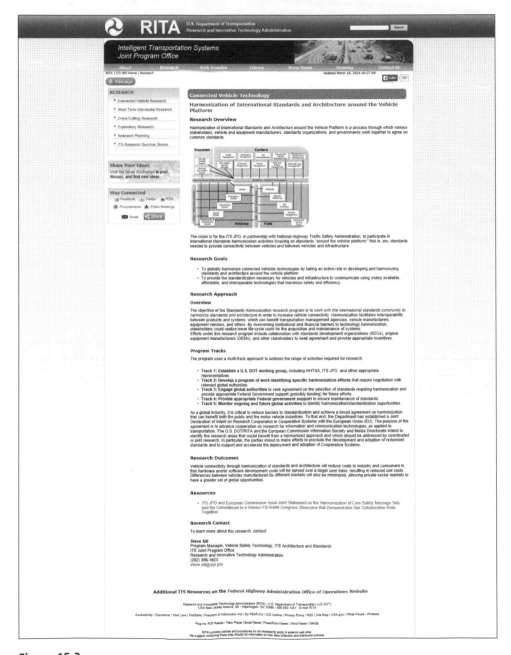

Figure 15.3
Sample from RITA showing how various stakeholders play a role in the research.

Source: U.S. Department of Transportation Research and Innovative Technology Administration webpage http://www.its.dot.gov/research/harmonization.htm.

Figure 15.4

Sample of data available from The Bureau of Transportation Statistics (BTS), which is a part of RITA.

Source: The Bureau of Transportation Statistics (BTS) webpage http://www.transtats.bts.gov/.

Government research in these areas is not only important to standardization and quality assurance in such programs and products, but also in developing innovative advancements that may be beyond the private sector's initial interests or resources. By funding and doing the research and then making the data available to all parties concerned, advancements appear more quickly in the marketplace than they would if solely pursued by private interests. This has always been the case, but now the data is flowing faster and bigger than ever before. Because of this trend in fast and widespread data sharing, you can expect new industries to develop quickly, more innovation to happen faster, and technological advancements to appear in the marketplace with accelerating speed.

Further, entities outside the transportation arena can also make use of this data in myriad ways. For one thing, you can expect wearable computing and mobile apps to become more tightly integrated with transportation. Already contact lists on phones can be uploaded to cars and voice conversations and social media used over the car instead of the phone. Users can even leave the car mid-conversation without a drop in the call. They just pick up the phone, keep talking, and leave the car.

We also see a number of apps related to traffic and vehicle routing and reporting. Not only are there a variety of mapping/GPS apps such as Google Maps on mobile devices, but also phone notifications to tell a user who just searched a destination how long it will take to drive there. There are also alerts, such as those issued by Google, that advise a smartphone user when they must leave in order to catch their flight based on traffic conditions. Such notifications and alerts are pulled from email and web-search data and require no special or further input from the user. The apps combine that user data with traffic and weather data to do their analysis for the benefit of the individual user.

Data Leads to Innovation and Automation

Such apps, alerts, and reminders are only the precursors of integration and convergence between data and devices, however. Soon wearable and implantable computing devices will serve as "keys" for cars, essentially identifying which drivers are approved for access and operation of the vehicle. These new devices will also summon a car to the driver rather than necessitate the driver walk the parking lot to the car. Such is not just a matter of convenience but a matter of practicality. Vehicles can be parked more closely together, stacked or parked in new ways such as vertically rather than horizontally, when it is no longer necessary to enable human egress or access. This is important for a world increasingly short on parking spaces. Building costs for parking facilities will also go down as the need for human elevators, stairways, and ramps and special parking places for the disabled diminish and then disappear.

Further, vehicles will be able to automate a number of seemingly miraculous tasks such as verify driver and occupant identities in security checkpoints using data the car has accessed or created itself (think fingerprint authentication from the steering wheel and vehicle surfaces checked against employer, driver license bureaus, and law enforcement databases) and through other devices courtesy of the expansion of the Internet of Things. The possibilities and opportunities in data convergence and fast analytics are nearly endless.

The Rise of Smart Cities

Meanwhile, the rise of smart cities is also reshaping ground transportation. "Smart cities" are generally defined as "digital cities" or "connected cities," meaning they are urban areas with an exceptionally high degree of connectivity among all or large parts of their infrastructure, including buildings, roads, connected cars, utilities, and other aspects. From all this flows data that enables a city to function "smarter" in several ways ranging from public policy development to implementations that protect and enhance human quality of life and the environment. At the moment, this is a goal that has yet to fully manifest in our reality, but it is a goal that many cities are rapidly working on achieving.

As the human population continues to grow, space and ecology issues also increase. For example, the need for more houses and more farmland increases in direct proportion to rises in population growth. Such requires cities and states to seek innovation and changes in transportation in order to free up more space and reduce ecological impact.

This problem also exists outside of cities. The sprawling suburbia model the United States has today will be unsustainable as traffic volume increases and land is at a premium. By reducing the amount of land now consumed by highway pavement and parking facilities, more land becomes available for more useful things such as farmland and housing inside and outside of metropolitan areas.

Big data tools, particularly predictive analytics, are extremely useful in identifying specific problems and when they are likely to occur but also in plotting new plans to prevent them from occurring and/or to overcome them. Already plans are afoot to redesign cities into smart cities and to change transportation completely. If you would like to see a few examples of these concepts, check out plans for The Bionic Tower, aka Vertical City, currently under consideration in both Hong Kong and Shanghai; Sky City 1000 in Tokyo; and, the X-Seed 4000, also planned in Tokyo, which is shaped like Mount Fuji but nearly 700 feet taller than the real mountain. In none of these cities is there room for ground vehicles as we know them. Yes, there are plans for transportation, but in more highly innovative forms. Plus, the entirety of these cities is connected. No things or living residents stand alone. Data flows to, from, around, and through all things. Advanced analytics everywhere make sense of it all.

Examples of Transportation Innovations Happening Now

Meanwhile, less futuristic cities, those already in our time and place, are busy converting into smarter, better connected communities. These too will ultimately change ground vehicles and road systems. Some corporations already see that and are changing their delivery models accordingly. Already retail giant Walmart has built a futuristic truck and trailer called the WAVE, short for Walmart Advanced Vehicle Experience. The vehicle is not only eco-friendly and extremely fuel efficient, it's slated to be driverless eventually. Figure 15.5 is an infographic of the WAVE, showing many of its features. It will literally be data-driven from its future self-driving capabilities to its onboard analytics. From monitoring and adjusting shifts in the load, and making automated adjustments to its shocks to fit the roughness of the road, to maintaining optimal load temperatures, be they refrigerated or not, data and analytics will be behind it all.

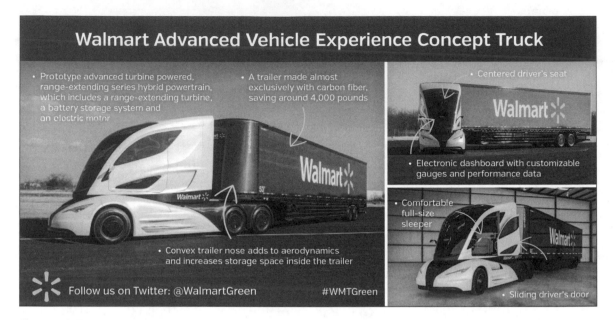

Figure 15.5
An infographic of Walmart's WAVE concept tractor trailer truck showing many of its features.

Source: Photo infographic from Walmart's media library at http://news.walmart.com/photos/walmart-advanced-vehicle-experience-truck-infographic.

Meanwhile fellow retail titan Amazon is exploring shipping packages to buyers via airborne drones in a program the company calls Amazon Prime Air. The company says it hopes FAA rules concerning the operation of drones will be finalized by 2015 and if so, it will be ready to deploy the drones then. If Amazon shifts many of its deliveries to drones, shipping companies such as FedEx and UPS will likely feel the pinch in revenue. If other retailers move to drone deliveries as well, the impact on incumbent delivery companies could very well prove to be devastating. Figure 15.6 shows the Amazon concept drone in-flight.

Figure 15.6
Amazon Prime Air concept drone in-flight. The orange-looking container underneath carries the package to the customer. The company says its goal is to deliver purchases in 30 minutes or less from time of purchase.

Source: Amazon's web page on the Prime Air drone announcement found at http://www.amazon.com/b?node=8037720011.

All of these changes bring pressures to bear on the transportation industry, which must keep up in order to stay in business. Already shipping and delivery companies are relying heavily on data and analytics to improve their operations and remain competitive. They will also need to use data analysis to reshape their entire business model and offerings in order to adapt and survive all these market changes.

DATA AND THE DRIVERLESS CAR

As amazing as progress has been in developing driverless cars and connected vehicles, these advancements are still in their infancy. We have not yet seen the peak of data's influence over the driverless car's evolution or that of connected vehicles. No doubt there will be data use cases we haven't yet imagined. For now most of the focus is on getting the data from sensors and other sources and connecting that with advanced real-time analytics in order to move people safely from point A to point B. But that doesn't mean that no one is working ahead. Nor does it mean that any given technology used now will be a mainstay throughout development. It's not so much that the technologies, including analytics, will become antiquated and replaced but rather that competition is high and innovators and disruptors continuously arrive on the scene.

RITA's Intelligent Transportation Systems (ITS) Joint Program Office explains the continuing need to look for more ways to improve connected vehicles but also to correctly analyze market forces at work on them, on its ITS Exploratory Research web page:

> Designed to explore technology outside of mainstream transportation research, the Technology Scan and Assessment project features two types of research reports. The Technology Scan focuses on long range, global and cross-cutting technologies. The Technology Assessment is specific to the U.S. DOT's plans for connected vehicle research, and highlights particular global technical risks such as security or uncertainties such as "game-changing" scenarios where a potential technological breakthrough or social or economic changes may tilt the playing field to favor one technology over another. Both reports are designed to explore technologies outside of mainstream transportation research, the Technology Scan and Assessment project examines technologies where the inclusion of said technology can tilt the industry and the future of connected vehicles to favor one technology over another.

> The research plan is to:

> 1) Cover technologies over three time horizons – science base (10 to 30 years perspective), emerging technologies (5 to 10 years), and pacing technologies (3 to 5 years applied on trial basis) in the information technology, telecommunications, transportation and energy sectors.

> 2) Focus on technologies centered on efficient data and information flow, from acquisition (sensors) and dissemination (wireless), to processing (computing) and management (decision support) systems.

Because market forces continuously affect change and create anything from minor shifts to outright upheavals, and such will end up in regulations accordingly, it behooves the transportation industry to detect, observe, track, and respond to these changes quickly. Big data tools enable them to do just that. Let's take a look at what decision factors ITS uses to make their ultimate judgments on implementations to see how such movements might relate to and affect those in the transportation industry.

In an April 2013 report titled "Longitudinal Study of ITS Implementation: Decision Factors and Effects," the ITS explained its implementation decisions:

> The set of decision factors were organized into four categories: technology or application factors, implementer factors, external environment factors, and user/market factors (shown in Figure 15.7). The relative importance of each of these categories and specific factors were explored qualitatively and quantitatively through the public sector interviews. These factors were modified and assessed with the trucking industry to identify factors of importance [to] this sector.

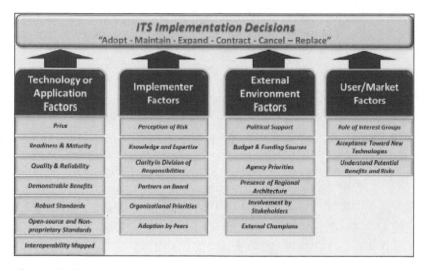

Figure 15.7
How the ITS makes its implementation decisions.

Source: ITS DOT study http://www.its.dot.gov/research/pdf/longitudinal_study.pdf called, "Longitudinal Study of ITS Implementation: Decision Factors and Effects."

Specifically that report says these are the factors most important to the trucking industry in making decisions on which technologies to invest in:

- Price of the technology/return-on-investment
- Readiness and maturity of the technology
- Compatibility with the existing systems
- System integration and flexibility
- Quality, reliability, service, and support

The report writers continued with their assessment of the factors of influence in the trucking industry and on the factors and assessments important to the ITS in its decisions:

> As expected, the factors demonstrate that the trucking industry places considerable importance on demonstration of monetary benefits and less emphasis on inter-agency coordination and cooperation.
>
> Looking overall at factors influencing the implementation of ITS, budget/funding, quality and reliability, demonstration of benefits, and compatibility/standards are most important. End-user awareness and acceptance were also rated as important factors for ITS implementation. A knowledgeable and skilled workforce, budget/funding, and compatibility & standards challenges were cited as critical barriers to ITS implementation. It has been noted that many of these factors are expressed in the framework for the Capability and Maturity Model developed for Transportation System Operations & Management (SO&M). The six

dimensions of that framework (Business Processes, Systems & Technology, Performance Measurement, Culture, Organization/Workforce, and Collaboration) are used to provide a structured approach to perform self-assessment and identify the incremental changes in agency capabilities that are essential to improving SO&M effectiveness.

Tremendous amounts of data go into these calculations. Coupled with the data and analytics used in driverless cars and connected vehicles, this means that data and data-centric tools are now the cornerstone of the transportation industry.

Connected Infrastructure

Once upon a time not so long ago, futuristic changes in transportation were envisioned in terms of rebuilding our entire road and highway system to include rails or other hardware meant for automated vehicles to follow. In reality, such an effort would be cost prohibitive and also disruptive to the nation's transportation needs in the meantime. Such would take years, if not decades, to complete. Instead, we are discovering that it is possible to use digitalized data to achieve much the same thing, only faster and cheaper. Our existing roads and highways are now being digitalized through the use of cameras and sensors. Data is collected and fed to different government agencies, some focused on law enforcement and others on improving traffic patterns and future transportation planning. Our vehicles are also using more digitalized data everyday using a range of sensors and technologies. Data analytics and reporting is done in-vehicle, between vehicles, and soon with the road infrastructure and surrounding structures, signs, and buildings.

But for now we have a hybrid infrastructure rather than a connected one. It is a hybrid infrastructure in that it is part legacy, the roadways and highways as we have always known them, and digitalized, through a variety of sensors installed on the infrastructure and installed in vehicles.

Additionally, other technologies such as wearable computing of the Google Glass ilk, as well as a number of mobile apps, can provide virtual layovers of augmented information over the real world views. For example, you can view a building or a road with Google Glass or Epson's upcoming Moverio BT-200 glasses, or you can use a camera on a mobile phone equipped with the right augmented reality (AR) app, and instantly see digitalized information about that structure and geographical area. You can also see other information such as which of your friends is nearby and where. Even more data will be fed to users as time goes by. This data will also converge with vehicles and infrastructure for even more complex computing and better, stronger, and faster analytics for a variety of end uses not yet imagined.

As innovation and data convergence increases, the transportation industry will be forced to keep pace and adapt. That too requires the use of data, particularly predictive analytics, to stay atop of what's coming next. Even a short delay in production changes and business model adaptations can cost a company everything.

Such analysis, in order to be effective, requires layering data from disparate sources. Top external data sources include data sets from the government, such as those found specific to transportation on the Data.gov website and those from specific transportation related agencies.

Figure 15.8 shows that at the time of this writing there were 7,797 data sets related to transportation data available on the Data.gov website. More such data will be added over time and existing data sets will be updated so it is important to frequently revisit the data set list and the data sets themselves.

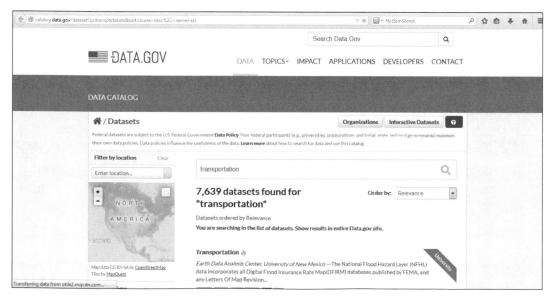

Figure 15.8
Data.gov catalog of transportation data sets showing that at the time of this writing there were 7,639 data sets related to transportation data available.

Source: U.S. government Data.gov data catalog.

Figure 15.9 shows a sampling of data sets specifically from the Department of Transportation (DOT) agency found on the Data.gov data catalog website.

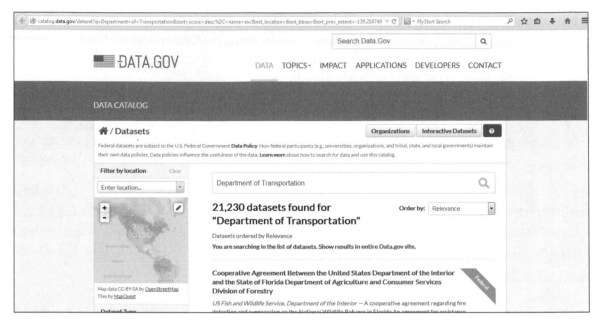

Figure 15.9
Data.gov catalog of transportation data sets specifically from the U.S. Department of Transportation (DOT) showing that at the time of this writing there were 21,230 data sets available.

Source: U.S. government Data.gov data catalog.

However, it is also important to check each government agency's own website too for additional information pertaining to tools and the means to sign up for update notices. Figure 15.10 is an example of just such a case wherein the DOT offers APIs and automated updates for developers.

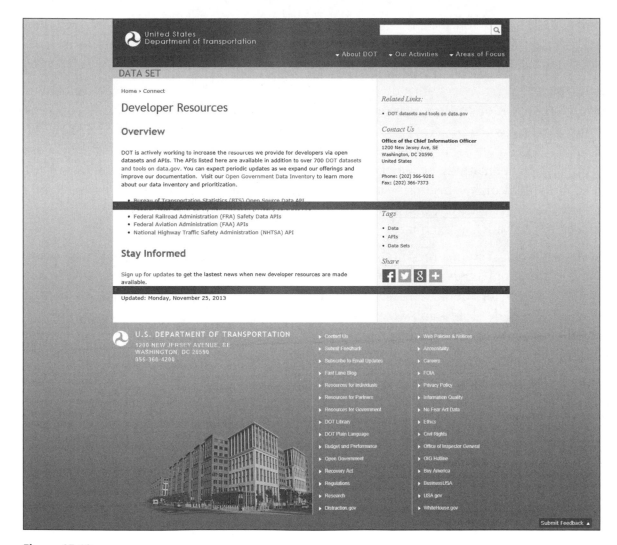

Figure 15.10
U.S. Department of Transportation's Developer Resources web page showing APIs and automated updates for developers.
Source: U.S. Department of Transportation (DOT).

CAR INSURANCE BRANDED DATA COLLECTION DEVICES

Some car insurance companies prefer to collect data on their own rather than be dependent on other entities, such as car manufacturers and driver assist services of the OnStar ilk, for their data needs. This is partly an attempt to cut data collection costs and partly a reaction to increased privacy concerns curtailing the amount of data available from these sources. That's why you see a number of insurance companies offering their own branded devices to drivers—even drivers who are not currently customers—with the promise of discounted rates for "good" drivers in return for the data.

Examples of such devices include Allstate's Drivewise and Progressive's Snapshot, but there are many more on the market. The prevailing assumption is that privacy concerns are not an issue when people voluntarily use these devices. However, most people have no idea how, where, and when this data might be used elsewhere in the future or for what purpose. Participants may be shocked to discover one day that they are turned down for a job or charged higher health insurance premiums because of these new driving records on their driving habits. Or, find that such data is demanded during discovery related to a car accident lawsuit, for example.

The point is that car insurance companies are typically not transparent nor necessarily forthcoming about how the data will be used. Perhaps they are unsure themselves but there's no hurry for them to figure out future uses right now. After all, once the data is collected, it will be stored and accessible to them for a very long time—perhaps forever. But they don't talk much publicly about that. Instead they focus their messaging on the fact that the device is "free" and the price discounts are flowing.

Take for example, Progressive's pitch on its web page, which explains Snapshot to its consumers:

> Great drivers get great rates with Snapshot. See what you can save on top of our already low rates:
>
> 1) We send you a free Snapshot device in the mail.
>
> 2) Plug it into your car (it's easy!) and drive like you normally do for 30 days.
>
> 3) Your good driving automatically turns into savings.
>
> Get Snapshot today with your auto policy!

It is important to always be cognizant of the fact that no company in any industry would go to such costs and effort just to reduce their own revenue. Although it is true that only drivers who self-assess themselves as "good" drivers would be likely to use these "free" and "easy" devices, car insurance companies are not likely to make the same assessment of their driving even if they are indeed good drivers by most definitions.

Consider how such data could be interpreted to the insurance company's advantage as pointed out by Brad Tuttle in his August 6, 2013 post in *Time*:

> *Some fear that those who don't sign up for the programs will be lumped into a higher-risk pool and assumed to be unsafe drivers, and therefore faced with higher rates. Critics also have a problem with some of the driving habits that are deemed unsafe. It makes sense to penalize drivers for superfast acceleration and repeatedly slamming on the brakes. But as a St. Louis Post-Dispatch columnist pointed out, drivers who work nights—and are regularly out on the roads during hours regarded as risky statistically—are less likely to get discounts. Ditto for workers who have long commutes, who suffer due to the theory that the more you drive, the more likely you are to be in a traffic accident.*

But even if insurance companies were to deem all these device users as good drivers, which certainly isn't going to be the case, such would serve as a good baseline from which to calculate risks pertaining to other drivers whom the insurance company most certainly would not label as "good." It is not the theory behind this use, but the vagueness of the labels of safe vs unsafe and good vs bad drivers and future uses of this data that concerns critics and consumer advocacy groups.

In any case, the goal of any big data user is to increase their revenues and profits, not to decrease them. It could be argued that these insurance companies do increase profits by virtue of limiting coverage to safe drivers or by increasing premium costs for "unsafe" drivers and therefore will voluntarily limit their data efforts to awarding good drivers discounts. But that simply isn't realistic nor is it in keeping with data usage trends in play across industries today. And indeed, players in the industry have admitted to such, as Tuttle reported in that same *Time* post:

> *But it's unclear whether this is how the system will work in the future. At its May presentation, Progressive told analysts and investors that it is an open question if usage-based programs will remain "discount-only models," the Wall Street Journal noted. In other words, insurers could change the rules at any moment and perhaps start jacking up the rates above the norm because drivers have been detected to be hitting the gas pedal hard, or just on the roads more often late at night.*

Expect at some point for car insurance companies to require the use of their devices in order for the driver to get and keep insurance coverage. You can also expect them to turn to other technologies as well, such as mobile phone detection to ascertain how many drivers are using a given vehicle and how they are driving it, as well as apps and sensors that detect and report breath alcohol content, and other metrics auto insurance companies consider pertinent to assessing driver risk. In nearly every case, such data will likely be contorted to drive premiums up, not to reduce them. But also expect an entire black market of counter-apps and counter-measures from savvy drivers that tie into technology to offset such individual metrics.

The auto insurance industry also faces business pressures from increased vehicle safety features that lower risk independent of the driver's operating skills, particularly those found in driverless vehicles and connected vehicles. Why? Because eventually, the vehicle and not the driver will be responsible for the driving, thus rendering the current model of insuring the driver obsolete. Insurance coverage will still be needed of course for driverless or connected vehicles, but such will likely be tied more to malfunction coverage rather than individual driver actions and skills. This will force a change in the insurance companies' business models and pricing structures. Such will require even more data collection and analysis to accurately compute. They will also need to use predictive analytics to assess the timing of the market shift, the new risks involved, and to power their business model transformations.

The shift in what risks auto insurance will cover in the future will not lessen the value of the data they gather on drivers today, however. Such data can be used for other purposes useful to other types of insurance coverage, employers, and other industries and business functions. For example, driver data can be used to assess the level of risk an individual will take and is comfortable with. Such could be useful to life insurance companies in assessing risk in insuring the life of an individual or to employers seeking personalities uniquely suited to taking risks in their work that may lead to new innovations.

UNEXPECTED DATA LIABILITIES FOR THE SECTOR

So far the major thrust of big data use in the transportation industry, as has also been the case in other industries, has been to improve profits for the players. It's been a bit of a free-for-all with little concern for liabilities outside a few privacy issues and most of those are really just PR problems for the moment. However, that is changing as the industry detects more liabilities coming from unexpected quarters down the road.

It was widely reported at the time that Jim Farley, executive vice president of global marketing at Ford, said at the 2014 International Consumer Electronics Show (CES), "We know everyone who breaks the law; we know when you're doing it. We have GPS in your car, so we know what you're doing. By the way, we don't supply that data to anyone."

Almost immediately Ford's then CEO, Alan Mulally, spoke to the press to counter Farley's statement. He said that Farley was in error and that Ford does not track driver data. He did confirm Farley's statement that the company does not share data without expressed consent from vehicle owners and drivers. That's a bit odd, in that if Ford does not collect vehicle tracking data, how could it share it with anyone even with consent. Perhaps Mulally meant his company only tracks vehicle diagnostic data and not driver movement data, but if so, that's a bit questionable too, as analysis of diagnostic data can reveal driver behavior simply by noting rate and occurrences of wear and tear on the vehicle. His statements then are still a bit confusing.

However, Mulally was beseeching regulators to protect consumer privacy by law despite whatever privacy practices Ford is already following. It's a bit odd for a manufacturer to deliberately seek more regulation, but the reasoning becomes a little clearer when you look at the issues closer.

In the absence of clear privacy protection laws, a company could conceivably be found liable for *not* sharing the data with appropriate authorities before or immediately after an event. Take for an example a drunk or ill driver who is driving erratically. If the vehicle reports that data to the manufacturer in real-time, as Farley seems to suggest, and the company fails to report it to authorities to help get that driver off the road before an accident happens, what then could the company's liability be in connection with that accident? For another example, what of the driver, perhaps a terrorist, aiming to ram a building or security checkpoint, or who is parking a car nearby loaded with explosives? If that terrorist succeeds, is the vehicle manufacturer liable if they had data indicating a problem in advance, while it was happening, or immediately afterward? Now multiply those and other scenarios over thousands of erratically driving drivers and what potential liability and arguments clever plaintiffs' attorneys may make—and what do you see?

Never before has a car manufacturer been held directly or vicariously liable for a driver's actions not linked to a malfunction. Yet that could very well come to be now that manufacturers have such strong new data and analysis capabilities. A manufacturer could not even plead innocence on the grounds that it does no such driver tracking and analysis or that it has no duty to act because the point is that it could if it wanted too and such resulting "losses" are obviously, given the limited examples provided here, foreseeable, which is a necessary element to successfully argue a party is guilty of negligence.

It is only under cover of strong privacy protection laws that vehicle manufacturers, and possibly other entities in the transportation space, can avoid this category of potential liabilities.

Now, Mulally's reasons for supporting privacy laws may have nothing to do with fears of future liabilities. His personal or business reasons for doing so are largely unknown. But if this isn't one of his reasons, it should be. For this rising threat is all but certain. Everything is pointing toward harsher legal liabilities in connection with unauthorized data use or data loss in every industry. Why? Because the foundation for all current big data use is to a) provide safety to an individual and the public at large and b) to provide a service or benefit for the user or users collectively. Therefore, sooner or later the law will inevitably hold data users accountable for such claims to an extraordinary degree.

Now add to those potential liabilities new threats in regard to product liability. Data from vehicles on the road, vehicles in testing, and vehicles on the production line will most certainly reveal product flaws and malfunctions faster. In turn, recalls are hopefully issued quicker and the reasoning for recalls cannot be easily dismissed. Vehicle manufacturers will then incur more liabilities if they don't "voluntarily" react in a timely fashion to solve the problem and prevent accidents. The irony is that recalls sometimes cost manufacturers more than lawsuits do. And sometimes product problems go undetected by others and never result in a lawsuit. But big data changes that. More knowledge of product problems earlier will lead to more accountability and responsibility on manufacturers in fixing them, whether or not anyone else knows of the problem's existence.

Summary

Once again, we see data-driven decision making is both an advantage and sometimes a disadvantage to the entity wielding it. However, use cases in this sector are nearly unlimited and carry with them exciting new opportunities as well as several disruptors.

Big data and predictive analytics can be used to foresee and respond to changes in the market and in the industry. Needed changes in products and business models can be better predicted, more clearly defined and tested earlier. Businesses processes can be improved and profits gained via new efficiencies.

Data tools can also be used to find production problems quicker and correct them before too much liability is incurred. Further, data from devices—be those mobile, wearable computing, in vehicles, or on infrastructure—are converging to make even more innovation possible and happen faster.

New external, open data sources, such as those available from various transportation related government agencies, aid greatly in corporate efforts to remain competitive and in compliance no matter what challenges they face.

In short, this industry, like many others, is now data-centric in all facets. This will only become increasingly true over time.

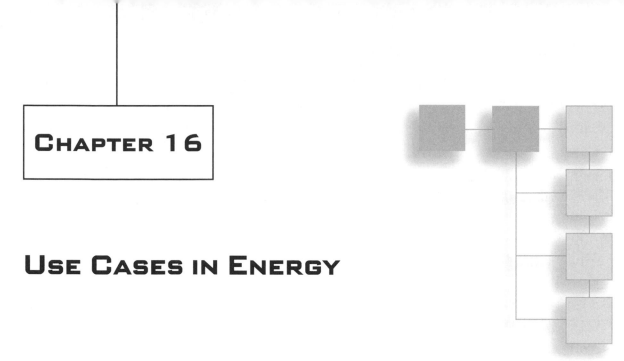

CHAPTER 16

Use Cases in Energy

Energy is a hot topic in its own right, given the increasing need for it and the dwindling supply of traditional sources. Political leaders in every country are struggling with this issue, albeit from different perspectives. Countries that historically relied upon being a top fossil fuel producer now worry about how to maintain a worldwide leading position despite growing support for alternative energy sources and continued global energy conservation efforts. Countries traditionally dependent on oil imports are now hurrying to become energy leaders via alternative energy exports or at least to become energy independent.

The Data on Energy Myths and Assumptions

In the midst of all this competitive positioning are worrisome public sentiment, nationalistic and intellectual bias, and a plethora of misinformation leading to bad judgment calls. Big data now makes it possible to overcome each of these obstacles, predict future energy needs, collaborate among experts, and even publicly crowd-source innovation, and most importantly, to correct faulty assumptions.

For example, most U.S. citizens continue to believe the country is unsustainably dependent on foreign oil. Actually the opposite is true. The United States is regaining its position as an energy superpower. According to the International Energy Agency (IEA)'s 2012 World Energy Outlook report, the United States will surpass both Saudi Arabia and Russia to become the world's top oil producer by 2016. Some reports, such as energy consultancy PIRA's in October 2013, conclude that the United States has already surpassed Saudi Arabia and is in fact the world's largest oil producer today.

While that is undoubtedly hailed as good news, at least by Americans, it's not the end of the energy story in the United States or elsewhere.

Energy conservation efforts are on the upswing globally and almost universally applauded. The payoff in those efforts are multi-fold, including reduced costs, better leveraging of existing supplies, and reduced environmental impact. But those benefits are also subject to misinformation and misinterpretation. In other words, those who believe that current energy conservation efforts are either sufficient or overkill are truly mistaken as the data shows otherwise.

It turns out that current conservation efforts are not sufficient to offset the growth in energy needs. Take the situation in the United States, for example.

According to a December 2013 report by Navigant Consulting, Inc. and SAIC (now Leidos) prepared for the U.S. Energy Information Administration (EIA):

> *Miscellaneous Electric Loads (MELs) comprise a growing portion of delivered energy consumption in residential and commercial buildings. Recently, the growth of MELs has offset some of the efficiency gains made through technology improvements and standards in major end uses such as space conditioning, lighting, and water heating. Miscellaneous end uses, including televisions, personal computers, security systems, data center servers, and many other devices, have continued to penetrate into building-related market segments. Part of this proliferation of devices and equipment can be attributed to increased service demand for entertainment, computing, and convenience appliances.*

In other words, the increase in the number and variety of devices is driving up the demand for energy and increasing consumption. Figure 16.1 shows how MELs, in aggregate, affect electricity consumption in both the residential and commercial spaces. Figure 16.2 shows that the largest MEL measured by annual electricity consumption (AEC) is televisions. The rest of that chart shows how other electronic devices rank in comparison.

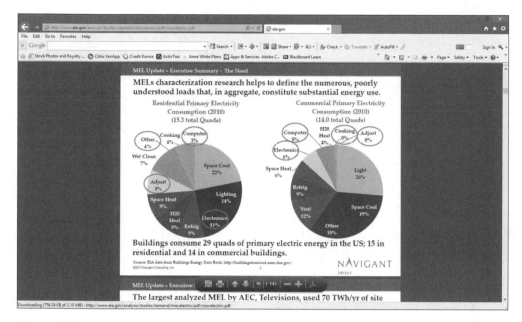

Figure 16.1

MELs characterization.

Source: The December 2013 report by Navigant Consulting, Inc. and SAIC (now Leidos) prepared for the U.S. Energy Information Administration (EIA) with permission from EIA.

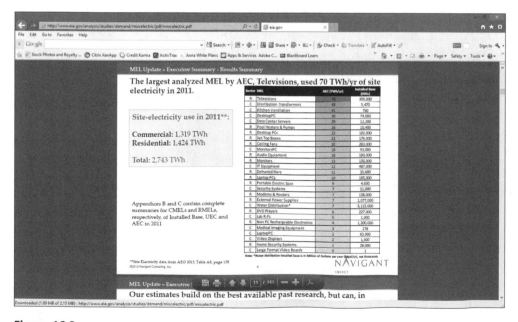

Figure 16.2

The largest analyzed MEL.

Source: The December 2013 report by Navigant Consulting, Inc. and SAIC (now Leidos) prepared for the U.S. Energy Information Administration (EIA) with permission from EIA.

Energy information is not solely of interest to country or regional economies. States, provinces, cities, and townships, as well as utility companies and businesses of all kinds and sizes seek to lower their energy use and costs. Each also seeks to know how energy trends and future predictions impact them and their constituents or customers. Hard data and advanced analytics can help each meet their goals and reduce risks.

Big data continues to inform and enlighten on matters of energy use and energy planning across industries. We'll get to some specific examples shortly, but before we look at specific use cases, let's first consider some prime energy data sources and developments.

EIA Energy Data Repository

Please note that by law, EIA's data, analyses, and forecasts are independent of approval by any other officer or employee of the U.S. government. The EIA implicitly states that its views therefore should not be construed as representing those of the U.S. Department of Energy or other Federal agencies. However, the EIA is part of the U.S. Department of Energy. The agency's work is focused on providing a "wide range of information and data products covering energy production, stocks, demand, imports, exports, and prices; and prepares analyses and special reports on topics of current interest."

The EIA has possession of energy data that is not otherwise collected by other parties but shares it publicly and freely through reports and the EIA.gov website.

"We use our federally mandated power to gather information," explained Kevin Jarzomski, Operations Research Analyst in Building Energy Consumption & Efficiency Analysis at the EIA, in a phone interview. "We output a lot of different things but if you don't find what you need, contact us and we'll help you find it or provide the information if it isn't on our site already."

You can contact staff and industry experts at the EIA on questions regarding energy data and statistics via the Contact Us page on the EIA.gov website.

"We have a lot of valuable information that may or may not be readily obvious so feel free to ask for what you need," said Jarzomski.

The EIA also provides comparisons of its analysis with that from other sources. In its hardcore commitment to accuracy in analysis, the EIA sometimes finds itself at odds with federal agencies and other studies. The agency is quick to acknowledge such and freely offers its reasoning. It is this transparency and willingness to explain its findings that adds meaningful value to its analysis. Figure 16.3 shows how the EIA directly compares its findings to other MEL studies and explains the differences.

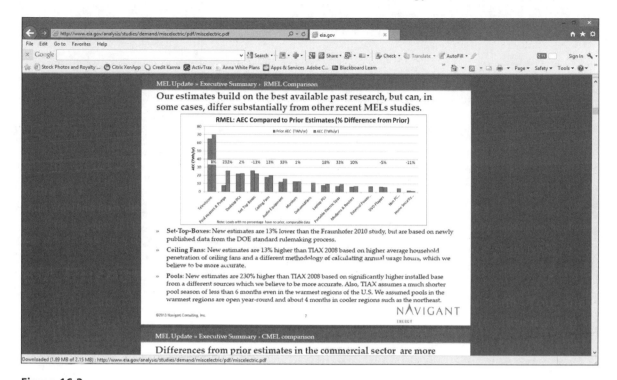

Figure 16.3
Chart showing how the EIA's estimates differ substantially from other recent MELs studies.

Source: The December 2013 report by Navigant Consulting, Inc. and SAIC (now Leidos) prepared for the U.S. Energy Information Administration (EIA) with permission from EIA.

EIA ENERGY DATA TABLE BROWSERS

The EIA's table browser is the easiest to view and manipulate output data. You can use tabs on the EIA.gov site to find projection data, analysis, models, and documentation specific to your interests or enter "table browser" in the site's search bar to browse tables on specific subjects. Use filters on the table browsers to drill down for more information. You can also download the table browsers in spreadsheet format and use the data in any way you wish from there. Figures 16.4, 16.5, and 16.6 are examples of EIA table browsers.

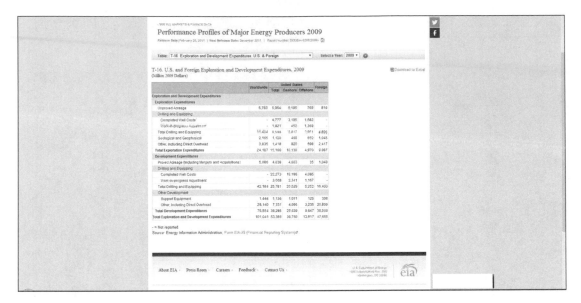

Figure 16.4
An EIA table browser: T-16: U.S. and foreign exploration and development expenditures, 2009.
Source: U.S. Energy Information Administration (EIA).

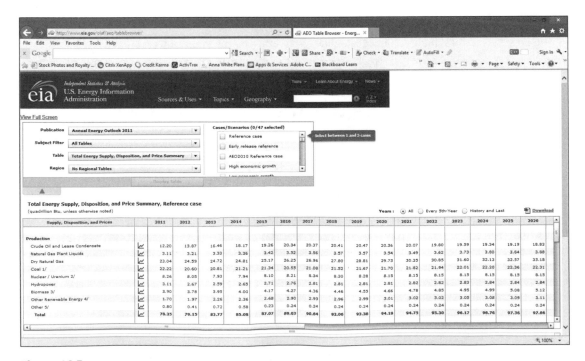

Figure 16.5
An EIA table browser: Total energy supply, disposition, and price summary, reference case.
Source: U.S. Energy Information Administration (EIA).

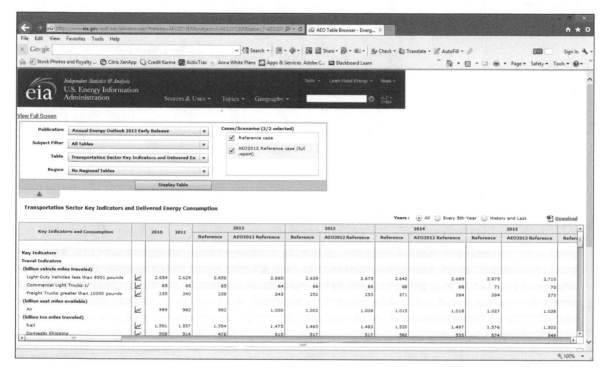

Figure 16.6
An EIA table browser: Transportation sector key indicators and delivered energy consumption.
Source: U.S. Energy Information Administration (EIA).

As to use cases for this data, which are limited only by your imagination, here are a few examples:

- Utility companies can use the data and projections to see how data usage is changing over time and plan accordingly. "The data is useful in planning capacity, supply side, growth, the equipment they need to use, and other factors," said Jarzomski.

- "Utilities trying to reduce demand through technologies can use this data as their baselines," added his team leader Erin Boedecker in that same phone interview. "Using the energy consumption and sector growth tables, companies can discover housing growth and commercial footage growth to determine where and when they'll have to increase connections and output."

- Researchers wanting to learn anything energy specific such as different distribution models or the state of or future predictions of traditional or alternative fuel production can easily access reliable data or ask for additional outputs.

- Companies—be they utilities, airlines, package delivery, or others—that are trying to compute or project energy costs can tap into this data and plan accordingly.

- Companies, news media, researchers, and other interested parties can check on new developments in energy, trends, analysis, and new input from industry experts by quickly checking the "Today in Energy" posts on the EIA.gov website homepage.

- Product developers can use the data to ascertain where their devices rank and where they might be improved in terms of energy use. They may also be able to use the data for insights leading to innovations in product designs.

Smart Meter Data Is MIA

If however, you're looking for data from *smart meters*—the new meters used by utility companies that are connected to the Internet and capable of numerous new capabilities as compared to traditional meters—you're in for a long wait. While most utilities, particularly electric companies, are quickly moving to use smart meters throughout their network, few have a clue as to what to do with the resulting data. The average utility company is gathering the data and storing it but leaving it to sit untouched for the moment. Like most companies in other industries, the average utility company is unsure how to proceed.

There is also the matter of complying with various regulations, which is somewhat complicating how utilities can use the data but is necessary in order to protect individual privacy. Data from smart meters can show when individuals are home or away, what appliances and devices they own and how they use them, and other revealing information. According to the National Conference of State Legislatures (NCSL), 25 states now have smart meter legislation (see http://www.ncsl.org/research/energy/states-providing-for-smart-metering.aspx).

But there are a number of problems in streaming smart meter data to the EIA.

"We are not in possession of smart meter data," said Boedecker. "There are issues of consistency and permissions. Smart meters vary greatly as do their outputs."

"We're getting aggregate data from utilities," Jarzomski explained. "But granularity hasn't made it to us yet."

The EIA largely relies on traditional survey and statistical methods to complete its work.

THE EIA'S API AND DATA SETS

Whatever your needs for energy data, the EIA is a prime source for data output. The agency also provides numerous tools to assist you in using the information including APIs for developers.

According to the agency, EIA's API currently contains these data sets:

- 408,000 electricity series organized into 29,000 categories
- 30,000 state energy data system series organized into 600 categories
- 115,052 petroleum series and associated categories
- 11,989 natural gas series and associated categories
- 132,331 coal series and associated categories (released February 25, 2014)

The API is a beta product and is offered as a free public service. However, registration is required and usage is monitored. In January 2014, the EIA added the bulk download facility. The facility provides the entire contents of each major API data set in a ZIP file. There is also a downloaded manifest, updated daily, containing information about the bulk files including all required common core attributes. "Downloading and ingesting entire data sets via the bulk files is 20 to 30 times faster than repeated API calls and is simpler to implement," according to the eia.gov/beta/api/ web page.

According to that same EIA web page, the manifest allows a consumer of EIA data to:

- Quickly check the manifest for updates
- Only download and process bulk data files with a more recent last_updated field in the manifest than your previous download
- Associate common core attributes, such as description and keywords, with the data
- Process the series that are newer than your last download
- Optionally ingest and replicate the data set's complete category structure

Figure 16.7 shows some of the information available on the EIA API bulk download facility found on the eia.gov/beta/api/bulkfiles.cfm web page.

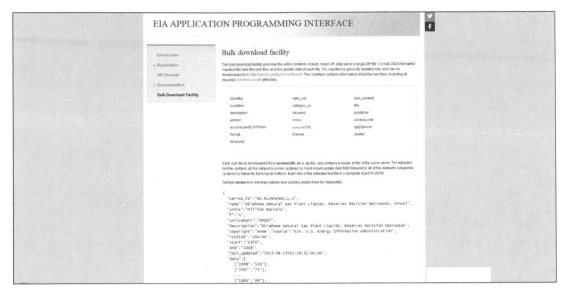

Figure 16.7
The EIA Application Programming Interface (API) bulk download facility page.
Source: The U.S. Energy Information Administration (EIA).

INTERNATIONAL IMPLICATIONS AND COOPERATION

As to the U.S. Department of Energy overall, look for fast development in new big data computing tools for use in the science end of things. Interestingly, the Russian Ministry of Education and Science recently awarded a $3.4 million dollar grant to Alexei Klimentov, Physics Applications Software Group Leader at the U.S. Department of Energy's Brookhaven National Laboratory for this precise cause. A February 26, 2014 article in *Scientific Computing* explains what hopes rest on Klimentov's efforts:

> *The project builds on the success of a workload and data management system built by Klimentov and collaborators to process huge volumes of data from the ATLAS experiment at Europe's Large Hadron Collider (LHC), where the famed Higgs boson—the source of mass for fundamental particles—was discovered. Brookhaven is the lead U.S. laboratory for the ATLAS experiment, and hosts the Tier 1 computing center for data processing, storage and archiving.*
>
> *"The increasing capabilities to collect, process, analyze, and extract knowledge from large data sets are pushing the boundaries of many areas of modern science and technology," Klimentov said. "This grant recognizes how the computing tools we developed to explore the mysteries of fundamental particles like the Higgs boson can find widespread application in many other fields in and beyond physics. For example, research in nuclear physics, astrophysics, molecular biology, and sociology generates extremely large volumes of data that needs to be accessed by collaborators around the world. Sophisticated computing software can greatly enhance progress in these fields by managing the distribution and processing of such data."*

Other big data tools and developments are underway so it behooves those with serious interest in energy analysis and the science in energy to continue to watch these sources closely.

Public-Private Collaborative Energy Data Efforts

That's not all the U.S. Department of Energy (DoE) is involved in regarding energy and big data development. In partnership with the Presidential Innovation Fellows, a public-private partnership between civilian members of the innovation community with top civil servants, the DoE invited the public to help with energy innovation by "doing amazing things" with DoE data.

In other words, the U.S. federal government turned to crowd-sourcing for energy data analysis and innovation. It offered over $100,000 in prizes for winners of the American Energy Data Challenge's call for "the best ideas, apps and visualizations using energy data to help address some of America's biggest challenges." The challenge consisted of four contests held from November 2013 to October 2014. The public was also invited to vote for the winners in the app contest, which was the second contest. To qualify, apps had to use one or more featured inputs to solve an energy problem.

Figure 16.8 shows the DoE web page on featured inputs for the app contest. It is found at http://energychallenge.energy.gov/a/pages/featured-inputs and shown here to illustrate how the government set contest parameters around a set of inputs to leverage the data and guide innovative efforts without limiting creativity.

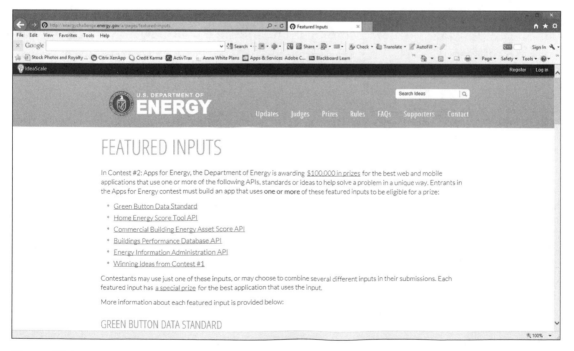

Figure 16.8
U.S. Department of Energy web page on featured inputs in American energy data challenge.
Source: U.S. Department of Energy at http://energychallenge.energy.gov/a/pages/featured-inputs.

As of this writing, there were 32 Apps for Energy II listed on the energychallenge.energy .gov site and voting had closed a few days earlier, on April 4, 2014. The most popular app idea was Black Sheep, "an iOS application that helps home buyers find energy efficient homes by combining real estate listings with energy efficiency and energy consumption data." According to the description on the energychallenge.energy.gov site, the app "also motivates homeowners to get home energy score assessments, which helps populate the Department of Energy's Home Energy Score database and encourages home owners to improve their energy efficiency."

The interesting thing to note in this example is how such an app, should it become widely used, could affect the real estate industry as much as the energy industry. Buyers' demands could shift, for example, and potentially make entire neighborhoods of older, less energy efficient homes far less marketable.

If you watch big data trends closely, you'll see that the lines between industries become quickly blurred and changes in one industry can affect change in one or more other industries seemingly overnight. Data, end applications, and market reaction cross over formerly well-defined sectors. It's not that changes and events in one industry didn't previously affect other industries. Certainly energy supply and costs have always affected other markets from food prices to car sales. But the intensity and speed of impact changes radically with the advent of big data; the trend in sharing data and pushing collaborations to rapidly speed innovation is new. More than one industry will inevitably be caught off-guard by new and rapid developments. And such surprises will happen almost continuously. Collaboration and convergence are the themes of the day.

UTILITY USE CASES

Utility companies look to data from smart meters and other sources first to improve cash issues both in raising revenue and cutting costs. The second most common use case of big data is to detect and resolve network issues such as breaks, stressed components, inefficient components and weak points, likelihood of outages, and future capacity needs. This will likely come as a relief to patrons as well since most utility companies formerly relied on customers to report problems as their sole indicator of network issues. In other words, utility companies were always working in a reactive state which slowed service restoration and costs the utility companies more money too. With the advent of new smart sensors, meters and other equipment capable of generating a constant stream of data, and the analytics needed to make sense of all that data, utilities can now work in a proactive state thereby preventing most outages and containing repair costs.

A third use case is in opening the network to receive more energy supplies, such as in customer buy-back programs where customers augment utility use with an alternative energy source, such as solar panels on a business or home. The utility can buy the customer's excess energy and add it to its general supply for resale. It will take big data tools to correctly track and monitor new incoming energy supplies and to properly track those costs and resale dollars.

A fourth use case is in early detection of a threat to the system be that a heavy squirrel population near a transformer, a developing weather system, or a terrorist or activist threat. As utilities increasingly turn to digital information to drive operations, those systems will be vulnerable to attack. It will take big data driven security efforts to detect, block, respond, and deter such efforts.

A fifth use case is in innovating the utility company overall. From changing inefficient internal processes to improving energy output and alternative energy input, analytics will eventually change everything in how a utility company and the energy industry overall operates.

Energy Data Use Cases for Companies Outside the Energy Sector

Energy supply and demand and related costs have always affected many other industries. Until recently nothing much could be done to accurately predict when changes in supply or prices might occur or to develop defenses against such. The most anyone could really do is buy energy efficient equipment and buildings to offset rising costs.

By using data so readily available from reliable sources, such as the EIA, your analysis of energy costs and availability impact, both in the moment and for the future, becomes infinitely more accurate. Because such data is regularly updated and often in real-time, updated predictions that reflect such things as supply chain problems and world events can be constantly provided for your own analysis within your own data projects. APIs make it easy to feed the information into your calculations and dashboards.

Further, businesses can use this information to inform their analysis on store, plant, or office locations as energy costs affect cost of living, and therefore payroll costs, as well as overall operational costs. Indeed, in its Annual Energy Outlook 2013 report, the EIA warns that:

> *The second-largest increase in total primary energy use, at 3.1 quadrillion BTU from 2011 to 2040, is in the commercial sector, which currently accounts for the smallest share of end-use energy demand. Even as standards for building shells and energy efficiency are being tightened in the commercial sector, the growth rate for commercial energy use, at 0.5% per year, is the highest among the end-use sectors, propelled by 1.0% average annual growth in commercial floor space.*

Figure 16.9 is an EIA chart from the previously mentioned report showing projected primary energy use by end-use sector. Having this data to include in your decision-making can greatly improve your planning capability, resulting in potentially higher profitability.

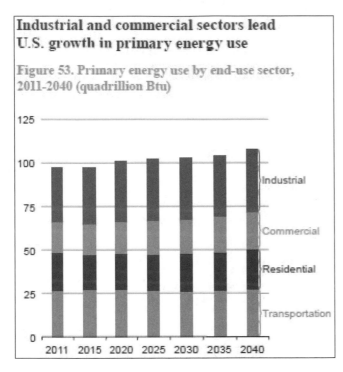

Figure 16.9
EIA chart from its Annual Energy Outlook 2013 report showing industrial and commercial sectors leading U.S. growth in primary energy use.
Source: The U.S. Energy Information Administration (EIA). http://www.eia.gov/forecasts/archive/aeo13/sector_commercial_all.cfm.

For companies in transportation and/or shipping and delivery, knowing the best places to refuel and route fleets to contain fuel costs is essential. Using up-to-date energy data is the best and fastest means with which to do so. A well designed algorithm can quickly compute the costs of rerouting vehicles to leverage lower fuel costs so that you can make the best choices with the highest end benefit.

For example, UPS, the shipping company, figured out that routing their delivery trucks in such a way as to only need right turns saved time and fuel and greatly reduced accidents. Left turns, they discovered, meant burning time and fuel waiting on lights to turn and traffic to give way. Left turns also exposed the trucks to higher risks in collisions because they meant maneuvering against or across traffic flows.

"Our entire delivery network has been re-engineered for more environmental benefit," Scott Davis, chairman and CEO of UPS, said in a speech. "You may have heard it described in the press as the UPS Right Turn Policy. We carefully map out routes for all our drivers to reduce the number of left turns they make. Now get this—In 2007 alone, this helped us shave nearly 30 million miles off already streamlined delivery routes, save three million gallons of gas, and reduce CO_2 emissions by 32,000 metric tons, the equivalent of removing 5,300 passenger cars from the road for an entire year."

For real estate companies and other companies involved in sales to the public or in business-to-business sales, it is vital to keep an eye on how data- and app-fueled changes in the energy industry, such as the Black Sheep app, can impact the value of goods and emerging buyer patterns.

The point here is that data-driven decisions and innovations in any industry, but particularly the energy industry, affect the entire marketplace. Big data tools enable you to use data beyond the scope of your business or industry to note, predict and respond to changes, opportunities and challenges across the board.

Summary

In this chapter you learned that energy data is plentiful and you saw examples of where to find it and how to use it in your company. But you also learned that some energy data is still under development, such as data from smart meters, and what the problems are there.

Although it is true that energy costs have always affected costs and prices in industries outside the energy sector, now those costs can be more easily contained and more accurately predicted in the future, thanks to modern analytics and publicly available energy data sets. One example of how data analysis can be used to increase profits and lower costs is found in UPS' Right Turn Policy, which saved time and fuel and greatly reduced accidents by routing trucks in such a way as to avoid making left turns. You also saw how publicly-available energy data may affect consumer buying patterns in the future such as in home sales. Further, you learned how crowd-sourcing is being encouraged by the U.S. government to speed innovation in this sector.

CHAPTER 17

USE CASES IN RETAIL

Over the past several years the retail sector has been bombarded with challenges. Brick-and-mortar stores have closed in record numbers and continue to do so. Indeed virtually every member of the entire industry is at high risk. They are vexed by several threats ranging from increased competition from online super-shopper sites such as Amazon to a plethora of more brand-specific problems, such as a lack of differentiators, pricing pressures, muddled marketing messaging, poor business processes, online pricing/brand comparison sites, customer reviews on their own websites, vulnerability to customer social messaging, and an overall disconnection with the buying public. Their former strategies in merchandising, merchandise selection, pricing models, customer service, and marketing are no longer working as effectively as they have in the past.

Consider these findings from an April 2014 report on apparel retailers by Stealing Share, a company that conducts brand research and provides corporate rebranding, marketing strategy, competitive analysis, brand positioning, brand training, and brand design for clients:

Despite what the retailers say, they are not. The major learning while Stealing Share strategists were looking at the retail market was how much it was full of blaring noise. Everything—from style to messaging to operations—ran together to form a ceaseless blob that consumers are increasingly tuning out.

The differences between retailers are as thin as blades of grass. It may be the most undifferentiated market we have ever seen. That is why the doomsday scenario is in play for many retail outlets.

Think about this. Only 10 years ago, The Gap was the 18th largest retailer in the nation. Last year, it was 33rd. The Sears Holding Company (which owns both Sears and Kmart) saw sales drop 9.2% in 2013. J.C. Penney's dropped a whopping 24.7%.

We could go on and on. But the future is coming and changes must be made. Take heed. If you don't, you will lose.

OLD TACTICS IN A BIG DATA RE-RUN

The state of the retail market can be clearly conceptualized by looking at Figure 17.1, which is a snapshot of month-to-month and year-to-year estimates for the industry from the U.S. Census Bureau's "Advance Monthly Sales for Retail and Food Services" report that was released on March 13, 2014. As you can see, this sector undeniably isn't doing well as of this writing.

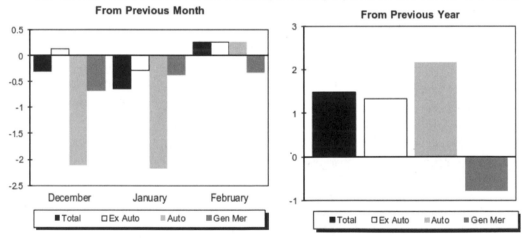

Figure 17.1
Month-to-month and year-to-year estimates for the industry from the U.S. Census Bureau's "Advance Monthly Sales for Retail and Food Services" report, released on March 13, 2014.
Source: U.S. Census Bureau News Release at http://www.census.gov/retail/marts/www/marts_current.pdf.

Retailers are aware of this, of course. But typically they are at a loss as to what to do about it. Therefore, they experiment with big data—usually focusing on transactional data but occasionally on a smattering of social media data—while they continue to beef up old tactics, such as loss leaders and product discounts offered to all buyers and often across all stores, in the hopes that something will work. In other words, instead of using data to figure out new tactics, most retailers are trying to fit more information into existing tactics.

Unfortunately, repeating old tactics will not change anything. At most they'll succeed in temporarily enticing a few shoppers in the moment, but it is unlikely they can hold onto them for any meaningful amount of time in the absence of brand loyalty and brand differentiators. So it is that shoppers come and go between store brands with little positive effect on the retailers' bottom lines.

Consider this analysis of the current retail clothing market from the aforementioned Stealing Share report:

> In this paradigm, and because of their polar positions, luxury retailers and discount stores already come with a built-in audience. Those shoppers seeking exclusivity for the privileged and top designer fashion will frequent the high-end markets, while those seeking a value will hit the discount shop.
>
> This then leaves the largest portion of the market in and around the middle. Here we find department and specialty stores lurking about, but without any real defining factors that separate them from the other contenders.
>
> In this realm, the department store aims to steal market share from both the luxury and discount category. The lunacy in that is the only way these stores can gain market share is by way of discounting merchandise and building store locations nearby. That's all.
>
> Obviously a growth plan based on both a revenue loss (discounting merchandise) and an increase in expenses (building more brick-and-mortar stores) doesn't have good odds at succeeding. The sector is badly in need of new business models and newer, more successful tactics—two things that big data excels at.

Retail Didn't Blow It; the Customers Changed

Part, but not all, of the problems that this sector faces comes from a radical change in consumer shopping behavior borne from the last recession. The recession of 2007–2009 created a lasting change in U.S. consumer mindsets wherein materialism and brand consciousness nearly disappeared. Retailers struggled to survive the recession, stripped of any former brand advantages and customer loyalties, and the subsequent downward pressures on pricing and already too thin margins.

Figure 17.2 shows a U.S. Bureau of Labor Statistics, Consumer Expenditure Survey chart, from a 2012 report titled "The Recession of 2007–2009." It shows average annual expenditures of all consumer units, aka households, in constant 2010 dollars, for the years 1984 to 2010. Note that in 1984, average total expenditures per household were $46,119 and in 2010, a year after the close of the recession, the average was a meager $48,109 nearly two decades later.

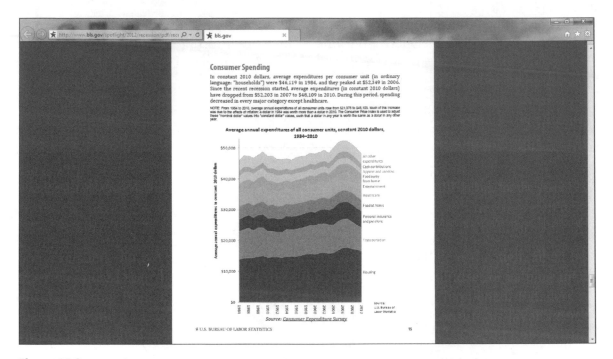

Figure 17.2
Average annual expenditures of all consumer units, aka households, in constant 2010 dollars, for the years 1984 to 2010.

Source: U.S. Bureau of Labor Statistics, Consumer Expenditure Survey at http://www.bls.gov/spotlight/2012/recession/pdf/recession_bls_spotlight.pdf.

Some retailers did not survive that recession. Those that did make it through, albeit battle scarred, pinned their hopes on a return of the traditional U.S. mindset of valuing materialism, favoring brands, and embracing debt. That so far hasn't happened. Retailers now fear that brand loyalty has been permanently put aside as most consumers favor steep discounts and an avoidance of debt when possible.

Brand Mutiny and Demon Customers

In fact, American consumers were showing signs of brand mutiny and a preference for steep discounts prior to the recession. This emerging shift did not go unnoticed by savvy brands. Some in retail thought it not only possible to fight back against these growing consumer behaviors but they also boldly and publicly stated that was their intention. The results were not pretty nor particularly helpful to the brands.

On July 6, 2004, CBS News reported that Larry Selden, a consultant that worked for Best Buy, called customers who were not loyal to the store and did things found unprofitable to the retailer "demon customers." Selden co-wrote a book titled *Angel Customers and Demon Customers* wherein he wrote "while retailers probably can't hire a bouncer to stand at the door and identify the value destroyer, they're not powerless."

And with that, the retail industry proactively began to seek ways to ditch customers who do deplorable things like buy stuff, get the rebate, and then return the item for a credit or a cash refund. But retailers didn't stop there. They began to turn their sights on discouraging and outright exorcising "demon customers" who only bought doorbuster sales items, without buying anything at regular price while doing so.

In other words, they ceased to see the sale of "loss leaders" as an expected loss and a necessary cost of doing business and instead came to see such losses as an attack on their profits by thieving "demon" customers. That mind shift in retailer thinking persists today and it's still not particularly helpful to retailers. The more profitable approach is not in culling customers from your customer base but in developing every customer in your base to increasingly higher levels of profitability. We'll get to that in a moment, but for now let's continue with our exploration of the notion of culling customers.

Retailers sought other ways to cull their customer lists too; keeping profitable customers while ditching as many unprofitable ones as they could identify. Typically they achieved this, at least in part, through the use of customer relationship management (CRM) software, which gave them insights to customer behavior primarily through transactional data. With CRM they could easily see who was buying what and at what price point and how regularly. From that information it became possible to offer incentives for good customers, other incentives for irregular customers, and none at all for the demonic bargain hunters.

Then along came the recession and good customers began to delay purchases and even stray from their favorite stores to find better prices. Customers who bought irregularly continued to do so or not at all. And thus the by-then broadly defined "demon customer" ranks (bargain hunters) grew to an unprecedented size. It became obvious that retailers could no longer be so picky about who they wanted to sell to. The race to the bottom of pricing was then on in earnest. However, pricing wars usually don't work as a long-term survival tactic because already slim margins get slimmer while business costs typically rise or stay the same. Of course, store closings and staff reductions quickly followed to reduce business costs. That in turn also decreased the customer experience thereby producing a further loss in sales and erosion of brand loyalty. The industry's business was now circling around the drain. Still, they held on as best they could and hoped for a better day.

Customer Experience Began to Matter Again

When things appeared to be improving a bit economically speaking, retailers turned to another tactic. This time it was to improve the customer experience in an effort to reestablish a brand differentiator and to rejuvenate brand loyalty. *Customer experience management* is a blended approach of using software by the same name, called CEM or CX for short, and affecting changes in both the real and virtual worlds. The intent was to view the entire operation from the customer's perspective and revamp anything necessary to make the shopping experience more pleasurable and memorable.

These efforts typically took everything into account from where shopping carts were placed in the parking lot, the lineup of vehicles on a dealer's lot, or other "outside the door" elements of the operation, through the door to the actual shopping experiences there, be it on a virtual or real store floor, and all the way through cash-out, the at home experience, and customer service afterwards. Although this effort continues today, it still hasn't produced the effects retailers hoped for—more cash in their coffers.

Big Data and the Demon Customer Revival

Then along came big data and the insights it could bring. At first retailers were enthralled with the ability to get to know their customers better and therefore make personalized offers they hoped would entice more sales per customer. But it wasn't long before many of the retailers moved from a "we're here to serve" motive to a "yeah, but what have you done for me lately, customer" attitude. In other words, many retailers reverted back to a version of the demon customer mindset. The effort was no longer pointed at attracting, rewarding, and maintaining good customers through loyalty programs and personalized offers, but to punish and drive away customers the retailers deemed not just unprofitable, but not profitable enough.

One example of this can be seen in a February 6, 2014 CBS New York report:

> *A warning if you shop online and have a habit of returning items, you may be in for a surprise—more retailers are starting to take notice and some are even punishing repeat offenders...*
>
> *"The days of using your living room as a fitting room are yes, going to be coming to a close," retail expert Carol Spieckerman said. "For retailers, returns are an absolute nightmare."*
>
> *In addition to charging restocking fees, stores may also start revoking free shipping, CBS 2's Kristine Johnson reported.*
>
> *Promotions and coupons may also be a thing of the past for customers who frequently return merchandise.*

And this, despite the fact that retailers are largely still unable to differentiate themselves to any appreciable degree and are still locked in an unsustainable pricing war. As the authors of the Stealing Share report put it, "the retail industry is amuck... What does the future hold? How can any retail environment survive when most retailers are simply copying one another? At the end of the day, is price, discounting, and over-saturating the market the only game worth playing? Are the department store websites eating their own young?"

Yes, the industry is a complete mess but to their credit, they are seeking ways to right the ship again. Big data is the best tool they have in doing so. But that's not to say that they've figured out quite how to use it yet. Even so, they'll have to keep trying and keep experimenting because really they have no choice if they are to survive and prosper.

You can always find data on where the retail sector stands as of the most recent reporting/survey dates at the U.S. Department of Commerce, U.S. Census Bureau, most notably on its website in the Monthly and Annual Retail Trade data sets and reports. Figure 17.3 shows a screenshot of the Bureau's data set lists in this category as of this writing. The Bureau regularly updates these data sets and provides new reports, so it is a good idea to check back often.

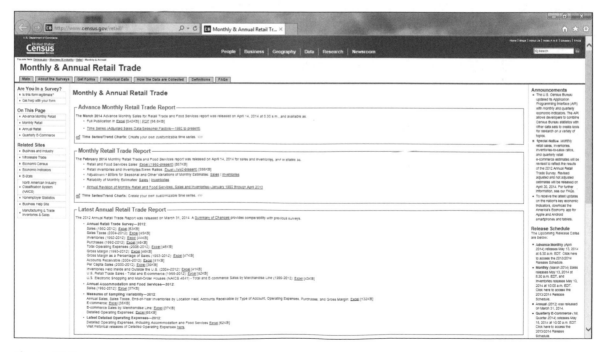

Figure 17.3
The U.S. Department of Commerce, U.S. Census Bureau's data set lists in this category as of this writing.

Source: U.S. Department of Commerce, U.S. Census Bureau at http://www.census.gov/retail/.

WHY RETAIL HAS STRUGGLED WITH BIG DATA

Big data tools, unlike any other, can show retailers what is happening now rather than merely dissecting what happened in the past, uncloak emerging threats and opportunities, and spur changes in innovation, processes, and future business model needs. Right about now, every retailer reading this is totally disgusted, having heard all this before but not seeing any of it actually work profitably—or at least not seeing it work to the extent proponents loudly and broadly claim. That disgust and aggravation is not unwarranted, however the fault lies not in the big data tools, but in how they are currently approached and used.

The problem retailers have run into so far using big data is two-fold. First, the data hygiene problem can lead to crippling big data failures. For one thing, "information certainty" gets fuzzier outside of structured data, that is, the retailer's own transactional data. In other words, the retailer knows that their own transactional data is both correct and uniformly structured in "conventional" databases, whereas much of the data they now import, such as from social media, is not. Well, the retailer presumes its transactional data is correct. In some cases that data is clean; in others, not so much. It all depends on how well the retailer breaches data siloes, integrates software, synchronizes file changes, and purges outdated information—as is the case in any other organization's data operations.

Dirty data and/or incomplete data lies at the heart of nearly 40% of all failed big data projects. Yes, it is hard to understand how such massive amounts of data, especially when combined with other data set inputs, could be incomplete, but that is often the case. Just because you have lots of information about some things doesn't mean the information you're still missing won't hurt your output. The key is to look for data and form algorithms that complete the puzzle you're trying to solve in such a way that you end up with an accurate and full picture. Otherwise, all you have is a picture of something unrecognizable or suggestive of something different than it should portray because it has too many missing pieces.

Second in the retailers' two-fold problem is the lack of creativity in the formation of big data questions. Like many organizations in every industry, retailers typically ask the same old questions of big data that they asked of smaller data. Namely those are in the vein of "who are my best/worst customers" and "which products are moving best/making me the most money?" While it's perfectly understandable to ask these questions repeatedly, they give too narrow a view if that is all you ask. Further, asking the same questions of big data that you've always asked in the course of your business keeps your mind in the same framework as before, thereby blocking new thoughts and ideas. The goal before retailers today is to change the organization into a highly distinctive, fully differentiated, profit-generating machine. How are you going to do that by doing the same things over and over again ad nauseam?

This trap of asking the same old questions of big data is harder to escape than you might think. Because the ultimate concern of any business is on costs and profits, the questions asked of big data tend to exclusively focus on those concerns too. Certainly the answers to these questions are pressing and important. However, they are also too pointed. You can poke a hole for a glimpse of what you need with these pointed questions, but you can't slice the blinders from your view with them. Just as many now-disappeared railroad companies of the last century failed to adapt because they narrowed their view to "we're in the railroad business" rather than the broader, and proper, question of "we're in the transportation business," retailers today need to call on big data to answer both the "small" familiar questions of profits and loss items but also the broader "meta" questions that can mean the difference ultimately between success and mere survival.

WAYS BIG DATA CAN HELP RETAIL

In a nutshell, these typical problems with using big data, or in plotting the path forward in general, is why retailers are having a tough time in finding their way. Instead, retailers find themselves continuing to resort to cliché advertising messaging, personalized marketing that is anything but, and broadly offered, deep discounts they can ill afford. If status quo continues to be projected into big data projects in retailing, than status quo will be the result of the efforts, i.e. small gains if there are any gains at all. Figure 17.4 is a table from the U.S. Census Bureau News' press release on its "Advance Monthly Sales For Retail and Food Services February 2014" report showing "Estimated Change in Monthly Sales for Retail and Food Services by Kind of Business" for the period. As you can see, in status quo, as depicted in this chart, is not where retailers would like to see their business stay.

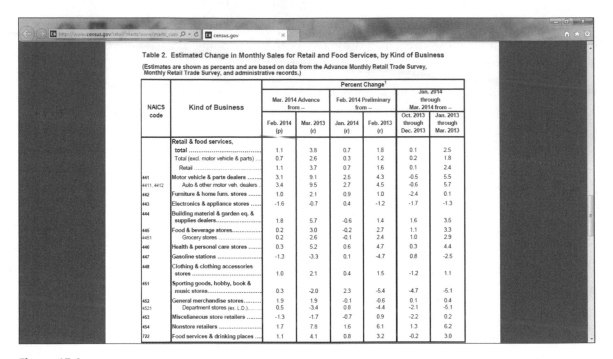

Table 2. Estimated Change in Monthly Sales for Retail and Food Services, by Kind of Business

(Estimates are shown as percents and are based on data from the Advance Monthly Retail Trade Survey, Monthly Retail Trade Survey, and administrative records.)

NAICS code	Kind of Business	Percent Change[1]					
		Mar. 2014 Advance from --		Feb. 2014 Preliminary from --		Jan. 2014 through Mar. 2014 from --	
		Feb. 2014 (p)	Mar. 2013 (r)	Jan. 2014 (r)	Feb. 2013 (r)	Oct. 2013 through Dec. 2013	Jan. 2013 through Mar. 2013
	Retail & food services, total	1.1	3.8	0.7	1.8	0.1	2.5
	Total (excl. motor vehicle & parts)	0.7	2.6	0.3	1.2	0.2	1.8
	Retail	1.1	3.7	0.7	1.6	0.1	2.4
441	Motor vehicle & parts dealers	3.1	9.1	2.5	4.3	-0.5	5.5
4411, 4412	Auto & other motor veh. dealers .	3.4	9.5	2.7	4.5	-0.6	5.7
442	Furniture & home furn. stores	1.0	2.1	0.9	1.0	-2.4	0.1
443	Electronics & appliance stores	-1.6	-0.7	0.4	-1.2	-1.7	-1.3
444	Building material & garden eq. & supplies dealers.........................	1.8	5.7	-0.6	1.4	1.6	3.5
445	Food & beverage stores.................	0.2	3.0	-0.2	2.7	1.1	3.3
4451	Grocery stores	0.2	2.6	-0.1	2.4	1.0	2.9
446	Health & personal care stores	0.3	5.2	0.6	4.7	0.3	4.4
447	Gasoline stations	-1.3	-3.3	0.1	-4.7	0.8	-2.5
448	Clothing & clothing accessories stores	1.0	2.1	0.4	1.5	-1.2	1.1
451	Sporting goods, hobby, book & music stores..............................	0.3	-2.0	2.3	-5.4	-4.7	-5.1
452	General merchandise stores..........	1.9	1.9	-0.1	-0.6	0.1	0.4
4521	Department stores (ex. L.D.)......	0.5	-3.4	0.8	-4.4	-2.1	-5.1
453	Miscellaneous store retailers	-1.3	-1.7	-0.7	0.9	-2.2	0.2
454	Nonstore retailers	1.7	7.8	1.6	6.1	1.3	6.2
722	Food services & drinking places	1.1	4.1	0.8	3.2	-0.2	3.0

Figure 17.4

U.S. Census Bureau News' press release showing estimated change in monthly sales for retail and food services.

Source: U.S. Census Bureau News' press release. See current version at http://www.census.gov/retail/marts/www/marts_current.pdf (Table 2).

In order to break that pattern, retailers need to do something different. That means looking at the business differently and deliberately seeking out new ways to find profit. To that end, additional big data projects should include, but not be limited to, the tactics discussed in the following sections.

Product Selection and Pricing

The goal here is to ultimately aid in differentiation through product selection, product bundling and grouping, and value-added services and incentives. This is also a way to note product fluctuations and product category movements and trends early and overall. This can help in determining which items to discount and what merchandise your buyers should be buying in the future.

For example, retailers have historically stocked apparel in their stores according to national apparel size averages. But this tactic may be costing them revenue when customers can't find their size on racks and shelves to buy. If the problem of size availability continues, customers may actually become discouraged and stop shopping at that store entirely. Meanwhile, the retailer has left-over product at the end of the season that it must now mark-down which further cuts into its revenue. If, however, a retailer stocks sizes according to customer needs and preferences in each store location, the opposite reaction occurs: more product is sold and customers regularly return as they know they'll likely find their size in most items at that store. This is the beginning of a brand differentiator and budding new brand loyalty.

Such sizing data already exists and brands can either act on that data alone or add it to their algorithms to further enhance their product buying and inventory decisions. It would be a mistake to determine size selections based on the store's transactional data alone as that data would not account for items not purchased (lost sales) due to size unavailability and therefore is unlikely to deliver the correct answer in the analysis.

So where is that existing apparel size data? One place you can find it is at Stitch Labs, a producer of inventory management control systems. The company says it analyzed more than $100 Million in apparel sales from tens of thousands of retailers to determine sizing trends across the United States.

"The data indicates that consumers in western states (California, Washington, Oregon, Idaho, Nevada, Utah and Hawaii) prefer smaller sized apparel, purchasing almost double the amount of X-Small apparel compared to the U.S. average," the company announced in its report released to the press on June 24, 2014. "Consumers in South Dakota, Nebraska and Iowa, on the other hand, purchase the most X-Large and 2X-Large apparel. One in three pieces of apparel purchased in these states is an X-Large or 2X-Large."

From this analysis, it is relatively easy to see how something as simple as changing the size selection of apparel in stores can significantly improve profits, customer satisfaction, and brand loyalty. Figure 17.5 is an infographic built from the Stitch Labs sizing data analysis for a fast overall view of customer size preferences per state.

The point is to use data in product selection and then work with data on optimum pricing to improve both your store profits and brand loyalty.

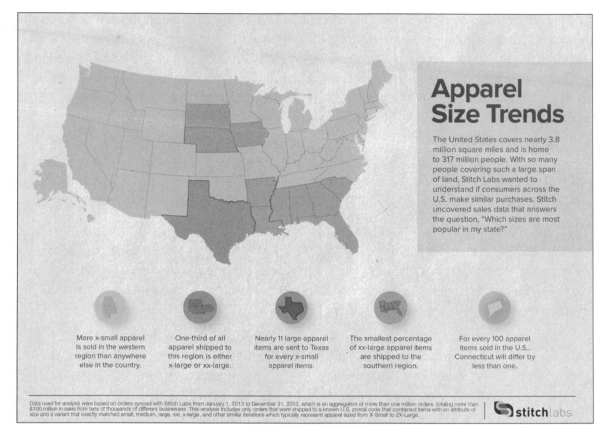

Figure 17.5
Infographic from Stitch Labs' data analysis on customer preferred apparel sizes per state.
Source: Stitch Labs. Reprinted with permission.

Current Market Analysis

This includes analysis in near-real-time to note any shifts and trends in the overall market. Retailers need to watch for patterns found among indirect competitors such as those within the collaborative economy discussed in Chapter 8, those outside your retail category (luxury, discount, specialty, and so on), and those in geographic markets where you also have a store.

Use Big Data to Develop New Pricing Models

This could allow retail chains to avoid broadly available discounts that may hurt their bottom lines if these loss leaders become sole purchases. Look instead to adjusting pricing in personalized offerings that reward good customers and entice irregular and new customers. Avoid any actions designed to punish customers. Such is self-defeating because many of these so-called demon customers are actually suffering from a jobless recovery after the recession or otherwise temporarily encumbered. You don't have to encourage their behavior, just avoid doing anything that will turn them off of your brand when they are in better financial circumstances. You also don't want to inadvertently spark new regulations intended to stop price discrimination and unfair business practices. Remember that using big data successfully means using it to improve both the short- and long-term results.

Find Better Ways to Get More, Better, and Cleaner Customer Data

Approach data gathering in a way that respects privacy and actively solicits customer partnerships to aid in brand differentiation and customer loyalty. Your data will be cleaner (more accurate and up-to-date) if customers give it to you willingly than if you try to collect it on the sly. Consider offering customers something tangible for their data and self-service data updates, such as an extra service, a discount toward their next purchase (and every purchase after a self-service data update), points towards price discounts in the future, or access to first views and buying opportunities of new inventory or inventory "reserved" for these special data-sharing customers (inventory not offered on your website or in-store to other customers).

Whatever you do, do not think that offering a "personalized ad" is in anyway compensation for their data. The truth is everyone hates ads. Distributing and displaying them are to your benefit, not the customers'—at least that is the case in the customers' minds. By all means you should be distributing highly-targeted, personalized ads—just don't think you're doing the customers a favor in doing so.

Study and Predict Customer Acceptance and Reaction

This should be done prior to investing in new technologies and changing stores. For example, analyze studies and tests for potential consumer reaction to service automation and self-service customer service before you fully invest in it. Also use big data to compute the mid- and long-term impacts of any changes you are considering.

Applebee's and Chili's Experiments

At the time of this writing, Applebee's and its rival Chili's are busy putting tablets on tabletops to enable customers to view menus, place their own orders, and cash themselves out, which will eventually reduce or eliminate the store's need for waitresses, waiters, and cashiers. This is very appealing to restaurants as it means they can eventually wave good-bye or reduce the impact of minimum wage increases and other employee costs such as health insurance mandated through the Affordable Care Act.

A December 2, 2013 *USA Today* article reports that the tablets have 7-inch screens, which are larger than a cell phone's but smaller than the tablets most consumers own. While the move clearly targets younger customers it may actually be a barrier to older customers who may have trouble viewing the screen or placing orders and making payments on it. This would be bad for restaurants as the U.S. population is aging, meaning that for years to come there will be far more older than younger customers in the market. Further, using tabletop technology reduces the personal interaction between restaurant staff and customers, thereby decreasing the chances of developing customer loyalty to the brand. So yes, it could reduce a restaurant's employee expenses but it may also cost it in sales. The *USA Today* report said that Applebee's plans to offset this somewhat by continuing to give patrons a traditional menu as well, at least for awhile. Even so, this move may very well backfire in the end.

For one thing, if the trend continues to automate every possible job, how far will that diminish the customer base? Think of it this way—if the recession harmed retailers to the extent that it did because of job losses and loss in consumer confidence, how can mass job reduction through automation affect retailers not only in the same time frame as a typical recession, but for all of the foreseeable future? Can retailers really afford to join the job elimination movement and cut off the hand that feeds it?

What Walmart Is Doing

Walmart isn't so sure and is considering a move to *increase* consumers' ability to buy from them through supporting an increase in the minimum wage. One might think, considering that Walmart is the largest private employer in the nation, that an increase in minimum wage would drive its payroll costs to untenable heights. But this is what Renee Dudley reports about the retail giant's thoughts on the issue in her February 19, 2014 article in *Bloomberg*:

> *"Walmart is weighing the impact of additional payroll costs against possibly attracting more consumer dollars to its stores," David Tovar, a company spokesman, said today in a telephone interview. "Increasing the minimum wage means that some of the 140 million people who shop at the chain weekly would 'now have additional income,'" Tovar said.*

> *In the mid-2000s, Walmart backed an increase in the federal minimum wage that eventually took effect in 2007. Asked whether Walmart would support another raise in the federal minimum wage, Tovar said, "That's something we're looking at. Whenever there's debates, it's not like we look once and make a decision. We look a few times from other angles."*

It is telling that Walmart, and not Applebee's and Chili's, is the poster child for big data use in retailing. It is also telling that Walmart is a super giant in retailing and not prone to mistakes in its market moves. Now think about that a moment. Which plan—eliminating jobs through automation or increasing minimum wage nationwide—is more likely to spur retail sales? A big data project run properly could easily determine that. There is no reason to guess or to cook up ideas and plans in an isolated bubble. Turn to big data and find out, and then make your move accordingly.

The J.C. Penney Failure

Consider J.C. Penney's woeful tablet tale and its disastrous move away from its established but older customer base to cater to a younger, hipper crowd. Note that J.C. Penney isn't a big data poster child either. If it had been, this scenario would never have come to be. Here is how Brad Tuttle reported in *Time* J.C. Penney's horrific fall and the subsequent firing of CEO Ron Johnson, former retail superstar at Target and Apple stores:

> As Johnson removed their beloved coupons and sales and increasingly focused on making J.C. Penney a hip "destination" shopping experience complete with boutique stores within the larger store, many of the chain's oldest and most loyal customers understandably felt like they were no longer J.C. Penney's target market. The return of "sales" hasn't proved to bring about a return of these shoppers.
>
> Johnson pictured coffee bars and rows of boutiques inside J.C. Penney stores. He wanted a bazaar-like feel to the shopping experience, and for J.C. Penney to be "America's favorite place to shop." He thought that people would show up in stores because they were fun places to hang out, and that they would buy things listed at full-but-fair price.
>
> But early and often during the Johnson era, critics pointed out that J.C. Penney was not the Apple Store. The latter features cutting edge consumer tech that shoppers have grown accustomed to purchasing at full price. J.C. Penney, on the other hand, is stuck with a "reputation as the place your mom dragged you to buy clothes you hated in 1984," as a Consumerist post put it. The idea that people would show up at J.C. Penney just to hang out, and that its old-fashioned shoppers would be comfortable with Johnson's radical plans like the removal of checkout counters almost seems delusional [checkout counters were replaced with tablets].
>
> In retrospect, Johnson and J.C. Penney seem like a horrible match. All along, Johnson insisted that he absolutely adored the venerable J.C. Penney brand. But if he loved it so much, why was he so hell bent on dramatically changing it, rather than tweaking and gently reshaping as needed?

Once again we see that gut instinct and past experience are not enough to steer a company in the right direction. Knowing the customer base intimately and leveraging their buying triggers is key and that requires a mastery of big data.

Sears and MetaScale—A Big Data Love Story

Sears was once the largest U.S. retailer by revenue count and enjoyed high ratings in consumer trust and brand loyalty. Since then, the very same problems that have plagued all of retail, such as shifting consumer shopping trends, the rise of online competitors and a major recession, have also tormented Sears. The giant retailer has tried several strategies to regain its footing in the market with mixed success. One of those strategies was an early foray into big data. It is still working hard with data to this day.

"We were already dealing with big data as we had already amassed a huge volume but it was expensive and inefficient to do much with it," said Sunil Kakade, IT Director at Sears Holding Corporation, in a phone interview for this book. "Everyone accepted the limits of the technology at the time. But, the nature of our business was changing so we needed to find a tech platform that would enable us to compute more information, more often and cheaper."

It was then that the company turned to Hadoop and took its first serious step into using big data to guide the company forward.

"We have thousands of jobs running at a time and we have learned a lot in this process," said Kakade. "Big data is not going to solve all your problems though, so use the best of both worlds."

Kakade offered a few more tips for retailers in that interview concerning using big data:

- Don't lock yourself in with vendors. The whole nature of big data is open source, leverage that. Plus, the industry is immature and if you lock-in with one vendor or distribution you risk their going out of business and having to start over.

- Dedicate multiple teams to big data because it is evolving and you have to stay on top of it. We also have software developers who are available if we need more help. You may want to do that too. It also helps to have teams dedicated according to functional expertise required by the systems, such as in supply chain, pricing, marketing, human resources, and so on.

- Move forward and start making decisions now. You need a smart strategy first to take advantage of big data and optimize everything.

Shortly after the company started using Hadoop for its own benefit, Sears launched MetaScale, a new big data subsidiary to serve not only Sears, but other companies too.

Rachel King reported in her April 30, 2012 piece in the *Wall Street Journal* how this came to be:

> *Sears is certainly not the first retailer to try applying advanced business analytics to create more targeted marketing to its best customers. But it may be the first retailer to turn that activity into a service it will sell to companies in other industries.*
>
> *On April 24, [2012], Sears launched MetaScale, a new big data subsidiary. For the last couple of years, [now former] Sears CIO Keith Sherwell has been using open source software called Hadoop that lets the retailer search through reams of information to better understand its business. For example, Sears discovered that many people who go into its stores to buy jewelry also buy tools.*
>
> *Sherwell realized as he was providing services to other divisions of Sears internally that other businesses might also benefit from the expertise Sears had built with Hadoop. MetaScale is selling managed Hadoop services that will be customized and implemented in a matter of weeks. MetaScale will target customers with revenue in the range of $1 billion to $10 billion in industries such as healthcare and entertainment. MetaScale will avoid selling services to its competitors, said Sherwell. The day-to-day operations of MetaScale will be run by Sears CTO Phil Shelley.*
>
> *These services can be used to better target offers to customers. For example, Hadoop software can search through raw transactional data from each cash register and online purchases at the item level to glean insights about a specific customer's preferences.*

While Sears' original big data masterminds, former CEO Lou D'Ambrosio and former CIO Keith Sherwell, have exited the company, Sears' big data efforts and MetaScale live on, albeit separately. The MetaScale website only mentions that it "grew out of a Fortune 100 enterprise" with no mention at all that the enterprise was Sears. Executives on the retailer end also make no mention of MetaScale when discussing their big data efforts. Presumably this is because MetaScale was spun off as a separate company and the two are trying to keep proper distance from one another even though MetaScale executives still speak fondly of their hard-won expertise with big data in the retail sector.

Figure 17.6 shows how MetaScale handles data migration from a mainframe using big data tools.

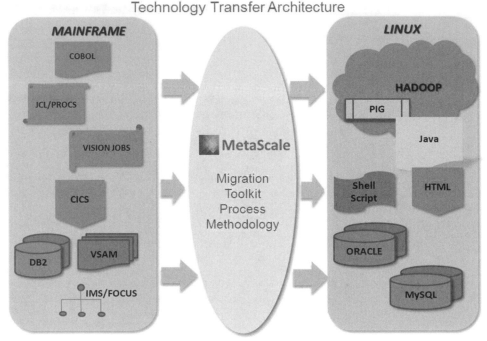

Figure 17.6
Mainframe migration with big data tools.
Source: MetaScale. Reprinted with permission.

Predict and Plan Responses to Trends in the Broader Marketplace

One mistake retail is notorious for repeatedly making is thinking it exists in its own bubble, unaffected by whatever else is going on in the world except maybe by changes in the economy. The rise of such disrupters as Amazon and eBay should have been a wake-up call to the industry and in some ways it was. But many retailers have yet to regain their footing since. Now there are more disruptors on the horizon and retailers will have to really scramble to catch up and surpass these challenges. Revisit Chapter 8 on the rise of the collaborative economy for an example of new challenges on that front.

Enter 3D Printers

There are other changes coming as well, such as 3D printers. Already manufacturers are using 3D printers, known in those circles as additive manufacturing, to produce goods faster, cheaper, and more precisely. Additive manufacturing means a device, a 3D printer, constructs the item by layering raw material to a precise, predetermined shape.

By comparison, the traditional way is to use subtractive manufacturing, which means cutting or stamping a shape out of the raw material. In other words, the process subtracts the shape from a chuck of raw material. Subtractive manufacturing produces a lot of waste; additive manufacturing does not. As of this writing, additive manufacturing is well underway and producing everything from car parts to human dentures.

In the near future, 3D printers will be in wider use. Instead of shipping goods assembled in a manufacturing plant or from a retailer to a customer, in many cases design codes will be sent to on-site 3D printers instead and produced there. This situation will enable on-site production in regional or local distribution centers as well as on customer premises. For example, companies of the Kinko's ilk can receive design codes and print items for customer pick-up or local delivery. This will of course diminish the need for long distance, overnight, and ground shipping services such as those provided by FedEx and UPS. Eventually, many items can be produced on the customer's own 3D printer in their business and home. This will be especially true of items made from common and easily handled raw materials. If an image of the Star Trek replicator has popped into your mind, you're not far off.

Home Body Scanners

Also in the near future will be the rise of home body scanners. Indeed these are in use today albeit in a limited fashion. Personal body scanners can be used in the privacy of the consumer's own home to take precise body measurements. Such measurements can be used to virtually "try-on" and order clothing and other items made to fit perfectly. This will decrease or eliminate the need to return items after purchase to retailers because of fit or "look" issues. The body scan can be uploaded to a device screen where the consumer can then see how the item looks on them before purchase. If the consumer likes what they see, their measurements can then be sent to the retailer to purchase the item in a precise fit, rather than a generic size. The retailer can then upload the measurements to their own 3D printers to produce it, send the adjusted code to the customer's 3D printer for production there, or send the measurements to a manufacturer to print and ship it.

The days of buying a piece of clothing in a size 6 or 12, or whatever general size grouping are quickly coming to an end. Instead, items will be ordered in "My Size" in whatever individual measurements are required. This will come to be because of the versatility of 3D printers in producing items individually rather than in bulk.

An example of such scanners in use today is Shapify, an online service that leverages hand-held scanners and software to produce a physical but miniature 3D model of the person scanned. A November 19, 2013 article by Elisabeth Eitel titled "Does This $59 3D-Printed Figurine Make Me Look Fat?" in *Machine Design* explains how this system works:

> *The service uses models made with a commercial game controller sold for use with the popular Xbox 360 console to make a detailed scan of a person's body and then additive manufacture a physical 3D model of it. More specifically, Artec's Shapify service uses models made with a Xbox Kinect (or Kinect for Windows).*

> *First, users scan themselves, friends, or family with the Kinect—one person at a time, please—and then upload the scans to the Shapify website. Next, software sends the models over a server to a 3D printer that generates the figurines. A week or so later, presto—the user gets her Mini Me (and Friends, where available) in the mail.*

Figures 17.7 and 17.8 show examples of figurines that Shapify produces on a 3D printer using a person's body scan made via an Xbox Kinect game console.

Figure 17.7
Figurine that Shapify produced on a 3D printer using a person's body scan made via an Xbox Kinect game console.
Source: Shapify/Artec Group.

Figure 17.8
Another figurine from Shapify produced on a 3D printer.
Source: Shapify/Artec Group.

PREDICTING THE FUTURE OF RETAIL

Obviously these changes, separately and together, will abruptly alter how retailing is done. It behooves the industry to prepare for such now. Some retailers may want to strive to be the first to offer such since first to market has its advantages. Others may prefer to incorporate upcoming market changes into their model to enhance customer experience and continue to entice customers to shop at their brick-and-mortar stores.

Former J.C. Penney CEO Ron Johnson was not wrong in thinking of shopping as a social event and in trying to leverage that aspect to entice and retain more shoppers. There are reasons why customers do not exclusively shop online and shopping as a social experience is chief among them.

Johnson's timing was a bit off and he followed his gut in creating what he thought a prime social experience for shoppers would be rather than building an experience more in tune with what the customer base defined the preferred social experience to be.

In the face of changes to come in retailing, such a plan may work marvelously well for other retailers. The point is that while Johnson's instincts were right on the money, his actions based on that gut call were not. Had he used big data to understand his customer base better and plan his actions accordingly, the end of this story would have been vastly different and Johnson would have likely been hailed as a visionary.

If the brick-and-mortar retail sector is to save itself, it must hasten and improve its use and mastery of big data and other technologies. It must also reinvent itself in ways previously never imagined. Retailers cannot afford to operate on gut instinct or stick to business as usual.

Summary

In this chapter you learned how the retail industry came to be in the position it is now. You learned that changes to the industry wrought by outside forces such as brand mutiny, online competitors, and the last recession have forever changed the marketscape for this sector. You also learned that retail companies have made some bad decisions along the way in their attempts to survive in the face of adversity and later to prosper in spite of it.

You also learned that the retail industry is still not in the clear as many challenges still remain and more change is coming. You now know what some of those are and how retailers might profitably address them.

Last but not least, you saw how retailers that have mastered big data, such as Walmart, compare to retailers that have not yet mastered it, such as Applebee's and J.C. Penney. You saw from these comparisons how radically different the thinking and implementations are as a result—and the differences in outcomes, either already achieved or likely to come soon.

The take-away is that retail has to reinvent itself to stay in business—not just once but repeatedly. Big data offers the best and safest means with which to do that.

CHAPTER 18

USE CASES IN BANKING AND FINANCIAL SERVICES

Banking and other financial services institutions are a study in contradictions. On the one hand they traditionally excel at calculating and containing risks, which means of course that they generally excel at using data effectively. On the other hand, they're not doing so well in using big data.

DEFINING THE PROBLEM

Big data tools are not so much the main problem for this group, although some are certainly struggling with those, rather they generally suffer from a "brain rut," where their thinking on the various aspects of their business models, product lines, risk calculations, and investments is so deeply rooted in tradition that they often have difficulty branching out into more creative approaches. When they do try to break free of their rut, they sometimes do so by throwing caution to the wind as we saw happen in the financial crisis leading to the last worldwide recession. Somehow far too many investment banks thought disregarding prudence and risk control was necessary in spurring innovation and creating new profits. That of course was not the case and the rest as they say is history.

When things went sour for financial institutions during and after the recession, most retreated to the old ways and clutched their on-hand cash with a tighter grip. Credit availability dipped to almost zero for a good while as a result. Now credit is more available from traditional institutions but nowhere near where lending was before 2008–09. The tendency is to still go overboard in risk reduction, a situation further channeled by increased federal laws and regulations enacted in recent years. The end result is to extend credit only to a small percentage of customers and prospects who are largely most notable for somehow escaping punishing blows from the recession. In other words, lending prospects who suffered losses in the recession but are otherwise responsible borrowers are almost entirely ignored by traditional lenders.

The problem with this approach in traditional lending is three-fold. For one thing, shrinking one's customer base is always a bad idea. Fewer customers generally equates to fewer sales, smaller profits, and a higher future loss in customer attrition. For another, this approach opens the door wide for competitors to encroach and even seize the bank's market share. Hunkering down in a defensive position encourages aggressive competitors to go on offense and move in on your territory. And third, while traditional financial institutions spurn potential customers and new alternative lenders welcome them with open arms, the public perception of banks shifts from essential financial service providers to nonessential, perhaps irrelevant, players in a crowded field.

In short, business-as-usual in financial services is crippling the industry.

Some financial institutions recognize this and are trying to change things by using big data more proactively and creatively but with mixed results. Gartner analyst Ethan Wang explained in his October 22, 2013 report what Gartner found is happening on this front:

> *In Gartner's recent survey, most organizations were at the early stages of big data adoption—and only 13% of surveyed banks had reached the stage of deployment. Many banks are investigating big data opportunities and initiating big data projects on a "me too" basis. Their executives have heard—though not seen—that their competitors are exploiting big data, and they are afraid of being left behind. They find, however, that it is difficult to monetize big data projects based on an explicit business ROI.*

To learn how to monetize data and calculate ROI, see Chapter 7. In this section, the focus will be on use cases and strategies for banks and financial services. To learn more about the current financial and structural information for most FDIC-insured institutions, you can download data on individual institutions or bulk data on the entire group from the Federal Financial Institutions Examination Council (FFIEC) Central Data Repository's Public Data Distribution website at https://cdr.ffiec.gov/public/. Figure 18.1 shows information on that repository.

Figure 18.1

The Federal Financial Institutions Examination Council (FFIEC) Central Data Repository and data sets.

Source: Federal Financial Institutions Examination Council (FFIEC) Central Data Repository's Public Data Distribution website at https://cdr.ffiec.gov/public/.

USE CASES IN BANKS AND LENDING INSTITUTIONS

Like organizations in many industries, banks have plenty of data on hand and more at their disposal. So the problem is not the lack of total information, but in figuring out how to use it and for what purposes.

Surprisingly, some banks are using big data successfully but fail to recognize that is what they are doing. By not recognizing these efforts for what they are, the banks fail to grasp and leverage lessons learned in big data projects. Gartner analyst Ethan Wang explains this phenomenon in the same report cited previously:

> It is worth noting that many banks are seeking or implementing what could be regarded as big data initiatives—frequently at the business-unit level—but are not referring to them as big data projects. Instead, they are often identifying them by the business problems or needs they are trying to address, such as real-time fraud detection and prevention, systemic risk analysis, intraday liquidity analysis or the offering of information-based value-added services. It is not unusual for both business-unit leaders and bank CIOs to fail to recognize the big data nature of these activities. Bank CIOs and business-unit leaders should review these current projects, where business cases and key performance indicators have already been established, and identify when these create opportunities to show the value and role of big data. This would save the efforts involved in building a business case and calculating a financial forecast from scratch.

Many banks are unsure where to start with big data. First, look to see if you already have projects in motion that are using copious amounts of data. If so, find and use the lessons learned within them as Wang suggests. Otherwise the best place to start is in any activity where you currently use data analysis. Choose one or a few of those that you judge to be in most need of improvement and then begin a pilot project or two accordingly.

"Almost every single major decision to drive revenue, to control costs, or to mitigate risks can be infused with data and analytics," said Toos Daruvala, a director in McKinsey's New York office, in a McKinsey & Company video interview online titled "How Advanced Analytics Are Redefining Banking."

Daruvala also gave examples in that video interview on how three banks specifically used big data to their advantage:

> Let me give you a couple of examples of real-world situations where I've seen this applied quite powerfully. There was one large bank in the United States, which had not refreshed their small-business underwriting models in several years. Certainly not post the crisis. And they were getting worried about the [risk] discriminatory power of these models.

> The Gini coefficient of their models—which is just a measure of how powerful a model is in terms of its ability to discriminate between good risks and bad risks—was down in the sort of 40- to 45% range. What these folks did was developed a 360-degree view of the customer across the entire relationship that that small business had with the bank, across all the silos. Not easy to do; easy to talk about, not easy to do.

> And then what they did was selectively append third-party data from external sources, trying to figure out which of those third-party pieces of information would have the most discriminatory power. And they applied the analytical techniques to redo their models and essentially took the Gini coefficient of the models up into the 75% range from the 40- to 45% range, which is a huge improvement in the discriminatory power of those models.

> Another bank that we were working with was in the developing markets, where data to begin with is pretty thin on consumers. And they decided that they would try to actually get data from the local telco. The paying behavior for the telco is actually a great predictive indicator for the credit behavior with the bank. And so they bought the data, appended that to the bank data, and again had a huge improvement in underwriting.

> Another institution, a marketing example, where we ended up using, again, that 360-degree view of the consumer and then appending some external data around social media to figure out what's the right next product to buy for that consumer and then equip the front line to make that offer to that consumer when they walk into the branch or when they call into the call center. And the efficacy of their predictor models on next-product-to-buy improved dramatically as well.

> So these are examples of things that you can do. And part of the reason why this is so important is that in the banking world, of course, in the current regulatory and macroeconomic environment, growth is really, really, really hard to come by.

While those are good examples, they are only a few ways big data can best be used by banks and financial institutions. Other use cases include strategic planning, new revenue stream discovery, product innovation, trading, compliance, and risk and security. For more information on how financial services can use big data in risk and security efforts, see Chapter 12, "Use Cases in Security."

Meanwhile, traditional financial institutions had better speed their use of big data in finding new business models and products because disruptive competitors are already on the scene.

How Big Data Fuels New Competitors in the Money-Lending Space

While banks and other traditional lending institutions struggle with how, when, where, and why to use big data, disruptive competitors are using big data to bore into their market strongholds. Where once people were at the mercy of traditional lenders and the only alternatives were pawn shops and predatory secondary lenders, there now exist alternative financiers that pose considerable threats to banks while opening substantial opportunities to borrowers. One example that immediately comes to mind is online banks that can compete more aggressively because they have less overhead since they do not carry physical bank branches and the associated operational costs on their balance sheets. But these are still banks that largely function like all traditional banks.

Examples of truly new alternative credit sources include PayPal Working Capital, Amazon Capital Services, CardConnect, and Prosper, as well as co-branded credit cards such as those offered by major retailers like Target, Macy's, and Sears in partnership with companies such as Visa, MasterCard, and American Express.

The New Breed of Alternative Lenders

Some of these new lenders, such as PayPal Working Capital and Amazon Capital Services, lean heavily on their own internal data to measure a loan applicant's credit worthiness. In other words, they are loaning money only to their own customers based on those customers' sales performance within the confines of the lender's business. But there are other new lenders on the scene that use a peer-to-peer model to issue personal and business loans for just about anything.

PayPal Working Capital

For example, PayPal doesn't require a credit check to qualify for the loan. Instead, credit worthiness is established by the borrower's record in PayPal sales. A PayPal spokesperson explained the process in an interview with me for my article on the subject in *Small Business Computing* (see http://www.smallbusinesscomputing.com/tipsforsmallbusiness/how-big-data-is-changing-small-business-loan-options.html):

> *"WebBank is the lender for PayPal Working Capital, and since WebBank is responsible for verifying the identity of the applicant, it must use a trusted third-party for this verification," says PayPal's spokesperson. "PayPal chose Lexis Nexis as the partner for this verification, and many large banks use Lexis Nexis. Buyers are qualified based on their PayPal sales history."*

> *There's also no set monthly payment, since PayPal allows a business to repay the loan with a share of its PayPal sales. When there are no sales, there is no payment due.*

> *"It's a revolutionary concept that allows PayPal merchants the flexibility to pay when they get paid," says PayPal's representative. PayPal Working Capital does not charge periodic interest. Instead it offers one affordable fixed fee that a business chooses before signing up—there are no periodic interest fees, no late fees, no pre-payment fees, or any other hidden fees.*

> *PayPal's rep pointed out how this practice compares to traditional credit, where "businesses report they seldom know how much they ultimately pay in interest and other fees."*

PayPal's model already competed with banks in payment and money transfers. Now with PayPal Working Capital it also competes with traditional financial institutions in small business lending. In addition to the additional revenue stream, PayPal also benefits by strengthening its brand and its stature as a solid financial services resource in the minds of small business owners.

Prosper and Lending Club

By comparison, Prosper and Lending Club operate a peer-to-peer lending model. Lending Club has been around since 2007 and as of March 31, 2014, it had issued over $4 billion in personal loans over its platform. Lending Club is even selling its paper to banks now. For example, on May 5, 2014, Lending Club announced "Union Bank will purchase personal loans through the Lending Club platform, and the two companies will work together to create new credit products to be made available to both companies' customer base."

Prosper Funding LLC, according to the company's website, is a wholly-owned subsidiary of Prosper Marketplace, Inc. The founders are former managing partners of Merlin Securities: Steven Vermut and Aaron Vermut. Sequoia Capital and BlackRock are among the investors backing Prosper Marketplace, Inc.

Prosper's loan originations grew by 413% in one year to exceed $1 billion in personal loans. As of this writing, Prosper said its community contained 75,699 investors and 93,321 borrowers and that the majority of the $1 billion borrowed to date was used for debt consolidation. This means traditional lenders lost revenue from interest payments in this deal as borrowers paid off debt early. Further, Prosper said much of the remaining money borrowed was for car loans and home renovations, which siphons business away from banks and traditional lending organizations.

In an April 3, 2014 press release announcing Prosper surpassed the $1 billion personal loan mark, the company said:

> *A driving factor in the company's growth has been the ease with which people can obtain a loan through Prosper compared to traditional methods of lending. Over 50% of the loans on the Prosper platform are funded within two days of the borrower starting the application process, and rates and loan options can be checked within a matter of seconds with no impact to a person's credit score. Loans are competitively priced, and based on a person's personal credit, rather than a generic rate across the board. They are also fixed-rate, fixed-term loans with no prepayment penalties. In addition, borrowers have the convenience of applying any-time day or night online, and receive their FICO score for free as part of the application process.*

How did the alternative financiers such as PayPal Working Capital, Amazon Capital Services, Lending Club, and Prosper come to be? First and foremost these models came from the ability to replace or augment conventional historical analysis with near- and real-time data analysis and to predict future risk via new predictive analytics. With these newfound big data capabilities, new competitors in the space were able to make loans to persons and businesses that traditional lenders turned away and to do so with minimal risk. Further, these new competitors were also able to fashion entirely new lending models that banks could not easily compete with.

RETAILERS TAKE ON BANKS; CREDIT CARD BRANDS CIRCUMVENT BANKS

Co-branded retail credit cards are also putting some pressure on the future of banks. These cards are easier for consumers to qualify for than bank-issued credit cards, although they are usually offered at higher interest rates. They should not be confused with store credit cards, which can only be used for credit in a specific store. Co-branded credit cards can be used anywhere just like a traditional bank-issued credit card. In other words, they work exactly like a bank-issued Visa, MasterCard, or American Express. Indeed, from a consumer's perspective they are, for all practical purposes, identical except instead of having a bank logo on the card, there is a store logo. Both of these credit card types also carry the payment card brand, such as Visa or MasterCard.

It should be alarming to banks that leading payment card brands such as Visa, Master-Card, and American Express are teaming with so many non-banks for the purpose of issuing credit. Further, these cards are generating a considerable amount of data for competing entities that was formerly contained and controlled by banks and traditional lending institutions. Plus, consumer use of these cards generates additional data from the stores on specific user shopping habits and other behaviors that can be further leveraged in many ways, not the least of which is to hone retailers' competitiveness and leverage against banks. Many retailers resent banks for charging what they perceive as high merchant and processing fees. They are eager to find ways to reduce or eradicate these costs, and indeed many options have arisen to fill the need.

Consider Walmart's continued encroachment into financial services as an example. The giant retailer and the nation's largest private employer already offers low-cost money transfers, pre-paid debit cards, check cashing services, and auto insurance. Are financial institutions worried about Walmart and other retailers competing on financial services? Yes, they are.

In an April 30, 2014 report in Yahoo! Finance titled "The Bank of Walmart: Can the retail giant unseat the big financial institutions?", Kevin Chupka wrote:

> *Walmart tried to become a bonafide bank back in 2007 but pulled their application after what* The New York Times *said was "a firestorm of criticism from lawmakers, banking industry officials and watchdog groups." Banks bristled at the potential competition and lawmakers were in the midst of crafting a bill to block non-financial companies from creating a bank in order to protect neighborhood banks and big bank profits.*

> *Still, their failure to become a real bank hasn't stopped Walmart from being the go-to place for low-income consumers who don't have a bank account. Check cashing fees and debit card refills are much cheaper at Walmart and they have taken a significant share of that business away from traditional financial service companies.*

As more consumers learn it's easier to qualify for credit cards from airlines, retailers, and other non-bank companies—and where the loyalty rewards are typically better too—fewer consumers will turn to banks for these services. As they learn other financial services are more freely offered and at lower fees by non-bank entities, consumers will drift further still from banks, which is not necessarily a "bad" thing in the aggregate. Nevertheless, when combined these trends erode market share for banks and other traditional financial institutions.

THE CREDIT BUREAU DATA PROBLEM

As mentioned earlier, banks and other traditional lending institutions over-tightened credit in response to the financial crisis and recession and have since loosened their grip some, but for some, not enough to maintain profitability over a longer timeframe. It is the classic pendulum over-reaction to past errors in their work. Granted, the repercussions were profound and thus a rapid reinfusion of prudence was certainly in order to stabilize individual institutions and the industry as a whole. However, lending decisions are still largely fear-driven to this day. By reacting out of fear rather than from knowledge gained through data, the banks lose billions in potential business.

On top of that, traditional lending institutions place too much faith in outside traditional risk-assessment sources, namely traditional credit bureaus. Therefore the lenders are further stymied by the problems in traditional credit bureau data such as too little data, irrelevant data, outdated credit rating systems, and virtually no distinction between potential borrowers who are truly a credit risk and those who were set back temporarily by the recession but otherwise pose little risk.

Further, there have been documented cases where traditional credit bureaus presented *dirty* data—corrupted or incorrect data—to lenders as though it were clean and factual. In many cases, once aware of errors in consumer data, credit bureaus are exceptionally slow in correcting it or otherwise make data correction a difficult process. Incorrect credit bureau data diminishes a traditional lender's ability to correctly assess risk in any given loan applicant. To add insult to injury, lending institutions pay credit bureaus for specific data that may have little to no actual value.

On July 26, 2013, Laura Gunderson wrote a report in *The Oregonian* on just such a dirty data case involving Equifax, one of the three major credit bureaus in the United States:

> *"A jury Friday awarded an Oregon woman $18.6 million after she spent two years unsuccessfully trying to get Equifax Information Services to fix major mistakes on her credit report," reported Gunderson. "Julie Miller of Marion County, who was awarded $18.4 million in punitive and $180,000 in compensatory damages, contacted Equifax eight times between 2009 and 2011 in an effort to correct inaccuracies, including erroneous accounts and collection attempts, as well as a wrong Social Security number and birthday. Yet over and over, the lawsuit alleged, the Atlanta-based company failed to correct its mistakes."*

Unfortunately, this case is not an isolated incident. The Federal Trade Commission (FTC) reported in February 2013 that its study uncovered a significant number of credit reporting errors. "Overall, the congressionally mandated study on credit report accuracy found that one in five consumers had an error on at least one of their three credit reports. One in 20 of the study participants had an error on his or her credit report that lowered the credit score."

Jill Riepenhoff and Mike Wagner wrote a May 6, 2012 report in *The Columbus Dispatch* on the Ohio paper's own investigation into the accuracy of credit bureau data:

> *During a yearlong investigation,* The Dispatch *collected and analyzed nearly 30,000 consumer complaints filed with the Federal Trade Commission and attorneys general in 24 states that alleged violations of the Fair Credit Reporting Act by the three largest credit-reporting agencies in the United States—Equifax, Experian, and TransUnion.*
>
> *The complaints document the inability of consumers to correct errors that range from minor to financially devastating. Consumers said the agencies can't even correct the most obvious mistakes: That's not my birth date. That's not my name. I'm not dead.*
>
> *Nearly a quarter of the complaints to the FTC and more than half of the complaints to the attorneys general involved mistakes in consumers' financial accounts for credit cards, mortgages or car loans. Houses sold in bank-approved "short sales," at less than the value of the mortgage, were listed as foreclosures. Car loans that had been paid off were reported as repossessions. Credit cards that had been paid off and closed years earlier showed as delinquent.*
>
> *More than 5% complained to the FTC and more than 40% to the attorneys general that their reports had basic personal information listed incorrectly: names, Social Security numbers, addresses and birth dates. An Ohio man said his report identified him as having been a police officer since 1923. He was born in 1968. A woman in her 60s said that her credit report listed her as 12 years old.*
>
> *More than 5% complained to the FTC that their reports contained an account that did not belong to them. Many of those accounts involved debts that had been turned over to collection agencies. A woman in Georgia complained about a medical-collection account on her report. It was for treating prostate cancer.*
>
> *Nearly 200 people told the FTC that their credit reports listed them as deceased, cutting off their ability to access credit.*
>
> *More than half of all who filed complaints with the FTC said that despite their best efforts, they could not persuade the three major credit-reporting agencies to fix the problems.*

Gunderson confirmed in her report in *The Oregonian* that the Oregon Attorney General office was seeing much the same thing across all three major credit bureaus: "Since 2008, Oregon consumers have filed hundreds of complaints about credit bureaus with the state's Attorney General. Those complaints include 108 against Equifax, 113 against Experian, and 70 against TransUnion."

While most traditional lending institutions add factors to their decision formulas other than credit ratings from the big three credit bureaus, they are still heavily dependent on that data and overweigh its worth in the final lending consideration.

For banks and other traditional financial institutions to better assess their risk and realistically expand revenue from loans and other credit and financial services, they have to import significant data from sources other than credit bureaus and develop better risk assessment algorithms. Further, they have to develop the means to assess the credibility, accuracy, and validity of data sources and the data they supply. In other words, they have to monitor the data supply chain closely and audit sources routinely and extensively. The days of meekly accepting credit bureau data, or any data, at face value are long gone. The business risk in that behavior is unacceptably high.

All internal data silos need to be immediately opened and the data reconciled so that all internal data is available for analysis. In this way, traditional financial institutions can better assess risk in existing customers and develop new ways to retain customers, despite the allure of offers from competitors both new and old. Financial institutions can also use data on existing customers to help identify characteristics they need to look for in prospects in order to add profitability and sustainability for their business.

A WORD ABOUT INSURANCE COMPANIES

As noted, Walmart began offering auto insurance to consumers through a partnership with AutoInsurance.com in April 2014. A *New York Times* report by Elizabeth Harris said the giant retailer explains that effort this way:

> Daniel Eckert, senior vice president of services for Walmart U.S., said the company is using its size to broaden its offerings for customers and to get an edge on the competition. While some companies have rebounded more easily from the recession, Walmart's core customer base, largely low-income people, has struggled to regain a foothold, so its sales have been sluggish. Mr. Eckert said this was just another way to help customers save money and simplify a complicated process... "What it does," he said, "is it engenders trust."

The issue of trust is huge in establishing and retaining customer loyalty and in brand building. While Walmart excels at both, despite collecting huge amounts of customer data, auto insurance companies are not quite hitting that mark. As discussed in Chapter 15, "Use Cases in Transportation," data collection devices provided to consumers by auto insurers to track driving habits and price premiums accordingly, are viewed with suspicion by consumers and watch groups alike. That's because a conflict of interest is inherent in the exercise. Detractors can easily discern that there is little motivation for insurance companies to reduce their premiums and thereby reduce the company's revenues. There is, however, significant opportunity and motivation to increase premium costs on most drivers for the slightest perceived driving infraction.

In contrast, Walmart, despite watch groups' concerns over many of its actions, has been able to position itself as a champion of its customers in part by offering services seemingly unrelated to its core business. Such offerings are generally perceived by customers as an effort to help them afford more than they would otherwise rather than an attempt to sell them more products and services.

Yet Walmart is very good at using big data to precisely target and increase sales at the micro and macro levels. Bill Simon, president & CEO of Walmart U.S., said as much at a Goldman Sachs Global Retailing Conference held on September 11, 2013. The entire transcript, redacted in parts, provided by Thomson Reuters StreetEvents is available online in PDF form. Here is part of what Simon said about Walmart's use of big data at that event (found on page nine of the transcript):

...while we don't have a traditional loyalty program, we operate a pretty big membership club that is the ultimate in loyalty programs. So we have that set of data that is available to us. If you take that data and you correlate it with traceable tender that exists in Walmart Stores and then the identified data that comes through Walmart.com and then the trend data that comes through the rest of the business and working with our suppliers, our ability to pull data together is unmatched.

We've recently stood up a couple years ago a group that's designed specifically to understand that and find ways to leverage that in the Company. And so, while data is a commodity today or an asset today, the opportunity for us to use it I think is as good as if not better than others because of the wealth and the breadth. Loyalty cards only give you kind of one dimension data and we get to see it from multiple different sources. We are using it in all kinds of ways today. So magically we know exactly which SKUs are bought in that particular geography because of our ability to understand the data. We think that gives us a competitive advantage that others would really struggle to get to.

Interestingly, *The New York Times* reported in the article cited above that "A Walmart spokeswoman said the company would not have access to customer data collected on AutoInsurance.com" through its new auto insurance offering. Harris, the author of that report, describes the relationship between Walmart and AutoInsurance.com this way:

The website, AutoInsurance.com, allows consumers to review prices at several insurance companies and contrast them with their current insurance. Effectively, Walmart and AutoInsurance.com will be marketing partners. Walmart will promote the website in its stores, and receive a monthly fee in return, while AutoInsurance.com will collect commissions when insurance is sold on its site. Customers will also be able to access the site from Walmart.com.

And so there appears to be the answer as to why Walmart, one of the best of all big data practitioners today, "would not have access to customer data collected on AutoInsurance.com" after the CEO said "...trend data that comes through the rest of the business and working with our suppliers, our ability to pull data together is unmatched." The answer is likely that Walmart will pull the data it needs from customers who access the site from Walmart.com. Truth be told, it's doubtful that the retailer needs very much of the data entered on and gathered by the AutoInsurance.com site anyway. After all, driving records are easily accessed elsewhere as are accident reports and vehicle repair records should Walmart ever decide it needs that information. For whatever reason, Walmart is not accessing the AutoInsurance.com data, and the statement that it won't is a great public relations move. It casts the company as respectful of privacy and self-restrained in its big data actions, whether or not that is actually the case.

Do not mistake the intent here, which is not to disparage or endorse Walmart in any way. I point to its excellent skills, some of which are beyond its big data collection and analysis, as a credible and serious threat to any industry it cares to take on. That is to say that should the company decide to try to move into insurance, be that health, life or auto, as it has tried with mixed success to move into banking, the insurance industry will have a serious new competitor with which to contend.

Further, helping customers save money on financial essentials also helps them increase their disposable income, which in turn might lead to an increase in sales for Walmart. The retailer is smart in cultivating and conserving its customer base much like a paper manufacturer would cultivate trees and diligently practice forest conservation to ensure its own continued existence and success. Far too few companies are this proactive in both customer service and customer conservation. Although this comment should not be seen as an endorsement of Walmart's tactics, it is acknowledgement of the company's business acumen and strategic use of data.

As insurance companies move forward using big data to mitigate risks and increase their business, they too should diligently watch for the rise of new disruptive competitors similar to those that have risen in other areas of financial services such as in lending. The one thing that is certain about big data is that it is disrupting and reshaping every industry.

SUMMARY

In this chapter you learned that banks have plenty of data on hand and more at their disposal. So the problem is not the lack of data but in figuring out how to use it and for what purposes. You also discovered that, surprisingly, some banks are using big data successfully but fail to recognize that is what they are doing. By not recognizing these efforts for what they are, the banks fail to grasp and leverage lessons learned in big data projects.

You learned that financial institutions should first look to see if they already have projects in motion that are using copious amounts of data. If so, find and use the lessons learned within them. Otherwise, the best place to start is in any activity where data analysis is currently and routinely used. Choose one or a few of those that are in most need of improvement and then begin a pilot project or two accordingly.

Other use cases for this sector include strategic planning, new revenue stream discovery, product innovation, trading, compliance, and risk and security.

You also learned that traditional lending institutions place too much faith in outside traditional risk-assessment and data sources, namely traditional credit bureaus. Therefore the lenders are further stymied by problems found in traditional credit bureau data such as too little data, irrelevant data, outdated credit rating systems, and erroneous data.

Finally, you learned that as insurance companies move forward using big data to mitigate risks and increase their business, they too should diligently watch for the rise of new disruptive competitors similar to those that have risen in other areas of financial services such as in lending.

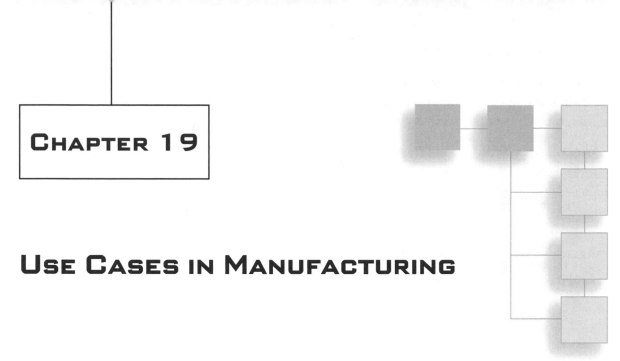

CHAPTER 19

USE CASES IN MANUFACTURING

Manufacturing in the United States today is struggling from various forces and challenging conditions. Chiefly, the sector is plagued with outdated legacy systems and too little talent left to run them. Indeed, numerous obstacles currently exist, often stemming from institutional memory loss due to massive layoffs and retiring talent that is proving difficult to replace.

"Many Gartner clients continue to share concerns about their manufacturing systems. The issues span from basic automated data collection to frustrations with the inability to scale software applications without added cost or disruption. Additionally, the skill sets to deploy and maintain these technologies continue to dwindle from years of staff reductions, a lack of focus on manufacturing in the educational establishment and technological change," write Gartner analysts Simon F Jacobson, Leif Eriksen, and Marc Halpern in a November 21, 2013 report titled "Predicts 2014: Manufacturing Operations."

Indeed several countries, the United States chief among them, in the push toward a "knowledge" service economy, lost sight of the economic value of manufacturing. The academic sector did too, hence the diminished attention to teaching manufacturing skills. Now there is little in place on any front in the United States to help manufacturers staff up and modernize to better fuel their own profits and add to the sustainability of entire economies. Yet they must find a way to do both.

"The decentralization of manufacturing activities on a global scale, digital business, and a resurgent focus on manufacturing as a critical contributor to economic prosperity and competitiveness are reshaping manufacturing operations," write the authors of that

Gartner report. "New business models, as well as new emphases on speed, productivity, and sustainability, are raising questions about the ability of traditional manufacturing systems and deployment models to keep pace."

The chief challenge before manufacturers today, then, is in reinventing themselves. That is no small task for an industry so far behind the times and steeped in the once fabulous and now seriously dated tradition of Henry Ford's assembly line.

They do have information at their disposal, however, that could be used to help them make the necessary transitions. Manufacturers have plenty of data of their own, and more at their disposal, yet few are equipped to make adequate use of it in this task.

"Big data is a virtually untapped asset for most manufacturers, a hunk of potential value that no one has quite yet figured out how to turn into lots more profit," said Michael Rothschild, founder and chairman of Profit Velocity Solutions, in an interview. His company is the maker of the PV Accelerator platform, designed to enable manufacturers to plan and control profitability. There's a sense it can and will be done, but for now the exact how-to seems elusive.

"Big data should be seen [as] an essential raw material for manufacturers competing in tough global markets, but precisely what should they do with that raw material?" continued Rothschild. "What's the highest short-term payoff from leveraging the big data they already have on hand? Which decision-making processes, if enhanced by the availability of better information, would have the biggest impact on the bottom line? Very few manufacturers have crisp answers to these questions."

This chapter discusses big data use cases deployed by a few manufacturers as well as the tactics that may prove useful to many.

Economic Conditions and Opportunities Ahead

This sector's recovery from the recent global recession has happened mostly in fitful starts and wheezing accomplishments, but the future is looking brighter for manufacturing. The *March 2014 Manufacturing ISM Report on Business* says that while the overall economy has been growing for 58 consecutive months, the manufacturing sector has only been growing in the last 10. However, there appears to be some real momentum there. From that report:

> *Manufacturing expanded in March as the PMI (Purchasing Managers Index) registered 53.7%, an increase of 0.5 percentage points when compared to February's reading of 53.2%. A reading above 50% indicates that the manufacturing economy is generally expanding; below 50% indicates that it is generally contracting.*
>
> *A PMI in excess of 43.2%, over a period of time, generally indicates an expansion of the overall economy. Therefore, the March PMI indicates growth for the 58th consecutive month in the overall economy, and*

indicates expansion in the manufacturing sector for the 10th consecutive month. Bradley J. Holcomb, CPSM, CPSD, chair of the Institute for Supply Management (ISM) Manufacturing Business Survey Committee, stated, "The past relationship between the PMI and the overall economy indicates that the average PMI for January through March (52.7%) corresponds to a 3.1% increase in real gross domestic product (GDP) on an annualized basis. In addition, if the PMI for March (53.7%) is annualized, it corresponds to a 3.5% increase in real GDP annually."

Figure 19.1 is the Institute for Supply Management's (ISM) depiction of the state of manufacturing as of March 2014. ISM is a highly respected association dedicated to leading and serving the supply management profession. The full text version of the Manufacturing ISM Report On Business is posted on ISM's website at www.ism.ws on the first business day of every month after 10:10 a.m. ET. Be sure to check the website for more current information.

MANUFACTURING AT A GLANCE
MARCH 2014

Index	Series Index Mar	Series Index Feb	Percentage Point Change	Direction	Rate of Change	Trend* (Months)
PMI®	53.7	53.2	+0.5	Growing	Faster	10
New Orders	55.1	54.5	+0.6	Growing	Faster	10
Production	55.9	48.2	+7.7	Growing	From Contracting	1
Employment	51.1	52.3	-1.2	Growing	Slower	9
Supplier Deliveries	54.0	58.5	-4.5	Slowing	Slower	10
Inventories	52.5	52.5	0.0	Growing	Same	2
Customers' Inventories	42.0	46.5	-4.5	Too Low	Faster	28
Prices	59.0	60.0	-1.0	Increasing	Slower	8
Backlog of Orders	57.5	52.0	+5.5	Growing	Faster	2
Exports	55.5	53.5	+2.0	Growing	Faster	16
Imports	54.5	53.5	+1.0	Growing	Faster	14
OVERALL ECONOMY				Growing	Faster	58
Manufacturing Sector				Growing	Faster	10

Manufacturing ISM® *Report On Business*® data is seasonally adjusted for New Orders, Production, Employment and Supplier Deliveries indexes.
*Number of months moving in current direction.

Figure 19.1
ISM's depiction of the state of manufacturing in March 2014.
Source: Institute for Supply Management (ISM) from its April 1, 2014 press release.

Chad Moutray, Chief Economist at the National Association of Manufacturers (NAM), also delivered an analysis of where manufacturing stood as of this writing:

The JPMorgan Global Manufacturing PMI edged lower, down from 53.2 in February to 52.4 in March. This was the lowest level since October, but it also marked the 16th straight month of expanding manufacturing activity worldwide. The underlying data in March were somewhat mixed. New orders (down from 54.6 to 53.2) and output (down from 54.6 to 53.4) were both off slightly, but still reflected modest increases. At the same time, the pace of growth for exports (up from 51.5 to 51.7) and employment (up from 51.3 to 51.5) was marginally higher.

As noted last month, the United States accounts for one-quarter of the weight in the Global PMI measure, making it somewhat more difficult to disentangle the strength of the U.S. manufacturing sector from the worldwide analysis. For its part, the Markit U.S. Manufacturing PMI declined from 57.1 to 55.5, but it still reflected relatively healthy gains in both sales (down from 59.6 to 58.1) and production (down from 57.8 to 57.5). Likewise, the competing PMI measure from the Institute for Supply Management noted a bit of an improvement in March (up from 53.2 to 53.7) as manufacturers have begun to move beyond the winter storms of January and February, with production turning positive (up from 48.2 to 55.9) and sales accelerating (up from 54.5 to 55.1).

Looking at the top 10 markets for U.S.-manufactured goods, all but China (down from 48.5 to 48.0) and Hong Kong (down from 53.3 to 49.9) saw manufacturing activity expand in March. South Korea's economy (up from 49.8 to 50.4) returned to slight growth for the month. In the remaining countries, the data were largely mixed. Most of our key markets had some easing in their growth rates for the month, but some of these nations continue to have decent growth, particularly our trading partners in Europe, such as Germany (down from 54.8 to 53.7), the Netherlands (down from 55.2 to 53.7) and the United Kingdom (down from 56.2 to 55.3).

Much of this is at least partially heartening news for the still struggling manufacturing industry, but it also underscores the need for speed in developing new business models and increasing efficiencies in business and production processes if the momentum is to be maintained and profits increased.

CROSSROADS IN MANUFACTURING

There are also a number of overall market and technology trends now pressuring manufacturing. Chief among them is the larger market trend toward personalization and the emerging trend of 3D printing in manufacturing. The two trends are related even though they may not appear to be at first glance.

The trend toward personalization is seen everywhere in the market today, from personalized marketing to personalized medicine. In every case, personalized means tailored to an individual and not bulk delivery to the masses.

When you look at traditional manufacturing, you see bulk production still underway, which is counter to the overlying market trend of personalization. However, manufacturing is currently undergoing a disruptive shift from subtractive to additive production that neatly dovetails with the personalization trend.

Subtractive manufacturing, that is, cutting, stamping, and otherwise extracting a shape from a raw material, is suited for bulk manufacturing and assembly. Subtractive manufacturing often requires expensive retooling to make any changes in production. By comparison, additive manufacturing, aka 3D printing, is conducive to personalized production as it adds materials in layers to form a given shape or a finished product, the specs of which can be easily, rapidly, and cheaply changed between printings. Cost and production efficiencies are not reliant on volume to reduce the per unit price in 3D printing but can instead be achieved at the individual unit level—meaning that the price of producing even just one unit is optimized. This is what makes personalized manufacturing possible and feasible.

Additive manufacturing also enables fast prototyping and testing, which in turn leads to a faster time to market. Take, for example, Rabbit Proto's recently launched project that enables 3D printers to deposit conductive material along with traditional plastic. The conductive material can be embedded within the 3D model and printed in the same 3D printing process, without any interruption in the printing. Among other things, Rabbit Proto can print a functioning circuit inside plastic. In other words, it is now possible to print interactive prototypes with capacitive and conductive features. This is a marked departure from the expensive production of individual components and the subsequent assembly typically required in traditional methods of producing prototypes.

Figure 19.2 shows the Rabbit Proto demo video from the company website (you can view it on YouTube at https://www.youtube.com/watch?v=mS6-Tzjeths). The demo shows Rabbit Proto being used to print a complete game controller in a single, uninterrupted printing. Traditional manufacturing prototyping requires many steps by comparison. The company says that "game controllers, wearables devices, and interactive art are just the tip of the iceberg of what is possible." Indeed, that is true. You can expect to see enterprising manufacturers quickly move beyond prototyping with this and similar technologies to produce entire, working products on-demand. When that happens, and it will, traditional manufacturers will not be able to compete using the slower, more costly and labor-intensive processes in use today.

Figure 19.2
The Rabbit Proto demo video from the company's website.
Source: Courtesy of RabbitProto. Used with permission.

But even before you get to the prototyping stage, designers, engineers, and workgroups can draw and change their ideas in the air using technologies like the Lix pen. This 3D printing pen works much like 3D printers. It melts and cools colored plastic that renders rigid and free-standing 3D drawings, i.e. structures, which can be formed in any shapes imaginable. Figure 19.3 shows an example of a structure drawn using a Lix pen. Figure 19.4 shows the Lix pen's design.

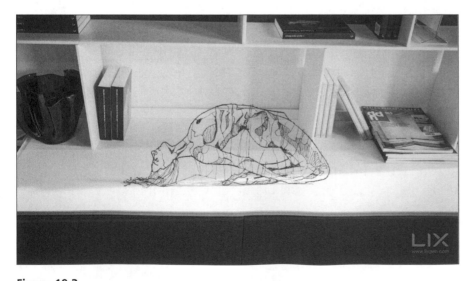

Figure 19.3
An in-air rendering using a Lix 3D pen as an example of the intricate work the pen is capable of performing.
Source: Lix press kit at http://lixpen.com/press.html.

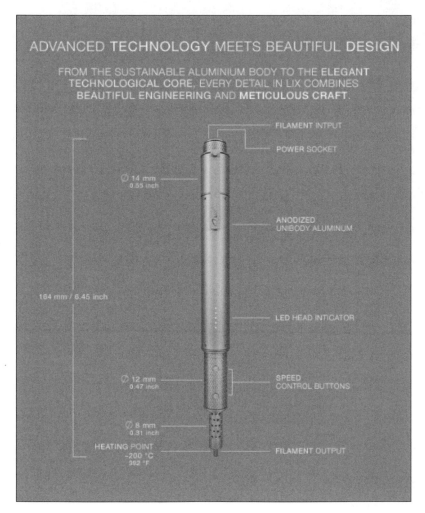

Figure 19.4
The Lix pen's design. Its power cable plugs into any USB port, making this 3D pen highly portable and useable anywhere.

Source: Lix press kit at http://lixpen.com/press.html.

In general, additive manufacturing requires little to no in-factory assembly to complete production whereas subtractive manufacturing often requires extensive assembly of parts. Additive manufacturing also produces little to no waste in the printing process; indeed, it can use industrial waste as "ink." Generally speaking, it is faster and cheaper than subtractive manufacturing.

In short, 3D printing is changing every aspect of manufacturing and is the most disruptive force seen in this sector since the industrial revolution.

At the Intersection of 3D Printing and Big Data

Traditional manufacturers can view this disruptive trend as a threat or an opportunity. But either way, they will have to increasingly compete against manufacturers that are using faster, cheaper, and greener 3D printing production techniques. Therefore, it is no longer profitable to merely turn to more robotics to perform existing production processes or to continue to eek small gains from increasing efficiencies in existing processes. Traditional manufacturers will have to discover and deploy new ways to remain competitive.

Big data is among the manufacturer's best tools in finding their way forward on what will increasingly feel like an alien marketscape. Unfortunately, most manufacturers have so far ignored or failed to master these tools.

"For the most part, big data, as it is used so far, is irrelevant to senior decision-makers in manufacturing," said Rothschild. Executives and managers can only impact the future. They cannot change history. But most big data efforts are focused on mining historical data, not future modeling. Decision-makers need very specific, near real-time answers as they weigh alternative plans—before they pull the trigger and make their choices. Unless big data can be harnessed to provide that kind of forward-looking decision support, it is not really of much value to senior manufacturing executives.

"ERP, SCM, MES, production control, and other advanced systems have endowed many manufacturers with huge treasure troves of raw big data," he continued. "But until these companies find a way to readily convert all those digits into timely, relevant business insights that lead to different choices being made—decisions that quantifiably impact the bottom line, nothing much of value is happening."

How 3D Printing Is Changing Manufacturing and Disrupting its Customers

To understand why having the ability to see data in real-time and to use predictive analytics is critical to manufacturers and their customers, consider the changes already being wrought from competitors wielding 3D printers.

WinSun Prints 10 Homes in a Single Day

Take for example, the story of China-based WinSun's breathtaking accomplishment in producing 10 homes in a single day. An April 23, 2014 article in *Gizmag* described the feat like this:

> *Rather than printing the homes in one go, Winsun's 3D printer creates building blocks by layering up a cement/glass mix in structural patterns (watch the process on YouTube at https://www.youtube.com/watch? v=SObzNdyRTBs). The diagonally reinforced print pattern leaves plenty of air gaps to act as insulation. These blocks are printed in a central factory and rapidly assembled on site.*

> *Each small house takes very little labor to assemble, and costs as little as $4,800. Winsun hopes to make them available for low income housing projects.*

But the company has far more in its sights than just low income housing projects. An April 2014 article in *T3-The Gadget Website* details the company's aspirations: "[WinSun's CEO, Ma Yihe] hopes his printers can be used to build skyscrapers in the future and has plans to build an entire villa using the same process."

The homes WinSun already built "are made using recycled materials [a mixture of cement and construction waste] and the process does not require labour, each house can be printed for just £3,000," reports T3. "The company also intends to build 100 recycling facilities around China to help keep up with demand."

WinSun's massive 3D printer measures 490 feet long, 33 feet wide, and 20 feet deep, according to a report in *Inhabitat* and was used to print, "each of the structural components from the giant concrete slabs to the inner cross bracing. To cut down on costs, WinSun fabricated the frame from layers of concrete partly made from recycled construction waste, industrial waste, and glass fibers. Each house is approximately 2,100 square feet."

The 3D Printed Landscape House

Lest you think WinSun's accomplishment an anomaly, consider how many such projects are already underway, and there are many. Take for example the Landscape House, a strip-shaped house designed by Universe Architecture in Amsterdam. A June 4, 2013 article in *Wired* describes that project thusly:

> *Designed by architect Janjaap Ruijssenaars, it will be printed in one go with a huge 3D printer created by Italian roboticist Enrico Dini.*

> *That printer—the D-Shape—creates a substance similar to sandstone by mixing sand (or any other similar aggregate material) with a binding agent and layering it. Layers can be as thin as 5mm, and its huge frame can handle objects as large as six metres in each dimension. Each one can handle as much as 2,500 m² of*

material per year, which is the equivalent of 12 small houses. They can also work in tandem if needed—imagine a future where not just houses, but entire streets are printed in one go. That's the potential of this technology, if it works.

According to Ruijssenaars, the Landscape House couldn't be built with conventional technology—the printed frame will be one huge piece of rock, entirely seamless, with steel and glass extras installed on the sides. Its shape is meant to "celebrate landscape," but it's also a demonstration of what might be considered the efficiencies of 3D printing rather than any kind of revolution.

Per square meter, it's meant to be four times faster than normal construction methods, and also a lot cheaper. Dini has built a large, nine-cubic-meter pavilion for a roundabout in Pontedera—an installation that looks more like a sculpture, but the whole thing only cost €200 (£170). And it runs (theoretically) by itself, so you don't need to hire builders, or worry about them injuring or killing themselves during construction.

Figure 19.5 shows the innovative design in the Landscape House. Notice the floor is also the ceiling in this design. The frame is created with a 3D printer as one solid, seamless piece.

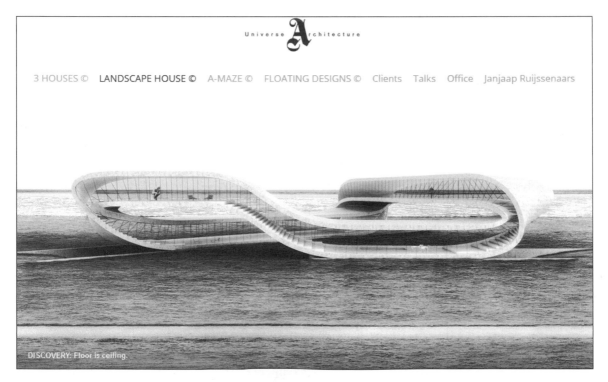

Figure 19.5
The 3D printable Landscape House.
Source: Universe Architecture and Janjaap Ruijssenaars, the Architect.

The 3D Printed Canal House

In another example, Dutch architects constructed a home in Amsterdam known simply as the "3D Print Canal House." Using a printer they dubbed KamerMaker, or "room builder," they print entire rooms that can then snap together to form a home or building.

According to a March 14, 2014 Associated Press (AP) report, Hedwig Heinsman of architect bureau Dus says "the goal of the demonstration project launched this month is not so much to print a functioning house—in fact, parts of the house will likely be built and re-built several times over the course of three years as 3D printing technology develops. Rather, it is to discover and share the potential uses of 3D printing in construction by creating new materials, trying out designs and testing building techniques to see what works."

In other words, homes are not only being built with 3D printers, but designs are being rapidly tested and tweaked to improve aesthetics, utility and delivery of various models. And all of these models can be printed, reprinted, tossed, and resumed quickly, easily, and cheaply.

The AP report explains how Dus is going about this:

It takes the Kamermaker about a week to print each massive, unique, honeycomb-structured block, layer by layer. The first block, which forms one corner of the house and part of a stairway, weighed around 180 kg (400 lbs).

The blocks will later be filled with a foam material, still under development, that will harden like concrete to add additional weight and bind the blocks together.

Dus expects to add more printers and change designs along the way, with help from Dutch construction company Heijmans, German chemicals manufacturer Henkel, and anybody else who wants to participate and can make useful contributions.

The Impact of 3D Home Printing on Manufacturing

As architects and construction companies increasingly turn to 3D printing to produce their work, their need for traditional building materials diminishes and then disappears. That will bring about massive changes in demands for everything from sheetrock manufacturing to secondary manufacturing such as engineered wood product production. Even home improvement stores will shift their buying patterns from traditional building supplies to stocks of "ink" suitable for printing whatever is needed. The stores may even provide the printing services. As you can see from this one example alone, traditional manufacturers, secondary manufacturers, and many of their customers will see their business dry up and blow away if they don't change with the times. Home builders and construction workers will also be heavily affected by this trend.

THE SHIFT TO ADDITIVE MANUFACTURING WILL BE MASSIVE AND ACROSS ALL SECTORS

But it isn't just manufacturers of building supplies and their customers that are being impacted by the shift to 3D printing. All manufacturing sectors are or soon will be affected.

Large companies such as auto manufacturers are already seeing 3D printing beginning to shape their industry not only in how parts can be made but in how entire vehicles can be manufactured. Consider this description of one such effort in a February 27, 2013 article in *Wired* entitled "3D Printed Car is as Strong as Steel, Half the Weight, and Nearing Production:"

> *Picture an assembly line that isn't made up of robotic arms spewing sparks to weld heavy steel, but a warehouse of plastic-spraying printers producing light, cheap and highly efficient automobiles...*
>
> *Jim Kor and his team built the three-wheel, two-passenger vehicle [called the Urbee 2] at RedEye, an on-demand 3D printing facility. The printers he uses create ABS plastic via Fused Deposition Modeling (FDM). The printer sprays molten polymer to build the chassis layer by microscopic layer until it arrives at the complete object. The machines are so automated that the building process they perform is known as "lights out" construction, meaning Kor uploads the design for a bumper, walks away, shuts off the lights and leaves. A few hundred hours later, he's got a bumper. The whole car—which is about 10 feet long—takes about 2,500 hours.*
>
> *Besides easy reproduction, making the car body via FDM affords Kor the precise control that would be impossible with sheet metal. When he builds the aforementioned bumper, the printer can add thickness and rigidity to specific sections. When applied to the right spots, this makes for a fender that's as resilient as the one on your Prius, but much lighter. That translates to less weight to push, and a lighter car means more miles per gallon. And the current model has a curb weight of just 1,200 pounds.*

Figures 19.6 and 19.7 show the Urbee 2.

Figure 19.6
The 3D printed car known as the Urbee 2.
Source: Courtesy of KOR Ecologic, Inc. Used with permission.

Figure 19.7
The interior of the Urbee 2.
Source: Courtesy of KOR Ecologic, Inc. Used with permission.

Even smaller manufacturers are feeling the effects of 3D printing. Take dental labs all around the world, for example. Many are moving to incorporate 3D printing in their operations but it may prove to be too little, too late. Once the sole source for dental appliance manufacturing from dental crowns to dentures, dental lab services are now being replaced with onsite 3D printers in dentist offices. This way, dentists can eliminate the third-party lab overhead and keep profits for themselves by creating dental appliances in house. Further, 3D printers eliminate the need for manual modeling, meaning they can replace traditional mouth mold impressions with cheaper and faster digital mouth scans. Further, dentists no longer have a need to store physical models on premise.

One might think that keeping abreast of such changes and producing new products is a function of Research and Development (R&D) departments rather than a task for big data. But it is big data that can reveal changes in the market overall as well as among competitors and within the ranks of customers as they are happening. These insights move manufacturers from a defensive position played in a continual catch-up mode to a proactive one, enabling them to adapt faster to rises and falls in demands and to produce innovations faster.

How Personalized Manufacturing Will Change Everything and Create Even More Big Data

Because 3D printing enables personalized manufacturing, that is, the ability to cheaply and quickly create unique items rather than produce identical items in bulk, everything downstream from manufacturing will change too. For example, traditionally clothing manufacturers have produced clothing in set size ranges. As an example, in the U.S. women's sizes come in even numbered sizes such as 4, 6, 8, 10, 12, 14, 16, and so on. Junior sizes for younger women come in the odd numbered sizes such as 5, 7, 9, 11, and so forth. Although there are slight differences in each size, as the sizes are not entirely standardized between manufacturers, those are the clothing size choices presented to consumers on retail store racks and online.

With the advent of personalized manufacturing, that is, 3D printing, the notion of clothing sizes will disappear. Instead, articles of clothing will be produced to precisely fit each person's body measurements. Those measurements will be made by scanners at home or in stores. Indeed, we see the early stages of this technology already in use. See Chapter 17, "Use Cases in Retail," for an example of how an Xbox Kinect is used by consumers in the privacy of their own home to scan their own bodies for the purpose of making a figurine that looks exactly like they do, only in miniature.

When this practice becomes common, and it will, clothing manufacturers can no longer sell bulk produced clothing. They may shift to 3D printing to produce clothes to exact customer body measurements or the industry may be replaced entirely by retailers and clothing designers much like dental labs are being replaced by dentists with 3D printers today. Or, consumers may elect to print their orders at home. In that case, the designer or the retailer ships the production code to the customer's at-home 3D printer with instructions to the customer on what "inks" to use.

Although consumers will likely be quick to embrace the advantages in personalized manufacturing from a highly tailored fit to the joys of adding one's personal touches to the design, there are disadvantages to consumers in this scenario as well. Personalized manufacturing of clothing will generate a good deal of digital exhaust, meaning there will be immense amounts of data on consumers' bodies and changes in body sizes that will likely be used by numerous parties, including manufacturers but certainly not limited to them. This data, like all other personal data, can be used in myriad ways that can benefit and harm consumers.

Similar changes will occur in other types of retailing, too. For example, car dealers in the future may no longer stock a large number of vehicles on their lots. Instead, they may have only a handful on a tinier showroom floor. In this way customers can see the finished product and take it for a test drive. But the actual vehicle they buy will be 3D printed to their personal specs—including a variety of traditional options plus a few more such as options in headroom and legroom that were not previously possible in bulk manufacturing. Consumers will also be able to order exterior and interior colors in any combinations they can imagine and even add personalized art elements.

The advantages in this scenario to car dealers include the reduction in real estate and flooring costs. They will no longer need large lots of land to display their merchandise. Nor will they need to get financing from vehicle manufacturers or financial institutions for flooring, aka floor plans, which are short-term loans that enable them to buy and hold vehicles they plan to sell to consumers. Flooring is expensive and there is no doubt that dealers will be thrilled to be rid of it.

The advantages to consumers include being able to purchase the precise vehicle they desire rather than choose from those on a dealer's lot. But even that may have limited appeal to buyers. A new collaborative economy is emerging. In a collaborative economy, the emphasis is on access to, rather than ownership of, material goods. See Chapter 8, "Rise of the Collaborative Economy and Ways to Profit from It," for more information on that.

So how is a manufacturer to know which way to go to survive and prosper among all these many changes? It's not enough to note that 3D printers are changing the industry and then go buy 3D printers. After all, that strategy will not necessarily save dental labs, now will it? No, it's not enough to look out and see changes on the horizon and follow suit. Nor is it enough to simply study what your traditional competitors are doing. Upcoming changes such as 3D printers are turning your former customers and retailers into your new competitors, and thereby substantially complicating your options. Consumers themselves are also changing. A new collaborative economy makes it possible for them to share and enjoy many goods without actually buying much from manufacturers or retailers.

Manufacturers are better served in using big data analytics to not only note upcoming sea changes but to predict the likelihood of success in various models to improve their competitiveness before they choose a path forward. In this way, risks are better managed and innovative ideas are made more certain.

New Data Sources Springing from Inside Manufacturing

Not all the forces of change are external, however. Some come from within. For example, many manufacturers are very aware of the value of data today and are busy collecting more of it. Unfortunately, they tend to think only in terms of the resale value of this data, primarily to marketers but to other parties as well.

It is the rare manufacturer that also thinks of these new data as a source for product and business model innovation. You'll find one example in Tesla, which is described in Chapter 15, "Use Cases in Transportation."

Be sure to note in the Tesla story how hard its own industry resisted Tesla's entry into the market, largely through political maneuverings. As of this writing, politicians in several states are blocking Tesla dealerships at the bidding of traditional dealerships that fear the disruption to their service model. Tesla vehicles do not require servicing. Further, Tesla improves vehicles it has already sold through software and hardware upgrades. That practice has the potential of disrupting the auto industry's new model every year sales plan.

It is even rarer for manufacturers to think about the potential consumer backlash from harvesting private data on the sly, that is, without consumer expressed consent and without providing the means for consumers to opt out. Examples of questionable data harvesting tactics used by manufacturers are plentiful. However, sometimes manufacturers go to considerable lengths to protect consumer privacy only to see their own liability increase. See Chapter 9, "The Privacy Conundrum," for more information on both of these situations.

Use Cases for this Sector

It would be prudent for manufacturers to look to analytics they place on and within their products with an eye to how this information can be used for the manufacturer's benefit in ways other than reselling the data to other parties. There are numerous ways such can be done.

As mentioned, manufacturers can use big data and predictive analytics to detect large and small trends and proactively and profitably react to them. Big data enables manufacturers to see beyond their own company and industry in order to detect emerging trends such as personalization and 3D printing that inevitably will lead to personalized manufacturing. Further, big data analytics will enable them to test several business models, thereby significantly reducing risks and failure rates ahead of implementation. Additionally, big data will enable manufacturers to see in near- or real-time if any business model or product tweaks are needed to refine the path to higher profits.

Product liability can also be substantially reduced or eliminated. For example, auto manufacturers can study vehicle diagnostics to determine potential product liabilities from malfunctioning parts and begin replacing those parts in the production line early to limit their liability exposure. Likewise, they can recall affected units faster, again limiting the liability potential. The same holds true for manufacturers of any product line that can carry diagnostic analytics. These days that includes all *durable goods* (goods that are intended to last for three or more years and that are infrequently replaced by consumers). But many soft goods or perishables such as refrigerated foods can similarly be controlled and improved to limit liabilities through the smart use of analytics in shipping containers and packaging.

However liability isn't the only thing manufacturers can improve with the help of big data. By studying how, when, and where consumers use their products, ideas for profitable innovations are more easily found. By comparing dealer, reseller, or retailer performance, a manufacturer can increase profits by better managing performance details in each and by identifying new requirements they should seek or impose on their distributors.

The possibilities in big data are almost endless. How well any given manufacturer profits from it depends almost entirely on the strength of its big data strategy and its willingness to quickly and efficiently act on the analysis.

SUMMARY

In this chapter you learned that manufacturing is struggling under a variety of forces and challenging conditions but that its future is looking brighter. The sector is plagued with outdated legacy systems and too little talent left to run them. Indeed, numerous obstacles exist that are borne from institutional memory loss due to massive layoffs and retiring talent that is proving difficult to replace.

The chief challenge before manufacturers is in reinventing themselves. That is no small task for an industry so far behind the times and steeped in the once fabulous and now seriously dated tradition of Henry Ford's assembly line. Manufacturers have plenty of data of their own, and more at their disposal, yet few are equipped to make adequate use of it in this task.

There are a number of overall market and technology trends now pressuring manufacturing. Chief among them is the larger market trend toward personalization and the emerging trend of 3D printing in manufacturing. When you look at traditional manufacturing, you see bulk production still underway, which is counter to the overlying market trend of personalization. However, manufacturing is currently undergoing a disruptive shift from subtractive to additive production, which neatly dovetails with the personalization trend.

Subtractive manufacturing—cutting, stamping, and otherwise extracting a shape from a raw material—is suited for bulk manufacturing and assembly. By comparison, additive manufacturing, aka 3D printing, is conducive to personalized production as it adds materials in layers to form a given shape or a finished product, the specs of which can be easily, rapidly, and cheaply changed between printings. In short, 3D printing is changing every aspect of manufacturing and is the most disruptive force seen in this sector since the industrial revolution.

Because 3D printing enables personalized manufacturing—the ability to cheaply and quickly create unique items rather than produce identical items in bulk—everything downstream from manufacturing will change too. The changes wrought in distributors, resellers, dealers, retailers, and even in consumer behaviors will in turn greatly impact manufacturing and in some cases replace traditional manufacturers outright.

Manufacturers are better served in using big data analytics to not only note upcoming sea changes but to predict the likelihood of success in various models to improve their competitiveness before they choose a path forward. In this way, risks are better managed and innovative ideas are made more certain. However, manufacturers who do innovate faster typically encounter strong resistance from their own industry. Getting to market with new innovations can be difficult as a result.

It would be prudent for manufacturers to look to analytics they place on and within their products with an eye to how this information can be used for the manufacturer's benefit in ways other than reselling the data to other parties. You learned that there are numerous ways that this can be done and that the possibilities are limited only by the manufacturer's imagination.

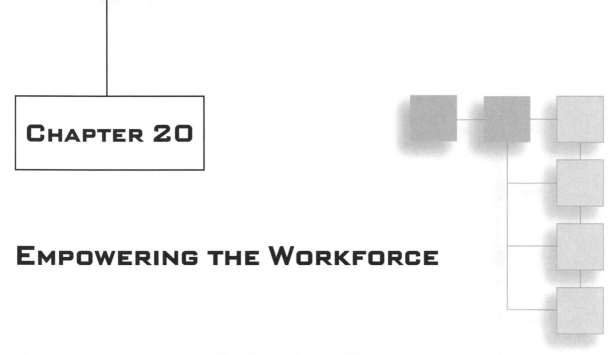

CHAPTER 20

EMPOWERING THE WORKFORCE

The typical big data project suffers from a host of ills, including bottlenecks and communication snafus between technologists, executives, and business users. Because the process is often clogged, output is often sluggish, results are frequently confusing or error-laden, and valuable time is habitually lost.

Empowering the workforce through big data analysis and solutions can dramatically change everything. And improving any current sub-optimized processes will be just the beginning. Fortunately big data is already beginning to trend toward data democratization and self-service tools and that is a clear indication that workforce empowerment is on the near horizon.

Big data will likely follow the path of every other major enterprise technology—from telephone to e-mail to business intelligence—all of which were quickly optimized when put in the general hands of the workforce. As big data follows suit, we will see organizations that accelerate this trend benefit from faster decision-making and marked competitive advantage. In order for that to happen, big data must be accessible to users in a self-service, readily available, user-friendly model.

This notion is likely to cause IT leaders to develop a few more ulcers as they rightly fear a possible spike in security issues. Additionally, some old school business leaders may resist this change for parochial reasons (knowledge is power, after all). But this change is coming and savvy organizations can accelerate its blessings while staving off its curses.

DEMOCRATIZING DATA

Democratization of data is rich in its promise to empower increasing numbers of knowledge workers in both big and small enterprises. However adoption rates are likely to trail in the early years simply due to low data literacy rates and varying levels of interest and ability in data-driven analytical thinking among the rank and file. Even so, the overall effect will be significant as first-adopters within the company begin to reshape how the company functions and competes. That effect will be magnified as more workers become comfortable with using data and data tools.

And true to expectations, self-service data access and analysis is already showing great results. Allowing workers to interact directly with information, and thus reducing or eliminating the need for highly trained data scientists or IT departments to get involved, adds agility to the organization overall by eliminating bottlenecks and speeding reaction times. Innovation ideally becomes a common occurrence since every ounce of talent on the organization's payroll potentially comes into play. IT also becomes more productive since some resources are eventually freed for other projects.

Directly plugging workers into data is the perfect blend of multi-processors: that of computer software and human wetware. After all, analysts are paid to think and generate knowledge in support of their organization's mission. Does it not make sense to plug them directly into the system rather than make them wait for a middleman to retrieve the data or do the analysis for them?

As mentioned earlier, data analysis offers insights but generating advanced inferences and producing actionable information from data is a decidedly human function. Giving workers direct access to data therefore shortens the formula for success. Forcing them to go through an IT department or data scientist or statistician achieves the opposite in that it introduces delay and bottlenecks.

Connecting analysts via self-service solutions also multiplies the advantages in computing. No human can handle the multi-dimensional correlations of factors present in data-intensive situations. The need to comprehend the arrays of data and how they interrelate is beyond human comprehension. And although the trained analyst takes steps to avoid bias, there are certain errors that humans are so prone to making that automation can at times help mitigate their occurrence.

FOUR STEPS FORWARD

Several things are required to help make this promise of user empowerment come true. Here is a four-step plan to develop a user self-service data program:

1. Articulate a vision.

2. Involve your analysts to understand how they need the program to work on their end.

3. Evaluate your current capabilities and determine what additional capabilities are necessary.

4. Derive action plans for a self-service system based on all of the above.

Your vision for user self-empowerment should of course flow from your mission. As described in Chapter 2, "How to Formulate a Winning Big Data Strategy," your vision will frame all other actions and your ability to engage analysts.

Regarding the evaluation of your own capabilities, this chapter presents three tables that capture a comprehensive look at capabilities enterprises will need for a truly empowered solution to be fielded. From these lists comes a matrix of capabilities that organizations should consider in optimizing this approach of user empowerment.

Many foundational capabilities are probably already in place in your organization today. Table 20.1 contains a review of key elements in the area of analyst facing capabilities; Table 20.2 covers enterprise IT capabilities; and Table 20.3 covers enterprise policy considerations. Evaluation criteria are included. The section concludes with an action plan that can help accelerate your movement to an analyst-empowered organization.

Table 20.1 Evaluating Analyst Facing Capabilities

Capability	Evaluation Factors
Operability	How well can the analysts in your organization operate their tools? To what degree do they require assistance from the IT department or from specialized outside contractors? Are technologies in place that funnel the right data and assessments to the right person? Do technologies support analysts' needs for social network analysis (SNA).

(Continued)

Table 20.1   Evaluating Analyst Facing Capabilities (*Continued*)

Capability	Evaluation Factors
Functionality	To what degree does the functionality of tools provided to your analysts support the full spectrum of functions (find who, what, where, and when, as well as connections and concepts and changes to all the above)? Do the capabilities your analysts use help them discover connections and concepts over large/diverse data sets? Can analysts evaluate data veracity? Can analysts evaluate data relevance?
Tailorability	When analysts need to tailor their capabilities for new data sources, can they develop them themselves? Or do they require assistance from outsiders?
Accessibility	Can analysts access enterprise capabilities where the mission requires it? Are there thin client and mobility options? Are there stand-alone options that can synchronize with the enterprise when reconnected?
Interoperability	Can analysts work with other analysts both inside and outside their organization? Solutions should be integrated and configurable across domains and work across internal boundaries and with partners.
Team Support	Can analysts work across the collaborative spectrum from one independent analyst to an entire enterprise collaborating together? Can analysts move their conclusions quickly to others on the team and to decision-makers? Have coalition-sharing capabilities been engineered that enable sanitization while protecting the essence of the information?
Knowledge Capture	As new conclusions and insights are developed, they need to be smartly captured to build upon and for continued fusion and analysis. This can include knowledge from partners and others outside the organization.

The above criteria in this table are best assessed in conjunction with experienced analysts who know your organization's mission and function and are familiar with available current tools. But keep in mind that analysts are not charged with the responsibility of keeping abreast of the full potential of modern technologies. Additional evaluation factors listed in Table 20.2 will be best evaluated in conjunction with your internal technology team and the broader technology community.

Table 20.2 Evaluating Enterprise IT Capabilities for Big Data

Capability	Evaluation Factors
Data Layers	Does your data layer connect all relevant data? Have you established a trusted information layer?
Data Grooming	Does your trusted information layer include incorporation of unstructured information into a semi-structured format? The key here is being able to crawl massive amounts of unstructured data, identify documents of interest, extract and know entities, and prepare this information for use.
Multi-Dimensional Security	Does your enterprise security model support getting all the information to those who need it? Have you engineered for a multidimensional security model that ensures your policies are always enforced and the mission is still always supported with the best possible analysis?
Synchronized	Have you engineered an ability to synchronize data sources? Does this enable smooth interoperability between single users, workgroups, and enterprises?
True Service Orientation	Do you have an architecture that facilitates sharing of secure information for both service (request/response) and notification (publish/subscribe) via widely supported standards and best practices? Does this architecture provide the flexibility and adaptability needed to keep pace with the change and evolution of the data type and volume, the analytic tools, and the analytic mission?
Enhanceability	Can enterprise IT staff tailor the capabilities for analyst use, or do they need to task an outside vendor to re-code capabilities?

Most modern enterprises, especially those in the national security community, have already been building toward more service-oriented, data-smart structures. Progress on these varies from sector to sector, but it is very likely that your organization has a good foundation along this path. But remember it is a journey, and the balanced approach your mission requires may well require changes to your configuration and perhaps even more modern technologies to optimize your ability to support the mission. See Table 20.3.

Table 20.3   Evaluating Enterprise Policy Factors for Big Data

---

Do your policies emphasize the need for automation for efficiency? Do you have measures of return on investment (ROI) or return for mission that are used to inform architecture decisions?

Do your policies seek out and eliminate barriers to collaboration that impact data design?

Do you seek out and reposition or remove capabilities that do not play well with others?

Before selecting new capabilities, do you conduct market assessments and solicit the opinions of others with similar mission needs?

Do you enforce mandates for open application program interfaces (APIs) and service-oriented architectures (SOA) best practices?

Whatever the status of your technology infrastructure, you will need a good governance process in place to move to a more optimized infrastructure.

Four More Steps Forward

Ready to move forward? Here are four steps to consider as you do:

1. Evaluate your enterprise in light of the recommended criteria. Use that to build your plan.

2. Enlist the aid of your analyst community to prioritize the analytical capabilities to deliver.

3. After prioritizing the analytical capabilities your mission requires, address the enterprise technology gaps required to enhance support to mission.

4. Track improvements to your enterprise like a project. Monitor costs, schedules and performance.

Every enterprise is different, with different missions, infrastructures, and architectures. You may find that many of the criteria outlined in this chapter are met by your existing enterprise. A quick inventory of existing capabilities and gaps will help you assess the challenge and prioritize how you architect for improvement.

A structured engagement with your organization's analysts is strongly recommended. They understand your organization's mission and vision and will likely be strong supporters in your move to bring more balance to your organization's approach to big data analytical solutions. Their prioritization of needs and capabilities should help guide discussions regarding organizational improvement plans.

However, keep in mind that your analysts are not paid to understand the power of modern computing. External advice and assistance in this area, including connecting with other organizations that have met similar challenges, will provide important insights into your road ahead.

We have observed organizations making this type of transformation around the globe, including commercial organizations, government agencies, and militaries. One thing they all seem to have in common is a deep need to automate with efficiency. For some this translates to a calculation of return on investment. For militaries, it can be a more operationally focused return on mission. But in every case, understanding a solution's efficiencies and total cost to the enterprise is critically important to ensuring success.

Expect to see a sharp rise in big data self-service soon and across all industries. If you are not empowering your team now with self-service, they will be at a huge disadvantage competitively speaking in the near-term.

Summary

In this chapter you learned that there are many advantages to democratizing data, chief among them being the leveraging of human talent throughout the organization. Indeed, big data tools are trending fast toward business-user-friendly applications for this purpose. However, adoption rates are likely to trail in the early years simply due to low data literacy rates and varying levels of interest and ability in data-driven analytical thinking among the rank and file. Even so, the overall effect will be significant as first-adopters within the company begin to reshape how the company functions and competes. That effect will be magnified as more workers become comfortable with using data and data tools.

This chapter presented three tables that capture a comprehensive look at capabilities enterprises will need for a truly empowered solution to be fielded. From these lists comes a matrix of capabilities that organizations should consider in optimizing this approach of user empowerment. You also learned steps to take to ensure you are empowering employees correctly.

Further, you now know to expect to see a sharp rise in big data self-service soon and across all industries. If you are not empowering your team now with self-service, they will be at a huge disadvantage competitively speaking in the near-term.

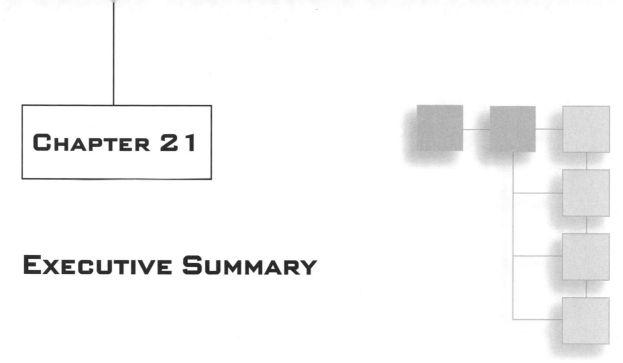

CHAPTER 21

EXECUTIVE SUMMARY

There are many details in each chapter of this book that you will likely find beneficial to your big data efforts and in developing your business strategy. There are so many changes wrought by big data in so many industries that the entire market-scape is changing as a result. Therefore, it behooves any business leader to be aware of changes in industries other than their own in order to predict, adapt, and profit from the fluidity of disruption and the continuance of cross-industry convergence happening now and continuing into the foreseeable future. To this end, the following summary is provided for those pressed for time or seeking a quick refresher after an initial read.

This is not an overly short summary; rather it is an attempt to flesh out the skeleton of the book so you can walk away with a working understanding. The following headings correspond to the chapter titles so that you can easily go to that chapter for details, real-world examples, and data resources.

WHAT IS BIG DATA REALLY?

The term big data is a bit of a misnomer as there is no consensus on the minimal size data must be in order to qualify for the designation. Further, the current definition is relative to current computing capabilities. This means that any data considered "big" today will likely not be deemed as such in the future when computing capabilities grow. Therefore the term is considered by technologists to be largely useless. Instead the technical world tends to favor a definition more attuned to data characteristics, that is, "containing volume, velocity, variety, and veracity." However, it is important to note that data is indeed getting bigger every day and extreme data is on its way.

Big data tools are highly adept at handling data sets of various sizes so business people should not think they only have value if the business owns very large data sets. Indeed, much of the data that is useful to any business, even very small businesses, comes from outside the organization and is quite large. One example is social media data and another would be publicly available data offered by governments and open data communities. Further the tools are inexpensive, some are even free, and thus well within the grasp of any business, even a microbusiness.

Big data is not universally viewed the same by business executives. This is important to understand if you are tasked with making a business case for big data before executives or in communicating analytical results to them. At the extreme ends of the spectrum are the "big data is omnipotent" and the "big data is just a spreadsheet upgrade" groups. Many executives fall somewhere between these two extremes.

It is important to assess where the executives you work with fit in this spectrum and assess how each executive learns and absorbs information in order to effectively manage expectations and expediently communicate outcomes via visualizations. If you don't know how the executive best absorbs information, you may choose the wrong visualization. Conversely, if you prefer more modern visualizations, you may discount executive preferences before realizing those preferences may not be as outdated as you thought.

How to Formulate a Winning Big Data Strategy

Strategy is everything. No amount of data or collection of big data tools will help you if you don't have a strong strategy in place first. Big data does not replace business acumen. Start at the end by identifying what you need to know and why you need to know it before you do anything else. Decide if that information is actionable, that is, something you can take action on immediately. If it is, computing and delivering ROI, and choosing tools and data sets will be infinitely easier.

IT can get things rolling by improving existing processes and workflows using big data. These changes typically relate to increased efficiencies of different categories and business divisions; as a result, metrics and ROI can thus be quickly measured and, in a best-case execution, actually realized.

Beyond that, you should develop an overall big data strategy as well as more pointed project specific strategies. The overall data strategy should be focused on continuously discovering ways to improve through innovation and solid returns both in the short and long terms. Project specific strategies should lead to a successful and actionable end to be immediately followed with ideas on what can be done from there, which in turn should ultimately lead to satisfying the goals in the overall big data strategy. Successful projects will also lead to refinements and changes in your overall strategy, as it is a living document.

Be aware that the most vexing challenges you are likely to encounter are people problems, not technical ones. People are simply unaccustomed to thinking in terms of using data to decide the way forward and to predict business impact. Further, people tend to limit their use of big data to familiar types of analysis already performed in the course of their work rather than imagine new uses. Fear is also a common problem that must be overcome. Common fears include a loss of power, loss of job security, or inadvertently creating a public relations backlash. Data literacy rates are also low. These skills must be taught throughout the organization to optimize data-driven decision-making and innovation but also to prevent errors in analysis that can lead to costly mistakes and embarrassments for the company.

Look for "big data diviners" in your organization to help speed the adoption of big data tools internally. These are employees who possess sufficient intellectual curiosity, analytical and critical thinking skills, and fearlessness of change to power true innovation through data use. They tend to be natural teachers who peers look to for answers about how to complete tasks. They also tend to be goal-oriented rather than clock watchers and they easily detect patterns in everything they see. Be sure to also cross-pollinate your interpretive team. To do list:

1. Consider adding a Chief Data Officer to manage your data.

2. Use prototype and iteration strategies to increase adoption throughout your organization.

3. Grow your own experts. Start with small projects, learn from those, and proceed to bigger projects.

4. Remember to also use big data to answer questions that no one has yet asked in order to find new threats and opportunities early.

5. Avoid the pitfall of focusing only on immediately profit-generating projects. You must also use big data to explore and discover the mid and far futures.

6. Watch out for cognitive biases and lurking hidden agendas in your team.

How to Ask the "Right" Questions of Big Data

While data analysis has always been important to business decisions, it has traditionally only been possible to do so after the fact. For example, analysis of the effectiveness of a marketing campaign is historically done after the campaign has run its course. The great thing about today's analytical tools is you can see what is happening in real-time, or near real-time, and therefore you can change course as needed to affect outcomes much sooner than was possible in the past. However, immediate actions can lead to problems in the mid- to long-term too, so be sure to use predictive analytics to consider those impacts as well before you take the action now.

Avoid data paralysis by forming the questions your company most needs answers too right now. Think in terms of what instant knowledge will make the biggest difference in moving the company or the department ahead immediately. For that moment forget about the data and the tools and focus only on what insights would offer the most business value.

All data analysis must be purpose driven to be useful. And that purpose is defined by the question asked of the data. Make sure that question is highly relevant to the business at hand and that the answer to that question will be something you can take action on or use in meaningful ways. Most of the time forming the right questions to ask will require a collaborative effort with people outside the data science team.

How to Pick the "Right" Data Sources

In the minds of data scientists and IT pros who deal with the intricacies of analyzing and storing data, the source of any given data set is not nearly as important as its form: structured or unstructured. And that is as it should be from a technical perspective, but from a business perspective the source of data matters a great deal.

Finding key insights and solutions to problems that can be solved with data analysis depends in large part on the quality of the data used, both in terms of its accuracy and the reliability of its source. Not all data brokers are created equal but we are now officially in a new data economy wherein data is the new currency and all and sundry are trying to cash in. Remember always "caveat emptor"—let the buyer beware.

A considerable amount of data is available free. You should check first to see if the data you need is available from a free source before you go off to purchase it. It is not uncommon for public data to be repurposed and then resold by commercial interests. Be careful that you don't buy that which is free for the taking.

A data seller's reputation for providing quality data must be taken into full consideration before a purchase is made but the buyer must also seek hard assurances that the data is regularly cleaned and protected from corruption. Further, since most of the data bought and sold today is not raw data but an analysis of that data, buyers need to examine and evaluate the algorithm(s) the seller used. It is no longer workable for algorithms to be trade secrets because data buyers need to know the modeling is sound in order to know the ultimate value of the data they are buying. Transparency is everything in determining data value.

Choosing which data brokers to buy data from becomes an easier task when you know what data you need before you go shopping. In many big data projects you will be adding information to existing formulas. The key to using big data successfully is not in just putting more data behind each of the variables you use now but in adding more variables to the equation.

For projects where no formula already exists, you must first define the problem you are trying to solve and then determine what information is pertinent to solving the problem. This will result in the formation of an algorithm. Double check the variables to ensure that you have enough inputs and that all inputs are relevant to the question. From there you can determine what data you need and whether such exists internally or externally. That enables you to define what data you need to purchase.

WHY THE ANSWER TO YOUR BIG DATA QUESTION RESEMBLES A RUBIK'S CUBE

The key point to remember is that "data-driven decision making" does not mean that analytics actually make decisions for you. They usually don't, with a few exceptions such as with prescriptive analytics. Using analytics generally means you have better and faster information with which you or others in your company can make a decision. Real-time analytics in particular, but high frequency runs of other analytics too, will send computed data results to you rapidly and frequently. What you do with that information is entirely up to you and beyond the scope of a machine.

Not all questions asked of data tender straightforward results. Many questions will have to refined, sometimes repeatedly, before you can ultimately learn whatever it is that you need to know and do. Sometimes you'll need to combine the results from two or more questions to get the answer you seek. You need to make sure you align everything correctly to solve the puzzle. Even if you make another algorithm to work that out for you, you still have to figure out how to weight each of those former results.

On still other occasions, the results will be so bizarre that you will feel compelled to test them and the algorithm to make sure they are correct. Testing and double-checking is important, as is making sure the data you are using is clean and relevant.

The most useful analytics are dynamic and not static. It generally is nonsensical to run analytics once and stop unless of course you are looking at a one-time event, such as a unique marketing campaign that had a definite beginning and ending. But not only is the work dynamic, so is the algorithm. A common mistake is to continue using the same algorithm as it is. Revisit and revise algorithms often or you risk missing important information.

In any event, analytics often spawn as many new questions as they do answers. Or at least they should because you should be learning continuously and the new knowledge should spark more questions. Data analysis is all about learning—machine learning and human learning. That being the case, you will never see a time when you have all the answers. It's impossible to know all the answers when you can never know all of the questions.

The Role of Real-Time Analytics in Rolling Your Strategy

When real-time analytics should be used is an individual call made by every company based on its overall strategy. Look at the advantages and shortcomings in real-time analytics in order to determine where they might best fit into any particular big data strategy.

Chief among the many concerns in real-time analysis is the speed in which the data is collected and whether the data itself is current enough to be considered real-time. With direct streaming of social media, for example, the speed and immediacy is readily evident. Not so much with other data.

In addition to the speed and immediacy of incoming data, one must consider reaction time on the other end of things. If, for example, marketing can do a real-time analysis on customer reactions to a marketing campaign but cannot act on the analysis for days, weeks or perhaps even months, then they are in effect reacting to a past event and not to a real-time analysis.

You must be selective in determining what information you need in real-time and how fast your company can react to it before you go to the effort and expense of analyzing it in real-time. Sometimes the slower and cheaper past-time analytics work just as well and are far more practical.

If you use real-time analysis too much, you're burning up resources needlessly. However, if you skip using it where needed you are hobbling the enterprise and putting it at a huge competitive disadvantage. Find the timing sweet spot for any given information and adjust your tactics accordingly.

However, even real-time analytics can reveal past events or decisions already made, so you may discover that damage is already done or opportunity is already lost. For example, you may find that a startup has produced a wildly popular product similar to the one you were planning to introduce six months from now or that completely disrupts your industry. In other words, the analysis you do in real-time may result in bad news that is difficult to influence or change to any significant degree.

With real-time analytics you can pivot mid-stride. Whatever you find in real-time analysis, you can find a way to cope with it and even profit from it despite the obstacles because you are now aware of the situation.

THE BIG DATA VALUE PROPOSITION AND MONETIZATION

Divining the value proposition of big data depends considerably on how well your company wields it. Therefore it is exceedingly difficult for a big data vendor to specifically answer your questions pertaining to ROI. It is not difficult, however, for you to calculate ROI for your company as presumably you do know the rest of the equation: how well your company strategizes and implements internal, market, and customer intelligence.

The value in big data is always found in the outcome. Unfortunately, that poses a problem for big data champions trying to make a business case for big data investment long before projects are started much less completed. Hence the recommendations by some experts to run small projects first and then make the case to scale that particular project, or to use the value found in the small test case as evidence that value does exist in other big data projects by extension. Many big data champions bank their business case on resolving existing data problems and costs and/or on increasing efficiencies in processes.

Outputs are intended for different audiences with different goals and the values of each are therefore determined differently. In other words, there is no one ROI calculation, but many. You will have to choose the formula that fits your expected business outcome. See the full chapter for a variety of formulas you can use.

Inevitably the question of data monetization surfaces in the ROI discussion. Data has already become a commodity and the prices are now so low that it is doubtful that selling your data would be worth the effort. The problem is that the data most data buyers want is the very data you would exclude or anonymize to oblivion in order to protect your company's competitive edge, secrets, and profitability. What is left after you do all that redacting is worth little to anyone. Raw data then is rarely of much value. Insights however are another story. There is a market for big data insights that big data users cannot arrive at on their own.

You can monetize your data by selling it if you create unique value in some way. Is it cooked to offer unique insights that are so fresh that they are a hot attraction? It's generally not of value if you serve it like sushi: raw and cold.

Rise of the Collaborative Economy and Ways to Profit from It

Big data's biggest impact is model shattering. One example of that is the emerging collaborative economy wherein people value access to goods and services over ownership and where they get such from each other rather than from retailers, manufacturers and other corporations.

The collaborative economy has three basic components: sharing economy, maker movement, and co-innovation. How much this new market shift will affect your company depends entirely on how well you respond to it. That means you will have to use big data to predict impact but also to deduce the means to compete in an ever changing environment. Successful adaptations will more likely than not be in the form of revised or new business models often put into effect on the fly. This is an example of why your big data strategy must be far broader than just improving how you do business now. It must also include a focus on the mechanisms and processes for how to change or adapt your business model as necessary to survive and capitalize on changes brought about by ever-evolving industry and market disruptors.

The definition of agile is quickly becoming antiquated. The new goal will be to become fluid, that is, to change the shape of the entire organization as needed to fit an ever-evolving market.

It will be the companies that master big data to the point that they can successfully use predictive analytics to change their overall company, processes, services and products rapidly to snare fast moving opportunities that will ultimately survive and profit. This is why you must use big data for more than just short-term goals. This is why ROI should not be your main focus or motivation in using big data. Make sure that your big data strategy is big enough to do all that must be done.

THE PRIVACY CONUNDRUM

Four major shifts in how data is collected and used have sparked public ire. The first is that data collection tactics are far more invasive than in years past. Secondly, more and a larger variety of data is collected, correlated and inferred which reveals far more telling details than most people are comfortable with others knowing. Thirdly, silos have crumbled, leaving the average person more exposed and vulnerable in data integration. Last but not least, companies and governments are gathering data far beyond the traditional business or mission scope and often doing so through surreptitious means.

The privacy conundrum is further complicated by the unfettered use of data in the private sector. If future regulation focuses on government use of data alone then the private sector will continue on unabated, thereby guaranteeing individual privacy will not exist. Further, the private sector is likely to profit from regulations forbidding governments to collect data as the corporate world will simply collect the same information and sell it, or sell the analysis of it on demand, to governments. Indeed, many are already doing so.

In addition, numerous corporate entities such as Facebook and Google have already collected sufficient information on individuals and businesses to infer behaviors for decades to come. It is also likely that the United States and foreign federal governments have as well. There is no realistic way to ensure data is permanently erased in any of these collections.

Lastly, there is no clear definition of who owns what data, making the argument to delete data on individuals harder to make and win.

This brings you to an important aspect in developing big data strategies for your organization: are your data collection processes and uses respectful of individual privacy and if not, is your organization prepared to cope with the inevitable repercussions?

Certainly liability issues should be forefront on your mind in determining what data to collect, how you collect it, and what you infer. However, few companies understand that they can also potentially be liable on other counts *because* of their efforts to protect individual privacy. Not reporting a clearly suspicious or illegal act, in the name of protecting customer privacy, could conceivably make a company complicit in the crime. A very good way to help limit this exposure is to make absolutely sure you collect no more data than is necessary to conduct your business in a "privacy by design" framework. Another good approach is in supporting the development and implementation of sensible privacy regulations and clear guidelines, so you know better how to safely proceed.

The one truth all data practitioners should hold fast is this—Big Brother is us and we are the individual. It is our data practices, and the practices of others like us, that collectively give life to the Big Brother concept. But each of us is also an individual and whatever data use horrors that we allow to exist will haunt each of us in turn. Together we know privacy or none of us do.

Use Cases in Governments

Very few local governments in the United States are working in big data now due largely to funding cutbacks and a lack of talent capable of doing big data projects. For the most part local governments are using traditional data collection and analysis methods largely contained to their own databases and local and state sources. Large cities tend to be far ahead of the curve in using big data and in offering public data sets. Eventually local governments will benefit from the growing spread of data from myriad sources and simpler analytics that can then be more easily used at the local level.

State governments vary greatly in their use of big data. Some states rely on a mix of their own existing data and that which they pull from the federal government or is pushed to them. Other states are busy integrating data from cities, townships, counties, and federal agencies as well as integrating data across state agencies. Most states are making at least public records data readily available online but you usually have to find that information in a state by state online search. Some state agencies also offer mobile apps that contain specialized data. As of this writing, no regional data sets have been created by state governments that are voluntarily combining their data with that of adjacent states for the benefit of their region—at least none that we have found.

The U.S. government has made substantial strides in making more government data available to citizens, commercial and non-profit interests and even to some foreign governments. The Obama administration's stated goal is to make the government more transparent and accountable. But the data provided also often proves to be an invaluable resource for researchers and commercial interests. Data.gov is the central site for U.S. government data and is part of the Open Government Initiative. The Data.gov Data Catalog contains 90,645 data sets as of this writing. You can expect that count to climb higher over time and for the data sets to individually grow as well.

The federal government is using big data to inform its decisions but also sharing data as a means of fueling or aiding private and commercial efforts as well as a public relations initiative. See the full chapter for more details.

USE CASES IN THE DEPARTMENT OF DEFENSE AND INTELLIGENCE COMMUNITY

There is nothing more frightening to the public psyche than the prospect of an all seeing, all knowing Big Brother government. The recent and ongoing leaks from Edward Snowden, a former Central Intelligence Agency (CIA) employee and a former contractor for the National Security Agency (NSA) turned whistle-blower, continue to feed that fear. Many of the resulting concerns are covered in the chapter on the privacy conundrum, but this chapter looks at the other side of those issues, from the government's perspective.

Given their urgent and important national security mission needs, it is no surprise that technologists in the Department of Defense (DoD) and Intelligence Community (IC) have sought out new approaches to analyzing and using data. After all, big data is uniquely suited to quickly and efficiently searching mega-sized data for markers that could indicate criminal and terrorist activity. Big data tools also make it possible to see and note personal relationships between criminals and terrorists that might otherwise remain hidden.

Modern data analysis can even accurately predict rising nation aggressors and impending war. Big data tools can also make it easier to find and respond to cyber-attacks in progress. Further, big data can power artificial intelligence and drive automated war machines to attack faster and more precisely than their human counterparts. Indeed, there are already so many ways to use big data in national defense that it boggles the mind. Even so, more uses for it will appear as mastery of big data improves.

Currently, the types of big data solutions being fielded include situational awareness and visualization, enhanced healthcare, information search and discovery in overwhelming amounts of data, logistical information including asset catalogs, big data in weaponry and war, and many more.

The DoD and IC Community's work with big data is more complex by nature, but they do share some data openly. For example, DARPA has made its Open Catalog available on a public website. It lists DARPA-sponsored software and peer-reviewed publications for interested parties to see and review. Obviously, such openness could lead to efforts designed to thwart DARPA's and other agencies' work as easily as it could enlist aid. Just as obviously, agencies don't list anything overly sensitive in their open data collections for precisely that reason.

Indeed, as of this writing, terrorist groups were already seen to be using intelligence gained from the Snowden revelations to implement encryption and other ways to shield their actions. Suffice it to say that the Department of Defense (DoD) and Intelligence

Community (IC) are now severely challenged in detecting and preventing threats. For all practical purposes, they must now create new ways to work from scratch. Big data will continue to play a central role in these new efforts.

USE CASES IN SECURITY

The cybersecurity and physical/facility security subsectors, for all practical purposes, have blended into one, given the digitalization of devices and sensors and the advent of the Internet of Things, which refers to all things being connected to the Internet. It is in this context that security experts must now work whether they are charged with cybersecurity, that is, protecting data, or in physical security (protecting facilities, events, and persons). Very little in security work relies on direct human observation anymore.

That's not to say that security work has gotten any easier. Despite all this data, all these additional mechanical eyes and other extensions of the security expert's manifested presence, the exponential growth of threats and the steady rise in the sophistication of the attacks is still outpacing security efforts.

Privacy problems increase when data is collected for security purposes. Once data is gathered, stored and shared it is impossible for that information to be retrieved, deleted or otherwise guarded by the person that information is about. This leaves the door wide open for future abuse.

On the other hand, security professionals can only do so much in identifying immediate threats in real time. It is often the case that forensics teams and infosec professionals need to backtrack through metadata, log files, and sometimes even generalized data to find the trail of evildoers and to predict what they are likely to do next. Hence, there is value in collecting and storing massive amounts of data over time.

Therein lies the rub. That which strengthens privacy is often "bad" for security and vice versa. Yet those who seek privacy also wish to be secure and those who seek to provide security also want privacy for themselves. Big data, then, is both friend and foe to both causes.

Use cases for big data in this category include those in any other cybersecurity effort as well as in the development of innovative protective measures. Such includes but is not limited to offline overrides in medical equipment that react to unauthorized changes in commands or performance and offline secondary and compartmentalized or containerized emergency and backup systems such as for electric grids, water and banking systems.

One of the biggest benefits of big data in security is in its ability to identify likely threats and afford the opportunity to design both prevention and responses.

Use Cases in Healthcare

These are already data-driven industries, albeit in a highly siloed and splintered fashion. Pooling data and analyzing disparate data sets for additional insights is the next logical step. Unfortunately, that is easier said than done. For one thing, many of the industry players are highly competitive and their information is proprietary.

For another thing, the industry is highly regulated. Revealing data could lead them to compliance troubles with existing privacy regulations such as the Health Insurance Portability and Accountability Act of 1996 (HIPAA) and its counterparts in other nations. How does one go about sharing meaningful data on thousands if not millions of patients when the barrier is so high on sharing data on just one patient?

Despite these challenges, efforts are underway to share data in order to speed cures, treatments, and vaccines. Big data helps speed the shift to personalized medicines to improve patient outcomes and to genetic-based medicines to replace current antibiotics that will soon no longer be effective. It also is invaluable in finding new and more effective ways to prevent health issues from developing in the first place and in innovating entire healthcare systems on a scale never before seen.

There are problems with using only data shared on the Internet. Consider the case of Google Flu Trends vs the CDC's traditional methods of tracking outbreaks of the flu wherein Google Flu Trends handily lost. This happened largely because that data which is online, or collected digitally online, is too limiting for accurate analysis. Further, for such data to be useful it must be exacting and precise. It must follow strict protocols and include traditional data collection methods and refined statistical analysis. Fortunately traditional health agencies are beginning to share more data online to aid the development of more comprehensive efforts elsewhere.

On the side of more informal data sharing and collaborations is the biohacker community. As is the case with computer hackers, they come in both the white hat and black hat varieties. Like computer hackers before them, the vast majority of biohackers in these early days of the movement are indeed white hats. They create cheap antibiotics in the field and hack DNA to experiment with creating genetic-based medicines, cures, and biological defenses. When they gather in groups, they learn from one another as well as collaborate on projects. Such gatherings happen all over the world and very frequently.

Data is used in healthcare to cure humankind of what ails it and to break bottlenecks in discoveries and innovations. It is used to better patient outcomes and to battle rising costs. Big data is used to inform policymakers and to proactively warn providers of impending compliance issues. Data reveals all from the drug abuser visiting multiple emergency rooms to get a fix to fraudulent insurance and Medicare/Medicaid claims to bad medical practices and price gouging by the industry.

It enlightens and improves healthcare but also illuminates and destroys healthcare as we know it. Those providers who wield data analysis well and take smart action will prosper. Those who don't, won't.

Use Cases in Small Businesses and Farms

Big data gives SMBs incredible business advantages that were once only in reach of the biggest companies. But it also makes large companies more agile and innovative, and their offerings more personalized—strengths that formerly belonged to smaller businesses. This means that large companies using big data can better compete with the SMBs' legendary personalized service and innovative capabilities. This poses a new threat to SMBs.

While big data can give you important and even vital insights, it can't think for you. Indeed, it is the best strategists that win using big data, not those who own the most expensive, fanciest big data tools. The three things SMBs should understand are that a) big data is not just for big companies, b) the information has little to no value unless you act on it, and c) it is your strategy borne out in this use that benefits or harms your company.

Fortunately for small businesses and farms on tight budgets, many big data tools are free or available for a very minimal fee. Specific examples and resources can be found in the full chapter.

One of the big advantages to using big data tools is the ability to augment your own data with data from other sources. There are many public data sets available for free and more showing up every day such as those found on Amazon Web Services (AWS), Yahoo! Labs, and Open Science Data Cloud (OSDC). Some of the most bountiful sources for free data sets come from government agencies from the federal level to the county or city level. Small businesses can use this information for a variety of purposes from identifying best locations for new stores to finding loans, grants, and a variety of other resources. Data is readily accessible and available almost everywhere. Decide what information you need first and let that guide your search for data sets.

Deciding whether to share your own company data is a bit trickier. Small businesses and farms should seek resolution and clarity before committing to any data sharing agreement or smart machine purchase. Conflicts of interest often do exist.

While small businesses are busy figuring out how best to use big data and whether or not to share or pool their data and if so then with whom, other industries are busy using big data to figure out how best to serve and profit from SMB customers. In many cases, big-data-spawned disruptors have arrived to change circumstances for the better for small businesses.

USE CASES IN ENERGY

Countries, states, provinces, cities and townships, utility companies, and businesses of all kinds and sizes seek to lower their energy use and costs. Each also seeks to know how energy trends and future predictions impact them and their constituents or customers. Big data and advanced analytics can help each meet their goals and reduce risks.

Several entities provide energy data for industry and public use. Among them is the U.S. Energy Information Administration (EIA). The EIA has possession of energy data that is otherwise unobtainable by other parties but shares it publicly and freely through reports and the eia.gov website.

If you're looking for data from smart meters, you're in for a long wait. While most utilities, particularly electric companies, are quickly moving to use smart meters throughout their network, few have a clue as to what to do with the resulting data. But there are also a number of problems in streaming smart meter data to the EIA including a lack of standardization in outputs and a variety of local regulations.

Utility companies look to data from smart meters and other sources first to improve cash issues both in raising revenue and cutting costs. The second most common use case is to detect and resolve network issues such as breaks, stressed components, inefficient components and weak points, likelihood of outages, and future capacity needs. With the advent of new smart sensors, meters, and other equipment capable of generating a constant stream of data, and the analytics needed to make sense of all that data, utilities can now work in a proactive state thereby preventing most outages and containing repair costs.

A third use case is in opening the network to receive more energy supplies, such as in customer buy-back programs where customers augment utility use with an alternative energy source, such as solar panels on a business or home. The utility can buy the customer's excess energy and add it to its general supply for resale. It will take big data tools to correctly track and monitor new incoming energy supplies and to properly track those costs and resale dollars.

A fourth use case is in early detection of a threat to the system, be that a heavy squirrel population near a transformer, a developing weather system, or a terrorist or activist threat. As utilities increasingly turn to digital information to drive operations, those systems will be vulnerable to attack. It will take big-data-driven security efforts to detect, block, respond, and deter such efforts.

A fifth use case is in innovating the utility company overall. From changing inefficient internal processes to improving energy output and alternative energy input, analytics will eventually change everything in how a utility company and the energy industry overall operates.

By using data so readily available from reliable sources such as the EIA your analysis of energy costs and availability impact becomes infinitely more accurate. APIs make it easy to feed the information into your calculations and dashboards. Further, businesses can use this information to inform their analysis on store, plant, or office locations as energy costs affect cost of living, and therefore payroll costs, as well as overall operational costs.

Use Cases in Transportation

At first, in-vehicle data collection was thought of in terms of advantages to the automakers, most notably in developing new revenue streams from drivers, insurance and lien holder sales. For example, features that offered emergency services for drivers, that is, those of the OnStar ilk, also provided data that was valuable to car insurance companies and vehicle repossession companies working for lien holders.

Car dealers also found new data-generating, in-car features to be financially rewarding. They discovered that by reading data on cars they could cut diagnostic and repair costs and increase the number of service department visits via automated customer diagnostic messaging and thereby increase revenue in the service centers.

However, the focus in using data from cars and in-car technologies has broadened beyond the auto manufacturers and dealers scope. Governments, from the township and county level all the way to the federal level, are also looking to this data to improve roadways, safety, and traffic flow and to eventually move to a connected transportation infrastructure.

While most people think of "connected vehicles" in terms of cars being connected to their owners' devices both in and out of the car, and connected to the Internet, the term actually has a different meaning. Connected vehicles as a specific term means connectivity between vehicles and road infrastructures, usually achieved with the aid of wireless technologies.

Our existing roads and highways are now being digitalized through the use of cameras and sensors. Data is collected and fed to different government agencies, some focused on law enforcement and others on improving traffic patterns and future transportation planning. Our vehicles are also using and generating more digitalized data everyday using a range of sensors and technologies. Data analytics and reporting is done in-vehicle, between vehicles, and soon with the road infrastructure and surrounding structures, signs, and buildings.

Trains, planes, ships and other forms of transportation including everything from drones and intelligent, autonomous war machines to ferries and golf carts, are being transformed. In each case, data generation, analysis and data-driven innovation are at the heart of the transformation.

Increasingly, data is being publicly shared. Entities outside the transportation arena can make use of this data in myriad ways. Already plans are afoot to redesign cities into smart cities and to change transportation completely. You can expect wearable computing and mobile apps to become more tightly integrated with transportation. The possibilities and opportunities in data convergence and fast analytics are nearly endless.

All of these changes bring pressures to bear on the transportation industry, which must keep up in order to stay in business. Shipping and delivery companies are relying heavily on data and analytics to improve their operations and remain competitive. They will also need to use data analysis to reshape their entire business model and offerings in order to adapt and survive all these market changes.

Insurance coverage will still be needed but such will likely be tied more to malfunction coverage rather than individual driver actions and skills. The shift in what risks auto insurance will cover in the future will not lessen the value of the data they gather on drivers today, however. Such data can be used for other purposes useful to other types of insurance coverage, employers, and other industries and business functions. For example, driver data can be used to assess the level of risk an individual will take. Such could be useful to life insurance companies in assessing risk in insuring the life of an individual or to employers seeking personalities uniquely suited to taking risks in their work that may lead to new innovations.

In short, this industry, like many others, is now data-centric in all facets. This will only become increasingly true over time.

Use Cases in Retail

Big data tools, unlike any other, can show retailers what is happening now rather than merely dissecting what happened in the past. They can uncloak emerging threats and opportunities and spur changes in innovation, processes, and future business model needs.

The problem retailers have run into so far using big data is two-fold. For one thing, "information certainty" gets fuzzier outside of structured data (the retailer's own transactional data). Even the retailer's own data can be "dirty," that is, incorrect or out-of-date and incomplete, as much of their data is still locked in siloes.

Second in the retailers' two-fold problem is in the lack of creativity in forming big data questions. Like many organizations in every industry, retailers typically ask the same old questions of big data that they asked of smaller data. While it's perfectly understandable to ask these questions repeatedly, they give too narrow a view if that is all you ask. The goal before retailers today is to change the organization into a highly distinctive, fully differentiated, profit-generating machine. How are they going to do that by doing the same things over and over again ad nauseam?

In a nutshell, these typical problems with using big data, or in plotting the path forward in general, is why retailers are having a tough time in finding their way. Instead, retailers find themselves continuing to resort to cliché advertising messaging, personalized marketing that is often anything but, and broadly offered, deep discounts they can ill afford. If status quo continues to be projected into big data projects in retailing, status quo will be the result of the efforts, that is, small gains if there are any gains at all.

The rise of such disrupters as Amazon and eBay should have been a wake-up call to the industry and in some ways it was. But many retailers have yet to regain their footing since. Now there are more disruptors on the horizon and retailers will have to really scramble to catch up and surpass these challenges.

There are other changes coming as well such as 3D printers. Already manufacturers are using 3D printers to produce goods faster, cheaper and more precisely. In the near future, 3D printers will be in wider use. Instead of shipping goods assembled in a manufacturing plant or from a retailer to a customer, soon design codes can be sent for many goods to an on-site 3D printer instead and produced there.

Aiding that shift to 3D printing is the advent of home body scanners, such as can be done via an Xbox Kinect game console now. Such precise body measurements can be used to virtually "try-on" and order clothing and other items made to fit perfectly. This will decrease or eliminate the need to return items after purchase to retailers because of fit or "look" issues.

Obviously these changes, separately and together, will abruptly alter how retailing is done. It behooves the industry to prepare for such now. Some retailers may want to strive to be the first to offer such since first to market has its advantages. Others may prefer to incorporate upcoming market changes into their model to enhance customer experience and continue to entice customers to shop at their brick-and-mortar stores.

If the brick-and-mortar retail sector is to save itself, it must hasten and improve its use and mastery of big data and other technologies. It must also reinvent itself in ways previously never imagined.

USE CASES IN BANKING AND FINANCIAL SERVICES

Banking and other financial services institutions are a study in contradictions. On the one hand they traditionally excel at calculating and containing risks, which means of course that they excel at using data effectively. On the other hand, they're not doing so well in using big data.

Big data tools are not so much the problem for this group, although some are certainly struggling with those, rather they generally suffer from a brain rut. Their thinking on the various aspects of their business models, product lines, risk calculations, and investments is so deeply rooted in tradition that they often have difficulty branching out into more creative approaches.

The problem with the traditional lending approach is three-fold. For one thing, shrinking one's customer base purposefully is almost always a bad idea. Fewer customers generally equates to fewer sales, smaller profits, and a future lost to customer attrition. For another, this approach opens the door wide for competitors to encroach and even seize the bank's market share. Hunkering down in a fearful position encourages aggressive competitors to move in on your territory. And third, while traditional financial institutions spurn potential customers and new alternative lenders welcome them with open arms, the public perception of banks shifts from essential financial service providers to nonessential, perhaps irrelevant, players in a crowded field.

New alternative credit sources are also beginning to pressure banks. They include in-house financiers such as PayPal Working Capital and Amazon Capital Services, peer-to-peer lenders, and co-branded credit cards such as those offered by major retailers like Target, Macy's, and Sears in partnership with companies such as Visa, MasterCard and American Express.

Further, these cards are generating a considerable amount of data for competing entities that was formerly contained and controlled by banks and traditional lending institutions.

As more consumers learn it's easier to qualify for credit cards from airlines, retailers and other non-bank companies—and where the loyalty rewards are typically better too—fewer consumers will turn to banks for these services. Combined these trends erode market share for banks and other traditional financial institutions.

Additionally, traditional lending institutions place too much faith in outside traditional risk-assessment sources, namely traditional credit bureaus. Therefore the lenders are further stymied by the problems in traditional credit bureau data such as too little data, irrelevant data, outdated credit rating systems, and virtually no distinction between potential borrowers who are truly are a credit risk and those who were set back temporarily by the recession but otherwise pose little risk. To add insult to injury, lending institutions pay credit bureaus for data that may have little to no actual value.

For banks and other traditional financial institutions to better assess their risk and realistically expand revenue from loans and other credit and financial services, they have to import significant data from sources other than credit bureaus and develop better risk assessment algorithms. Further, they have to develop the means to assess the credibility, accuracy and validity of data sources and the data they supply. The days of meekly accepting credit bureau data, or any data, at face value are long gone. The business risk in that behavior is unacceptably high.

Financial institutions can also use data on existing customers to help identify characteristics they need to look for in prospects in order to add profitability and sustainability for their business. Other use cases include strategic planning, new revenue stream discovery, product innovation, trading, compliance, and risk and security.

Use Cases in Manufacturing

There are a number of overall market and technology trends now pressuring manufacturing. Chief among them is the larger market trend toward personalization and the emerging trend of 3D printing in manufacturing. The two trends are related even though they may not appear to be at first glance.

The trend toward personalization is seen everywhere in the market today from personalized marketing to personalized medicine. In every case, personalized means tailored to an individual and not bulk delivery to the masses.

Manufacturing is currently undergoing a disruptive shift from subtractive to additive production, which neatly dovetails with the personalization trend. Additive manufacturing, aka 3D printing, is conducive to personalized production as it adds materials in layers to form a given shape or a finished product, the specs of which can be easily, rapidly and cheaply changed between printings. Additive manufacturing also produces little to no waste in the printing process; indeed, it can use industrial waste as "ink." Further, it is very much faster and cheaper than subtractive manufacturing.

Traditional manufacturers will have to increasingly compete against manufacturers that are using faster, cheaper and greener 3D printing production techniques. Therefore, it will soon be no longer profitable to merely turn to more automation to eek small gains from increasing efficiencies. Traditional manufacturers will have to discover and deploy new ways to remain competitive.

Big data is among the manufacturer's best tools in finding their way forward on what will increasingly feel like an alien market-scape. Unfortunately, most manufacturers have so far ignored or failed to master these tools.

Because 3D printing enables personalized manufacturing, everything downstream from manufacturing will change too. For example, homes can be printed faster and cheaper than they can be built in the traditional way. As architects and construction companies increasingly turn to 3D printing to produce their work, their need for traditional building materials diminishes and then disappears. That will bring about massive changes in demands for everything from sheetrock manufacturing to secondary manufacturing such as engineered wood product production. Even home improvement stores may shift their buying patterns from traditional building supplies to stocks of "ink" suitable for printing whatever is needed. The stores may even provide the printing services.

Similar changes will occur in other types of manufacturing. For example, car dealers in the future may no longer stock a large number of vehicles on their lots. Instead, they may have only a handful on a tinier showroom floor. In this way customers can see the finished product and take it for a test drive. Consumers will also be able to order exterior and interior colors in any combinations they can imagine and even add personalized art elements too.

The advantages to consumers include being able to purchase the precise vehicle they desire rather than choose from those on a dealer's lot. But even that may have limited appeal to buyers. A new collaborative economy is emerging. In a collaborative economy the emphasis is on access to, rather than ownership of, material goods.

Manufacturers are better served in using big data analytics to not only note upcoming sea changes but to predict the likelihood of success in various models to improve their competitiveness before they choose a path forward. In this way, risks are better managed and innovative ideas are made more certain.

It is prudent for manufacturers to look to analytics they place on and within their products with an eye to how this information can be used for the manufacturer's benefit in ways other than reselling the data to other parties or placing ads. There are numerous ways such can be done, such as in product innovation and reducing product liability and product recall costs.

By studying how, when, and where consumers use their products, ideas for profitable innovations are more easily found. By comparing dealer, reseller or retailer performance, a manufacturer can increase profits by better managing performance details in each and by identifying new requirements they should seek or impose on their distributors.

Empowering the Workforce

The typical big data project suffers from a host of ills including bottlenecks and communication snafus between technologists, executives and business users. Because the process is often clogged, output is often sluggish, results are frequently confusing or error-laden, and valuable time is habitually lost.

Empowering the workforce through big data analysis and solutions can dramatically change everything. And improving the current sub-optimized processes will be just the beginning. Fortunately big data is already beginning to trend toward data democratization and self-service tools and that is a clear indication that workforce empowerment is on the near horizon.

Big data will likely follow the path of every other major enterprise technology—from telephone to e-mail to business intelligence—all of which were optimized when put in the hands of the workforce. As big data follows suit, organizations that accelerate this trend benefit from faster decision-making and marked competitive advantage. In order for that to happen, big data must be accessible to users in a self-service, readily available, user-friendly model.

Democratization of data is rich in its promise to empower increasing numbers of knowledge workers in big and small enterprises. Adoption rates are likely to be lean in the early years simply due to low data literacy rates and varying levels of interest and ability in analytical thinking among the rank and file. The overall effect will be significant as first-adopters begin to reshape how the company functions and competes. That effect will be magnified as more workers become comfortable with using the tools.

True to expectations, self-service data access and analysis is already showing great results. Allowing workers to interact directly with information, and thus eliminating the need for highly trained data scientists or IT departments to get involved, adds agility to the organization overall by eliminating bottlenecks and speeding reaction times. Innovation becomes a common occurrence since every ounce of talent on the organization's payroll comes into play. IT also becomes more productive since resources are freed for other projects.

Expect to see a sharp rise in big data self-service soon and across all industries. If you are not empowering your team now, they will be at a huge competitive disadvantage in the near-term.

Now that you can see the big picture in big data, you can fashion your own strategies and projects to move your company meaningfully ahead. Remember you—and your competitors—are only limited by the imagination and business acumen at hand.

Good luck to you all!

INDEX